T0113661

Why America Loses Wars

How can you achieve victory in war if you don't have a clear idea of your political aims and a vision of what victory means? In this provocative challenge to US political aims and strategy, Donald Stoker argues that America endures endless wars because its leaders no longer know how to *think* about war, particularly wars fought for limited aims, taking the nation to war without understanding what they want or valuing victory and thus the ending of the war. He reveals how flawed ideas on so-called "limited war" and war in general evolved against the backdrop of American conflicts in Korea, Vietnam, Iraq, and Afghanistan. These ideas, he shows, undermined America's ability to understand, wage, and win its wars, and to secure peace. Now fully updated to incorporate the American withdrawal from Afghanistan, *Why America Loses Wars* dismantles seventy years of misguided thinking and lays the foundations for a new approach to the wars of tomorrow.

Donald Stoker is Professor of National Security and Resource Strategy at the Dwight D. Eisenhower School of the National Defense University in Washington, DC. He was Professor of Strategy and Policy for the US Naval War College's Monterey Program at the Naval Postgraduate School in Monterey, California, from 1999 until 2017. The author or editor of thirteen books, his *Carl von Clausewitz: His Life and Work* is on the British Army professional-reading list. His *Purpose and Power: American Grand Strategy Since 1775* will be published by Cambridge University Press in 2022.

Why America Loses Wars

Limited War and US Strategy from
the Korean War to the Present

Donald Stoker

CAMBRIDGE
UNIVERSITY PRESS

CAMBRIDGE
UNIVERSITY PRESS

University Printing House, Cambridge CB2 8BS, United Kingdom

One Liberty Plaza, 20th Floor, New York, NY 10006, USA

477 Williamstown Road, Port Melbourne, VIC 3207, Australia

314–321, 3rd Floor, Plot 3, Splendor Forum, Jasola District Centre, New Delhi – 110025, India

103 Penang Road, #05–06/07, Visioncrest Commercial, Singapore 238467

Cambridge University Press is part of the University of Cambridge.

It furthers the University's mission by disseminating knowledge in the pursuit of education, learning, and research at the highest international levels of excellence.

www.cambridge.org
Information on this title: www.cambridge.org/9781108479592
DOI: 10.1017/9781108611794

© Donald Stoker 2019, 2022

Hardback first published 2019
Paperback first published 2022

A catalogue record for this publication is available from the British Library.

ISBN 978-1-108-47959-2 Hardback
ISBN 978-1-009-22086-6 Paperback

To Hal Blanton and Mike Jones. Great colleagues. Greater friends.

CONTENTS

1 ARE WE AT WAR? WHAT DO WE WANT? AND DO WE WANT TO WIN?

There is no such thing as a *little war* for a great Nation.
Arthur Wellesley, Duke of Wellington (1838)

The Political Rules

The ethereal image has the green-yellow tint of a night vision scope. It was August 31, 2021, 11:59pm Kabul time. The commander of the 82nd Airborne Division, Major General Chris Donahue, the last American soldier in Afghanistan, approached the ramp of the last American transport aircraft departing Kabul. America's twenty-year war in Afghanistan was over. The United States was leaving in defeat.[1] Its NATO partners were already gone.

It was a long road to America's most recent loss in a war fought for limited political aims. The timing of the final act incontrovertibly demonstrated the dominance of the political in war. The US military had not suffered stunning reverses on the battlefield, and mass protests against the war in Afghanistan hadn't rocked American cities or universities. Most Americans hardly seemed to notice America's and NATO's long-running war in Afghanistan. But the president of the United States, Joseph Biden, had decided the war was not in the US interest – his prerogative as president – and on April 14, 2021 announced America's coming withdrawal.[2] Perhaps unaware of the implications, the administration made a political decision to choose defeat.

American warfighting since the Second World War is rife with such judgments. America's leaders – and those who advise them – too often do not understand war. Critically, they don't understand how to *think* about war and even have difficulty distinguishing between war and peace while failing to grasp the dangers of their confusion. How did we come to this place?

Are We at War?

On June 29, 1950, President Harry S. Truman held an after-noon press conference where he took questions about the recently erupted war in Korea. Four days before, Kim Il-Sung's Communist North Korean regime had launched a surprise offensive designed to conquer American-supported South Korea. Within forty-eight hours Truman had decided to commit US forces to the fight. General Douglas MacArthur, the commander of US forces in the Far East, received orders to "throw the North Koreans out of South Korea." Republican Senator Robert Taft agreed with Truman's deci-sion, but not the president's refusal to seek Congressional approval for taking the US to war. "If the incident is permitted to go by without protest," Taft wrote, "we would have finally terminated for all time the right of Congress to declare war, which is granted to Congress alone by the Constitution of the United States." Others echoed Taft's views. Truman ignored them all and began pulling together a United Nations-sponsored coalition to counter what many Western observers saw as the first move in a possible Soviet offensive aimed at the West. A reporter at the press conference prodded Truman: "Everybody is asking in this country, are we or are we not at war?" Truman replied, "We are not at war," and told those assembled that "the members of the United Nations are going to the relief of the Korean Republic to suppress a bandit raid." Another journalist asked: "Mr. President, would it be correct, against your explanation, to call this a police action under the United Nations?" "Yes," Truman replied. "That is what it amounts to."[3] The US was now at war, but its president disagreed. This initial confusion – or perhaps intellectual dishonesty – was only the beginning of the troubles the Truman administration faced in regard to what mistakenly has been called America's first limited war. The first step to solving any problem is to admit you have it.

In late-November 2015 testimony before Congress on the new Iraq War, President Barack Obama's Secretary of Defense, Ash Carter, said: "We're at war." But during the questioning he went on to say: "It's not war in the technical sense, but this is serious business. It feels that way to our people." Secretary of Defense Carter added: "We will win. We are going to win." Why is this relevant if the US is not actually at war? Additionally, President Obama repeatedly insisted there would be no American "boots on the ground" in the war against Islamic State (IS). At the time of Carter's testimony, there were 3,500 US military personnel in Iraq.[4] In the eyes of some analysts, war now is an exercise in risk management for too many political leaders.[5]

What was seen as an anomaly in 1950 has become the norm. US presidents do not ask for declarations of war. The practice of instead going to Congress for approval has been institutionalized in a bipartisan manner and is thus very unlikely to change. The 2001 Authorization of Military Force (AUMF) that President George W. Bush secured in the wake of the 9/11 attacks was particularly strong, and even though it did not officially declare war, it "bound the bureaucracy to frame the conflict as a 'war' rather than a law enforcement problem." Unfortunately, as political scientist Audrey Kurth Cronin observed, unlike the declarations of war upon Germany and Japan issued by Congress in 1941, which instructed President Roosevelt "to bring the conflict(s) to a successful termination," the 2001 AUMF had no such provision.[6] President Obama used the parameters of this same document to take the US to war in Iraq in 2014.

But What about So-called Limited War?

But how does all of this relate to so-called "limited war," and particularly modern American views of it? There are many weaknesses with the American approach to war since the end of the Second World War, but chief among them is a failure to deal successfully with the problems of so-called "limited war." The Korean War was quickly branded America's first "limited war," but there is no consensus on what this meant. It came to mean any war, particularly any US war, as long as it didn't look like the Second World War, or perhaps result in a nuclear exchange. Thinking on this subject quickly grew contradictory and confused, and the resulting misconceptions became underpinnings of the US failure to consistently, clearly, and decisively win its wars since the end of the Second World War. Why? The manner in which we write and think about limited war intertwines *all* US thinking about war, and this is so broken and illogical that it has poisoned the US ability to fight *any* war.

Franklin Roosevelt provided a past example of clearer thinking in his January 1942 State of the Union address, one delivered a month after the Japanese attack on Pearl Harbor brought the US into the Second World War. "Our own objectives are clear," Roosevelt insisted, and then he gave them: "the objective of smashing the militarism imposed by war lords upon their enslaved peoples, the objective of liberating the subjugated Nations – the objective of establishing and securing freedom of speech, freedom of religion, freedom from want, and freedom from fear everywhere in the world." This is not as clear and clean as "unconditional surrender," which became the US and Allied political aim after the January 1943 Casablanca Conference, but does provide solid aims: smashing militarism (meaning Nazi Germany, Fascist Italy, and Imperial Japan), and freeing "subjugated Nations." These are political aims to which military force can be rationally directed. Roosevelt then summoned the specter of failed post-First World War peacemaking and gave the US people a vision of what victory looked like – and meant: "We shall not stop short of these objectives – nor shall we be satisfied merely to gain them and then call it a day . . . this time we are determined not only to win the war, but also to maintain the security of the peace that will follow."[7] Roosevelt was thinking clearly about war *and* peace. Modern political and military leaders, policymakers, and academics who write on these matters consistently do not. The US failure to pursue victory, the US failure to understand the nature of the wars into which the country enters, the US failure to wage wars decisively: all of this is rooted in confused ideas about war in general and wars for limited political aims in particular. Why do I say this? And how do I prove this point?

Defining "Limited War"

It is imperative to begin our discussion by laying a firm, universally applicable groundwork for our approach. Simply put, we don't know what we mean when we use the term "limited war." Here are two examples from what are considered classic texts on the subject: 1) "Only conflicts which contain the potentiality for becoming total can be described as limited";[8] 2) "Limited war is a conflict short of general war to achieve specific political aims, using limited forces and limited force."[9] Both of these definitions explain limited war in relation to other types of conflict that also lack clear, generally agreed-upon definitions, i.e. "total war" and "general war" (we will revisit these in the next chapter). The best-known theorist of limited war, political scientist Robert Osgood, in his 1957 work defined limited war in terms of the objective sought and (among other things) by the fact that the combatants "do not demand the utmost military effort of which the belligerents are capable."[10] This is nebulous at best and fails to offer a firm and usable explanation of "effort," or what some would term the means used. The definitions haven't improved with the passing decades. A 2010 book noted that "The term limited war implies regular military operations by one nation-state against the regular military force of another nation-state and excludes irregular operations by terrorist organisations against state or by other non-state actors like warlords against a state or against other warlords."[11] This is another variation of a definition based upon means with the addition of the opponent's doctrinal warfighting methods. All of this demonstrates the potentially fatal problem: if we cannot even clearly define limited war, how can we understand its nature? And if we don't understand what "limited war" means, *we don't understand what we mean when we describe any war.*

Unfortunately, this type of conceptual muddle is typical in the theoretical and historical literature, as the given definitions of limited war generally imply that the level of means used by the combatants determines whether or not a conflict is a limited war. The problem here is this: defining a war by the means used – which is generally what current limited war theory and most similar literature does – fails to provide a clear, universally applicable foundation for analysis. Wars, as Carl von Clausewitz wrote in *On War* and in *Strategie*, should be defined by the political aim sought, not the means or level of violence employed, nor the amount of destruction inflicted upon the enemy. Clausewitz wrote: "War can be of two kinds, in the sense that either the objective is to *overthrow the enemy* – to render him politically helpless or militarily impotent, thus forcing him to sign whatever peace we please; or *merely to occupy some of his frontier-districts* so that we can annex them or use them for bargaining at the peace negotiations." Wars are fought for regime change or something less than this. Building upon Clausewitz's foundation, British maritime theorist Sir Julian Corbett, in his *Some Principles of Maritime Strategy*, gave us the terms "unlimited war," to describe a conflict waged to overthrow the enemy government (an unlimited political aim), and "limited war," for a war fought for something less (a limited political aim).[12] This typology provides an ironclad foundation for substantive analysis, because dissecting wars by beginning with the political aims sought provides a constant upon which to base any discussion or analysis, as well as a foundation for building a coherent theory in regard to wars fought for limited political aims. The means used certainly help determine the nature of the war being fought; indeed, this is one of the key factors (others are addressed in Chapter 4). But defining a war based upon the means used (or not) lacks universality, because it is not concrete. Moreover, it helps determine *how* the war is fought, but it is *not* what the war is about – the political aim – *and this is what matters most because it is from here that all else flows*. This clearly demonstrates part of the problem regarding how the US and other modern liberal democracies think about waging war: they too often fail to clearly define what they're fighting for or fail to understand the effects of this on what they must do to win and the actions of other powers.

Why does all of this matter for us? First, *all* of the wars in which the US has been involved since the Japanese surrender in 1945 have been branded limited wars. This is done regardless of whether or not the term accurately depicts US political aims or explains the nature of the war. The Korean War, the Vietnam War, the war in Afghanistan, and all three Iraq wars are consistently branded limited wars: a term that most writers and speakers on the subject fail to define, or that is a catchall for nearly every type of conflict.[13] For example, Seymour Deitchman, in his 1964 *Limited War and American Defense Policy*, provides a list of thrity-two wars fought between 1945 and 1962 that include such different conflicts as the Chinese Civil War (1927–49), the Philippine Huk Rebellion (1946–54), and the 1962 Bay of Pigs Invasion of Cuba. All are classified as limited wars. He has another list of fifty-nine conflicts that occurred – or almost did (a particularly unique element in his approach) – during this same period and breaks these struggles into three types: conventional wars, unconventional wars, and deterred wars. He does this while never clearly defining limited war.[14] Blindly throwing the "limited war" blanket over all of these examples is a flawed method of attempting to analyze and understand these wars, and – more importantly – to fight current and future ones. This remains part of the conceptual problem Americans have in regard to *all* wars.[15]

Second, the problem of not understanding the nature of the war is directly related to how we currently define – or more accurately – fail to define limited war. In a 2014 article, a *Washington Post* journalist described what the US began doing in Iraq in June 2014 as a limited war. He gave no clear definition of limited war and seems to believe that the most recent war in Iraq was a limited war because the US was making a minor effort.[16] But this does not define the war – or its nature: it simply explains the means being used. It does not in any way describe what the US hoped to achieve, and the political aim being sought is the keystone for what is being done – or at least it should be.

This is also illustrative of another problem: the Third Iraq War was arguably being waged for an unlimited political aim, i.e. "to degrade and destroy Islamic State," yet early discussions of the conflict branded it a limited war because of the low level of military means the US committed.[17]

This lack of clarity is not unusual and is far from new. Modern writing about limited war (which is rooted in Cold War works and concepts) is generally of value only as examples of how not to examine conflicts. The authors of these works – particularly the twenty-first-century examples – often fail to even define what they mean by limited war.[18] Moreover, when they do, the definition tends to mix political ends and military means, or political ends, strategic and operational ways, and military means, thus failing to provide a solid definition for critical analysis.[19]

Third, limited war writers, as well as the Cold War itself, helped teach many in modern liberal states not only that victory in war should not be pursued, but that its achievement was actually bad. John Garnett, one of the founding fathers of modern strategic studies, wrote: "In limited war 'winning' is an inappropriate and dangerous goal, and a state which finds itself close to it should immediately begin to practise restraint."[20] Former US Secretary of State and retired general Colin Powell once noted that "As soon as they tell me it [war] is limited, it means that they do not care whether you achieve a result or not. As soon as they tell me, 'surgical,' I head for the bunker."[21] A veteran of more than two decades in the US Foreign Service criticized examinations of US wars as being too "victory centric," faulted them for using a "victory-tinted lens," and insisted that searching for a reason for not winning a war "treats victory as the norm and military frustration as an aberration, an attitude that distorts our understanding of conflict and its unpredictable results." Instead, the focus should be upon cutting one's losses to avoid a protracted conflict.[22] In other words, the US should learn to lose more quickly at a lower cost. Even the Taliban's decisive August 2021 victory (there is no other word for it) over the United States, NATO, and Afghanistan's elected, democratic government, failed to staunch such thinking as the featured article in October 2021's Naval Institute *Proceedings* magazine argues the US military should not be in the victory business.[23] Such thinking sells short the seriousness of war and thus undermines the ability of the US and other Western powers to clearly identify the political aim or aims for which they are fighting any war (the ends), create intelligent strategy for achieving this (the ways), and harness national power – especially military power (the means) – *sufficient* for achieving the desired end.

Fourth, bad limited war theory has helped rob the US and other Western nations of the awareness that wars should be waged decisively. If leaders cannot clearly define what they want, how can the military hope to deliver it? And if the means dedicated to getting the job done are insufficient merely because the war has been branded limited, how can one win? The result is that "victory" – both in battle and in war itself – has generally disappeared from statements of analysts and policymakers. Many of these same figures view the term itself with suspicion.[24] One author writing in 2005 insisted, in a chapter titled "The End of Victory," that "The first notion the military strategist must discard is victory, for strategy is not about winning." He provides this elaboration: "Battles and wars may end, but interaction between individuals and states goes on," and "one can no more achieve final victory than one can 'win' history." Because of this, the strategist should not concern themselves with victory in the war itself; victory is only the concern of the tactician.[25] Among the many theoretical problems here is the false assumption that strategic analysis of potential future conflicts and events will stop if victory in a then current conflict is achieved and so named (the North Vietnamese and Taliban certainly understood the reality of victory). It also ignores the distinction between war and peace, and encourages drawing the false conclusion that strategic thinking will stop when the war ends.

Why does all of this matter? *If you aren't trying to win the war, you usually aren't seriously trying to end it.* Refusing to pursue victory can produce an endless war. Swedish political scientist Caroline Holmqvist, writing in 2014 about the conflicts in Afghanistan and Iraq, illustrates this problem by noting that "war is becoming perpetual or endless quite simply because the liberal world is *unable to imagine conclusive endings* to the wars it is currently fighting." She partially attributes this to the current practice of focusing on the present while detached from any reference to the past, accompanied by the inability to imagine a future different from the present trouble. This contributes to concentration on the immediate (and thus the tactical), and a focus on the means rather than the political end, the "how" rather than the "why" and "what for." The use of force becomes equated with the political aim, and the tactical mistakenly becomes the political, with the result that the point of the war becomes war itself.[26] Additionally, US and other Western leaders now forget this truth: *your enemy is trying to win*. General Rupert Smith observed that "unlike all other socially acceptable behaviour except some sports, wars and fights are not competitions: to be second is to lose."[27] Only Western liberal democracies in the post-Second World War era go to war without the expectation of victory. Fortunately, the political leaders who fought against the Nazis understood the necessity of victory. Winning (or losing) a war *matters*, particularly to the people who live directly with the results.

The refusal to value victory in warfare, or to define it, as well as the refusal to seek it when one is fighting a war, is a political problem that affects the ability of the military to fight the war effectively and deliver victory. American political leaders are ordering men and women into combat without having a clear idea of what they mean by victory, and sometimes with no desire to even achieve it. Since the time of the Korean War, US political leaders have too often sacrificed the lives of American men and women in wars these political leaders don't believe are important enough to actually win (the Korean and Third Iraq Wars spring instantly to mind). These political leaders don't often phrase it this way, but that is the reality of the result of their decisions. Waging war in this manner is either an expression of ignorance, or an example of incompetence on the part of political and military leaders. If it is not important enough to win, it is not important enough to go to war. One of the jobs of America's leaders is to *win* the wars into which they lead the United States. Using force – decisively – is the most important wartime tool for doing this.

What Do We Want? And Do We Want to Win?

The event crystalizing American views of the Korean War was President Truman's April 1951 firing of General Douglas MacArthur on well-justified grounds of insubordination.[28] Memories of this unfortunate clash cloud a key issue that contributed to the problem: confusion at the top of the Truman administration in regard to what political aim MacArthur was supposed to achieve in Korea. MacArthur's victorious United Nations forces had been sent into North Korea after liberating the South, but the Chinese Army that intervened in Korea on October 25, 1950 threw the US and UN forces out of North Korea and below the pre-war 38th-parallel border. By February 1951, the UN coalition forces had recovered and started pushing back the Chinese and North Koreans. This same month the US Joint Chiefs of Staff (JCS) complained that the US State Department would not give them political aims in Korea until its officials knew the military's capabilities. Both MacArthur and the Joint Chiefs protested – correctly – that the political decision needed to come first so that the military could then determine the courses of action that would allow it to fulfil the wishes of its masters.[29] The previous month, the National Security Council (NSC) had begun reexamining US war aims in Korea amidst the depth of the Chinese offensive. This political limbo dragged on – unresolved – until Truman signed NSC Directive 48/5 on May 17, 1951. The US political aim became the reestablishment of peace based on the pre-war frontiers.[30]

What does this mean? It means that from October 1950 until May 1951 the official political aim of the US forces fighting in Korea was the unification of Korea under UN supervision. This had been decided in NSC 81/1 by political leaders in Washington on September 9, 1950, *before* the US and UN forces under MacArthur landed at Inchon on September 15, and *before* they were ordered to invade North Korea on September 26 (this was a shift from the initial political aim of restoration of the antebellum border at the 38th parallel).[31] After MacArthur's relief, his successor, Matthew B. Ridgway, operated under the same orders to seek the unification of Korea. But this is something for which he was not given the means, and his instructions from the Joint Chiefs tied his hands in so many ways that he could not possibly achieve his government's official political aim. Here is the manifestation of the problem we have just discussed: the Truman administration struggled to define the political aim – to define victory.

Also, after the Chinese entry into the war the Truman administration failed to pursue victory wholeheartedly, even when opportunity stared at them. The following spring, during the last two weeks
of May 1951, Lieutenant General James Van Fleet, Ridgway's relief as
commander of the 8th Army in Korea when Ridgway replaced
MacArthur, saw an opportunity to decisively defeat the Chinese and
North Korean armies. The Communist forces were exhausted from
their most recent failed offensives and suffering immense logistical
difficulties. Breaking them would have given the US a solid chance
to conclude peace with the enemy. Many other senior US generals and
admirals shared Van Fleet's assessment of the military situation, and
post-war information confirmed the shattered state of the Communist
forces in Korea. Ridgway disagreed. He refused to give Van Fleet his
leash because the necessary operations would have meant attacking
north of a line drawn across the peninsula by the Pentagon.
Additionally, rumors of a ceasefire were in the wind, and Ridgway
considered the US forces exhausted. Instead of trying to land the
decisive blow – instead of trying to achieve a military victory that
would have a chance of forcing an end to the war and delivering
political victory – the UN forces began slowly and methodically
pushing back the Communist armies. The Communists then asked
for armistice talks, and the US pressure subsided. The Chinese then
dug in and reconstituted their forces.[32] The opportunity passed
untaken; and the war went on for two more years.

Extended armistice talks ensued. Vice Admiral C. Turner Joy
led the US/UN team through much of this drama. One of the sticking
points in the negotiations was the Truman administration's decision to
not force the repatriation of prisoners held by the US and UN who didn't
wish to return. The Communist powers demanded this, but neither side
would bend. Admiral Joy (though he never disagreed publicly with the
position of his political superiors) believed this decision put the security
of enemy POWs over that of US/UN prisoners. "Since we were not
allowed to achieve a victory," Joy explained, "I wanted the war
halted."[33]

A second thing that is widely remembered about the Korean War
is MacArthur's remark that "In war there is no substitute for
victory." What is forgotten is the sentence he uttered before this: "War's
very object is victory, not prolonged indecision."[34] MacArthur, for all his
many faults, understood the importance of victory better than Truman. In

the Korean War, not seeking victory meant the struggle devolved into a bloody stalemate. Most Americans supported US participation in the conflict, as long as their political leaders sought victory – meaning, to win.[35] Indeed, early in the contest the American public outran its political representatives in its desire to mobilize and do what was necessary to win the war.[36] But as it dragged on with seemingly no conclusion in sight, American support began eroding in a fashion foreshadowing the Vietnam War.

Other senior US officers shared MacArthur's views on the importance of achieving victory. During his presidential campaign, Eisenhower promised that, if elected, he would visit Korea. He did so on December 5–8, 1952, and met with Ridgway's successor, General Mark W. Clark. General Clark asked "to be allowed 'to win in our first test of arms against communism.'" He had a plan to do so, but was not permitted to present it to Eisenhower. Clark remarked later that "The question of how much it would take to win the war was never raised." When an armistice finally brought the fighting to an end, Clark bitterly noted: "In carrying out the instructions of my government, I gained the unenviable distinction of being the first United States Army commander in history to sign an armistice without victory ... I believe that the Armistice, by and large, was a fair one – considering that we lacked the determination to win the war."[37]

Why, then, did US leaders here fail to seek a military decision that would deliver a political victory? And was this decision correct? Something important to remember is the Cold War context. The US fought the Korean War under the umbrella of a Cold War great power competition against the Communist bloc. Thus, the US was seeking multiple political aims. The aim of the initial strategy of containment authored by George F. Kennan was to force the collapse or mellowing of the Soviet Union, but the US had a political aim in Korea as well. This is the problem with what is sometimes called a nested war, meaning a conflict waged in the midst of a larger political or military struggle. The contributing factor of the pursuit of additional aims can complicate the drive to achieve the political aim for which the limited war is being fought. In Korea, US leaders mistakenly deferred resolution of a very bloody problem to deal with a hypothetical, potential future conflict that never arrived. They took council of their fears, and this prevented them from solving the situation at hand, with ill effects for both the US and the world. Truman and his advisors feared escalation and a possible widening of the war – and they were right to do so – especially if they took the war into China. But the US had the capability of ending – and winning – the war in Korea without doing this. Indeed, as we have seen, General Van Fleet had wanted to try and had a plan for doing so: defeating a much-weakened Chinese army. Dutch political scientist Rob de Wijk insists that "to be successful, liberal democracies must use force decisively."[38] This seems a statement of the obvious, but it is no longer so obvious to American political leaders, journalists, and academics.

Bad Habits Die Hard

On November 16, 2015, US President Barack Obama held a press conference during a meeting of the G20 in Turkey. His reaction to hard questions from a usually sympathetic press was widely described as "peevish." Islamic State terror attacks had occurred three days before in Paris, and media reports depicted America's president as perceiving *himself* as under siege. His strategy for the war against the Islamic State in Iraq and Syria (ISIS) – or Islamic State (IS) – certainly was being critiqued, and not just by his Republican opponents and habitually critical talk radio pundits. Even Democratic California Senator Dianne Feinstein did not shy away from criticizing the administration's failures in dealing with IS.[39] Worsening President Obama's situation was his insistence the day before the Paris atrocity that IS was contained. This fueled administration critics and fed increasing concerns about its foreign policy competence, strategic acumen, and its general ability – and particularly willingness – to lead.[40]

The US president may have been "peevish" as his critics insisted, but what Obama said was vastly more important than journalistic speculations on his temperament. His answers to press questions raised two issues about the administration's view of and approach to Islamic State: Did they understand the nature of the war? And did they want to win?

One should not get the impression that President Obama is the sole source of US foreign policy ills. His predecessors, from Harry S. Truman to George W. Bush, have all contributed to the too-often disastrous approaches the United States has followed in the prosecution of its wars since the end of the Second World War, particularly so-called "limited wars." He is merely the most recent US president to take the country to war without admitting (or perhaps even realizing) that this is what they have done, while simultaneously not understanding the nature of the struggle upon which they've embarked. This last point is illustrated in three ways: his description of Islamic State as "killers with fantasies of glory," his insistence that the US plays into the Islamic State "narrative" by acting as if IS was a state, and his refusal to describe IS as "Islamic."[41] Yes, Islamic State was violent. Yes, its members were thuggish killers. But their violence was conducted with a clear political purpose in mind: the reestablishment of the ancient caliphate. They see themselves as true Muslims waging a justified and necessary "Holy War" against infidel unbelievers – and not just the West. To state these truths does not make all Muslims IS supporters. Indeed, the adherents to the Shi'a branch of Islam are seen as apostates in the eyes of Islamic State, as are Yazidis, Christians, and Jews. But to not call them what they are is a failure to honestly face part of the nature of the opponent, and thus the nature of the war. Obama's refusal to admit that IS was a state is equally puzzling and perhaps more dangerous. No, Islamic State never had official, *de jure* recognition from any other government – to IS, other states were themselves illegitimate – but they possessed a state's trappings: a leader, a government, a bureaucracy, taxation, and an army in the field that could be attacked. IS was *de facto* a state in the very ways the US was a state from 1775 to December 1777 when it received official recognition from France. To say that IS was not a state is – at best – a failure to understand the opponent and the nature of the struggle. And when Western intellectuals begin describing events with terms such as "narrative" and "discourse," they are sometimes trying to delegitimize the opposition argument, not address its substance.

But why is not understanding the war's nature a problem? In *On War*, the famous Prussian military theorist Clausewitz wisely insisted that understanding the nature of the war (especially, what one hopes to achieve by it) is the first and most important task of both political leaders *and* military commanders entering into a conflict.[42] If one fails here, winning the war is increasingly costly and perhaps impossible. How do you win if you don't understand your enemy? How do you win if you don't understand the myriad conditions dictating *why* and *how* the war in which you are engaged will be fought? Most importantly: how do you achieve victory if you don't even know what you want from the struggle, or even know what victory means?

None of these complex issues seem to have been a problem in the view of President Obama, many of his predecessors, numerous intellectuals and pundits who write about war (particularly limited war), and scores of leaders in the West. Why? Because they have no interest in winning. In a November 19, 2015 press conference, President Obama attacked the idea of victory:

> But what I'm not interested in doing is posing or pursuing some notion of American leadership or America winning, or whatever other slogans they come up with that has no relationship to what is actually going to work to protect the American people, and to protect people in the region who are getting killed, and to protect our allies and people like France [sic]. I'm too busy for that.[43]

This, of course, provoked criticism. One American commentator remarked: "I don't know that we've ever had a president who didn't really care about America winning – and who announced it to the public."[44]

It's not surprising that Obama professed his disinterest in winning a foreign war. He is merely expressing the view of much of the present intellectual milieu. In defending Obama's Turkey comments, journalist Matthew Yglesias inadvertently revealed as much: "the hardest problem in US counterterrorism policy is in some ways as much a speechwriting challenge as anything else. The next time something goes wrong and an attack hits the United States, how do you sell the American people on the idea of not really doing anything about it?"[45] The problem with such an approach is that it ignores a critical point: the enemy is using violence to try to kill you in pursuit of their political aim. This brings to mind Leon Trotsky's biting but realistic observation: "You may not be interested in war, but war is interested in you." French writer Bernard-Henri Lévy noted the larger problem with the president's remarks: "What is it about this war that the America of Barack Obama, at least for the moment, seems not to really want to win? I do not know the answer. But I know where the key lies. And I know the alternative to using the key: No boots on their ground means more blood on ours."[46]

This leads us to a larger point: what was the US political aim (or political end) sought in regard to Islamic State? When he explained his decision to embark upon the Third Iraq War in a September 10, 2014 speech on the subject, President Obama said that the US political aim was to "degrade and ultimately destroy" IS. His announced strategy for doing this: inserting US military advisors and working with coalition partners.[47] How long would this take? Three years, administration officials insisted, and the problem would be handed over to the next president. The new US war (and it is a war because combatants are using violence to impose their will on opponents in order to achieve a political aim), *The New York Times* reported, was driven by the fears created by the murder of two American journalists and Islamic State's lightning advance across Syria and Iraq (unfortunately, not the cold, rational calculation with which President Obama was so often credited). "These American forces will not have a combat mission," President Obama promised, "we will not get dragged into another ground war in Iraq."[48] Yet, this is exactly what happened.

Part of how one demonstrates an understanding of the nature of a war is by possessing a clear political aim (the end), a clear, logical strategy for getting there (the ways), and allocating sufficient strength and resources for achieving the end (the means). What Obama presented in his September 2014 speech did not possess these basic strategic building blocks. It confuses aims and strategy. "Destroy" is an aim. "Degrade" is how one gets there. And the strategy depended upon coalition partners that had already failed because they did not field competent military forces. Moreover, the primary US ally on the ground – the Iraqi government – was dominated by sectarian politics and seen as illegitimate by much of the Iraqi populace. The president sent US troops into a combat zone without giving them the means to achieve the aim he declared important enough to require the potential sacrifice of their lives and much American treasure. The cynic could suggest the administration dusted off Obama's 2009 West Point speech on US strategy in Afghanistan, rebranded it, trimmed it, and cut its personnel requirements.[49]

As we've seen, many modern governments, particularly democracies, sometimes refuse to acknowledge that they are indeed fighting wars when they have committed large numbers of people to a combat environment and some have been killed. The US has been particularly guilty of this since the Korean War. The Obama administration did this when it first came into office and its officials branded the US wars being fought as part of the so-called Global War on Terror "overseas contingency operations."[50] Obama launched US troops into the Third Iraq War in June 2014, but in September 2014 his Secretary of State John Kerry insisted that the US was not actually at war.[51] There are, of course, political reasons for doing this, as well as constitutional ones.[52] If one actually labels the conflict a war, the people and the military might demand decisive action. The US Congress might take up its duty pre-scribed by the Constitution to declare war when the United States embarks on a conflict that is not a result of a direct attack upon the nation.[53] All of this can be expensive – and politically risky domestically and internationally. But allowing cynicism and personal political interest to cloud the reality of sending US men and women to fight a war – without honestly addressing the truth of the matter – demonstrates a failure to lead and to take responsibility on the part of American officials, one repeated far too often over the last seven decades, and for which the US has paid enormous costs in blood and treasure. Secretary Kerry's state-ment is particularly incomprehensible because it comes from a man who is a combat veteran of the Vietnam War who knows far better than most political officials and pundits *exactly* what war means to the men and women who have to fight it. Refusing to call a war a war is an effort to spin reality into what one wishes it to be rather than honestly facing what is going on there. The badly named Global *War* on Terror and the *war* against Islamic State are wars. For a nation to be *at* war, and not admit that it is *in* a war, allows its leaders to see the conflict as something not particularly urgent. This gives them the option of not winning it, as well as to only support it enough to keep from losing face with their allies while avoiding potential domestic criticism.

This also demonstrates another significant and dangerous con-ceptual problem plaguing American strategic thinking: a failure to distinguish between war and peace and to understand what this means. War is violence purposely directed at an opponent for a political aim where one is trying to impose one's will upon the opponent.[54] The test is simple: can someone die there in combat? If the answer is yes, it's war. Whether or not the nation is at war deter-mines the means it can use military *force*, which is distinct from the possession of military *power*.

Again, one should not get the idea that President Obama and his administration are the sole source of such US problems. One can also point a blunt finger at his immediate predecessor, George W. Bush. President Bush demonstrated solid signs of not understand-ing the nature of the war that he launched when his administration declared a "Global War on Terror." Historian Hew Strachan makes a particularly cogent critique by labeling the Bush administration's approach "astrategic" because it chose as one of its aims the destruction of a particular fighting approach instead of establishing a clear political aim or goal. British comedian Terry Jones called it "war on an abstract noun." Another observer argued that the Bush administration failed to ask the key question: "What do we have to do to earn the peace we want?"[55] This conceptual debacle was furthered by declaring the war "long." What began in 2001 as a war against Al Qaeda in Afghanistan, and then added a war to democratize Iraq in 2003, was rebranded the "Long War" in February 2006. This is horribly inexact and unclear (as well as demoralizing) and can only be defined in relation to something just as undefinable – short. In 2007, the US Principal Undersecretary of Defense for Policy, when asked to define the "Long War," replied: "things get fuzzy past the five-year point." The official, when defending the term, said: "We in the defense department feel fairly confident that our forces will be called on to be engaged somewhere in the world in the next decade where they're currently not engaged but we have no idea whatsoever where that might be, when that might be or in what circumstances that they might be engaged."[56]

The more significant mistake, though, was a failure to define victory in the "Long War." One could argue that launching such a war is so intellectually and conceptually flawed that defining victory is impossible. Bush sought to destroy terror; Obama to destroy (or perhaps degrade) IS. These are aims, of a sort. But they are not clear political aims with solidly envisioned and obtainable end states with a clear vision of the post-war environment. Destroying terror is a nebulous and undefinable aim. Destroying Islamic State was possible, but what was to replace it? What, in both cases, was victory? It can be difficult to form a clear aim and express it, but this is no excuse for failing to take this first, important step.

Traditionally, being victorious in war meant something. Clausewitz said that "there is only one result that counts: *final victory*. Until then nothing is decided, nothing won, and nothing lost."[57] Sun Tzu wrote that "victory can be created."[58] Victory once mattered to US political leaders; it mattered to the people of the nation called upon to make the sacrifices necessary to fight the wars. This has changed. Theorist Edward Luttwak wrote: "The West has become comfortably habituated to defeat. Victory is viewed with great suspicion, if not outright hostility. After all, if the right-thinking are to achieve their great aim of abolishing war they must first persuade us that victory is futile or, better still, actually harmful."[59] As if to illustrate Luttwak's point, one author insists in a 2015 book that "We live in an age of unwinnable wars, where decisive triumph has proved to be a pipe dream."[60] The Taliban suffered from no such illusions.

US Presidents Obama and Bush demonstrated that they either aren't interested in victory (Obama) or failed to define it (Bush). There seems to be a bipartisan lack of understanding of the importance of victory, as well as what "victory" means. Here is a definition: the achievement of the political purpose for which the war is being fought. (This is distinct from victory in a specific battle or campaign.) Moreover, if the political leaders have done their job, their definition of victory includes a clear vision of the post-war situation. Ultimately, as Cicero tells us, war is about the restoration of peace; if it does not seek this, the war is not just.[61] Union General William Tecumseh Sherman insisted that "The legitimate object of war is a more perfect peace."[62] War is fighting for the peace *we* want.[63]

The Point of It All

What becomes clear in all of this is that the US and other Western democracies have a deep-seated problem: their political and military leaders too often do not understand how to *think* about waging wars, and thus don't wage them effectively. This is rooted in an inability to determine rationally the nature of the war and pursue it to a victorious end. Gaining an understanding of wars fought for limited political aims – what this means and how to wage them – will give us an understanding of *all* wars. This is imperative, as post-1945 US conflicts have been generally misunderstood and bad theory has undermined US thinking in regard to war. Wars fought based upon shoddy thinking have a price, one the US and its allies have paid far too many times, and for which the country gains little or nothing.

All of this demonstrates a Western world intellectually at sea in a strategic sense while facing conflicts and competition for which current strategic thought does not provide proper analytical tools.[64] Consistently, Western leaders don't know how to set clear political aims, don't understand how to conceptualize the wars they launch in pursuit of often fuzzy political aims, and don't value victory – or tell their people what this means. Waging war in this manner is either an expression of ignorance or an example of dishonesty – intentional or not – on the part of political leaders for short-term political purposes that have long-term effects on public opinion and the men and women who are being sent to fight wars their leaders don't call wars and have no intention of winning. As General Rupert Smith observed: we no longer understand the use of force.[65] To purposefully fight a war one must – at a minimum – know why one is fighting and what one hopes to achieve, understand the enemy, know what victory looks like, chart a sensible path for getting there, and plan for maintaining the peace.

The US cannot change what it does and how it does it in regard to waging war until it changes how it *thinks* about war. That is what this book seeks to do.

2 THE WAY WE THINK ABOUT WAR (PARTICULARLY SO-CALLED LIMITED WAR) IS BROKEN: HERE IS HOW WE FIX IT

Since words are hard to kill ...[1]
Urs Schwarz

The Task at Hand

Robert Osgood, one of the most prolific writers on our subject, insisted upon the impossibility of the construction of a functional limited war theory. "What we are almost certain not to witness," he wrote in 1969:

> is the perfection of limited-war conceptions and practice in accordance with some predictable, rational calculus and reliable, universal rules of the game. The conditions and modalities of international conflict are too varied, dynamic, and subjective for limited war to be that determinate. Any search for the strategic equivalent of economic man on the basis of which a grand theory of military behavior might be erected is bound to be ephemeral and unproductive.[2]

Osgood is utterly mistaken. Like nearly every other writer on limited war, he does not understand the purpose of theory. Clausewitz gave us the first steps to understanding: "The primary purpose of any theory is to clarify concepts and ideas that have become ... confused and entangled."[3] Theory, as Corbett tells us, "can assist a capable man to acquire a broad outlook." Theory should teach us to think critically, to analyze, to bring a testing but informed eye to the problem at hand and consider both its depth and breadth. It provides conceptual tools, and grounds us by defining our terms and providing us a firm foundation for analysis while teaching us to distinguish between what is important and what isn't.[4] It teaches us to ask the most important question: why?

But this can't be the "pie-in-the-sky" theorizing of which academics like myself are so often guilty. The results of theory, Clausewitz insists, "must have been derived from military history, or at least checked against it," thus ensuring "that theory will have to remain realistic. It cannot allow itself to get lost in futile speculation, hairsplitting, and flights of fancy." Most importantly, particularly in any theory addressing warfare, it "is meant to educate the mind of the future commander."[5] Historian Peter Paret made similar points on the value and importance of solid theory: "A theory that is logically and historically defensible, and that reflects present reality, has the pedagogic function of helping the student organize and develop his ideas on war, which he draws from experience, study, and from history – the exploration of the past extends the reality that any one individual can experience."[6]

Osgood also did not understand that Clausewitz not only told us why good theory is necessary, he also gave us the intellectual basis for building a solid theoretical approach to wars fought for a limited political aim. Chapter 1 poured the foundation of our analysis: the classification of wars based upon the political aim sought. But Clausewitz, though he provided a firm foundation in On War, did not finish the intended revisions to his text regarding the theoretical and strategic issues directly bearing upon wars fought for a limited political aim. He made clear his intention to rewrite his unfinished opus based upon his epiphany that all wars are fought for regime change or something less, but did not live to do so.[7] Corbett built upon Clausewitz's work to construct a theory of maritime warfare that deals with wars for limited political aims, but this work also does not finish the task, and suffers at times from a mixing of ends and means that confuses his message.

Why does this matter? Using Clausewitz's definitional and methodological approach, some of Corbett's ideas, and relevant historical examples, we have the tools for building a strategic theory for analyzing wars fought for limited political aims. Such an approach will clarify a muddled field, and provide military professionals and

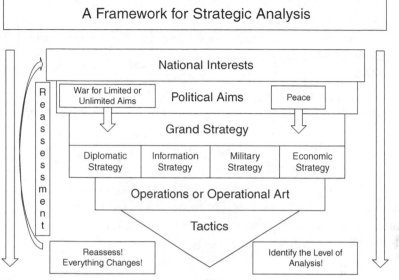

Figure 1

policymakers with a methodology that will help them better understand a type of conflict that nations have always faced – and that the US has forgotten how to win.

First, though, in order to further establish the basis for our discussion, we must (as Clausewitz says) "clarify concepts" and untangle the muddled theorizing regarding war in general. This will give us something that other works on limited war lack, as well as what is of fundamental importance: a firm foundation for analysis. Without this secure base we cannot build a theory that is consistently and rationally instructive.

One way to conceptualize the relationship between the political aim and how power is used to achieve it is to view war's dominant elements as distinct but interrelated realms. Figure 1 is presented as a conceptual, analytical tool. We start, as it does, in a top-down approach. Our foundational element is national interests, usually things of core necessity to a state's survival or prosperity. These often vary over time, can be subjective, and are sometimes determined by a unique situation. National interests usually underpin why nations select certain political aims and drive the actions of its leaders. But this is not an absolute; there are few absolutes in such matters. When examining this, we must be careful to avoid confusing interests with political aims. At times, something can be both, which complicates the analytical problem.

For example, it is in the interest of the United States to have security but seeking security for the nation can also be a political aim.

Next, are political aims. As Clausewitz, Corbett, Machiavelli, and other theorists make clear, states go to war for political reasons: there is something they want to achieve, or they want to protect what they have. These objectives might be masked in religious terms or various euphemisms, but, in the end, when states or political entities go to war they are using violence to get something they want, violence that is inherently political in nature in which they are trying to impose their will upon an enemy; this divides war from peace. To ignore the political aim sought is to forget the essence of what any war is about (this also ignores war's instrumentality), and to forget the bloodshed involved is to refuse to accept the truth of war's nature.[8] Indeed, one of the problems with some limited war theorizing is that it ignores the fact that wars fought for limited political aims are indeed *wars*. It is certainly true that states pursue political aims without resort to war (one wishes this were the preferred method), but the sweep of history demonstrates a human predilection for war – whether one likes this or not. Finally, elaboration of the political aim should include a vision of what victory looks like or what it means. When nations pursue their political aims – whether defensive or offensive – they use various elements of national power to try to achieve them. This is the realm of grand strategy. Here we find the tools of the state beyond just military power. Sometimes this is represented by the acronym DIME (Diplomatic, Informational, Military, Economic).[9] This is not a bad way to think about grand strategy, as it grants breadth and applies to the pursuit of political aims in both peace and war, and "grand strategy" can be utilized in both. One should not forget, though, internal political influence upon national decision-making.

The term "strategy" is too often used without bothering to define it. It boils down to the use of power. Military strategy is generally discussed in the context of warfare, but "strategy" certainly applies in peacetime as well. For our purposes, military strategy is defined as the larger use of military power in the pursuit of a political aim. It is how a nation uses military force to get what it wants and is the military element of grand strategy. Some examples of military strategy include attrition, exhaustion, and protraction.[10] This is addressed further in Chapter 5.

Military operations are the campaigns one conducts to implement wartime strategies. Operations bridge the gap between strategy and tactics and provide purpose for the subsequent tactical engagements. Operational art is the manner in which one conducts these campaigns and is defined by the US Army as "the pursuit of strategic objectives, in whole or in part, through the arrangement of tactical actions in time, space, and purpose."[11] Operations should support the implementation of strategy, and both should affect the enemy's will or material ability to wage war, ideally both. If they are doing neither, you must question their efficacy and whether you understand the use of force, and realize you're wasting time, resources, and – more importantly – lives.

The specific methods military forces use to conduct campaigns are known as doctrine (though this does not appear in Figure 1). This is important for our discussion because what is alternatively called Guerrilla War, Little War (*Petite Guerre, kleiner Krieg, Kleinkrieg*), or Partisan War (*Parteigängerkrieg*) is sometimes branded "limited war." It is not. These are methods of waging war, fighting methods, if you like, not what the war is about. Little War is a doctrinal practice governing the use of light troops or militia in independent detachments that dates to the eighteenth century. It is often confused with modern guerrilla warfare because the tactical activities of forces implementing Little War closely resemble those of the modern guerrilla: hitting outposts and messengers, attacking supply lines and detachments, etc. But the guerrilla is usually an irregular or a non-state actor and not part of a regular army (at least not at first).[12]

"Tactics," or the tactical realm, deal with how military forces directly fight the enemy. Weapons technology and methods for using them drive tactics more than any other factors, and the constant roiling of technology means tactics are never still. The operational and tactical realms are indeed important but beyond the scope of our study.

"Total War" and Other Terms That Mean Nothing

Discussion and analysis of all wars and their various elements fits within the same framework by beginning with the starting point of both Clausewitz and Corbett: all wars are fought either for the political aim of regime change or something less than this. But there is another problem we must first address. Peter Paret pointed out in 1960 that "any discussion of war is bedeviled by a confusion of terms ... the definitions have undergone repeated modification – and in different countries not always to the same effect."[13] Paret's point applies not just to wars fought for limited political aims, but to analysis and discussion of war in general. To properly explore war for limited aims, we must first destroy the shaky edifice that is the current approach to defining wars.

The modern use of the term "total war" can be dated to the French push in the last year of the First World War for *guerre totale*, which meant renewing the nation's ideological and political dedication to the struggle.[14] It is also often associated with German Field Marshal Erich Ludendorff's 1935 work *Der totale Krieg*, which appeared in English as *The Nation at War*.[15] Discussions of total war very often pick the First World War as the first example, though sometimes the French Revolutionary Wars and the US Civil War are branded the first total wars. These efforts focus generally – if not exclusively – on the means utilized or mobilized for the struggle in their effort to define it and are often tied to discussions on escalation that are based upon nations increasing the means they dedicate to the war.[16] As with limited war, the definition is built upon means.

The terms "absolute war" and "total war" are sometimes used interchangeably – and mistakenly – to depict Clausewitz's view of how wars should be fought, even though the term "total war" is not in the original text.[17] When using the "ideal type" methodology, the writer sets up a theoretical ideal that cannot be reached. Various factors intervene to prevent ascension to the ideal. Clausewitz used this method of analysis in *On War*. To him, "absolute war" is the unreachable "ideal type." War, if the state could utilize all of its resources and never stop moving toward its goal, would be absolute, but reality intervenes. Politics, friction, the actions of the enemy, and other forces unite to produce the reality of war, something that is violent and is always waged for regime change or something less than this.[18]

The most significant problem with the term "total war" is that it is used to mean everything and thus means nothing.[19] Historian Brian Bond calls total war a "myth."[20] Historian Eugenia Kiesling compares discussions of total war to medieval "ruminations about angels cavorting on pinheads."[21] Total war is rarely defined but generally is used to mean a "big" war, particularly the twentieth-century world wars. Explications of total war also usually include wars fought for the overthrow or complete conquest of the enemy regime and sometimes include other elements, such as the use of nuclear weapons and genocide, or the extermination of an enemy. Some similar terms often used interchangeably can be thrown in the same bowl: general war, major war, big war, national war, all-out war, central war, and others in this vein. A related (though valueless) definition commonly accepted in certain academic circles is: "Major war means an operation where the United States deployed over fifty thousand troops and there were at least one thousand battle deaths."[22] Critically, all of these definitions are dependent upon a variable that is consistently fluid: the means used to wage the war. Rationally, we cannot do this because it does not provide a foundation for critical analysis.

Robert Osgood offers us one of the better definitions of total war, though it also reveals the analytical and critical failure demonstrated by the use of this term as part of a theoretical approach: "that distinct twentieth-century species of unlimited war in which all the human and material resources of the belligerents are mobilized and employed against the total national life of the enemy."[23] This definition has several problems. First, it is limited to the twentieth century, and thus is not consistently applicable as an analytical tool. Second, it insists upon the mobilization of all of a state's "human and material resources." This is impossible. A state cannot harness "all" of its resources for war or anything else. During the Second World War the Soviet Union's leaders mobilized more of their nation's human and physical resources than any nation in history, but even Stalinism could not mobilize "all" of the state's power. During the US Civil War, nearly 80 percent of the Confederacy's white male population aged 15–40 served in uniform at some point during the conflict.[24] But even this extreme number is not "all."

Osgood's definition also mixes ends and means, which is not unusual. Indeed, the nearly universal element in definitions of total war is the emphasis upon means. Wars cannot be defined by the means, because this is a nebulous, subjective factor and thus does not pass the test of building upon solid ground. The means nations dedicate to pursuing political aims are a manifestation of the value they place upon that aim. The means used to fight the war are also one of the contributing factors helping to create the nature of the war. But they do not explain the war itself. The political aim sought is the only basis for analysis. The next two chapters address these elements.

Other discussions of total war center upon the use of technology, particularly technology that intensifies the bloodshed and destruction delivered at the tactical level. This is yet another example of defining total war by the means used. Technology and the increasing power of the modern centralized state simply feed and intensify war's inherent escalatory nature.

In military and political writing "limited war" and "total war" are often defined in opposition to one another. For example, in 1957 one author insisted that there existed no satisfactory definition of limited war, and that no one could explain when a conflict stopped being this and moved to being "total."[25] He makes this point by comparing one poorly defined thing with another defined equally badly.

The US Department of Defense once insisted that the term "total war" is "not to be used."[26] Unless someone is discussing war in a theoretical sense, "total war" should never appear in historical or policy writing. It has no analytical solidity, fails to clearly illuminate the nature of conflict, and destroys analysis rather than aiding it.

Limited War: A Bad Idea Whose Time Has Come

Current thinking on limited war is as intellectually unsound as that on total war and suffers from a number of fatal conceptual problems. First, it is largely designed to address a specific, no longer extant geopolitical situation – the Cold War, and particularly the early Cold War. Second, "limited war" is inconsistently and poorly defined. Third, its archetypal case study – the 1950–53 Korean War – is poorly understood by those who write on limited war, resulting in the creation of theory based upon falsehoods. Fourth, too often the authors of limited war theory assume the existence of supposedly predictable, liberal democratic views of rational behavior on the part of combatants, even when writing about the Soviet Union or one of its clients.[27]

A Now Non-Existent Cold War Context

As historian Hew Strachan correctly observed: "We live with the intellectual legacy of the Cold War more than we recognise." He also pointed out part of the problem with this: "The wars which actually occurred were defined, in the jargon of the 1960s, as 'limited wars' or 'low-intensity conflicts': in other words they were not assimilated into mainstream thinking about war, but were treated as exceptions to the rule."[28] This flawed view of post-Second World War conflicts has helped feed US and Western misunderstandings about waging war.

Modern limited war theory was born and developed under this Cold War cloud of a potential war between the United States and the Soviet Union. The most important concern of the era's limited war theorists was preventing violence escalating into a nuclear exchange between the superpower blocs. Avoiding nuclear war so ingrains early limited war literature that the cover of Robert McClintock's book on the subject depicts a mushroom cloud with a giant negating "X" superimposed over it. McClintock – confusingly but not atypically – defines limited war as "a conflict short of general war to achieve specific political aims, using limited forces and limited force. As between the great nuclear powers, the maintenance of the global strategic nuclear balance of power would preclude the use of strategic nuclear weapons, and fear of escalation would inhibit the use of tactical nuclear weapons."[29] Bernard Brodie, William Kaufmann, and others were driven by similar fears, especially after the development of the hydrogen bomb.[30]

A theory developed largely as a means of preventing escalation to a nuclear exchange has limited value as a theoretical approach for fighting wars that don't fit this specific model. Driven by dread of nuclear war, it became US practice to focus on deterrence, on "using policy to prevent war – and on a theory of limiting conflict – actually preventing escalation – should deterrence fail." US leaders saw themselves as having constraints – often self-imposed – "or saw conflict itself as limited," especially in regard to the means used. Their potential adversaries did not have the same views of warfare. But, again, it is a theory designed to deal with a Soviet–US clash.[31]

The Cold War no longer exists (though one could argue a new form of it is developing), and thus the theory constructed to meet this unique historical situation is obsolete. But we must not overlook that we certainly face some similar issues. The Western powers are confronted by a revanchist and nuclear-armed Russia. China, India, and Pakistan live in a very dangerous nuclear-armed neighborhood. All of these powers have fought a number of wars for limited political aims. How does theory deal with this, especially when we might have multiple nuclear-armed powers clashing with one another? This is addressed in Chapters 4 and 5.

Limited War: A Definitional Morass

"Limited War" is hardly a new term. Indeed, historians generally argue that eighteenth-century Europe endured "The Age of Limited Wars." But the effort to develop limited war as a typology of conflict distinct to itself is a recent development partly deriving from the Cold War desire to avoid a Third World War between the US and the Soviet Union.[32] The first modern piece on so-called "limited war" seems to be Basil Liddell Hart's March 1946 article "War, Limited."[33] Liddell Hart is thus the modern concept's likely but unintentional father.[34] The term possibly reentered our modern, public lexicon during the famous Senate hearings on the military situation surrounding the Korean War. In May 1951, General George C. Marshall (then Secretary of Defense), when asked to describe the war in Korea, said: "I would characterize it as a limited war which I hope will remain limited."[35] Numerous authors since have written on limited war and related topics, but the three whose work defined the modern approaches to the subject are Bernard Brodie, Robert Osgood, and Thomas Schelling.

Much of the thinking on limited war builds upon the work that historian and theorist Bernard Brodie began for the RAND Corporation in 1952 in the midst of the Korean War. Brodie notes that he did his first writing on this when most still believed that all wars had to be fought as "total wars." The fact that he suggested something different – limited wars – was, he insists, met with amazement.[36] Brodie himself was "converted" to limited war thinking by the work of Liddell Hart, of whom he became "a follower," also in 1952. This was probably the result of his reading Liddell Hart's 1947 book *The Revolution in Warfare*, about which Brodie noted Liddell Hart's linking the existence of atomic weapons to an "appeal for a return to limited war," which they generally define as limitation of the military means.[37] Among other things, the English theorist argued that Second World War area bombing, combined with the development of rockets and pilotless planes, demonstrated that warfare had moved "from a fight to a process of devastation," a point the development of the atomic bomb made definitive. Warfare had become so potentially destructive it was impossible for major powers to wage war against one another.[38] The ending of the US atomic monopoly in 1949 convinced more than one observer that this was indeed the case, but there was also the problem of potential Soviet aggression, particularly by a Soviet client state, as well as the hard reality that wars simply continued to be waged, regardless of the potential risk. Limited war theorizing filled what was perceived as a gap.

Brodie wrote an immense amount on limited war, but his seminal work here was *Strategy in the Missile Age*.[39] His extended definition of limited war bears quoting, as so many successive writers on the subject draw upon his work:

> What distinguishes limited war from total war? The answer is that limited war involves an important kind and degree of restraint – deliberate restraint. As a rule, we do not apply the term "limited war" to conflicts which are limited naturally by the fact that one or both sides lack the capacity to make them total (for example, the colonial war in Algeria). We generally use it to refer to wars in which the United States on the one side and the Soviet Union or Communist China on the other may be involved, perhaps directly but usually through proxies on one or both sides. In such wars the possibility of total or unrestricted conflict is always present as an obvious and immediately available alternative to limited operations. That is why we must emphasize the factor of deliberate restraint.
>
> The restraint must also be massive. One basic restraint always has to be present if the term "limited war" is to have any meaning at all: the strategic bombing of cities with nuclear weapons must be avoided.[40]

One sees here a basis of our theoretical problem. Brodie does not provide a coherent definition of limited war and defines limited war in opposition to the insubstantial term "total war." He does not define limited war by the objective sought, but by various factors that contribute to the waging of the war and its nature: whether or not the war is between the US and one of the great Communist powers, the possibility of escalation, and restraint in regard to the use of nuclear weapons.

The second key figure in limited war studies is one we have already encountered: political scientist Robert Osgood. His extended definition of limited war from his seminal 1957 book is also worth recounting in full, because it is generally cited in limited war writing and illustrates some of the problems in limited war thought:

> A limited war is one in which the belligerents restrict the purposes for which they fight to concrete, well-defined objectives

that do not demand the utmost military effort of which the belligerents are capable and that can be accommodated in a negotiated settlement. The battle is confined to a local geographical area and directed against selected targets – primarily those of direct military importance. It demands of the belligerents only a fractional commitment of their human and physical resources. It permits their economic, social, and political patterns of existence to continue without serious disruption.[41]

We see here key elements of much limited war thinking: a limited purpose (or limited political aim); the level of force is limited (sometimes proportionally); the bulk of a nation's political, social, and economic forces are not required; the geographical scope is restricted; and what is attacked is restricted.

Osgood elaborated on his definition:

Limited war, however, is not a uniform phenomenon. Such a war can be limited in different ways; it can be limited in some respects and not in others, depending upon its physical characteristics and the perspective of the belligerents. Thus, conceivably, a war can be limited in geographical scope but virtually unlimited in the weapons employed and the targets involved within the area of combat.

Later, he repeats his insistence that a limited war required the limiting of political aims and the limiting of means. All of this only clouds the issue by contradicting what he said in regard to the level of means. His definition of limited war provides no firm foundation for analysis because he does not – and indeed cannot – define "means" in a universally applicable manner. In Osgood's defense, he does say the following: "there is one characteristic of overriding importance in distinguishing among wars: the nature of the objectives for which the belligerents fight."[42] But the other items he heaps onto his definition are not a basis for defining a limited war; *they are factors contributing to the war's nature possessed of infinite variation*. They illuminate how the conflict is waged, but they do not define what it is about. Osgood did not sufficiently apply Occam's Razor and conclude the truth: the objective sought is *the* defining element.

Brodie and Osgood are in good company. An American officer writing in 1957 said that a limited war is "any war however large or small, regardless of the geography, objectives, weaponry, or strategy, in which the national survival of the US and the USSR is not at issue."[43] Some treatises are worse. In a discussion probably inspired by a RAND publication, one early limited war author breaks limited war into "High Order Limited Wars," by which he probably means a war by China in which the Soviets are not involved and where China can't attack the US, or a Soviet attack on Western Europe; "Middle grade" limited wars, such as the Arab–Israeli Wars; and "Low grade" limited wars or quasiwars, which are wars that are elements of the Cold War in such areas as South Asia, Africa, Latin America, and the Middle East.[44] Such an approach is a meaningless typology built upon seemingly random examples and lacking disciplined thought. It is worthless because it can't be applied consistently, and dangerous because it creates political and intellectual confusion.

One common point raised in efforts to define limited war is the necessity of the non-use of nuclear weapons.[45] This is not a universal requirement and as early as 1957 Henry Kissinger was writing about "limited nuclear war."[46] Brodie said there might be limited wars in which nuclear weapons were used.[47] Despite their destructive power, nuclear and atomic weapons are means for pursuing a political aim. They are particularly dangerous means, whose use (or potential use) is wrapped in unique political consequences, but they are still a manifestation of a combatant's means. One cannot define war by the means used. We revisit nuclear weapons in Chapter 4.

Other authors attempt to lay out requirements for defining a limited war by insisting upon restrictions upon such factors as the level of violence, the conflict's duration or time, and the geographical boundaries of the theater of war.[48] In 1972, Swedish political scientist Nordal Åkerman wrote that a limited war was a conflict in which a nation used only part of its "total military capacity," and where the "capacity for total war must not be affected by the conflict, nor must there be any engagement of the superpowers' home territory." He adds that the war must be confined to "a territorially limited area," and the combatants "must exercise voluntary restraint and have limited and well-defined objectives." Other restrictions include the types of weaponry, the geographical area, what can be attacked, the military objectives, "and the nature and number of the combatants involved."[49] Åkerman mixes ends and means, repeating the previously discussed error of basing parts of his definition on nebulous factors. He also adds "limitations" to his definition, but these are more accurately described as factors contributing to the nature of the war that govern where and how it will be fought: weapons, geography, the other combatants, and so on. All wars have geographical limits, even the Second World War (as some countries did not participate). Geographical limits cannot constitute part of a useable definition of limited war; they contribute to its nature, as do all other "limits" (though it is better to deem them "constraints"). These often describe how the war will be waged, but they don't define what the war is about. We will revisit the key constraints in Chapter 4.

Various descriptors for conflicts are thrown into the limited war pit even though they might not describe wars fought for limited political aims: "It has become fashionable," one author noted as early as 1957, to brand guerrilla wars, civil wars, wars between small states, and between big states and small ones "limited wars, and to attempt to arrive at some sort of magic formula for coping with them."[50] Low-intensity conflict, "big war," and "small war" also appear. "Big war" is sometimes used to mean a major national war or a so-called "total war." "Small war" is often used with the implication that a limited war must be a "small war," and is another fuzzy, badly defined designator. Political scientist and Iraq War veteran Craig Whiteside gives this tongue-in-cheek definition: "a small war is one in which you're getting shot at but no one cares." Well-known nineteenth-century soldier C. E. Callwell defined small wars as conflicts waged by regular forces against irregulars.[51] Thomas Schelling, the third member of our limited war triumvirate, provides us with this example: "Small wars embody the threat of a larger war; they are not just military engagements but 'crisis diplomacy.'"[52] To say this is to try to analyze war without talking about war, a common criticism leveled at Schelling, Osgood, and some other limited war theorists.[53] Unfortunately, this legacy has continued into the post-Cold War era. Too often US leaders and commentators on political and military affairs fail to realize that diplomacy is diplomacy, war is war, and that all wars should be analyzed beginning with the political aim sought. One author clearly explains the problem: "the big war/little war typology itself is not particularly useful because of its inherent ambiguity and lack of theoretical content."[54] Unclear thinking produces muddled ideas on this most important element of statecraft – waging war.

A 1961 article criticizing the use of the term "limited war" noted that "the wars envisioned by most people when they use the term 'Limited War' seem to be those in which non military [sic] constraints significantly limit the area of the conflict, the weapon and force mixture used, and the selection of military objectives and targets." There have always been such constraints upon warfare: geography, means, even international law. These are factors that contribute to the conflict's nature that must be examined to understand the war, but they do not lay a foundation upon which to base critical analysis. The same critic pinpointed the key problem: "The term has become a catch phrase describing a wide variety of past and possible circumstances and has been used by a variety of different people in a number of different contexts."[55] This has never been overcome.

Related to this is an ever-expanding group of buzzwords that generally describe the methods and means of warfighting (usually at the tactical level) and sometimes carry the added unintended evil of allowing political leaders to not call a war a war: Fourth Generation Warfare, Fifth Generation Warfare, Hybrid War, the Gray Zone, Measures Short of War, Low-Intensity Conflict, Political Warfare – the list goes on. They are generally part of the continuing (often unintentional) effort in the political science, international relations, and policy-wonk fields to repackage the old in a new wrapper.[56] There are many, many more examples of this, and such terms invariably define war by the means and methods used or confuse war and peace.[57] They also offer nothing new. For example, the war launched against Ukraine in 2014 by Vladimir Putin's Russia sparked discussions about gray zone war. In his 1954 book *Power and Policy*, former American Secretary of the Air Force Thomas K. Finletter wrote about war in "Gray Areas," deeming this "the countries outside of NATO which are in contact or nearly so with Russia and China."[58] Henry Kissinger built on Finletter in a 1957 article, and Osgood's 1957 book on limited war has a section title *Limited War in the Gray Areas*.[59] This is old wine in new bottles, often cracked ones.[60]

We see in all of this that the various definitions of limited war insist upon some or all of the following: limiting the aim (what is meant by this is rarely defined), limiting the means,[61] the prevention of escalation (particularly into so-called "total war");[62] constraints of various types that usually revolve around targeting or the level of violence, non-use of nuclear weapons (usually),[63] geographic limits,[64] and the awareness of limits on the other side. None of these provides a solid, useable foundation for critical analysis. Beyond the political aim sought, these are factors contributing to the nature of the war being waged.

One of the criticisms sometimes leveled at Clausewitz's *On War* is that he doesn't concern himself with various types of war, such as civil wars. Baron Antoine-Henri Jomini in his famous *Art of War* provides a laundry list of types of war.[65] What these works actually demonstrate is the weak reasoning offered by the authors of such texts. Jomini's treatment is really a discussion of the *reasons* for the wars and factors influencing their nature, one that doesn't differentiate by the political aim. More modern efforts on this line often mirror Jomini without knowing it. They all miss the point and fail to realize that the typology advanced by Corbett and Clausewitz, where one begins their analysis by examining the political aims of the combatants, encompasses all wars: civil, guerrilla, or whatever other moniker is composed.

Another problem with using such a variation of definitional types is that it makes impossible the construction of a coherent theory of war. Hence, we are back to reducing this to its essence and basing our discussion on the political aim sought. One must keep in mind the critical distinction between the political aim – which is defensive or offensive – and the strategy and operations conducted during the war. One may have a defensive political aim but use an offensive military strategy in pursuit of it. In turn, this may require defensive and offensive operations. One must also remember that all of these things – the objective, the strategy, the operations – are subject to change from the defense to the offense, and then back.

Also relevant to this discussion is the so-called "Spectrum of Conflict." This is a commonly used explanation that seeks to classify conflict (whether war or not) between nations, usually by the scale and type of means being used.[66] Harry Summers pointed out that this notion entered the US military lexicon as the "spectrum of war" via the US Army's 1962 *Field Service Regulations*. Then the spectrum stretched from "Cold War" to "Limited War." Summers also correctly identifies a "serious flaw": the spectrum fails to delineate between war and peace.[67] This type of defective thinking continues to feed current American misconceptions. We continue to confuse war and peace, something manifest in the discussions of hybrid war, gray zone war, and cyber war. In a 2016 article, General James Dubik made a similar argument, observing that US leaders are fuzzy about just what war is, a problem fed by the 1994 adoption (really, re-adoption) of a "spectrum of conflict" approach to strategic analysis."[68]

We need to kill the "spectrum of conflict" as a concept. Whether or not the nation is at war is the only proper delineation. One must not forget that nations can be in competition with one another and not be at war and involved in killing the soldiers (and usually civilians) of the other state. Competition is a norm and to be preferred but allowing our analysis of a war to be based upon a system that fails to consider the critical distinction between war and peace means there is no foundation for the argument.

All wars – civil wars, guerrilla wars, limited wars, religious wars, and the list goes on *ad infinitum* – fit within Clausewitz's typology because *all* wars are fought for political aims. There are no so-called "new wars."[69] The insistence of Clausewitz and many of his intellectual forebears that wars are driven by political considerations solved this key analytical problem centuries ago: wars are fought for political goals. Together, Clausewitz and Corbett provide the foundation for evaluating wars: it is the political aim or objectives sought – does the combatant seek regime change, or something less than this; the means and methods used in an effort to achieve the political aim are not the basis for analysis, but its indispensable enablers.

The Korean War, 1950–53: The Archetype That Isn't

The Korean War provided the cornerstone case study for the development of limited war theory and an example that ties all of the previously mentioned issues together.[70] This war is often presented – inaccurately – as "America's first limited war," and this term even features in the titles of works on the conflict.[71] This depiction has many problems.

When Kim Il-Sung's Soviet-backed North Korean regime launched its invasion of US-backed South Korea in June 1950, the North's political aim was clearly unlimited: conquest of the South. Initially, the US and UN fought the war in pursuit of a limited political aim: protecting South Korea. The US constrained the size of the force it employed to prosecute the war (the means) – particularly initially – and considered using, but never unleashed, its atomic arsenal (another means issue). Hence, we have why Korea is branded America's first limited war.

However, on September 9, 1950, *before* US forces under General Douglas MacArthur landed at Inchon on September 15 and subsequently completed the liberation of South Korea, the US altered its political aim and chose to eliminate the North Korean Communist regime.[72] What is almost universally ignored in the war's literature is that when the US crossed the 38th parallel into North Korea – a decision made by the Truman administration (which we address in detail in Chapter 4) and not MacArthur (who is often falsely blamed for this)[73] – the US was no longer fighting a war for a limited political aim. The US was now pursuing an *unlimited* political aim, because it was seeking to remove the regime ruling North Korea. The political aim changed – thus the nature of the war changed – whether US leaders realized it or not. The Chinese intervention decisively altered the nature of the war yet again. The Chinese political aim against South Korea was an unlimited one, because Mao sought the conquest of the peninsula. Against the US, Mao's objective was limited, as he sought the expulsion of US and UN forces from the peninsula and not the overthrow of the US government.[74] In May 1951, after much policy confusion, the US decided once again that it would settle for a limited aim: the status quo antebellum.[75] Two years later, the Chinese and North Koreans agreed. The Korean War is an example of a conflict where the political aims – and thus the war's nature – were in constant flux. Classifying this as a so-called "limited war" ignores the reality of the conflict.

Improper scrutiny of this struggle fed the construction of bad theory. Thomas Schelling, one of the best-known writers on limited war, likens the Korean War to a "negotiation" over the fate of that country.[76] One of the many problems with Schelling's analysis is that he seems to see everything as a negotiation, something probably arising from being overly influenced by his groundbreaking work in game theory. The struggle in Korea was not a negotiation. North Korea sought to annex South Korea using military force – violence – to achieve a particular political aim. The US and UN used military force – more violence – to keep this from happening. It was a war – plain and simple; to say anything other than this obscures the true nature of the problem at hand. To explain a war as a negotiation is yet another example of removing "war" from writing about war. Schelling, like so many other limited war writers, depict war – mistakenly and tragically – as something it isn't by branding the killing of hundreds of thousands of people as a business transaction. We must see things as they are, not as we wish them to be.[77]

Schelling's work provides other building blocks for some of the resultant cloudy thinking and false lessons arising from studies of the Korean War. For example, most definitions of limited war insist that the combatants will restrain themselves, particularly in regard to the means they're willing to commit to the struggle (we saw this earlier from Brodie and Åkerman). Schelling insists that the Korean War

> was fought with restraint, conscious restraint, and the restraint was on both sides. On the American side the most striking restraints were in territory and weapons. The United States did not bomb across the Yalu (or anywhere else in China) and did not use nuclear weapons. The enemy did not attack American ships at sea (except by shore batteries), bases in Japan, or bomb anything in South Korea, especially the vital area of Pusan.[78]

There are many problems with Schelling's assessment. The scale of the war was immense, no matter how one measures it. How, in any way, did the Chinese Communists practice restraint? Their entry into the war entailed an initial commitment of 260,000 troops.[79] The combined North Korean and Chinese forces in Korea in June 1951 numbered 1.2 million – and this was after absorbing nearly half a million casualties since the previous November. In May 1951, the UN forces consisted of 256,000 American, 250,000 South Korean, and 28,000 other troops. In July 1953, the South Korean Army had 568,994 men.[80] Moreover, Schelling is simply wrong about the lack of Chinese air attacks being an example of "restraint." The reality is that the US and UN forces controlled the air during most of the Korean War and had little fear in regard to air attacks on their bases in South Korea and Japan because of their air superiority.[81] The US did refuse to use atomic weapons in Korea, but this was as much because of their military impracticality in relation to the situation on the ground as it was to any other factor.[82] Moreover, in the spring of 1953, US President Dwight D. Eisenhower examined using atomic weapons if the Chinese and North Koreans would not sign an armistice.[83] This does not amount to a picture of "restraint."

What Schelling got right was that the US did not cross the Yalu River and expand the war into China. But this does not provide a corrective to the larger problem with Schelling's analysis. What he has actually identified – again – are means-and-methods issues representing some of the various factors contributing to the nature of the war. All wars have constraints placed upon their conduct. This is normal. There is political control. There are restrictions on means. In the Second World War, the US limited the size of its army in order to build a larger air force. Wars fought for limited political aims are more likely to have geographical constraints, but wars fought for unlimited political aims have them as well. These are factors contributing to its character and nature but fail to provide a foundation for a coherent examination of wars fought for limited political aims. Using the Korean War as the archetype for the development of limited war theory is flawed when one examines the facts within a consistent, rational context. The Korean War has its unique aspects – as do all wars – but it is also very similar to other wars in regard to the factors forming its nature.

The Assumption of Rationality and the Persistence of Irrationality

All of this leads us to our final point: the assumption of rationality made by limited war thinkers, particularly in regard to predicting the behavior of the enemy, especially the now-defunct Soviet Union. Historian Louis Morton raised this criticism of limited war thinkers in 1961: "Nor can one assume, as many of the proponents of limited war do, that the conduct of war will always be rational, and that the decisions of statesmen and soldiers will be governed in war by the same logic as in peace."[84] Nordal Åkerman wisely notes that "The special assumption of rationality on the part of one's opponent lends many works on limited war a cast of unreality." More importantly, he identifies the danger in such thinking:

> It is no problem to construct a logical system of reactions and counteractions if you are convinced that the enemy will consistently think in exactly the same categories as yourself. But if you take into consideration such matters as a different cultural framework of reference, different strategic cultures and traditions, utterly disparate and antagonistic ideologies – to mention only a few decisive factors – then its seems wishful thinking simply to assume that the enemy will react to one's gambit in the manner one has oneself defined.[85]

In this, Schelling is also the most important figure for our discussion. He proposed his own way of thinking about limited war in his 1960 *Strategy of Conflict*:

> To characterize the maneuvers and actions of limited war as a bargaining process is to emphasize that, in addition to the divergence of interest over the variables in dispute, there is a powerful common interest in reaching an outcome that is not enormously destructive of values to both sides. A "successful" employees' strike is not one that destroys the employer financially, it may even be one that never takes place. Something similar can be true of war.

Schelling went on to write: "Rather it is asserted that the assumption of rational behavior is a productive one in the generation of systematic theory."[86]

There are many problems with Schelling's approach here. First, as mentioned earlier, war is not "bargaining." It is, as Clausewitz tells us, a violent clash of wills, a duel on a larger scale. To describe it as a simple transaction is to refuse to see its true nature. War is violence, and the desire to pretend it is something other than this is the greatest failing of limited war theorists (one that remains with us). Author William Olson dissects a key problem here: "There was, for example, implicit in limited war theory a concept of tacit bargaining which maintained that belligerents continue to negotiate but use violence or its threat as an instrument in their 'dialogue.'" He goes on to note that limited war theory "was based on the notion that the belligerents had a common interest – to avoid nuclear holocaust," and that because of this there were certain "implied" ground rules "whereby the opponents recognised escalatory steps and thus were attuned to signals that communicated intentions and recognised the need to impose limits on means and actions – limits on intent. While this may have been true for the US–Soviet confrontation, the fact was that for many situations the US faced, there was not such a reciprocal concern."[87]

To Schelling, tacit bargaining – "bargaining in which communication is incomplete or impossible" – and "rationality" would produce mutually agreed-upon limits in warfare. Tacit bargaining was a form of "jockeying for limits in limited war."[88] The problem with this is that Schelling assumes the sides are "jockeying for limits." The reality of warfare – even in wars waged for limited aims – is that combatants tend to escalate the use of force and remove constraints when they are not achieving what they want but really, really want it. Combatants jockey for advantage. The Vietnam War gives us a fine example of this. When he became the US president, Richard M. Nixon used diplomacy with China and the Soviet Union to make it possible in the international political context for him to remove the self-imposed constraints on bombing North Vietnam and mining North Vietnam's Haiphong Harbor. He also removed many of the prior constraints regarding air and ground operations in Cambodia, at least for a time.[89]

Schelling also presents a theory that assumes rationality is sufficient to deal with irrationality, and his work speaks of a continuum stretching from rationality to irrationality.[90] At first glance his analysis appears to be a version of the "ideal type" method, but when insisting that rationality explains irrationality he is actually presenting opposites and not a lesser form of an acted-upon ideal. Moreover, we also know from Clausewitz's "Trinitarian Analysis" of rationality (usually manifested in the government), passion (generally arising from the people), and chance and creativity (primarily the military's domain), that governments aren't always rational and don't always do things purely because it is in their best interest to do so. Schelling – unintentionally – gives us an example of bad theory based upon faulty reasoning that isn't a universally applicable foundation upon which to build a theory of limited war. It is far more practical to simply seek to understand the reality of the other government's ideology and actions than to try to frame a government – or its actions – as rational or irrational, because in such a context these terms are very subjective and can be politically loaded. Deeming a political opponent "irrational" is a typical ploy used to delegitimize them. They are branded "irrational" because they don't agree with us or our solution.

This issue is further illustrated by the reality that the Soviets didn't agree that US thinking on limited war was correct – or even rational. In the early era of US limited war writing, the Soviets did not have a limited war theory, as their ideology assumed continuous struggle between Communism and capitalism: the capitalist system had to be completely destroyed; there was no other acceptable result. The Soviets also assumed the use of atomic or nuclear weapons in any future war (unlike some limited war theorists), but they also believed this hadn't removed the need for conventional units, because achieving victory would require defeating the enemy's forces and occupying their territory. Any future war would also be a global affair requiring full mobilization of forces and material.[91] Soviet leaders came to see US limited war concepts as a reaction to the shift in the strategic (meaning nuclear) balance in the Soviets' favor, and believed the US hoped to fight limited wars in order to prevent nuclear retaliation by the Soviet Union in the event of conflict. The Soviets saw concepts such as "graduated restraint" and "limited" and "local" wars as examples of the bankruptcy of the 1954 concept of "massive retaliation" (a reference to Secretary of State John Foster Dulles' speech in which the US reserved the right to meet Communist aggression with atomic or nuclear weapons). The Soviets saw "massive retaliation" as arising because of growing Soviet nuclear strength; US limited war ideas were merely its supplements. The Kremlin also perceived "limited war" as a US tool for suppressing "national liberation" movements as part of the US Cold War grand strategy of containment. When executed, a US "limited war" would be merely a prelude to the US fighting a bigger war against the Soviet Union.[92]

Soviet views, though, changed. In a speech delivered on January 14, 1960, Soviet Premier Nikita Khrushchev denounced limited war as "nonsense."[93] But, the next year, Khrushchev identified several types of limited war, and soon Soviet writers were discussing limited war in a manner very much like US writers: they had no consistent definition of what made a conflict a limited war, and concerned themselves primarily with geography and the fear of escalation, particularly toward a nuclear exchange.[94] But Soviet theorizing showed no interest in bargaining – tacit or otherwise. Schelling – and his ideas – failed Clausewitz's supreme test: the necessity of the statesman and commander understanding the nature of the war in which they are involved. Schelling and many other limited war writers did not understand the Soviet mind, and thus how Soviet leaders would perceive US limited war ideas.[95]

Schelling also ignores the possibility of small powers acting on their own when they are part of a larger alliance bloc of the East or West. This is a problem with much limited war literature: the failure to recall that all nations – even small ones – have their own agendas and will fight wars when larger powers do not want them to, even if they are clients of a larger state. For example, Cuban adventurism in Latin America, epitomized by Cuba's 1967 Bolivian debacle in which

Che Guevara was killed, angered the Soviet Union greatly. Moscow preferred less risky adventures on the part of its allies. This did not stop the Cubans.[96]

Schelling's work – and the man himself – arguably exerted the greatest effect on the execution of an American limited war because his ideas on bargaining and signaling underpinned the prosecution of the US air war in Vietnam, especially the failed Rolling Thunder bombing campaign, something addressed in Chapter 5.[97] "The dark side of Thomas Schelling," journalist Fred Kaplan noted in 2005, "is also the dark side of social science – the brash assumption that neat theories not only reflect the real world but can change it as well, and in ways that can be precisely measured."[98]

The Next Step . . .

In 2001, Indian author V. R. Raghavan noted this truth: "The fact remains, however, that limited war is not yet a fully developed idea, even at the turn of the 21st century."[99] We will now fix this problem by doing what Osgood said could not be done: construct a coherent theory of wars fought for limited political aims.

3 THE POLITICAL AIM: WHY NATIONS FIGHT WARS

What has gone wrong with the twentieth century? Why has the Western World, in spite of its great efforts to stand up for liberty, justice and truth, and its desperate yearning for peace and higher standards of living, brought itself to the very brink of universal disaster?

I think that one very important reason is that we have lost sight of our object in war, and have allowed the means to obscure the end.[1]
Air Marshal Sir Robert Saundby (1955)

Introduction

In an August 2, 1990 meeting that included then Secretary of Defense Dick Cheney, Undersecretary of Defense for Policy Paul Wolfowitz, and JCS Chair Colin Powell there was a back-and-forth discussion about how the US should respond to Saddam Hussein's conquest of Kuwait. Powell, fearing the US public would not support it, was reluctant to use military force over the fate of Kuwait. As the conversation extended, Cheney pressed Powell for options regarding how the US could use its military power against Iraq. Powell, for his part, insisted that his civilian leaders first provide the political aims they wanted to achieve. Growing irritated, Cheney exploded at Powell, growling "I want some options, General." "Yes, Mr. Secretary," Powell replied, and the meeting ended.[2] Powell's critics could argue that his efforts during the Gulf War to discourage fighting a war over Kuwait were out of bounds, but his insistence upon his political superiors deciding what they want before they take the country to war is to be applauded loudly. Powell was asking the right question.

The Political Aim: Why Nations Go to War

In war there is nothing more important than understanding the political aims of the combatants involved. This is the *why* of the war: the reasons the warring states are spilling blood and spending treasure. Sometimes the aim is masked by religious or ideological terms, but there is always some underlying political concern. Despite what they might say publicly, states always go to war to get something they want or to preserve what they have. The keystone of our analysis bears repeating:

> War can be of two kinds, in the sense that either the objective is to *overthrow the enemy* [unlimited] – to render him politically helpless or militarily impotent, thus forcing him to sign what-ever peace we please; or *merely to occupy some of his frontier-districts* [limited] so that we can annex them or use them for bargaining at the peace negotiations.[3]

Our theory of wars fought for limited political aims builds upon this foundation, as does any systematic analysis of a conflict or military plan. Clausewitz makes clear the immense importance of this: "The first, the supreme, the most far-reaching act of judgment that the statesman and commander have to make is to establish ... the kind of war on which they are embarking; neither mistaking it for, nor trying to turn it into, something that is alien to its nature. This is the first of all strategic questions." Critically, Clausewitz insists this is the job of *both* the military and political leaders, and gives a related admonition: "No one starts a war – or rather, no one in his senses should do so – without first being clear in his mind what he intends to achieve by that war and how he intends to conduct it." The last part of the passage demonstrates a key reason why understanding the political aim is so important: *everything else flows from this*. He makes this truth abundantly clear: "The polit-ical object – the original motive for the war – will thus determine both the military objective to be reached and the amount of effort it requires."[4]

Others have made similar observations:

Political objectives [aims] and constraints dominate the conditions under which the military action is conducted; that is, they
exert a decisive influence on the decisions as to when, where,
and in what manner the war is fought. For example, they
determine the amount of its total military capability a nation
will commit to the war. These political factors, moreover, act
continually in time, and to a large extent, continuously
throughout the levels of action, from the over-all strategic
direction of the war down into subordinate parts of the field
commands.[5]

Types of Political Aims

The political aim underpins the nature of the war and where and
how it will be fought. What though, are these aims? In theory, there can
be as many aims for which nations go to war as there are political
leaders, but the reality is usually more concrete. States go to war for
territory, trade rights, access to resources, eliminating opposition armed
groups, forcing political concessions, in defense of an invasion, and so
on. Some analysts insist there is no example of an accidental war.[6]

The first thing to think about is whether the state is fighting
for defensive or offensive political aims, though offensive aims can be
billed as the opposite. The state could have both. Offensive wars for
limited aims, unsurprisingly, generally require either contiguous or
expeditionary operations. Defensive political aims are usually as simple as retaining what one has at the beginning of the conflict because
you are the victim of invasion or insurrection. Defensive wars can be
easier to wage for a number of very obvious reasons. It is easier to
rally people against an invader; it is easier logistically because of
proximity to sources of supply; it is easier to bring forces to bear;
and one accrues the traditional advantages offered by the defense.
There is also the added issue of whether or not the war is fought to
defend ourselves or an ally. Here, as in all conflicts, the time and level
of sacrifice we are willing to make will be influenced by the value of
the object being sought. If we are defending ourselves, meaning protecting territory or an interest that is ours, we are more likely to fight

longer for this and pay more than we would for the survival of an ally or one of the ally's possessions.

Moreover, whether or not the objective is defensive or offensive should not be confused with the importance of the political aim being sought to the state pursuing it. At first glance, a defensive limited aim might not seem as important, because to some "defensive" connotes something small or insignificant. But the state pursuing a defensive war for a limited political aim might be fighting for the regime's survival. For example, in 1950 South Korea fought a defensive limited war for survival. It had numerous allies assisting it under the UN umbrella, the US being the most important.

Generally, when people think about wars fought for limited political aims, they think of an offensive or aggressive war, and with good reason. Historically, one of the most important and most common political aims is territory. Sometimes wars have been fought over the opportunity to trade or invest in certain areas, or for access to or possession of resources. In Asia in the nineteenth century, for example, it was very common for the United States and European powers to use force to open Asian states to trade (the Opium Wars spring immediately to mind), or to prevent another state from enjoying such access. But again, territory is usually the political aim. Frederick the Great fought one of his wars for the possession of Silesia. Prussian Chancellor Otto von Bismarck engineered wars against Denmark, Austria, and France in which territorial control ranked high among his political aims.

One of the clearest and most calculating examples of this in US history is President James K. Polk's 1846–48 war against Mexico. Polk intended to fight a short war for limited political aims that cost the US very little and hoped to annex Mexico's northern provinces of New Mexico and California.[7] Traditionally, states wanted to seize territory from other states, while those that have it want to keep it. This went out of fashion among liberal democracies after the Second World War and, for the US, after the First World War.

There can be more creative aims as well. In the 1973 Arab–Israeli War, Egypt's Anwar Sadat did not seek territory but a political crisis that would shock the regional political system and thus open the way for negotiations. Henry Kissinger said of Sadat: "Rare is the statesman who at the beginning of a war has so clear a perception of its political objective." General Rupert Smith wrote: "we see here an example of a statesman seeking to resolve a confrontation by initiating a conflict to alter minds."[8]

The Failure of US Political Leaders to Understand the Importance of the Political Aim

As we saw in our example above, military commanders should ask their political masters to provide the desired aim if they have failed to do so. What do the political leaders want to accomplish? Sometimes, as General Anthony Zinni has pointed out, there is something they want to prevent. The problem is that political leaders can fail to provide the political aim. This might be due to short-sightedness, being overwhelmed by their responsibilities, simple incompetence or ignorance of their duties, or perhaps fear of having to commit to something in writing that in the event of failure political enemies can use against them. Leaders who put what they want to achieve on record create something by which they can be measured and thus judged. A result can be broad or not clearly defined aims. Some argue that this is good, because it can smooth the ending of the conflict.[9] This is wrong. Not having clear political aims demonstrates shoddy thinking, incompetence, or indecision. This lays a foundation for failure, not success, because you either do not know what you want or are afraid to admit it, even in secret. If settling the conflict has become more valuable than the aims being sought, then the aims can be altered. True leaders take responsibility for such a change.

This failure of US political leaders to provide or explain the desired aims is more prevalent historically than generally realized. Truman rightly fired MacArthur for insubordination, but what is forgotten is MacArthur's accurate complaint in the wake of China's intervention in Korea that he hadn't received clear political guidance from his civilian and military superiors regarding what he was supposed to achieve now that the Chinese had intervened and the nature of the war had changed. MacArthur testified about this in the Congressional hearings held in the wake of his relief: "I felt that the position I was in, the military position, was untenable without having some directive, some mission which was more realistic than that which existed at the time; and I felt, in all con-science, I could not go on ordering men to their deaths by the thousands, in such a complete vacuum of policy decisions."[10] One can certainly take issue with MacArthur's reference to this being his "whole effort," as well as his early December 1950 insistence that, in the face of the Chinese offensive, he might have to evacuate the entire peninsula unless he received reinforcements and the relaxation of the constraints on the use of air power,[11] but the larger complaint against the Truman administration is backed by the simultaneous experience of the Joint Chiefs of Staff (JCS) and MacArthur's interaction with them and the Truman administration.

After the Chinese intervention in the Korean War, the JCS gave MacArthur a directive that told him to hold nine points and three other defensive lines that MacArthur had suggested, all north of the UN's old Naktong defenses in the Pusan area, and "to damage the enemy as much as possible, subject to the primary consideration of the safety of his troops and his continuing responsibility for the defense of Japan." He was also eventually advised that if the Chinese reached an arc about 30 miles north of Pusan, a decision on withdrawal would be made by the JCS at that time. They would control this because of the political ramifications.[12]

US Army Chief of Staff J. Lawton Collins, MacArthur's superior, clearly described the dilemma his subordinate faced, and he and the other JCS members sympathized. "MacArthur radioed the JCS on January 10, stating that the two courses of action were incompatible in that they could not be carried out simultaneously," Collins noted, and he believed that what MacArthur wanted "was a spelling-out of the continuing political aims that should govern the decision whether the United Nations forces should remain in Korea and under what conditions." Collins also noted the key problem: the military leaders kept trying to get the State Department to detail the political aims now that the Chinese had intervened, but the diplomats would only respond by asking for the delineation of military capabilities. General Matthew Ridgway corroborates Collins' assessment of MacArthur's views, noting that in a December 26, 1950 meeting MacArthur said they seemed to be operating in a "mission vacuum." The JCS stuck to their December 30, 1950 directive that it was "in the national interest to hold as long as possible so as to permit diplomatic and military consultations with other United Nations members, to maintain United States prestige throughout the world, and to sustain confidence in the United Nations and, among our allies, in NATO."[13]

As the UN forces continued their retreat and approached the 38th parallel, the JCS and representatives of the State Department met to discuss the future course of action. Collins noted that, just as in January, the Department of State refused to deliver a political aims in

Korea "until military capabilities there were established," while the JCS wanted a political decision so they could determine the required military courses of action.[14] Collins eloquently described the problem:

> The State Department representatives were laboring under the same basic difficulty as the Chiefs: the lack of a clear United States or United Nations *policy* [aims] with respect to Korea in the light of the existing circumstances. Such a policy could only be determined by the National Security Council for the United States – and, for all practical purposes, for the United Nations – and by the heads of state of the nations actively participating in the war. On the other hand, the National Security Council needed recommendations from the State Department staff and the JCS to assist it in determining the basic policy. This was what the State–JCS discussions were struggling to provide. But under our American philosophy that the military should be subservient to civilian control – to which the JSC fully subscribed.[15]

What Collins failed to do here was to point out the obvious: President Harry S. Truman and his chief foreign policy advisor, Secretary of State Dean Acheson, had utterly failed in their responsibilities as leaders by not addressing this critical issue.

The confusion over policy continued through the winter and early spring of 1951. At a February 13, 1951 JCS–State Department meeting, JCS chairman Omar Bradley said that the political aims needed to be decided, and then the military requirements for achieving this then could be determined.[16] When General Matthew B. Ridgway replaced MacArthur he encountered the same problem: the lack of a clear political aim. But he also suffered from unclear military guidance. One of Ridgway's first acts as commander was to have his staff review all relevant directives. He found confusion and contradictions, and at one point even tried to write his own orders, an effort the JCS rebuffed.[17]

The JCS issued an April 5, 1951 memorandum to the National Security Council that said "the Korean problem cannot be resolved in a manner satisfactory to the United States by military action alone." Collins insisted that there was a military stalemate. They also made a number of recommendations, and discussions between the military and State Department officials continued. Meanwhile, the MacArthur hearings focused a lot of attention upon issues surrounding the war. On May 17, 1951, Truman approved NSC 48/5, which essentially agreed with the JCS recommendations of April 5, 1951, and sought to secure the Republic of Korea below the 38th parallel.[18] Finally, the political had been clarified.

Collins had a new directive written for Ridgway that was sent on May 31, 1951. It laid out Ridgway's responsibilities under his two hats. His tasks as Far East Commander remained unchanged. His job as the UN commander changed greatly and was a result of the policy review then being undertaken by the National Security Council. Essentially, Ridgway's orders became to terminate the war at the 38th.[19]

All of this demonstrates terrible problems at the top of the Truman administration. Moreover, a firm decision regarding the political and military objectives being sought by the administration was only made "after General MacArthur, the Joint Chiefs of Staff, and the senatorial investigating committee investigating General MacArthur's dismissal had attempted to discover what we were trying to accomplish in the war."[20]

The Vietnam War illustrates this issue in a different way. Soldier-scholar Harry Summers, author of the influential *On Strategy*, argued that the United States lacked a clear political aim during its war in Vietnam. He backs this by demonstrating the numerous justifications given for US intervention in Indochina, as well as revealing the results of a survey of US Army general officers holding commands in Vietnam that showed 70 percent of them did not understand the political aim.[21]

Summers was mistaken regarding the political aim. Secretary of Defense McNamara clearly articulated the US political aim in South Vietnam in a March 16, 1964 document that became National Security Action Memorandum (NSAM) 288. "We seek an independent non-Communist South Vietnam," it noted.

> We do not require that it serve as a Western base or as a member of a Western Alliance. South Vietnam must be free, however, to accept outside assistance as required to maintain its security. This assistance should be able to take the form not only of economic and social measures but also police and military help to root out and control insurgent elements.

McNamara also explained the object's value, insisting that "Unless we can achieve this objective in South Vietnam, almost all of Southeast Asia will probably fall under Communist dominance (all of Vietnam, Laos, and Cambodia)." This would then make many other states in the region susceptible to Communist influence or domination and threaten America's allies in the hemisphere.[22]

Why Summers' account is important is because it reveals two related problems: the failure of the Johnson administration's civilian and military leaders to ensure its general officers were aware of what the government sought to achieve in South Vietnam, and the failure of these generals to find out for themselves the purpose of the war in which they were fighting. This is a dangerous situation to have.

This problem – which is also a civil–military relations issue – has remained and is bipartisan. In a 2014 speech, then JCS chairman Martin Dempsey noted that when the military leaders are consulted by their civilian superiors, the military leaders want to know the objective being sought. The civilian leaders respond by asking for options for how to deal with a particular problem.[23]

Since the time of the Truman administration, American political leaders too often have failed to understand the overwhelming importance of knowing what they want to accomplish and what this means. If they don't understand this, they don't understand anything else, because they haven't grasped the context of their actions, nor those of the enemy. Clausewitz railed against this nearly two centuries ago in 1827 when asked to evaluate a pair of defensive war plans sent by a former subordinate, replying that he couldn't usefully assess them because he did not know the political aim, meaning what the plans were supposed to achieve.[24] This persistent problem can only be solved by better educating our civilian leaders in regard to their roles in the formulation of strategy and policy. Undoubtedly, on too many occasions this task will fall to US military leaders (see the Powell example above), and it will be a thankless one that could very well endanger the leader's career. But it is imperative that it be done when the problem is obvious, and will require great moral courage from the unfortunate military commander in this position.

The Value of the Object

Critical for understanding the nature of the war is to understand the value of the object being sought. Clausewitz says that "Since war is not an act of senseless passion but is controlled by its political object, the value of the object must determine the sacrifices to be made for it in magnitude and also in duration. Once the expenditure of the effort exceeds the value of the political object, the object must be renounced and peace must follow."[25] This is one of Clausewitz's most useful concepts – the value of the object – because its gives us a superb tool for analysis. How much value does each combatant place upon the object being sought? To understand this is to understand much about the nature of the war. The more valuable the object, the more the combatants are willing to pay, and the longer they are willing to pay it.

Clausewitz also correctly believed that the value of this object to the combatants would determine the duration of the struggle, as well as its cost, and the means the combatants were willing to expend. When one side is no longer willing to pay the price necessary to achieve the aim, peace will break out. The value of the object directly affects the impact of the various constraints upon the war, as well as the termination of the struggle. Clausewitz wrote: "The smaller the sacrifice we demand from our opponent, the smaller presumably will be the means of resistance he will employ, and the smaller his means, the smaller will ours be required to be. Similarly the smaller our political object, the less value shall we set upon it and the more easily we shall be induced to abandon it."[26] This is a depiction of the relationship between the end sought and the means used to obtain it.

But how does one judge this value in a concrete manner? I have not discovered a way to objectively quantify this, as "value" has such a personal and subjective sense. A simple (arguably simplistic) and very unscientific method is to simply ask: "On a scale of one to ten, how does each combatant rate the value of the objective they are seeking?" For example, during the Vietnam War, the North Vietnamese sought – primarily – to conquer South Vietnam. How valuable was this object to North Vietnam? When I ask this of students the answer is invariably "ten." But when the same question is posed in regard to how much the US valued the objective of keeping South Vietnam free, the answer is generally "six." This certainly does not tell us who will win the war and gives us only a subjective feeling for relative value and the fact that different polities place different values upon the same object, but it does force us to concentrate on the importance of trying to understand the effects of the value of the aims being sought upon the conflict and to consider their relative value. What makes this an even more difficult endeavor is that the value of the object can change during the course of the war based upon events and what one has already paid.

The value of the object has many effects upon the waging of the war. One effect – especially if the state is not at risk – is that if the value of the objective is on the lower end of the scale, it is difficult to raise the passions of the people in support of the war. The people are important, and become even more so if the war proves long or costly. Clausewitz warned that "if policy is directed only toward minor objectives, the emotions of the masses will be little stirred and they will have to be stimulated rather than held back."[27] This is also vital because the level of popular passion contributes to the amount of *time* one has to prosecute the war. But this can in turn be reduced by the casualties and other physical and psychological costs incurred.

The value of the object is critical. Most would readily agree that this applies to wars fought for survival against an invader or something easily identified as an existential threat, but it also drives a state to go to war for aims that might not seem so important to outside observers – and to fight hard for these. It is the object that matters, and the circumstances surrounding it, and one must not forget the importance of relative value in analyzing them. For example, when Japan launched its war against Russia in 1904, Tokyo sought limited aims: Korea, control of Manchuria, removal of Russian influence in key areas. Former Japanese Prime Minister Itō Hirobumi commented on February 4, 1904: "if Russia is left alone, she will go on to take complete possession of Manchuria, and after that, would invade Korea, and eventually threaten Japan. In these circumstances, there is no alternative. We are bound to fight, even at the price of our national existence. I say frankly that I expect no success."[28] Foreign Minister Komura Jutarō noted the stakes of the game the year before, on June 23, 1903: "Korea is like a dagger pointing at Japan's heart and she could never endure its possession by a foreign power. Russia's activities in Manchuria and Korea are leading eventually to her domination over Korea ... In order to ensure Korean security, Japan should limit Russia's activities in Manchuria to those permitted under existing treaties."[29] The Japanese also feared that they lacked the military power to achieve them, a very rational assessment when one considers that Japan was fighting greatly above its weight. But Japan feared Russian expansion even more, particularly Russian domination of Korea, which they considered potentially fatal to Japan's independence. Thus, the value of the objective was extremely high, so high that they were willing to assume the enormous risk of fighting the Russian empire, mobilize every possible man, mortgage the state, and fight as hard as possible for as long as they could.[30] Their political aims were limited ones, but they placed immense value upon them. How the combatant views the aims is key.

When North Korea invaded the South on June 25, 1950, Truman reacted immediately, authorizing air and naval support for the South that evening.[31] Truman compared intervening in Korea to the post-Second World War struggle in Greece and believed acting here would affect stability in the Middle East, because if the US didn't act, the Soviets would simply move into Iran and then overrun the Middle East.[32] He also believed the Soviets were trying to get Korea for free and betting the US would not respond, said it looked like a larger-scale version of what the Soviets tried in Berlin, and insisted the Soviets were probing to see where the US was weak.[33] Truman met with the leaders of both parties in Congress to explain how critical it was to act to stop the Soviets here.[34] He also told US allies that success in South Korea would make the Soviets less likely to try something similar again; this would make peace more likely.[35] Western leaders saw the invasion as part of a larger Soviet plan, or possibly a diversion. US JCS chairman General Omar Bradley branded it a "softening-up operation." Some feared a commitment of forces in a peripheral, unimportant place like Korea because the Soviets might move against something important like Europe or Iran.[36] Not a few worried this might be the beginning of a Third World War. Also, if the US failed to act in Korea, US credibility would be injured. The international stakes were too high to do nothing.

In Vietnam, Lyndon Johnson's decision to dramatically increase US involvement was driven by the value of the object in relation to his future domestic political situation, as well as Cold War fears. Johnson's political and military advisors made it abundantly clear that South Vietnam would fall if the US did not intervene militarily. Johnson feared the political fallout from this – the loss of a Cold War ally to Communist aggression – would leave him open to charges he had "lost" Vietnam in the same way Truman had "lost" China. He believed this would undermine his administration and ruin his chances of pursuing his domestic legislative agenda.[37]

In the Gulf War, US leaders valued the object in a number of ways. They certainly feared the possible economic results of Saddam Hussein's control of a significant part of global oil production, but the fears of what would happen if they did not act were also critical: other dictators might be encouraged to follow Saddam's example.[38] Moreover, US leaders believed that Saddam's keeping Kuwait would "erode the delicate balance of power in the Middle East with disastrous consequences to the world's industrial powers."[39] President Bush compared not acting to 1930s-era appeasement, and considered opposing Saddam so important that he later insisted: "In truth, even had Congress not passed the resolutions I would have acted and ordered our troops into combat. I know it would have caused an outcry, but it was the right thing to do. I was comfortable in my own mind that I had the constitutional authority. It had to be done."[40]

The necessity of understanding the object (the aim) being sought and its value cannot be underestimated. Everything else flows from this.

The Problem of Nested Wars and the Political Aim

One problem that can arise when waging a war for a limited political aim is that one is fighting what some call a nested war, meaning a war being fought in the midst of a larger struggle, one that is military, political, or both. What is clear from the examples in the previous section is that the US faced this problem in both Korea and Vietnam, as these wars were fought in the midst of global great power competition, the Cold War between the West and Communism, a contest that US leaders feared could become hot. This concern acted as a constraint on US policymakers – sometimes. This is addressed further in the next chapter.

The value of the object of the nested war is directly affected by the connected war or competition. The other contest can both increase or diminish its value; indeed, it may even determine it. Bernard Brodie remarked that, for the Korean War, "the real objectives were political and lay outside Korea."[41] What he got wrong is that there were multiple political aims being sought, when one takes into consideration the conflict in Korea as well as the larger Cold War competition. The initial aim of the Cold War strategy of containment was to force the collapse or mellowing of the Soviet Union, but the US sought separate (though changing) political aims in Korea: preservation of South Korea, then unification, then preservation again. This was all done amidst the Cold War. This is *the* key problem of a nested war. The contributing factor of other aims being pursued can complicate the pursuit of the political aims in the war being fought for limited aims. It also acts as a constraint upon strategy and means, because there are other concerns that cloud decision-making in regard to both because of the difficulty of clearly determining how actions in one realm affect the other – or don't.

Additionally, one can make one war part of a larger struggle – artificially – thus creating problems instead of solving them. The 2001 war the US launched in Afghanistan and the 2003 Iraq War are more easily understood and analyzed as separate conflicts, but they were subsumed by the George W. Bush administration under the "Global War on Terror" or "Long War" monikers. One critic observed that "By aggregating them within a wider conflict we have made them bigger than they are, even less amenable to strategy in its pragmatic sense, and incomprehensible to the electorates of the democratic states which are waging them."[42]

The Problem of Absent, Unclear, or Unobtainable Political Aims

What a state is doing to wage the war should be directed at achieving the political aim. The problem is that sometimes leaders are not so clear in their minds what they want, or they change the aim (sometimes for good reasons, sometimes not), or the nation simply lacks the strength to achieve it.

If the leaders do not have a political aim when they go to war (or fail to decide one, if they represent the power being attacked), they have failed on the most basic level, and their incompetence and lack of vision are on glaring display. This is exceedingly rare and examples are difficult to identify. Some have charged that Imperial Germany went to war in 1914 without clear political aims and only began to clearly discuss its war aims in September 1914. But it is probable that – at a minimum – Germany sought to break what it viewed as a form of encirclement by bordering states.

Unclear political aims can result from the war having taken an unexpected turn. The entry of a third party into the conflict may have brought defeat or great physical or psychological shock. Chinese entry into the Korean War provides an excellent example of this. Success during the 1990–91 Gulf War produced in US leaders a back and forth over what they wanted to achieve. We address this in Chapter 6.

Discovering that your political aim is unobtainable – whether because of the strength of the opponent or the unwillingness or inability of your state to continue the struggle – is often very difficult for leaders to handle. One obvious reason for this is that it can be a glaring indicator of having lost the war (though not always). Moreover, the cost of defeat may be so great as to result in the destruction of the regime. If one cannot achieve the political aim, it is probably time to change it. This is also often a time to try to make peace.

Nixon believed he faced just such a situation when he became president. The feelings and beliefs of both Nixon and Kissinger toward the ending of the war in Vietnam are certainly complex, but when he came into office Nixon believed that the war could not be won and that the US must end its commitment there.[43] In diplomatic wrangling with both the Chinese and the Soviets, Kissinger made it clear that he wished the separation of the military result in South Vietnam from the political, meaning that the US wanted out and would watch from afar to see how the political situation evolved after the US departure. The US wanted, he said, "a decent interval" between the US withdrawal and the possible fall of South Vietnam. Nixon and Kissinger had similar discussions amongst themselves but also hoped to move South Vietnam to a position where it could defend itself. They believed the fall of South Vietnam likely, but they didn't think it written in the stars.[44]

Changing the Political Aim

Sometimes the political aim changes. This is a critical point when reassessment of the situation *must* occur. This change is not necessarily good or bad; it depends upon the circumstances. A nation might increase or lessen the number of political aims sought as the war goes on. The enemy may have revealed itself to be more dangerous – or more incompetent – than they originally appeared. The aim can change and remain a limited one. During the War for American Independence, the Colonies initially sought the "redress of grievances." After July 4, 1776, the US fought for independence. The political aim changed, but both are limited aims because their achievement did not require the destruction of the British regime but merely, in the end, the theft of a few of its outlying possessions.[45]

Sometimes the combatants decide to settle for less than what they originally or previously desired. Why? The fact that one is losing is certainly critical. Survival may hinge upon not insisting that the state retain all of its land when perhaps the invader can be bought off with a province or some other concession, so the defender moves from insisting upon keeping all of its territory to keeping less than this. The rising cost of a conflict can convince a state that the pursuit of its aim is simply no longer worth it, so they settle for something less. In the Korean War, the Chinese sought the expulsion of all UN forces from Korea. This aim was unachievable because the US refused to abandon South Korea and was eventually dropped.[46]

In his 2009 Afghan War speech, President Obama gave as his political aims "to disrupt, dismantle, and defeat al Qaeda in Afghanistan and Pakistan, and to prevent its capacity to threaten America and our allies in the future."[47] In June 2011, little more than two years later, he changed the US aim, an action firmly within his powers as president. The aim became: "No safe haven from which al-Qaida or its affiliates can launch attacks against our homeland or our allies." This was a marked retreat from his 2009 speech. One critic argued that the US changed its aim based upon the evolution of the military situation in Afghanistan, one that had resulted from the fact that the Obama administration never committed sufficient military means to achieve the declared aims. Ideally, the political aim should determine the military commitment, and not the other way around. Though the reality is that aims change when political leaders conclude that they cannot get what they wanted, or they simply don't want to pay what it will cost to achieve it for as long as this will take.[48] More important was that Obama never had any intention of trying to win the war in Afghanistan. Obama removed from his 2009 speech "any language that spoke of winning or victory." Obama sent troops to fight a war he didn't intend to win while building in an expiration date: eighteen months.[49]

The Trump administration's strategy for, and execution of, the war in Afghanistan addressed some past failings: it removed overly restrictive rules of engagement, restored tactical control to commanders in the field, increased the military means, and put much-needed pressure on Pakistan. Despite this, and despite seventeen years of war, in late 2018 one observer insisted that the Taliban controlled, or contested control, over 60 percent of Afghanistan, the greatest percentage since before 9/11. Some deemed the war a stalemate. Critically, the Trump administration did not deliver victory. Why? One critic offers this reason: "Trump, like Obama, was never committed to winning in Afghanistan."[50]

There are also cases where wars fought for limited aims become wars for unlimited political aims. This is not escalation. Political aims don't escalate – *they change*. The level of force used escalates (or does not). The reasons for such a shift are as varied as people, but there are common drivers. One of the chief is opportunity. Nations at war see a chance to grasp for something more than what they originally intended, the enemy might be weaker than originally thought, or perhaps there has been a disaster that creates opportunities worth grasping. Again, this is not necessarily a good or bad thing: the situation influences this.

There could be very good reasons for abandoning a limited aim and seeking an unlimited one. This must be very clearly and deeply considered, because when political leaders decide to begin fighting a war for an unlimited aim, *they are now embarking upon a new war, perhaps even an additional war*, even though to many this might not appear so. When you change the aim, you change the nature of the war. One must then reassess because *everything* else has changed. The mission has changed; thus the force requirements have changed; thus your strategy probably no longer applies. Third-party actors now see the situation differently and may change their behavior. All of these factors have bitten the US before, with bad effects, something explored further in the next chapter.

One of the great myths of the Korean War – one that underpins much historical, political science, and international relations literature on conflict – is that the invasion of North Korea was entirely MacArthur's doing. Truman administration officials such as Secretary of State Dean Acheson successfully painted MacArthur as the villain for a decision they made. Acheson, for example, insisted that the UN resolution passed on October 7, 1950 "encouraged MacArthur's adventurism." Acheson also said that "General MacArthur at once stripped from the resolution of October 7 its husk of ambivalence and gave it an interpretation that the enacting majority in the General Assembly would not have accepted. Nowhere did the resolution declare that the Eighth Army would impose a unified and democratic government on all Korea."[51] That MacArthur made the decision to invade North Korea is simply a lie, one that ignores the Truman administration's decision to change the political aim, as well as the text of the UN resolution itself, which calls for a unified government.[52] Truman glossed over the decision to invade North Korea in his memoirs: "This decision to take the offensive in Korea made it necessary to consider on a high policy level what our subsequent course of action should be. This was done in National Security Council discussions which finally resulted in a policy statement that I approved on September 11, 1950."[53]

Numerous other sources – including from others "present at the creation" – make it very clear that this decision was not MacArthur's.[54] Army Chief of Staff and JCS member J. Lawton Collins wrote in his memoirs: "There remained no question but that the UN General Assembly, President Truman, the US Secretaries of State and Defense, and the US Joint Chiefs of Staff all had approved the crossing of the 38th Parallel. Most of the questions concerning the wisdom of this decision came after the event."[55] The primary-source documents are equally clear.[56] Critically, the Truman administration made this decision *before* the successful execution of the September 15, 1950 Inchon invasion. UN approval was obtained afterward. Works claiming the US was seized by a kind of "victory fever" are equally mistaken. The most important question for our purposes: why did the Truman administration change the political aim?

There was an intense debate in the State Department regarding whether or not the US aim should be the unification of Korea under the auspices of the UN. Key among the supporters was John M. Allison, the director of the Office of Northeast Asian Affairs, who pushed for this as early as July 1, 1950, and his Asia desk superior Dean Rusk.[57] Allison was even willing to risk a global war over crossing the 38th. Secretary of State Acheson dispatched a draft statement on the necessity of liberating Korea on August 1, 1950.[58]

It had long been a point of consideration when it occurred, and sometimes of public discussion. MacArthur was already considering the necessity of crossing the 38th parallel by mid July 1950. Truman said in a July 13 press conference that this was on the table. Truman also made it clear to reporters on this day that his administration was considering what to do once US forces reached the 38th and said he would decide when the time arrived. The same day, South Korean president Syngman Rhee said that the invasion had "obliterated the 38th parallel" and insisted that there could be no peace in Korea if this division remained, and Republic of Korea (ROK) troops would cross it (though a US Army spokesman insisted that force would be used to prevent this).[59]

Among dissenters was George F. Kennan. He urged Acheson to ignore those pushing to take North Korea, warning that it risked war with the Soviet Union and China. Kennan noted – with great clarity – that if the US had acted to save South Korea, the Communists could certainly do the same for North Korea.[60]

The decision to cross the 38th was partially based upon fears of what would happen if the US failed to do so. A July 31, 1950 Department of Defense memorandum insisted that "a return to the status quo ante bellum would not promise security." Some in the Department of Defense also saw an opportunity to "roll back" Communism. Truman conducted a public campaign to garner support for the move.[61] The US sought unification because it believed that this was the only way to prevent a future attack by North Korea. The JCS believed that stopping at the 38th did nothing to prevent a future attack and that the North Koreans could simply move south again when they were ready.[62]

Truman declared a political aim of unification of Korea in a September 1, 1950 speech. NSC 81/1 of September 9, 1950 made it official. The US decided to reunite Korea under the South's government, using three pre-war UN General Assembly Resolutions in favor of Korean unification as a basis. They would also seek UN approval, which followed on October 7, 1950 via a UN Resolution authorizing the invasion.[63] The new Secretary of Defense, George Marshall, sent MacArthur orders to advance north of the 38th parallel on September 27, 1950.[64]

Why does this matter? Truman moved the US and the UN from fighting a war for a limited aim to waging a war for an unlimited political aim. He changed the political aim. Thus, he changed the nature of the war. Moreover, this was done without sufficiently deep consideration of the effects. The administration had envisaged the worst-case scenarios – the intervention of China and the Soviet Union – but did not take this seriously. Moreover, the Truman administration was feared the war's expansion.[65] Truman later insisted in his memoirs that everything he did in Korea was to prevent a Third World War.[66] If this was true, why did his administration invade a Soviet client state?

But why does this discussion matter? One must ask whether changing the aim is wise. The situation might be one where changing it is in the best interest of the state, so issuing a blanket statement regarding whether or not it is correct to alter the political aim is wrong because one does not know what the future holds. What one can say with certainty is that this is a critically important decision requiring much thought and analysis, because changing the objective changes what the war is about for you, the enemy, and potential third-party actors who are *always* observing what is going on and may now see their interests threatened by your decision. They may also see opportunities in your failure to act. Also, whether or not you think changing the aim threatens the interests of others is irrelevant if they see it as doing so. One should also consider how the change affects not only neutrals and potential enemies but also friends and allies.

Critically, when the political aim is altered, the Ends-Ways-Means relationship is completely altered, too. If the objective changes, the mission changes; if the mission changes, the needed strategy changes, and so do the force requirements. Moreover, a complete reassessment of the situation is made necessary because – like it or not – *a different war is now being fought.*

An example of the effect of multiple political aims is found in Iraq in 2003. The Second Iraq War (2003–11) is often described as a limited war, even though it certainly did not begin that way. The political aims were decided in August 2002. The Bush administration sought regime change (an unlimited political aim) and the creation of a democratic Iraqi government. Strategically, Saddam and his closest followers would be removed, governance put into the hands of other Iraqis and returning exiles, and American troops quickly withdrawn. The expectation was that this would spark something in Iraq and the rest of the Middle East not unlike what occurred in Eastern Europe in 1989. Occupation and nation-building were not part of the original strategy.[67]

The initial post-war stabilization operation and the transition to Iraqi control was guided by retired Lieutenant General Jay Garner's Office for Reconstruction and Humanitarian Assistance (ORHA). Garner planned to remove the key Baath Party officials and use the existing Iraqi ministries to run the country, appointing American advisors to help them. He also planned to summon the Iraqi Army back to its posts (it had essentially demobilized itself in the wake of the American campaign), and use it to keep order and rebuild. After Garner had a few months to ensure there was no humanitarian crisis, a former American ambassador or governor was to become the face of the US mission. In a March 12, 2003 meeting of the Security Council, Bush agreed to this strategy.[68]

But the US found a much worse situation than expected. The infrastructure was a wreck and was further injured by the unexpected looting that took place after Baghdad's fall. The administration decided to accelerate the replacement of Garner. On April 30, 2003, former ambassador L. Paul "Jerry" Bremer III was named head of what became the Coalition Provisional Authority (CPA). The choice of Bremer was driven by Secretary of Defense Donald Rumsfeld. Garner had been in Baghdad for only two weeks.[69]

Bremer prepared for his new job by reading a RAND report on the reconstruction of Germany and Japan. At a meeting with Bush he received the power to do virtually anything he wanted in Iraq. He shunted aside US diplomat Zalmay Khalilzad, who had already pulled together key Iraqi leaders to form an interim government. Bremer decided to build a new Iraq.[70] This now became a war for a limited political aim as the US sought to preserve its own political creation. The objective was now a defensive, limited one. Moreover, what was intended as a liberation now became an occupation.

Bremer also immediately made a number of controversial decisions. The most critical was disbanding the Iraqi military and security forces, thus throwing several hundred thousand armed men out of work, and forbidding the top four tiers of Baath Party members from serving in government positions.[71] This made reconstruction and building a new government infinitely more difficult.

Why does this matter? You are now pursuing a different political aim; thus you have changed the nature of the war. You have changed the mission; thus you have changed the mission's requirements. What you are doing now also influences the actions of the other nations who are watching what is going on and have their own interests to pursue.

Moreover, Bremer had also changed the strategy but not told the military beforehand, which caught them unprepared.[72] One of the pre-war public controversies was the debate over the force requirements for the war and any post-war stabilization operations. US Secretary of Defense Rumsfeld and his allies won the fight for a light footprint for both the war and the post-war operations. They successfully argued that US military superiority would easily carry the day against Iraq as it had done in Afghanistan, and do it with ease. They proved correct, but built into this thinking was a belief that the US would immediately hand over control to Iraqi military and police forces after removing the top ranks and begin withdrawing. Critically, it takes a lot more troops to occupy and rebuild a nation than to topple the government, install new leaders, and leave.

The US and its coalition partners soon faced perhaps the most diverse insurgency in history. American and coalition forces now had new threats and a new war. This meant US leaders needed to deeply reassess everything they were doing, something requiring enormous intellectual flexibility and creativity, and not a little courage. Critically, securing the democratic government required eliminating the insurgency, something that demanded *more* forces and *much more* time than achieving the aim of regime change.[73]

This also reveals another problem. One of the more pernicious concepts in post-Second World War limited war theorizing is that the force used must be "limited," meaning "small." The reality is that sometimes a war for a limited aim requires *more* forces than a war fought for an unlimited political aim. The 2003–11 war in Iraq provides an example of this. This is a means issue explored in the chapter on constraints (Chapter 4).

One related question that could be raised is this: was the US aim both limited and unlimited simultaneously because the US sought the elimination of the insurgent threat? No. The elimination of the insurgents was a military objective, one accomplished by violence and nation-building, but also achieved by co-opting some of the Sunni groups when they turned against Al Qaeda in Iraq. Accomplishing this military objective was a necessary step on the road to achieving the political aim.

One final thing that must be said in regard to changing the political aim (which will be addressed in another fashion in the next chapter) is that it is a near certainty that no matter the depths of the reassessment of the situation when altering the aim, there will be effects no one considered or imagined.

Coalitions and the Political Aim

What is sometimes forgotten in discussions of the political aims is the complicating factor added by the existence of coalitions. It must be recalled that the political aims of one nation may not be the same as those of their coalition partners. This becomes even more complex when the war is being waged between two coalitions. This makes it difficult to simply brand a conflict a "limited war." For example, during the Korean War, one of the reasons the Communists were in no hurry to sign an armistice was the possibility of the breakdown of the alliance between the US and South Korea over Syngman Rhee's desire to unify Korea.[74]

In Vietnam, the United States pursued a limited political aim against North Vietnam, as did its coalition partner, South Vietnam. Neither sought the overthrow of the enemy regime. The North Vietnamese sought the destruction of the South Vietnamese regime, as well as the installation of Communist regimes in Laos and Cambodia. North Vietnam's political aim against the US was limited: the removal of the United States from the conflict. Doing this would place the North well on the road to achieving its other political aims.

Clausewitz offers this caution on the actions of coalition partners: "if one of them shows bad faith the others will be paralyzed."[75]

A Criticism of Wars Fought for Limited Political Aims: They Do Not Solve Problems

One common critique of wars fought for limited political aims is that they fail to resolve the issues that caused the war because, since the aims are limited, they do not result in complete defeat of the enemy. One author believes that "The most it can hope to achieve is to restore and reinforce the status quo because the threat of escalation would prevent the enforcement of a permanent solution unless it is acceptable to both sides."[76] Another says that "Limited wars, by definition, end inconclusively, with an enemy, at best, seriously weakened."[77]

Certainly criticisms such as these are warranted, but the same could be said of wars fought for regime change. British author Robert Saundby disagrees with the critics: "In the past, wars fought for a limited object – keeping that object firmly in view – have often been successful. Wars having an unlimited object have seldom if ever succeeded, in the sense of creating a world situation more favourable than if there had not been a war."[78] But one cannot take Saundby's word on the success of wars fought for limited objectives as writ. Every war – regardless of the aim – is different. Their settlement and results will be unique.

Admiral John D. Haynes wrote that "Limited wars never seem to get settled or settle anything. But man's affairs never get settled anyway. Life is a process of living with problems, not of settling them ... we must be ready to accept a corollary: negotiated settlements."[79] The weakness of Haynes' criticism is that it ignores the fact that a negotiated settlement *is* an acceptable resolution to the problem. A flaw in some of the writing on wars for limited aims is a belief that only a Second World War-style ending of the conflict – one involving the complete destruction of the enemy – is the norm and the only acceptable outcome. The problem with this expectation is that is goes against the historical record, particularly in wars fought among nation states in the modern era. The conflicts are generally ended by negotiation and generally do not involve the complete destruction or complete defeat of the enemy. Haynes' comment that "Life is a process of living with problems" is worth remembering.

Wars of Choice versus Wars of Necessity

One of the criticisms leveled at George W. Bush's decision to go to war in Iraq in 2003 was that this was a war of choice, not of necessity, as he did not have to fight this war. He certainly did not, but that doesn't really matter, as what we see with this argument is yet another example of faulty reasoning producing artificial distinctions.

The modern parlance on "wars of choice" seems to have arisen from Israeli Prime Minister Menachem Begin's 1982 speech at America's National Defense University. Begin defined a war of choice as one that was not fought in defense of one's national existence. Often, when people use this term the implication is that "wars of choice" are illegitimate, even illegal, especially if they aren't waged under UN auspices. But what is embarked upon as a supposed "war of necessity," such as the 2001 US war in Afghanistan, can come to be seen as a "war of choice." But, as has been pointed out elsewhere, such an observation discredits both terms.[80]

The reality is that *all* wars are "wars of choice" for all of the combatants involved.[81] Gerry Segal, the former director of the International Institute for Strategic Studies (IISS) made this same observation. "War of choice" is a term used to oppose a war that one doesn't believe should be fought. One can choose to defend one's state or not. One can choose to embark upon a war or not. Logic pretends to dictate that resistance will occur, but this is still a choice. In 1938, the leaders of Czechoslovakia could have resisted Nazi aggression; they *chose* not to. In 1939, the Finns could have bent to Soviet power. They *chose* to fight. Whether the choice is morally justifiable is a different matter, one that does not alter the reality that there is always a choice whether or not to fight. Lawrence Freedman writes:

> The problem with the distinction lay not in the idea of wars of choice but in the idea of wars of necessity. Because of the strong legal and ethical presumption against war, it is not surprising that when committing to combat, governments like to assert that they are following some unassailable strategic logic that permits no alternative. Talking of a war of choice opens up debate; asserting a war of necessity closes it down. Choices can be good or bad; necessity chooses for you.[82]

Freedman is certainly correct. Dividing wars into wars of necessity and choice has no explanatory value. It is easier and more useful to base our analysis on the political aims, the reasons *why* nations go to war. With this we have returned once again to Clausewitz's stress upon understanding the object sought and its value.

Unilateralism and Multilateralism

Unilateralism in and of itself is no sin. But one must evaluate the costs that will be paid for this and be willing and able to absorb them. Aggressive and totalitarian states, and states that deem their interests threatened, do not allow themselves to be bound by the aforementioned prescription – unless it serves their interests at the time. Free states should not tie their own hands out of a deluded sense of what *should* be the norm in international relations when in truth they are ignoring the *reality* of state behavior. Critics will say this is the sin of realism. The realist will say it is simply a fact of human history.

In both politics and war there are those who will oppose you no matter what you say because they deem it in their interests to do so. Some domestic and foreign political opponents will brand you "unilateralist" regardless of whether it is true. For example, when George W. Bush launched the Second Iraq War in 2003, his political opponents pilloried him by deeming the action "unilateral."[83] Though the US bore the weight of the war, it was by no means unilaterally waged, as the Bush administration assembled one of the largest coalitions in history to support it – thirty-eight countries.[84] One could certainly argue this was a paper coalition, and in some respects that is correct. But this does not negate the fact that the war was broadly supported – as long as it was

going well – and thus far from a unilateral act. Political commentator
Charles Krauthammer suggested the term "pseudo-lateral" to describe
wars where the US and its host nation carried the burden, and other
supporters dispatched essentially token forces.[85]

Political scientist William O'Brien observed that:

> The United States, in particular, has seemed to be greatly con-
> cerned with bringing an additional dimension of legitimacy to
> its participation in a conflict by introducing allies in a collective
> war effort. It seems to be believed by the US government,
> presumably in the conviction that this belief is widely shared,
> that there is a basic political, legal, and moral superiority to col-
> lective recourse to armed coercions over individual, unilateral
> recourse to force.[86]

Other critics insist that acting without UN support makes the
action unilateral. The UN is not the final arbiter regarding the activities
of sovereign states, and the belief that a nation must have allies and must
have UN sanction to act is a self-imposed constraint. Failing to get UN
support only means failing to get UN support. The question is whether
one is willing to pay the cost of this.

When President Obama made his speech launching the Third
Iraq War in 2014, he did not seek UN approval as both President Bushes
had done for their Iraq Wars (with mixed results).[87] Obama also endured
charges of unilateralism from both the American political left and right.[88]

Preemptive and Preventive War

These terms must be addressed, because they are too often used
to brand wars without bothering to reveal what the wars are about. The
two major problems with the terms preemptive and preventive war
revolve around definition and connotation. Also, these terms are often
conflated, which increases the confusion. The term preemptive war is
also often used interchangeably with the term preventive attack. This
demonstrates part of its analytical inadequacy, because sometimes its
users overlook the fact one is starting a war. A "preventive war" is
generally defined as a conflict launched in the face of a clear threat of
attack. Usually, such action is considered acceptable historically
because the state is being pushed into a position where its leaders must
either wait for the blow or seize the initiative.[89]

Bernard Brodie defines a preventive war as "a premeditated attack by one country against another, which is unprovoked in the sense that it does not wait upon a specific aggression or other overt action by the target state, and in which the chief and most immediate objective is the destruction of the latter's over-all military power and especially its strategic air power."[90] The term preventive war bears the connotation of being underhanded or perhaps illegitimate, a war waged to destroy a threat even before it has been clearly manifested. The Peloponnesian War is given as an example of this because of Sparta's decision to attack Athens before its power became overweening.[91]

German Chancellor Otto von Bismarck frowned upon the idea of launching a preemptive war, particularly because of the uncertainty involved: "I would ... never advise your Majesty to declare war forthwith, simply because it appeared that your opponent would begin hostilities in the near future. One can never anticipate the ways of divine providence securely enough for that."[92]

The idea of fighting a preventive war against the Soviet Union was a common part of early Cold War defense discussions in the United States. Academics, soldiers, even *The New York Times* presented arguments in support of this.[93] Bernard Brodie was skeptical about this for very practical reasons: "Actually there probably never was a time when preventive war would have been technically – not to say politically – feasible. When we had the atomic monopoly, we did not have enough power; and when we developed the necessary power, we no longer had the monopoly."[94]

Brodie was also very much aware of the moral issues relating to preventive war, "however much we confine ourselves to what we fondly regard as unemotional logic."[95] The reality is that a significant portion of the American public would oppose launching a war for these reasons. This was a point made in NSC 68 in regard to preventive war by the US against the Soviet Union.[96] Critically, as always, one must understand the political aim.

Declaring War: Yes or No?

Traditionally, declaring war was an expected and normal part of the relations between states. This is now *passé*, as many wars in the modern period have been launched without a declaration, and formally declaring war has essentially disappeared since the end of the Second

World War.[97] Moreover, most wars fought from 1920 to 1970 not only began "without a declaration or ultimatum," but also "have usually ended without a peace treaty, and the laws of war and neutrality have been grossly violated."[98] The US has not officially declared war on another nation since the Second World War, but one should note that the last time the US declared war was also the last time the US properly ended any war that required significant commitment of forces and time.

It should also be noted that of America's wars, only five involved formal declarations of war: The War of 1812, the Mexican–American War, the Spanish–American War, and both World Wars. In comparison, and depending upon how one counts such things, the US has fought perhaps 200 undeclared wars, nearly all fought for limited aims. Moreover, contrary to what some believe, it is not unconstitutional under all circumstances for the United States to be involved in a war without a declaration from Congress. It was established in the late eighteenth and early nineteenth centuries as a result of legal rulings related to the Quasi-War with France that if the US was attacked by a foreign power, it was then technically at war and thus there was no necessity of Congress declaring it so.[99] The US president's ability to take the US to war is constrained not only by the Constitution but also the 1973 War Powers Resolution. This states that the president can only insert US forces in a war "pursuant to (1) a declaration of war, (2) specific statutory authorization, or (3) a national emergency created by an attack upon the United States."[100] The president is also required to report to Congress on any commitment of troops every six months.[101]

Officially declaring war has both advantages and disadvantages. One advantage is that it makes it very clear to everyone the situation at hand.[102] It provides clarity to the leaders and citizens of the country at war, something too often lacking in regard to many post-Second World War US conflicts. In the case of the US, Harry Summers argued that "a declaration of war makes the prosecution of the war a shared responsibility of both the government and the American people."[103]

There are, of course, disadvantages. The late political scientist Paul Seabury correctly pointed out that "paradoxically the very act of declaring war, like the act of peacemaking, confers some legitimacy upon both sides." Another potential disadvantage is that the first state in a conflict to declare war risks condemnation under the UN Charter because they could be deemed an aggressor. A declaration of war might mean the enemy state activating treaties with allies who enter the conflict. Traditionally, declaring war triggered certain agreements and produced certain rights and responsibilities under international agreements such as the Geneva Convention. Avoiding a formal state of war might save a combatant from some obstacles arising from this, but it could also create others.[104] Declaring war could be a disadvantage politically in regard to international law and relations with other nations, particularly those opposed to you. Moreover, if Congress won't vote to support the war, then perhaps the president should reconsider. Weak political support could diminish popular support and increase the chances of defeat. But there are undoubtedly times when presidents feel they must act regardless of the political opposition.

Historian Stanley I. Kutler insisted that "a president who ignores the congressional role assumes greater risks for failure."[105] This allows Congress to not support the president's political aim because it is not Congress' aim, as it has not voted for it. Having Congress on board is usually beneficial. It gives a president political cover, but it also helps ensure the funding for the war. For example, President Richard Nixon lost the support of Congress after the 1972 elections. Nixon knew the new incoming Democratic Party-controlled Congress would cut the funding for the Vietnam War. He raced the clock to bring US involvement in the war to an end.[106]

The United States has not declared war on another nation since December 1941, yet it has fought numerous wars since then, including very long ones in Vietnam and Afghanistan. Instead of Congressional declarations of war, US leaders have asked for and received various other forms of legislative approval. Many constitutional scholars believe Truman and Johnson launched their wars without proper approval from Congress. Congress voted to support the 1990–91 Gulf War, but Bush insisted he had the authority to launch the war regardless.[107] There is no reason to believe that the practice of not asking Congress to declare war will change.

In the post-Cold War era, regardless of whether the wars the US president launches are for limited or unlimited political aims, they go to Congress for approval of their actions and not for declarations of war. President Barack Obama told an interviewer in December 2007 that "The President does not have power under the Constitution to unilaterally authorize a military attack in a situation that does not involve stopping an actual or imminent threat to the nation." He elaborated on the matter of defense, giving his view that:

> As Commander-in-Chief, the President does have a duty to protect and defend the United States. In instances of self-defense, the President would be within his constitutional authority to act before advising Congress or seeking its consent. History has shown us time and again, however, that military action is most successful when it is authorized and supported by the Legislative branch. It is always preferable to have the informed consent of Congress prior to any military action.

In the same interview he also remarked that "The President is not above the law."[108] It is difficult to argue with his remarks. Unfortunately, even his own administration did not work this way when he took the US into the Third Iraq War in 2014. He is in good company.

War without a Declaration – Theory in Practice

The Korean War

North Korea invaded South Korea on June 25, 1950. When Truman received word of this he immediately ordered MacArthur to throw the North Koreans out of the South before consulting Congress or the United Nations. Only a little more than seventy-two hours after the North Korean attack, the Truman administration had gathered an international coalition and won a vote of support for intervention from the UN Security Council.[109]

This, though, as we saw in the beginning of our study, did not settle the debate on US entry into the Korean War. Chief among the issues was whether the US should declare war. This matter was so contentious that it marks the beginning of the preface to the memoir of then Army Chief of Staff, J. Lawton Collins: "The Korean War was the first large-scale war in American history that began and ended without a declaration of war by the Congress of the United States."[110] By not getting Congressional approval to go to war in Korea, Truman missed an opportunity to get bipartisan support behind the move. He also left an opening for critics – who wasted no time – and by June 27 began charging that Truman was ignoring the Constitution.[111] The obvious questions are why did the Truman administration break with US tradition? And what were their arguments for doing so?

Truman asked Democratic Senator Tom Connally for his advice, and Connally warned that asking for a declaration of war might produce a long debate and tie Truman's hands. Connally also insisted that Truman had the needed authority "as commander in chief and under the UN Charter." Truman also didn't bother with Congress because he knew he had the support of the American people behind him. No one questioned whether or not a vote in Congress would be in Truman's favor (it would have been). What the Truman administration feared was a prolonged debate.[112] Acheson worried about attacks from the conservative Taft wing of the Republican Party and their use of Korea as a means of attacking the Truman administration's Asia policy, particularly the abandonment of Chiang Kai-Shek, and feared providing a platform for attacking how the administration had dealt with defense matters. On his part, Truman "wanted to avoid any action that would make his commitment more warlike in the eyes of his foreign and domestic allies and critics."[113]

The administration was correct about the potential source of Congressional criticism. Senator Taft argued, among other things, "that Democratic policies shaped by the ultimate appeaser, Dean Acheson, had brought on the war in the first place."[114] Acheson criticized Taft's Wednesday, June 28, 1950 speech as "bitterly partisan and ungracious, but basically honest." Taft insisted that Truman had done the right thing in the wrong way by intervening in Korea without a Congressional resolution, one Taft would have supported.[115]

Truman proceeded to argue that since the US Senate had approved the UN Charter that the US had transferred its war-making authority – in certain circumstances – to the UN Security Council. The Security Council had voted to use force: thus, the US was covered.[116] Critics could call this disingenuous, considering that his administration had raised the issue of intervention at the UN.

Truman continued to address the constitutional issue in early July 1950. His administration considered introducing an Acheson-authored resolution supporting Truman's decision.[117] At a July 3, 1950 meeting, Acheson "recommended that the President should not ask for a resolution of approval, but rest on his constitutional authority as Commander in Chief of the armed forces. However, we had drafted a resolution commending the action taken by the United States that would be acceptable if proposed by members of Congress." Unfortunately, Acheson's discussion of whether or not to obtain Congressional approval completely ignored the issue of the constitutional requirement for the Congress to declare war, as the US had not been attacked. He condemned any criticism of the move as partisan politics – which was doubtless partially true – and justified the move based upon a memorandum issued by *his* State Department on July 3, 1950 that listed eighty-five prior incidents where a president had initiated military action on his own authority. He also insisted that the inevitable ensuing debate in Congress would have generated unnecessary criticism that would undermine the morale of US troops fighting a desperate rearguard defense in Korea.[118] This is, of course, quite a bit of *ex post facto* justification of actions he endorsed, and also ignores the fact that the desperation of the defense in Korea was a result of his administration's failure to have a properly prepared military.

When one reads what Acheson used to support the decision the administration had already made, one is struck by its illogic. The State Department reprinted a 1941 list of eighty-five incidents of the use of US military forces outside the nation from 1812 to 1932. Most are instances where the US acted to protect endangered American nationals. There is nothing here that compares to the US decision to fight in Korea to protect the sovereignty of the South Korean government. Moreover, the authorities cited in the document note that the Constitution deems the president commander-in-chief "evidently for the purpose of enabling him to defend the country against invasion, to suppress insurrection and to take care that the laws be faithfully executed." The second authority says the Constitution gives the president "power to send United States forces outside the country in time of peace."[119] Neither of these were applicable to Korea.

Acheson's document also justifies these interventions as being necessary to protect the interests of the United States. Because enforcement of the UN Charter and its Resolutions was considered in the interests of the United States, intervention in Korea was also permitted.[120] But under this reasoning, any foreign act could be considered contrary to US interests and thus possess the required grounds for US military intervention.

Constitutional scholars of the day wasted no time rejecting the document. One branded it a "lengthy list of fights with pirates and bandits." Another protested based upon the scale, observing that

Acheson's list "contains not a single military adventure that comes close to the dimensions of the Korean War." Congress and Truman had also already tackled the relevant issues via the 1945 United Nations Participation Act, which said the US could only send troops to back UN actions if Congress approved. At the time, Acheson, serving as an Undersecretary of State, "had testified before a congressional committee that a president could commit troops requested by the UN Security Council only after he had received approval of Congress."[121] The UN Charter does not supplant the US Constitution in American law.

In the end – and fairly quickly – Truman let the matter drop and went on with the war.[122] The issue resurfaced the following year. When asked in the later 1951 MacArthur Senate hearings whether or not it would have been preferable to ask for a declaration of war, Acheson said: "If you ask me whether it would have been better, all I can say is to recite the facts of the situation. I doubt whether it would have made any difference." He insisted there was no time and added: "But certainly I do not believe the President would have gone to Congress for the purpose of asking for a declaration of war against anybody, because this was an action of the United Nations to repel an aggression and was not a question of war against any other country."[123] If it was not a war against North Korea (and, at the time of his testimony, China as well), what was it? His argument collapses even more quickly when one considers his driving the change in political aim leading to the invasion of North Korea.

The US had difficulty figuring out a name for what we call the Korean War because of the problem of calling it a "war" when there was no declaration of such, something with which Americans are now familiar.[124] As we saw at the beginning, Truman branded the Korean War a police action. He then gave approval for this as an official term, "and used it throughout the summer of 1950."[125] Moreover, in his memoir Truman resisted calling the Korean War a war, referring to it with terms such as "action," "situation," or "affair."[126] Does a refusal to acknowledge reality undermine America's willingness and ability to win here? This can't be proven, but denial of the reality to yourself and the people you have to count on to wage the war is not a good start.

Procuring a Congressional resolution of support would not have silenced all criticism, but it would have put some shackles on Truman's critics. If they voted for the war, publicly turning against it would become more difficult.[127] The oddest thing in this entire debacle is that Truman could have easily secured a declaration of war. He and Acheson were indeed correct that their political opponents would have ensured a contentious debate, something that happened anyway. But they also would have voted for a declaration of war if Truman asked and told him this. What is easily forgotten from our distant perch is the bitterness of the debates on politics and strategy of the previous five years, particularly the contention over the fall of China to Communism and the "Red Scare." It is understandable that Truman and Acheson wanted to avoid a new and public revisiting of recent events. But they launched the modern American practice of refusing to call a war a war. They also gave Congress an out, and critics started calling the Korean War "Mr. Truman's War."

The Vietnam War

In his 1964 election campaign, President Lyndon Johnson insisted that Americans weren't going to be fighting in Asia. He made these statements while simultaneously planning for just such an event, something he brought to pass the next year.[128] Indeed, by this time it was already beginning to happen. By the end of 1964, Johnson's advisors were telling him that he would have to dramatically increase the American military commitment in order to achieve stability in South Vietnam.[129] He already had in his hands the Gulf of Tonkin Resolution, which had been passed by Congress on August 7, 1964. This was as close as the US came to declaring war on North Vietnam.

On August 2, 1964, the destroyer *Maddox* was attacked by North Vietnamese patrol boats. On the night of 4 August, *Maddox* and *Turner Joy* reported another attack, though this one did not occur and resulted from bad radar and sonar readings in the poor weather. The administration decided that they could not let the attacks go unpunished. Retaliatory bombing followed.[130] The North Vietnamese knew the second attack never took place, but, seeing the incursions as provocative, they had thus launched the first attack.[131]

Johnson used the events to get Congress to pass the Gulf of Tonkin Resolution, which gave him the power to escalate the war in Vietnam.[132] It faced minimal Congressional opposition. Democratic Senator Ernest Gruening of Alaska opposed and criticized it. Democratic Senator Wayne Morse of Oregon predicted "history will record that we have made a great mistake in subverting and circumventing the Constitution of the United States ... We are in effect giving the president ... war-making powers in the absence of a declaration of war. I believe that to be a historic mistake." They were the only negative votes in Congress. Public support, meanwhile, was overwhelmingly behind the president, as 85 percent of Americans backed Johnson's retaliatory air strikes. The public was not told that the US had been supporting surveillance of and a raid against the North Vietnamese coast.[133]

The State Department had prepared the draft used for what became known as the Gulf of Tonkin Resolution a few weeks before.[134] Johnson, unlike Truman, believed Congressional approval imperative for any future action he felt necessary to take in Vietnam. One critic insists "the administration had been looking for an incident that would bring the United States openly into the conflict, a scenario in which it would respond to provocation, and that would enable the executive to get something like a declaration of war, which it might want down the road."[135]

Johnson believed he had to fight in Vietnam, but he never considered seeking a declaration of war. Doing so would have been too provocative in a Cold War setting. A declaration of war against North Vietnam might be taken as a threat to destroy it. This could provoke intervention by China, which had occurred in Korea, or perhaps even the Soviet Union. Either of these events could lead to a Third World War.[136] The Gulf of Tonkin Resolution gave Johnson the political cover he needed while reducing the risk of intervention by third parties that had occurred in Korea. It also provided future administrations a precedent for how to take the US to war.

Why did Johnson choose to escalate heavily in Vietnam? He said in 1964: "I don't think it's worth fighting for, and I don't think we can get out."[137] It is important to remember the backdrop of the Cold War. US policymakers did not become involved in Vietnam because they had any interest in making the US an imperial power, or because they necessarily disliked the North Vietnamese. The US became involved in Vietnam because its leaders feared continuing Communist expansion in Southeast Asia and wanted to stop it. The US war here can be seen as a nested war as it was a war fought in the midst of a larger struggle.

Moreover, Johnson would have preferred to not fight this war. He was more interested in pursuing his "Great Society" legislation.[138]

But he came to believe it was necessary to intervene in Vietnam because he feared that a North Vietnamese victory would provoke a debate so divisive that it would destroy his presidency and injure American democracy. Johnson himself might be blamed for "losing" South Vietnam the way that Truman was blamed for "losing" China.[139] For Johnson, the value of the object – an independent, non-Communist South Vietnam – was high enough to justify war, but the North Vietnamese wanted South Vietnam far more.

An odd result of the Gulf of Tonkin incident and Johnson's response relates directly to an underpinning of US strategic theory. At the time, Thomas Schelling was working as a consultant for the Department of Defense, some of whose key members were heavily influenced by Schelling's ideas on deterrence. In 1966, Schelling published *Arms and Influence*, which "made Johnson's Tonkin Gulf reprisal a centerpiece example of rational signaling."[140] A book based partially upon a false representation of an event, that pushes signaling ideas discredited by their strategic failure in Vietnam, is a standard text for strategic studies, international relations, and political science training in the US, and inevitably cited in any article dealing with the issues Schelling raises. Perhaps this is a problem that should be addressed by the people teaching in these fields.

The Gulf War

President George H. W. Bush never considered a declaration of war against Iraq in response to Saddam Hussein's conquest of Kuwait in 1990. By this time, it had been half a century since the United States had declared war. What was most important politically was the sanction of Congress. United Nations support was also valued. The Bush administration set about securing both.

There was, of course, resistance from the political opposition. Democratic Senator Sam Nunn's televised Senate Hearings on the Gulf War featured a long list of figures who were against or skeptical of the use of force, or who preferred to give sanctions against Iraq a chance to work, including recently retired Admiral William Crowe. The US Chargé in Iraq, Joe Wilson, relayed to Bush that Crowe's testimony convinced many in Iraq that the US would never attack. Bush believed the hearings had been stacked against him.[141] Such is political reality in a democratic state. Nevertheless, Bush succeeded. The House of

Representatives voted 250 to 183 to approve military action. The Senate approved in a 52 to 47 vote.[142]

The administration proved exceptionally successful at the UN. Bush had the able and energetic cooperation of British Prime Minister Margaret Thatcher, who remarked on August 5, 1990 that "Iraq's invasion of Kuwait defies every principle for which the United Nations stands. If we let it succeed, no small country can ever feel safe again. The law of the jungle would take over from the rule of law." UN Resolution 660 of August 2, 1990 condemned Iraq's invasion and demanded immediate withdrawal; it received no dissenting vote. On August 6, 1990, the UN passed Resolution 661, which imposed an embargo on all trade with Iraq and Kuwait, except for humanitarian and medical supplies.[143] On November 29, 1990, the UN Security Council approved Resolution 678, which set January 15, 1991 as the deadline for Iraq to obey the Security Council resolutions.[144] One important factor to remember here is that Bush believed he had the legal ability to act even if he did not receive the support of Congress.

It would be wise for future US presidents to force the American Congress to take more responsibility for taking the nation to war. Hopefully, this would encourage more oversight – in the best sense of the word – and thus more eagerness to bring conflicts to a successful and quick conclusion.

Conclusion

Secretary of Defense Weinberger tried to address the problem of unclear political aims and the related use of force after the Ronald Reagan administration's disastrous 1983 intervention in Lebanon. The Weinberger Doctrine had six tests for committing American troops: it must be a vital US interest; the US had to commit sufficient forces and intend to win; the US should have clear political aims and military objectives, know how its forces can accomplish them, and commit sufficient strength; the relationship between the political aim and forces dispatched must be constantly reassessed and altered as needed to win, and if the U.S. wasn't going to win, it shouldn't go; the commitment must be supported by Congress and the American people; and sending combat troops "should be the last resort." To support his insistence upon clear political aims and understanding how to achieve them, Weinberger quoted Clausewitz: "no one starts a war – or rather, no one in his senses ought to do so – without first being clear in his mind what he intends to achieve by that war, and how he intends to conduct it." This approach wasn't institutionalized.[145]

General Colin Powell, Reagan's last National Security Advisor, expressed things similarly in what is called the Powell Doctrine or the Powell Corollary to the Weinberger Doctrine. He was reluctant to use military force because of America's Vietnam War experience and his own. He wrote in 1995: "War should be the politics of last resort. And when we go to war, we should have a purpose that our people understand and support; we should mobilize the country's resources to fulfill that mission and then go in to win."[146]

Establishing the political aim is critical. It gives direction to the struggle. It can explain the *why* of the war. But it must be clearly conveyed to the men and women who have to fight the war to achieve it. This is an important first step, but only that. Knowing what you want is one thing. Figuring out whether or not you can get it is another. We consider next some of the major things affecting the pursuit of this aim and shaping the conditions for how the war waged for it will be fought. Connected to this are three important questions that must ride in the forefront of the minds of both political leaders and military commanders when entering a war: What are the risks involved? What are the rewards we hope to gain from this? And are the risks worth the rewards? Understanding the political aim can illuminate the first question. The next chapter helps with the second. The political leaders decide the third.

4 CONSTRAINTS: OR WHY WARS FOR LIMITED POLITICAL AIMS ARE SO DIFFICULT

The man who sacrifices the possible in search of the impossible is a fool.[1]

        Carl von Clausewitz

Introduction

In *War and Peace*, Leo Tolstoy's Prince Andrei said: "War is not a polite recreation but the vilest thing in life, and we ought to understand that and not play at war. Our attitude towards the fearful necessity of war ought to be stern and serious. It boils down to this: we should have done with humbug and let war be war and not a game."[2] Historian and philosopher Raymond Aron wrote: "To guarantee that wars remain limited is it not to accept permanent war? Will not limitation in means have as its corollary absence of limitation in time?"[3]

In other words, if we constrain our efforts too much, if we fail to use the means necessary to finish the struggle, unless one is willing to accept defeat, the war will go on and on. As we've seen, the result has been what some observers call "forever wars." Since 2001, US and other Western policymakers have failed to understand this. This is a great evil that has cost thousands of lives and trillions of dollars, one arising from the failure of US leaders to cogently understand and wage America's wars. We see this clearly in the imposition of unwise constraints, ranging from unnecessarily narrow rules of engagement in Afghanistan, to a refusal to deal with Taliban sanctuary in Pakistan, to the failure to isolate the battlespace in Iraq because sufficient forces were never committed, to the initial piecemeal effort against Islamic State intended to kick the can down the road to the next administration. US leaders need a deeper understanding of the concept of and effects of constraints upon American warfighting, as well as their respective failures in placing them – or not.

Exemplifying our intellectual weaknesses are limited war literature discussions surrounding "restraints" or "limits," and the related building of arguments upon the assumption that combatants can reach mutual understanding on what will and will not be done even if they have no formal communication.[4] One of many examples of this appears in political scientist Nordal Åkerman's work in an argument influenced by Schelling: "Agreements as to these limitations [constraints] and the level at which war is to be pursued can be reached either tacitly, by negotiation, or by signals."[5] Counting upon the enemy observing tacit limits is unwise, as one can't control what the enemy sees, *thinks* they see, or feels. Moreover, depending upon signaling to be understood (we will return to this later), and banking upon this to alter the enemy's action, is wishful thinking and not sound strategic analysis. Such an approach shunts aside the history of warfare and the human desire to actually win wars (at least until the post-modern era), and the reality of war's general (though not universal) tendency to become increasingly violent the longer a conflict drags on. Historian Michael Howard explained this problem: "if the belligerents can be reasonable enough to accept extraneous limitations on its conduct and regard the enemy almost as a *frère adversaire*, they should be reasonable enough to avoid fighting altogether ... Agreed limitations on warfare imply rational understanding with an enemy who, if he can be reasoned with, should not be an enemy."[6]

A related critical problem is that "limited war" is generally defined in terms of the various factors that can supposedly "limit" it, such as the means or the geography. Nearly all works discussing "limited war" suffer from this error.[7] As we've seen, these are *not* elements of a definition of a war fought for a limited political aim; they are factors contributing to its nature. This is the definition of constraints. Again, all wars have constraints, but in wars for limited political aims, the constraints intrude more fiercely.

Constraints and Wars for Limited Aims

The foundational thought in regard to constraints can be found – not surprisingly – in a quote from Clausewitz: "We can thus only say that the aims a belligerent adopts, and the resources he employs, must be governed by the particular characteristics of his own position; but they will also conform to the spirit of the age and to its general character."[8] Similarly, Corbett says "a war may be limited [constrained] physically by the strategical isolation of the object, as well as morally by its comparative unimportance."[9]

The reality of war – any war – is that there are constraints on its conduct. This is true regardless of whether the war is fought for limited or unlimited political aims. Wars fought for limited aims (especially offensive ones) usually have more constraints placed upon their conduct because the aim or aims sought usually are not existential and thus possess less inherent value. Because they have less value, the political masters are usually willing to pay less and thus limit – constrain – what can be done militarily, how it can be done, with what, for how long, and numerous other things. The ways and means strictures usually intensify and prove dominant constraints.

There are certainly exceptions to this rule of generally increased constraints. Indeed, one could argue that to successfully wage a war for a limited political aim, one must remove as many of these constraints as possible, or at least control their effect. The war that Japan fought against Russia in 1904–05, as well as its war against the United States from 1941 to 1945, are examples of Japan pursuing limited political aims while trying to mobilize as much of its military power as possible in the pursuit of its political aims. In the first case, it was successful; in the latter, it was not, but the opponents were different, as were innumerable other factors.

It is also theoretically possible that a war for a limited political aim will be fought with no significant contributing constraints on ways and means. This might be irrational, but that does not prevent its occurrence. War is the most complex thing humans do. To seek to always impose rationality upon war – and to expect "rational behavior" from an opponent whose mind and passions it is impossible to fully fathom – is to ignore the reality of human behavior and experience. The abandonment of constraints is less likely by the nation waging an offensive limited war because (usually) the stakes are not as high, but there is greater potential for this by a nation fighting a defensive war for a limited aim because the regime's survival could be at stake. The Japanese decision to arm women and children with bamboo spears in late 1945 as part of their *Ketsugo* defense plan to oppose an American invasion is an example. Continuing to fight a war one has little hope of winning and being willing to sacrifice in such a manner to do so does not figure as rational in the eyes of most Western observers, yet this is exactly what the Japanese intended. There is no doubt they would have executed this plan if necessary.[10] The problem analysts have in accepting this line of thinking is that they confuse the political aim with the scale of the means being used. The "size" of the forces is not how one explains the struggle. As always, analysis must begin with the political aim. Overall, current limited war theory ignores the logic and history underpinning the reality in regard to constraints.

Actual and Self-Imposed Constraints[11]

As noted at the beginning of this chapter, constraints are a reality of warfare. The problem for leaders and strategists is to determine how to use force to achieve the political aim within the dictates of these constraints. The most important constraints are addressed below. But before evaluating them individually, we must taackle the issue of whether the constraints are actual – meaning one has no choice but to act based upon their presence – or whether the constraints are self-imposed – meaning a combatant power *chooses* to allow them to exert influence upon their war effort. Constraints help determine the nature of the war, and where and how it will be fought. Analysis of them and their probable effects should be part of any rational assessment of the coming challenge. As one writer put it in a discussion related to terrorism that presents solid, general advice: "The fact that these limitations [constraints] – both structural and self-imposed – exist is a source of great consternation for many defense intellectuals ... The problem, however, will not go away."[12]

How one determines an actual constraint can be quite easy. When a nation goes to war, there will be factors that no amount of will or military power can hope to eliminate. Actual constraints are generally imposed by the physical environment. Korea is a mountainous peninsula. One cannot escape this any more than the fact that Russia becomes cold in the winter. Often, you cannot control these constraints, particularly if your opponent can determine them, but your actions or the enemy's reactions might change their respective effects.

Self-imposed constraints are those a state places upon how it wages the war. Some see this as bad. Others assume it an absolute and positive good. Both stances are foolish. Sometimes constraints are proof of wisdom, but at others they demonstrate naivety, incompetence, or an honest mistake. The difficulty is determining when constraints should be imposed and in what fashion. Politics usually provides the answer here (though this hardly means the constraints aren't foolish), especially at the beginning of a war, when the strategic and political situations can be particularly unclear. The value of the political aim sought, the relationships among the various states involved (including those between coalition partners and friendly states, as well as interested neutrals), additional military and political commitments, and other threats or future demands are among the most important factors that should influence decisions regarding which constraints we impose upon ourselves and how they affect our waging of the war. There will also be many more issues that will impose constraints, including some not directly linked to the war.

Deducing self-imposed constraints is more difficult. First, some of the past criticism of limited war theory and the manner in which the US has waged wars for limited political aims insists that US failures derive from "limits" on the use of force. This leads to the specious argument that the level of military force should not be "limited" (constrained), and the related contention that "limits" of any kind can fatally injure America's chances of success. One also sees the opposite argument: that force should not be used or cannot achieve the political aim. Neither of these responses are useful. The reality is that sometimes military force is the best tool a state has for addressing a threat, and when this force is used there are constraints, no matter the political aim.

Second, what is also often left out of the argument is a key question: are these self-imposed constraints wise? Obviously, sometimes they are. Just as obvious is the fact that sometimes they aren't. One of the many difficulties is in determining when this is the case. Here – yet again – politics enters the equation. The constraints will be decided by the political masters, though not always correctly, and influenced by factors already mentioned, particularly the value of the political aim. The military leaders will of course also play a role here. British Air Marshal Sir Robert Saundby observed:

> It is the duty of the military commander to advise his political chiefs as to the correct strategy to adopt in any given circumstances. It is also his duty to protest against restrictions [constraints] which jeopardize the attainment of the objective and

lead to unnecessary casualties. But having ensured that the politicians understand the price that will have to be paid if they decide, for reasons of their own, to adopt restrictions and limitations, it is equally the duty of the military commander to accept the position and do his best. He is justified in refusing to do so, or in resigning, only if he is convinced that the task he has been set is practically impossible or will compel his forces to accept a wholly unreasonable rate of loss.[13]

One could make the argument that all limits are self-imposed, even those generated by the physical environment, because we can find ways to overcome such things. But it seems more logical to accept the effect of the natural world upon the nature of the war, though this does not negate the fact that creative combatants adapt to meet natural challenges – or suffer the effects if they don't.

Identifying with absolute certainty what will drive the imposition or not of constraints (beyond the value of the political aim and whether or not the threat is existential) is impossible. The placement of self-imposed constraints often arises from the fear of an expanded war (especially the intervention of a third party) or the related injuring of relations with other states. These matters factored heavily into US decision-making during the Korean and Vietnam Wars. The fear that commitment will lead to overextension is also sometimes a driver (this was particularly true during the Korean War), as are apprehensions about the level of military means that will be needed, though this is often tied to the prior point. Sensitivity to casualties can also be important, as well as the internal political concerns of the leaders of the combatants, which is certainly linked to the issue of casualties. These are factors influencing the prosecution of all US wars, particularly after 1945.

The Key Constraints

As mentioned above, constraints are inevitable and universal. What is not universal are the constraints that uniquely bear upon a particular conflict. But there are also commonalities.

The key constraints (not necessarily in order of importance, as this will vary with the war and its constant evolution) are as follows:

1 the opponent's political aim and the relative value of the objects sought

2 time
3 the internal political environment, including public opinion
4 the international political environment
5 geography
6 military means (including nuclear weapons)
7 unknowns not considered or envisioned.

Sometimes these constraints are interrelated, but it is important to understand the effects of all of them, because they influence the nature of the war and thus the strategy and operations of each combatant.

1   **The Opponent's Political Aim or Aims and the Relative Value of the Objects Sought**

It is critical to consider the aims of the opponent or opponents.[14] This is the most weighty constraint, because the value of the object or objects they want – and how this conflicts or interacts with what you want – is a major factor contributing to the nature of the war. As we've seen, the problem with branding conflicts as "limited" is that the enemy's aims might *not* be limited. One work provides a solid, related admonition: "While it is meaningful to characterize a war as limited or unlimited for particular actors, it is not meaningful to designate a war itself as either limited or unlimited."[15] This is why analysis must be done for each combatant, and it must start with their political aims.

From a theoretical perspective, then, how do we address this important problem? *The aim your opponent is seeking becomes one of your constraints* – a factor contributing to the nature of the war – and arguably the most important constraint, because this is the *why* of the war for the enemy. The value of the object is still key, but the analysis must be extended beyond one's own aim to understand how the value of the enemy's aim affects the nature of the war and the enemy's willingness to fight it, as well as how one's own aim affects the equation. Critically: *the importance and effects of the other constraints flow from this.* How hard the enemy will fight for the goal affects how hard we will have to fight for ours. If you are aware the enemy is willing to fight in the last ditch, this should have a bearing upon how you impose constraints upon yourself, as well as many other issues. The problem one may encounter here is that the opponent's political aim may be unknown. If possible, it must be discovered or deduced.

The Vietnam War (or Second Indochina War, 1959–75), provides a good example of the problem. The United States pursued a limited political aim against North Vietnam, as did its coalition partner, South Vietnam. Neither sought the overthrow of the enemy regime but simply to force them to accept the independence of South Vietnam. The North Vietnamese sought the destruction of the South Vietnamese regime, as well as the installation of Communist regimes in Laos and Cambodia. These were unlimited aims. North Vietnam's aim against the US was limited: the removal of the United States from the conflict. But Vietnam is generally branded a "limited war."

One must make the utmost effort to try to control the various factors that affect the value of the aim. One cannot expect perfection here, but one can expect and indeed demand heroic effort, as this so directly affects one's ability to prosecute the war and for how long. Interestingly, not only are the effects of the enemy's political aims generally ignored in limited war theorizing, but also in theoretical discussions of warfare in general. When doing this analysis, *it must be done for each combatant.*

2   Time

When the war starts, the clock begins to tick. How long each state has to prosecute the war is unknown. One of the primary tasks of each combatant is to affect the ticking in their favor. They must slow the clock for themselves, while speeding it for the enemy. How long the clock ticks – and how fast or how slow – depends upon many factors. What determines the available time is the value of the object or objects sought, and the price that one is paying for it (usually consisting of blood, treasure, political capital, and prestige), combined with how long one must pay. The only "time out" allowed is the arranging of an armistice or ceasefire, something discussed in Chapter 6.

What the respective combatants do with their elements of national power will affect the clock. The most important of these is the available military means. Clausewitz tells us that what we are doing militarily should affect the enemy's will to wage the war or their ability to do so. If our actions fail to do either of these, we should reconsider them.[16] One should not expend blood and treasure for merely the sake of acting. Sun Tzu rightly cautions his sovereign about the seriousness and costs involved in war.[17] These things should always be kept in mind.

An important question to always ask is this: whose side is time on? This, of course, raises the larger issue of how to determine this. There is no single answer, as all wars are different, but the effects of the actions of both sides will act upon this. There are some things to consider. First, be aware of the international environment, which is addressed momentarily. This can have innumerable effects upon the will and ability of the various combatants to fight. Second, consider the relative military strength of all of the combatants, as well as from where this strength is derived, what will affect it, when, and how. Third, understand the relative internal political situations of the combatants. Under what terms will their people and governments keep up the fight or abandon it? What will affect this? When? And how? Finally, consider the other factors specific to the situation at hand. Every war has its own unique characteristics and must be understood on its own terms.[18] This fact is one of the great obstacles in constructing useful military theory.

A related concept is the idea of "decisive battle." Clausewitz is skeptical of this: "We regard a great battle as a decisive factor in the outcome of a war or campaign, but not necessarily as the only one. Campaigns whose outcomes have been determined by a single battle have become fairly common only in recent times, and those cases in which they have settled an entire war are very rare exceptions."[19] Simply put, he believes a battle can determine the results of a campaign (what we would now call an operation), but only rarely determine a war's outcome.

But winning a campaign or battle can buy time. Success feeds the will and public opinion, which feeds the nation's ability to continue the war. Gaining time can be particularly critical if one is in a poor position, as its passage can create a change in the situation to one's benefit. Moreover, "time can become a factor in the conqueror's strength as well; but only on condition that a counterattack on him is no longer possible, that no reversal is conceivable – when indeed this factor is no longer of value since his main objective has been achieved, the culminating crisis is past, and the enemy, in short, laid low."[20]

Generally, the longer the duration of *any* war – but particularly one fought for a limited political aim – the greater the weariness of the combatant nation's population with the struggle; this delivers a commensurate growth in their discontent with the war. Bernard Brodie noted that, as such a war continues, "In their frustration, the people begin to listen to those politicians who urge that whether or not it was wise for us to become involved in the first place, the only way out now is to loosen or even abandon the limitations on our fighting."[21] How this plagued Johnson during the Vietnam War is well known, but Truman suffered similar, though much less intense, public disenchantment.

How does one judge how long a people will tolerate the pursuit of a limited aim in a war that does not immediately deliver victory? There are a number of things to consider. First, again, we must consider the value of the object pursued, but in the eyes of the people, not the policymakers. Determining this is of course extremely difficult. But leaders *must* do everything they can to gauge public sentiment while also arguing for the war's support. In a totalitarian state, simple propaganda may prove sufficient, as the government has tighter control over the people. But in a pluralistic, educated, democratic society that enjoys basic freedoms, basic propaganda (strategic communication or information operations are our preferred terms today – *propaganda* is what the *enemy* does), as well as explanations that demonstrate governmental contempt for the populace by insulting their intelligence, can undermine popular support for the war and the government itself, while simultaneously discrediting the leaders.

For example, the Lyndon Johnson administration famously did almost nothing to prop up support for its war in Vietnam. The administration generally assumed support for the war, and for many years proved correct, especially if the US was seen as progressing in what can be depicted as the Vietnam front in the Cold War competition. But then the 1968 Tet Offensive struck, and many saw it as proof that the Johnson administration had been less than forthcoming.[22] The administration's "communications failures" fatally injured it, damaged the US ability to maintain public support, and thus trimmed the length of time it had for prosecuting the war at the level needed to produce victory. Nixon, Johnson's successor, felt he had little choice but to begin reducing US troop levels because of falling public support.[23]

Additionally – and this is also directly linked to the value of the object – is the ongoing blood cost. The higher the casualties in relation to the value of the object, the more quickly the people will abandon support for the war. In theory, if the cause has some value in the eyes of the population, and the casualties and financial costs continue to fall only upon a small percentage of the populace, the war could be prosecuted for a very long time. This, of course, brings with it its own problems. Sun Tzu, as we've seen, argued vociferously against a protracted war.[24]

Additionally, the duration of the conflict – in theory – could be affected by the financial burden imposed upon the state and thus the people from whom the money is drawn. It is better to impose a short-term burden and win, than long-term costs that might not bring victory based on the assumption that fighting a low-cost war is better. Despite this caution, one has a difficult time identifying a war in the modern period in which a combatant was defeated because they exhausted their financial means. During the War for American Independence, the US, Britain, France, and Spain were all racing toward bankruptcy, and the costs of the war to all powers involved certainly helped push them to the peace table, but none of them quit because of financial reasons. Modern states – especially large states – seem invariably capable of procuring at least the minimal financial resources needed to continue the war. Arguably, the most important factor here is the political will of the leaders. If the leaders have the nerve to carry on the struggle – even in the face of adversity and setbacks – while also making the case for the war and keeping the costs acceptable, the modern nation (this is more likely to apply to larger states) usually possesses the resources to fight for a very long time. This, of course, assumes enough strength to resist the enemy's efforts.

It is often argued that during the Vietnam War the US simply ran out of time because the support of the people collapsed. This is overly simplistic. There was indeed significant opposition to the war in Vietnam, but what is forgotten here is that Richard Nixon was reelected in a landslide in 1972 despite the fact that the US had been fighting its war in Vietnam in a dramatic fashion since 1965. The counterargument is that Nixon's party lost control of Congress to his political opponents, the Democratic Party, which had little will to continue the war its leaders had made. In theory, if the political leadership had been willing, the US could have maintained a low level of military involvement in Vietnam where the American effort stood on the backs of US air power and significant advisory forces, as it did in 1972–73. The fact that the draft was abandoned in 1973 and the US began relying upon a volunteer force theoretically makes this possible – if the casualties were not too high, and the South Vietnamese forces continued to improve, and many other potential "ifs" fell into place. The long struggle in Afghanistan from 2001 to 2021 argues in favor of this. Public support had indeed waned, but the political classes of both parties had tired of the war in

Vietnam and did not think it worth the costs. This proved the deciding factor.[25]

3   The Internal Political Environment, Including Public Opinion

One of the many original areas of analysis in Clausewitz's *On War* is his emphasis on the importance of the people in any nation's wars. The people will bear its costs in every form. They will pay in blood and treasure. They will serve or have family members who do. Consequently, having them support your cause, or perhaps having the enemy's people refuse to support their cause, are critical to winning. Public opinion – depending upon how it swings – feeds or undermines national will. Political scientist Seymour Deitchman discussed "Human Factors in the Environment," by which he meant the type and number of people and their society.[26]

The media are, of course, a critical factor in shaping public opinion, something that was not always apparent. One observer wrote that journalists on the battlefield in the Crimean War "led to a real awakening of the official mind. It brought home to the [British] War Office the fact that the public had something to say about the conduct of wars and that they are not the concern exclusively of sovereigns and statesman."[27] The development and continual evolution of social media drive home how important it is for leaders to understand the effects here, and how to use or counter them. Potentially, this can be a powerful constraint on the government's ability to fight. The media effects from both social media and traditional sources can be even more potent in free societies, as they have extensive access to information.

As General Rupert Smith makes clear, the media will be involved from the beginning, and this must be kept in mind, as it plays perhaps the dominant role in the shaping of public opinion and thus support for the war. The military and political leaders need the media to tell their story, but the media needs them in order to get the story. Smith also warns that the media will not be objective, despite their claims to be so, and notes that "Nowadays we have an international media that cannot be controlled, whose communications are frequently better than those of the military and that acts to inform on the theatre as a whole to both the players and the audience."[28]

Some observers point out that the problem of public opinion – or maintaining the support of the people – in wars fought for limited aims has its own peculiar problems. Sometimes the war isn't considered particularly important. Indeed, for US public opinion, the aim of the war as well as the view of the "rightness" of the cause in the eyes of the people are the key things leading to public support. Demonstrating success, or showing that one *will* succeed, also wins public support for the government's aims.[29] Casualties also affect support, as does the size of the deployment. Americans are less likely to support intervention in civil wars, and multilateral actions are generally more popular because others bear part of the burden.[30]

American leaders should keep these things in mind, as the support of the people – and their will to fight the war – will directly affect the duration of the war and sometimes how it can be waged. The erosion of US public support for the Vietnam War is well known, but most are unaware that similar problems afflicted political leaders during the Korean War, though on a drastically smaller scale. Like their 1960s successors, Truman administration officials worried that the American public leaned toward overreaction in a dangerous situation. This drove a careful restraint of administration rhetoric. But they also had to mobilize the population, and feared that if they did too much to rouse the people they wouldn't be able to control them.[31] The administration was fortunate to enjoy substantial popular support. In a July 1950 poll, 77 percent of Americans said the US should keep fighting in Korea, 12 percent said stop and leave, while 11 percent held no opinion.[32]

This would not prove the norm, as backing for the war dropped steadily as it continued. Public support in Ohio, for example, fell after Chinese intervention, plunging from 77 percent to about 50 percent, and remained around the lower number for the duration.[33] After MacArthur's firing, Truman's approval rating never topped 33 percent, and approval for the war never rose above 50 percent. Most Americans now viewed the war as a mistake.[34] In an April 2, 1951 poll, 51 percent of Americans felt the war was a mistake, 35 percent did not, and 14 percent had no opinion.[35] Support among allies also waned.[36] Truman's public approval had dropped to less than 30 percent when he decided to not run for reelection. Lyndon Johnson's numbers when he made the same decision were only a little better.[37] Something that appears in US fiction dealing with the Korean War is the frustration of US combatants that the war only affected themselves and their families.[38]

Contrary to popular myth, American public opinion initially supported the Vietnam War. Johnson wanted to fight the war in "cold blood," in the words of one well-known historian of the conflict. The president feared that if he did too much to rally the opinion of the American people, they might push for a bigger war than he wanted.[39] Johnson's January 10, 1967 State of the Union Address gives us a picture of this:

> Whether we can fight a war of limited objectives over a period of time, and keep alive the hope of independence and stability for people other than ourselves; whether we can continue to act with restraint when the temptation to "get it over with" is inviting but dangerous; whether we can accept the necessity of choosing "a great evil in order to ward off a greater"; whether we can do these without arousing the hatreds and passions that are ordinarily loosed in time of war – on all these questions so much turns.[40]

The problem, though, was that he tried to fight a war *without* doing anything to maintain public support. This is a problem when you are conscripting hundreds of thousands of men each year and sending them to a foreign nation to fight a war in which often they see no value. The Johnson administration eventually realized the problems in their approach and in 1967 launched a number of efforts to build support for the war. By this time, though, it was probably too late, especially when the American public saw the Tet Offensive break across South Vietnam in 1968 – just after General Westmoreland had testified before Congress that the war was nearing its end.[41] Johnson administration figure Dean Rusk remarked later:

> we never made any effort to create a war psychology in the United States during the Vietnam affair. We didn't have military parades through cities ... We tried to do in cold blood perhaps what can only be done in hot blood, when sacrifices of this order are involved. At least that's a problem that people have to think of if any such thing, God forbid, should happen again.[42]

One critic sums up Johnson's handling of public opinion with this assessment: "He failed to communicate his goals to the nation, and often appeared devious and deceitful. He suppressed internal dissent within his administration, he misled Congress and then sought to stifle legislative criticism, and he assaulted his public critics, denouncing them as 'nervous Nellies.'"[43]

The erosion of public support for the war ground away American will. When Richard Nixon came to the presidency in 1969, this decline limited his options for fighting the war. Ending American involvement became more important than winning.[44] One, though, should be careful to not oversimplify the complexity of this issue because, as we've seen, Nixon was reelected in 1972 even though he had not yet extricated the US from Vietnam.[45]

The Gulf War was also generally popular among Americans. There were protests, but they bore no comparison to those of the Vietnam era. But military success in a quick war did not keep George Bush from losing his presidential reelection race, though this was a unique election because of the participation of a third-party candidate.

4   The International Political Environment

The war will not be fought in a political vacuum. Any actions taken – particularly in an offensive war for limited aims – will likely impinge upon the interests of other nations, both enemies and neutrals, and thus potentially provoke diplomatic, economic, military, or informational reaction. One must also consider the replies of allies and friends – especially coalition partners.

One of the most devastating results is the intervention of other states, which can be public or discreet. This can affect both sides, and weak states as well as strong. "The weaker the country," political scientist Fred Iklé observed, "the more ought its military planning to take account of the possibilities for outside help, both for itself and for its enemy." "But," he warned, "government leaders are easily absorbed by what they see just across their border; and if their ambitions are focused on the province next door, their military vista may fail to extend much farther."[46] Jomini articulated the danger quite well: "In an offensive movement, scrupulous care must be exercised not to arouse the jealousy of any other state which might come to the aid of the enemy. It is a part of the duty of a statesman to foresee this chance, and to obviate it by making proper explanations and giving proper guarantees to other states."[47] Unfortunately, sometimes such assurances – even if honestly given – will not be believed. The reasons for this are myriad: ideology, credibility, fear, interest, and so on.

The worst result can be war with more nations than intended. Deducing the chances of the entry of other powers can be difficult. Iklé advised considering the following: "How likely is each larger round and how might it end? Is the enemy emboldened by the expectation that his allies will always bail him out, or is he afraid to lose their support and hence inclined to make peace?" The issue is indeed complex.[48]

The Japanese handling of the threat of third-party intervention when planning their 1904 war against Russia provides several lessons. One of the reasons for Japan's success was its isolation of the theater diplomatically, partially via an alliance with Great Britain. Related to this is an example of a self-imposed constraint in regard to the international environment. The Chinese offered to help Japan against the Russians, but Japan feared public cooperation with China might provoke European powers to come to Russia's aid, thus making it impossible for Japan to wage a successful war. Keeping China out of the war ensured that Kaiser Wilhelm's Germany would not conjure the racist specter of a "Yellow Peril" to rally nations against Japan. Tokyo proved perfectly content with clandestine Chinese cooperation.[49]

Truman's decision to conquer North Korea provides an opposite example. The administration's members spent little time analyzing the response of China to the US entry into the Korean War. Washington figures were more concerned about the Soviet response.[50] Moreover, they did not prepare militarily for *either* possible event. The State Department received a number of messages on October 3, 1950 relaying China's insistence that it would enter the war if US troops crossed the 38th parallel (China did not consider an advance by South Korean troops a trigger). Similar information came from Moscow, New Delhi, and Stockholm. These included the statements of Chou En-Lai, the Chinese foreign minister, to India's ambassador to Beijing, K. M. Panikkar. But Panikkar, Truman wrote, had no credibility in Washington because he "had in the past played the game of the Chinese Communists fairly regularly, so that his statement could not be taken as that of an impartial observer. It might very well be no more than a relay of Communist propaganda."[51] Paul Nitze, the director of Truman's Policy and Planning Staff, had also seen reports of Chinese warnings, but these had come from Panikkar, about whom Nitze held the same views.[52] Truman famously met MacArthur on Wake Island in October 1950 to discuss the issue.[53] Like nearly every other US military and diplomatic official, MacArthur saw China as lacking the interest in or capability to intervene.[54]

The general assessment was that China wouldn't intervene, out of fear of what might happen if they went to war with the US, the danger to the Communist regime from the subsequent encouragement of anti-Communist forces, and a belief that the Communists wouldn't care to injure their chances of gaining the China seat on the UN Security Council. If they did enter, and didn't have Soviet air and naval support, they would suffer grievously. But if they received Soviet aid, it would make them dependent upon Moscow and expand Soviet control in Manchuria. The military intelligence branches simply saw little chance of Chinese intervention unless the Soviets had decided to launch a world war.[55] Regarding the intelligence assessments of possible Chinese intervention, Army Chief of Staff Collins wrote: "As was to prove the case in later years, notably the Cuban Affair in the 1960s, the Central Intelligence Agency and all other United States Intelligence agencies which based their conclusions on probable intentions of the enemy rather than his capabilities were wrong. This time the Central Intelligence Agency had plenty of company; everybody was wrong."[56] There were, of course, voices advising otherwise. As noted earlier, George F. Kennan was among the dissenters.[57]

Neither Truman nor his advisors successfully calculated the chance of third-party intervention. The subsequent Chinese entry produced one of the greatest debacles in American military history, as US and UN forces were driven down the peninsula and below the 38th parallel. In the end, Truman and Acheson had made the call. Acheson, passing part of the blame to others for a decision driven by his State Department, wrote: "With the cast of characters as it was, however, the [UN] resolution of October 7 [authorizing the invasion] increased the hazards, for which I must bear a measure of responsibility."[58]

The existence of sanctuaries in other nations feeds the risk of more active third-party involvement (though one can argue that furnishing sanctuary already denotes involvement). The nation providing the sanctuary risks the war coming home. Whether or not the host nation truly controls the sanctuary area can be irrelevant in the view of the power suffering the attacks. Since the time of the Soviet invasion of Afghanistan in 1979, Pakistan has provided sanctuary to various Afghan groups, including evolutions of the Taliban. During the Soviet war, Pakistani sanctuary proved instrumental to the survival of Afghan opposition forces but did not lead to a Soviet invasion of Pakistan.

After September 11, 2001, Al Qaeda and its Taliban ally became targets of the US. Afterward, Pakistan consistently played both sides in the struggle in a very dangerous game, something proven by the sanctuary provided to Al Qaeda leader Osama bin Laden and numerous Taliban elements. Pakistan took US aid while also actively opposing the US and helping Taliban forces destabilize Afghanistan. US drone strikes in Pakistan are also an example of the war spilling over into a sanctuary area. The US widened the war in a minor way when it attacked the Pakistani compound holding bin Laden. When a nation is providing sanctuary to your enemies, they are not your friend, even if they take your money. This was something US leaders proved exceptionally slow to understand. Pakistani sanctuary was the key reason the Taliban survived after 2001. And it was from here they waged the war culminating in America's 2021 defeat.

Nations provide sanctuary for their own reasons, but a fear of expanding the war, particularly of a third party intervening, is one of the reasons nations get away with this. The Truman administration never allowed attacks into China because it feared Soviet intervention in support of its Chinese ally. Parts of North Vietnam essentially functioned as sanctuary areas because they were at times off-limits to US air attacks during the 1965–68 Rolling Thunder air campaign.

The disaster of Chinese intervention haunted the Johnson administration, which feared Chinese entry in support of North Vietnam, a worry backed by a 1965 CIA paper arguing (correctly) that China would militarily support the North in the event of a US invasion. Some administration members even wondered if intervention in South Vietnam would provoke Chinese or Soviet entry.[59] These fears drove the imposition of constraints upon US forces in Vietnam, some wise, some not. One result was to restrict US ground forces to fighting only in South Vietnam during the Johnson administration. This had spill-over effects on the region's strategic situation. It gave the North Vietnamese sanctuary above the 17th parallel in North Vietnam and neighboring Cambodia and Laos, because they couldn't prevent the Communists from sending forces into their countries. This made possible Viet Cong and North Vietnamese supply routes such as the Ho Chi Minh and Sihanoukville Trails, as well as base areas within easy striking distance of much of South Vietnam, including its capital, Saigon.

The Johnson administration's self-imposed constraint regarding US forces invading North Vietnam was indeed wise. Invading North

Vietnam would have produced another US struggle with China, which had troops in North Vietnam until 1970, and had promised to support North Vietnam in the event of an American invasion.[60] Moreover, China exploded its first atomic device in 1964. An invasion of North Vietnam would have meant ground combat against another nuclear-armed power, something that should generally be avoided because of the potential risks (though the other side should always know you are willing and able to fight if needed). No matter what was said publicly about the aims of such an invasion – whether limited or unlimited – the 1950 US attempt to eliminate the North Korean regime would have driven the Chinese to conclude that the US intended to conquer North Vietnam. Moreover, such an invasion would have been costly diplomat-ically for the US, because it would have allowed the Communist bloc to paint the US as the aggressor.

But should the Johnson administration have done more to tackle the problem of sanctuary? If it had launched operations into Laos and Cambodia, this probably would not have produced an inter-vention on the part of China or the Soviet Union, a particular fear of US leaders in the Cold War. This also would not have required much more means than the US eventually committed to the war in Southeast Asia. One can also argue that expansion of the war into Laos could have resulted in the war requiring *fewer* forces than the US ultimately com-mitted. Why? In the early 1960s, as it became increasingly apparent that the civil war in Laos was going the way of the Communist forces, the Kennedy administration considered numerous plans for intervention in Laos. One of these boiled down to effectively partitioning Laos by inserting 150,000 US troops into the theater to support the non-Communist forces that then controlled southern Laos.[61]

Doing this would have utterly changed the nature of the war in Southeast Asia. Such a substantial US force would have prevented most North Vietnamese infiltration into South Vietnam and thus lowered the US force requirements there. Critically, it would have severed the Ho Chi Minh Trail, North Vietnam's key infiltration and supply route into South Vietnam. This could have given South Vietnam time to root out the Communist insurgency behind a screen of US forces stretching from the coast to the border of US-allied Thailand, which was actively involved in Laos and solidly anti-Communist. This could in turn have produced in Vietnam a situation not unlike that existing in South Korea after 1945 (it is generally forgotten that South Korea also had to suppress a Communist insurgency). But this raises other questions: Are you willing to suffer the political costs of a probable *de facto* partitioning of Laos? As well as run the risks of Chinese intervention there?

There is also the issue of Cambodian sanctuary. Blocking the infiltration routes from North Vietnam via Laos would have removed the primary factor in the destabilization and destruction of the Cambodian regime: North Vietnam. Though the North Vietnamese could supply their forces fighting in the South via Sihanoukville to a point (at least until the US naval blockade), they depended upon the Ho Chi Minh Trail through Laos and into Cambodia for infiltrating troops.

In both the Korean and Vietnam Wars, concern about the possible effects upon third-party nations also produced constraints on how the US used air power. The Truman administration limited air attacks along the Chinese border early in the war.[62] Some constraints for strikes in this area later went away, but they never entirely disappeared. Johnson constrained aerial attacks on North Vietnam because he feared that if the US mounted heavy raids against the North, its Soviet and Chinese protectors would believe the US intended to destroy North Vietnam. This could provoke their entry.[63]

During the First Iraq War (1990–91) (also called the Gulf War), the end of the Cold War, combined with near universal international disapproval of Saddam's invasion of Kuwait, removed the threat of third-party intervention in the conflict on the side of Saddam Hussein. This greatly eased the US effort to build an extensive coalition, as well as to fight to expel Saddam Hussein's forces from Kuwait. The US faced no other threat and could use as much of its military power as it deemed necessary to do the job.

The possibility of third-party intervention is far from the only event one must consider in regard to the international environment, though it is generally the most influential. The international environment can produce innumerable effects arising from the unique situation at hand, but there are well-known commonalities. Economic and political sanctions may arise as a result of your actions – and not necessarily against the enemy. Other states may dislike what you are doing and align against you. Your power will bear directly upon what they're willing to do beyond words, diplomatic notes, and votes in international organizations that often impose little or no real costs.

But there are examples that break the mold here as well. Trade is perhaps the most common. Excepting South Korea, Britain was the most important UN partner and US ally during the Korean War. When the Chinese intervened in Korea in 1950, a British contingent was part of the United Nations force fighting in Korea, but neither the British Labour government nor its Conservative successor ended trade with the Chinese, though they did institute restrictions.[64]

Another likely third-party action will be the arming of one or both of the powers by other allied or interested parties. This can be pivotal for the prolongation of the war – especially for a weaker state. The North Koreans could not have fought the United States without the arms they received from the Soviets and Chinese. Similarly, North Vietnam's ability to fight the US and continue its war against America's South Vietnamese ally rested heavily on Communist-bloc supplies and arms.

International law (including the law of war) acts as a potential self-imposed constraint, and sometimes a wise one, particularly in the case of the Geneva Convention rules, for example. One legal scholar notes that: "The historic function of the laws of war has been to impose restraints upon international violence in the common interest of the community of the states."[65] But Michael Howard points out a harsh problem that too often arises here: "'Laws of war,' *jus in bello*, do imply a rather sophisticated warrior culture in which adversaries are conscious of an overriding common interest in preserving the rules of the game; and it may be precisely this kind of aristocratic society that a war is being fought to destroy."[66] But this constraint is invariably self-imposed, as there are usually few consequences for its violation, particularly in wartime, and particularly if you win, and especially for "Great Powers." If you lose, this can be different. The Nuremberg trials, as well as the proceedings at the Hague after the Yugoslavian civil war, spring immediately to mind.

Historically, combatants ignore international law the moment its provisions impinge upon what they want to do or achieve. This is particularly true of revolutionary movements. The Algerian rebels fighting France recognized no constraints on their actions – international, legal, moral, or otherwise. The North Vietnamese Communists also committed whatever atrocity they believed supported the achievement of their political aims.[67] Why was this possible? In the Algerian case, the French resort to torture alienated their allies and some of their own people. In both wars, many international political and media voices sympathized with the goals of the insurrectionists, often ignored their actions, and sometimes depicted the perpetrators as victims of Western, outsider "Great Powers."

Smaller states are more likely to support international law because it is to their advantage to do so.[68] They also run more risks when violating international law, because larger states have the strength to hold them accountable after the war. Powerful states – including liberal democracies – are only constrained by international law if they wish to be. Sometimes it can be advantageous to obey the rules in order to garner popular support at home, abroad, or at the UN, or prevent problems such as sanctions. This is governed by the situation. The question is whether or not the offending states are willing and able to endure the consequences of disobedience.

5   The Geography

Directly related to the international political environment – and sometimes inextricably intertwined with it – are issues connected to geography. Many definitions of "limited war" include discussions of geography, meaning that the war is declared "limited" because there are "limits" placed upon where it will be fought. Julian Corbett argues that:

> A war may be limited not only because the importance of the object is too limited to call forth the whole national force, but also because the sea may be made to present an insuperable physical obstacle to the whole national force being brought to bear. That is to say, a war may be limited physically by the strategical isolation of the object, as well as morally by its comparative unimportance.[69]

All wars are shaped by geographical constraints: even the Second World War did not engulf every nation. But wars fought for limited aims tend to include more geographical constraints. These are always driven by the value of the object (it is simply not worth the costs to expand the war), but fear of the conflict's expansion to third-party nations is one of the most important factors underpinning the imposition of geographical constraints.

One must be careful to differentiate between actual and self-imposed geographical constraints. This is not easily done, because of the flux in the related political circumstances. How will allies, neutrals, and other enemies with whom you are not at war react to where the conflict is being waged, and the added issue of expanding it? Geographical constraints can be wise even though they increase the difficulty of achieving the political aim. It depends upon the circumstances. A danger in imposing geographical constraints is that it can result in situations where a combatant possesses sanctuary, something discussed above.

Geographical constraints can generally be grouped into physical geography (mountains, river, etc.) and lines of political control or borders. Most of the issues of constraint deriving from physical geography are self-evident. But it is important to note that here we are not generally concerned with the ways in which geography affects tactical matters. This is important, but beyond our purview. If one is fighting for an isolated island, the war will generally be fought on, over, and around that island. The geography – as well as the aim, the island – have imposed a constraint.

Physical geography can also apply to man-made geographical features that act as constraints, though these are more likely to affect operations. Roads, ports, railways, cities, canals, and their level of development have a direct effect upon the means that will be needed, as well as the type of force required. A less developed theater of operations will make it more difficult to operate.[70]

Corbett believed that certain geographical positions could be especially suited for waging a war with a limited aim. Regarding the Russo–Japanese War, he wrote:

> Owing to the geographical position of Korea and to the vast and undeveloped territories which separate it from the centre of Russian power, it could be practically isolated by naval action. Further than this, it fulfilled the condition to which Clausewitz attached the greatest importance – that is to say, the seizure of the particular object so far from weakening the home defence of Japan would have the effect of greatly increasing the strength of her position. Though offensive in effect and intention it was also ... a sound piece of defensive work.[71]

Sea and air lines of communication also must be considered. For example, the problem of geographically restricting to Europe a war that breaks out there is complicated by the fact that the logistical lines (particularly for the US) run across the Atlantic and can be targeted.[72] The US entry into the First World War was, of course, heavily driven by attacks at sea.

Potential problems and possible expansion of the war can arise from trying to cut off an enemy via blockade. Iranian blockade efforts against Iraq during the 1980–88 Iran–Iraq War saw Iran attacking Kuwaiti and other tankers. An American commitment to protect Kuwaiti ships brought the involvement of the US and some of its allies in the Gulf, and clashes between US and Iranian forces saw the Iranian navy pummeled.[73]

Self-imposed geographical constraints dictated much about the Korean War, especially the most common factor here: where one's forces are allowed to fight. The Truman administration consistently restricted combat operations to the peninsula and its surrounding waters. This was done because they feared expansion of the war into China or the Soviet Union, and the possibility of a Third World War. Even after China entered the war, Truman maintained this constraint, even though it provided the Chinese a number of advantages, such as untouchable bases of supply and airfields. The question to ask here is whether or not this was a wise constraint. MacArthur certainly pushed to have it removed. He never wanted to put US troops into China, as some have said, but he did want to bomb Manchuria and blockade the Chinese coast.[74] MacArthur was far from the only one to push for military action against China. Though they sometimes posited different circumstances, these advocates included Air Force Chief of Staff General Hoyt Vandenberg and Chief of Naval Operations Admiral Forrest P. Sherman. Former Secretary of the Air Force and the Truman administration's chair of the National Security Resources Board Stuart Symington also advised attacks on Chinese military industry in Manchuria.[75] Sometimes, as was the case during the Korean War, one may be able to isolate the battlespace in most respects, but in a war such as that waged in Vietnam, this may not be possible.

For a short while, the 38th parallel also functioned as a geographical constraint in Korea. Most of the UN member countries fighting in Korea worried about crossing it, something of which Secretary of State Acheson was aware. Early in the war, he asked Secretary of Defense George Marshall to revise a September 27, 1950 JCS directive in order to restrict the UN advance. Acheson also said that crossing the 38th unilaterally might result in the withdrawal of allied forces, and that the US needed the approval of other governments before doing this.[76] Acheson, as we've seen, did not worry about this for long.

As the war in Vietnam lengthened, the US began lifting the geographical constraints (which are tied to the international environment and discussed above). The US would conduct a covert war in Laos, partially to interdict the Ho Chi Minh Trail, which it was also bombing (ineffectively), while the South Vietnamese launched an abortive effort into Laos to cut the trail in 1971. The US bombed Communist sanctuaries in Cambodia in 1969 and attacked the same areas in 1970. This injured the North's war effort but did not remove the sanctuaries.[77]

Lines of political control, obviously, are such things as boundaries, latitude lines, and so on. Schelling noted that: "They are merely lines on a map, but they are on *everybody's* map."[78] This is not always the case, as nations have different maps, but it does demonstrate a big piece of why these lines matter. People get upset when one crosses or moves them, particularly if they are *their* lines. Most wars fought for limited aims are about where these lines will be drawn. After the Second World War, most Western nations abandoned the idea of war as a tool of conquest, meaning adding to their own domains (this differs from regime change). Historically, usually this was what wars were about. Human nature hasn't changed. There are always rulers and states wanting to erase the lines on the map. Islamic State did this – temporarily – in Syria and Iraq in 2014. Putin's Russia did it by seizing Crimea in 2014.

Concerned about the possibility of a nuclear exchange, India imposed a geographic constraint upon itself during the 1999 Kargil conflict by publicly announcing its forces would not cross the Line of Control in Jammu and Kashmir. This was criticized by some active-duty and retired Indian Army generals because it created operational restrictions that forced the Indians to accept higher casualties. The government bent to the pressure by bringing in more troops in case it became necessary to widen the war. This put added pressure upon Pakistani military leaders. One author observed: "It was fortuitous that the Kargil conflict ended when it did."[79]

6   Military Means (Including Nuclear Weapons)

Air Marshal Saundby wrote: "It is idle, however, to pretend that political restrictions designed to limit the scope of war do not greatly impede the effective use of military force, as they often cut right across the requirements of sound military strategy."[80] Relatedly, Clausewitz explains how the value of the object being sought affects the means one is willing to use:

> The smaller the sacrifice we demand from our opponent, the smaller presumably will be the means of resistance he will employ, and the smaller his means, the smaller will ours be required to be. Similarly, the smaller our political object, the less value shall we set upon it and the more easily we shall be induced to abandon it.[81]

As noted at the beginning of this chapter, one of the greatest weaknesses of existing definitions of limited war is the nearly universal insistence that those waging so-called "limited wars" must use "limited means," a line of thought precluding the use of overwhelming force. This is a self-imposed constraint that fails to recognize the nature of the war. A number of things prove this.

First, this line of thought is flawed, because describing the force used as "limited" is undefinable and is relative to the combatants. For example, in Operation Allied Force in 1999, NATO used only a tiny part of its air power, but from the Serbian perspective it didn't seem particularly "limited."[82] Second, this demonstrates how "means" is a fungible term, as well as a relative one in regard to scale. Third, one cannot use "unlimited" means (all one has), because this is impossible, due to friction in the form of innumerable factors that constrain one's actions.

One of the great failures of US policymakers when fighting wars for limited aims is that they do not commit *sufficient* means to achieve the goal they have decided to pursue. Sufficient means should be provided to accomplish the task as quickly as possible at as low a cost to the state and its people as possible. MacArthur wisely observed that "once war is forced upon us, there is no other alternative than to apply every available means to bring it to a swift end."[83] MacArthur, as is often the case, elides into hyperbole, but his larger point should be taken to heart, as the longer the war goes on, the longer the killing and dying continue. Other authors have noted the West's self-imposed constraint on the use of force, and one correctly observed: "if limited war is fought in an environment that permits only piecemeal commitment of forces, it is not likely to be a short war."[84]

The primary factor underpinning the fears of Cold War limited war theorists regarding the use of force was that any conflict could lead to a nuclear exchange between the US and the Soviet Union, and thus the use of force had to remain "limited." If not, it was generally argued, the result could be General War or Total War – nebulous terms, yes, but indicative of their fears. The assumption became that one could control what happened, and tacit agreements with enemies would keep things from getting out of hand. This, though, is simply not possible. Authors writing in the 1950s had already pointed out that "There is always the possibility that all available force will be brought to bear." War is so unpredictable that to think that one can control the amount of force used by the *opponent* is ridiculous.[85] The inherent tendency of war's violence is to increase. Though one must overlook the use of the term "general war," General James Gavin correctly observed:

> No opponent will ever accommodate us to the extent of allow-
> ing us to fight a limited war merely because that is what we want
> to fight, and, more significantly, because that is all that we are
> capable of fighting. Actually, a nation dare not risk a limited
> undertaking without possessing the obvious capability of fight-
> ing a general war. And to the extent that we have the latter
> capability, we may indulge ourselves in the former.[86]

Rationality in the use of means in the pursuit of one's political aim demands the employment of *sufficient* means. One should bring the forces to bear that are needed to achieve the political goal. As this cannot be definitively calculated, it is wisdom itself to bring more than one believes necessary, as this stacks the deck in favor of victory and allows for the opportunity of overwhelming force to make up for the other errors one will undoubtedly make assessing the future course of the war and during its execution. One must match the means used to achieve-ment of the end desired.

Just because theory dictates that one is allowed to use sufficient means (which could mean overwhelming force) in a war fought for a limited aim, this does not mean that one is either willing or able to do so. There are constraints. The regime may have other commitments that require use of its finite military power and are thus either unwilling or unable to commit more to the limited war at hand. It might not be politically feasible, or a mobilization of this scale could be unacceptable domestically.[87]

A problem in past limited war theory is that it doesn't permit the use of overwhelming force. History teaches us differently, and when history disagrees with theory, the theory is wrong. In the Russo–Japanese War, the Japanese fought for limited political aims. Part of their strategy for achieving this was to use overwhelming force to quickly defeat the Russian armies before the tide of war turned against them. In the end, the force they used proved sufficient, and they scored important victories at the battles of Mukden and Tsushima in 1905. In Japan's case, this required enormous exertion, sacrifice, and risk-taking.

One can use abundant, overwhelming means to achieve a limited aim, or to defend it. Using sufficient means increases the likelihood of a quick victory – though this does not ensure it. Generally, a quick end to the war saves lives, lowers the costs, and reduces the chances of escalation of the violence or expansion of the conflict (which tend to increase in direct relation to the war's duration). There are, of course, exceptions to this. An aim could be achieved so quickly that it unnerves others so much they align against you, but this would be an anomaly as, historically, quick victories cow potential enemies.

In December 1950, at the height of the Chinese intervention in Korea, the Truman administration decided to send four army divisions to Europe to meet its NATO commitment. At that moment Chinese troops were driving outnumbered US forces out of North Korea. In addition to disappointing MacArthur, the decision caused so much internal US political consternation that a resolution was introduced in the Senate insisting that the president lacked the authority to order these troops to NATO until Congress acted. In mid February 1951, Truman officially announced his decision to dispatch four divisions to Europe to reinforce NATO.[88]

The Truman administration also had demonstrated previously its reluctance to commit forces to Korea (partially because the US had essentially disarmed). On July 3, 1950, MacArthur asked for the army's amphibious experts. On July 7, he asked Washington for four-and-a-half divisions to bolster the 8th Army's four to support his amphibious invasion at Inchon and a counteroffensive. This was not well received in Washington, because it "forced the JCS to move along the road to wartime mobilization. It was not a trip the chiefs wanted to make because Harry Truman and [Secretary of Defense] Louis Johnson were not ready to admit that the United States was at war." MacArthur was told by the JCS that they simply could not fulfill his request, though they did begin sending smaller units.[89]

On December 19, 1950, in the wake of the Chinese intervention, MacArthur again asked for reinforcements. JCS Chairman Bradley and new Secretary of Defense Marshal resisted the dispatch of forces to Korea in case the war there was a Soviet diversion, and the JCS members in general feared a new European war. The British opposed diverting US forces from Europe to Korea after the Chinese invasion, while Acheson also saw Korea as a distraction from the real potential area of conflict.[90] MacArthur remarked that after the Chinese intervention "I could obtain only a trickle of soldiers from Washington, under the plea that they were needed in Germany where there was no war."[91] The US and British leaders took counsel of their fears (which is understandable), but they failed to commit sufficient forces to the war they actually faced from worry over a possible war that never occurred, and long refused to create the military forces they so obviously needed.

It slowly became clear to Truman and his advisors that the US would have to build up its military and economic strength to fulfill its NATO commitments and possibly fight a "major war" with China. The National Security Council (NSC), acting on a November 22, 1950, JCS recommendation, elected to expand the US army to 18 divisions by June 30, 1954. A December 5, 1950 JCS recommendation approved by the NSC on December 14 set the date for this as June 1952, and also included comparable expansion of the air force and navy. Truman ordered two National Guard divisions to report in January 1951 and declared a state of national emergency on December 15, 1950.[92]

Meanwhile, the JCS argued that the war in Korea was a drain on US military and economic resources that benefited China and the Soviets. In the event of another world war, primarily against the Soviets, the Chiefs deemed Korea "strategically unimportant."[93] This, though, leads to the question: why did they push for the invasion of North Korea if it was "strategically unimportant" in the event of the US receiving one of its worst-case results?

Later, more than one US military leader expressed their distaste over how the US allocated its military means to Korea. General Gavin wrote:

> Having failed, therefore, to quench the flame of aggression at the outset, the next decision was determined by the rapidity of our build-up and, again, the superiority of our means. In

my opinion, in both of these we were again lacking. And this very shortcoming on our part contributed directly to the prolongation of that "police action," as we now call it, until our casualties reached 142,000 killed, wounded, and missing.[94]

Failure to allocate sufficient means for the task can prolong the war and cause more deaths than if one uses enough force to bring the war to an end quickly. General Ulysses S. Grant concluded this in 1864. The US Civil War ended the next year.

    The US wasted no time committing its air power to the war in Korea. Here, the self-imposed constraints were more often wise, but American leaders too often failed to realistically consider whether or not air power could accomplish what its advocates promised. Under pressure from his air force commanders, George E. Stratemeyer and Earle E. Partridge, and even though he did not have clear permission from his superiors to do so, MacArthur immediately ordered strikes against North Korea when the war began. US forces hit North Korean airfields on June 29, 1950, twenty-four hours before the Truman administration removed restrictions on bombing north of the 38th.[95] In the early months of the war, the US Air Force (USAF) had understandable constraints on what it could bomb along the border with China and the Soviet Union, as an attack here could provoke the intervention of one or both states, but the service's leaders objected to being allowed to do only precision bombing against military targets.[96]

    In July 1950, after winning air superiority, and with MacArthur's permission, the USAF began a strategic bombing campaign against North Korea like those it executed during the Second World War. Here, too, they still faced constraints. The hydroelectric plants along the Yalu that supplied China and the Soviet Union, as well as the city of Najin near the Soviet border, were dropped from the target lists by the State Department for obvious reasons.[97]

    Along the North Korean border with the Soviet Union and China remained an area where the Truman administration imposed constraints on air attacks. Even after the Chinese entry into the war in November 1950, the Truman administration temporarily blocked a MacArthur request to bomb certain Yalu bridges. Soon MacArthur was allowed to attack the Korean sides of the bridges, but he was forbidden from attacking power plants and dams.[98] MacArthur wrote in his memoir (with a MacArthuresque dose of exaggeration), "The order not to bomb the Yalu bridges was the most indefensible and ill-conceived decision ever forced on a field commander in our nation's history."[99] Ordering him across the 38th parallel was much worse, but that one he agreed with.

But the Chinese entry meant constraints on the use of air power began falling away. MacArthur ordered something the USAF had earlier desired and began using incendiaries against population centers, as had been done against Japan during the Second World War. No longer were the bombers limited to military targets. The administration did not protest.[100]

MacArthur sought to expand the use of air strikes to China itself. He believed that since China had forced war upon the United States, the US should respond appropriately.[101] The Truman administration refused to countenance attacks upon the Chinese homeland in any fashion because they feared this would lead to the Soviet Union's entry into the conflict (China signed a military alliance with its Communist comrade in 1949). The consensus is that this was a wise constraint, but there are certainly those who disagreed then and later. The primary counterargument: we are at war with China, why not fight China? MacArthur argued that the risk of Soviet intervention was as high at the beginning of the war as at any other time.[102] Truman also considered attacks against China, and, after the political aim changed in May 1951, the JCS planned for this along the lines MacArthur had advocated.[103]

Constraints on the use of air power continued to erode as the war went on. During the summer of 1952, the formerly off-limits hydroelectric facilities on the Korean side of the Yalu were bombed in order to increase pressure on the Chinese to negotiate an end to the war.[104] In May 1953, the US began striking the dams of the reservoirs in North Korea in the ultimately futile belief that targeting these would destroy rice production and result in farmers blaming the North Korean government for the war.[105]

The US also continuously launched interdiction strikes against Communist lines of supply and communication. This was critically important for hindering the enemy's operations and hurting his forces, but it was not something that could end the war. General Matthew Ridgway, writing during the Vietnam War, critiqued the use of air power in Korea as:

> a prime example of how mistaken it is to imagine that an enemy's supply lines can be "interdicted" through air power

alone. We had almost no opposition in the air over the battle-fields in North Korea and we were free to attack the enemy's supply lines without hindrance except from ground fire, and not even that during the first year.

He went on to say: "There is simply no such thing as 'choking off' supply lines in a country as wild as North Korea, or in jungle country either."[106]

The manner in which the US constrained the use of its military means in the Korean War is a mixed picture. In regard to ground forces, the US unnecessarily constrained its use of force. The desire to support NATO commitments is understandable, but this injured the United States' ability to support allies in Asia and fight the war it had decided to fight and then expand. This remained a pattern throughout the war as the US simply refused to commit what was necessary to win quickly, and, in the end, to win at all. America and its UN allies paid a heavy price in blood for this, because the war went on much longer than it should have. If the war continues, the costs rise and the risks increase. Constraints on the use of air power are understandable in regard to targets along the Chinese and Soviet borders, especially before the Chinese entry. But one can argue that the Truman administration should have imposed more constraints on the use of air power. It is difficult to see how incendiary raids against North Korean cities helped the UN along the road to victory.[107] The Chinese were not pressured by bombing North Korean civilians. Moreover, it is possible it made a settlement less likely, because the Chinese and North Koreans publicly vowed they wouldn't bend to such a blatant, tactical use of force.[108] The first rule for the use of air power is to bomb the right people.

In discussions of the Vietnam War, one of the consistent criticisms leveled at Johnson's administration is that it never matched the means to the end being sought, and that the constraints it placed on the use of these means doomed the US effort. There is no simple answer to this, and to address it properly one must separate the air war from the ground war without forgetting they are connected. We address the Johnson administration's constraints on means in the chapter on strategy (Chapter 5), as they are too interrelated to properly discuss separately.

The Gulf War, or First Iraq War, like the Russo–Japanese War, is an example of using overwhelming military force in an effort to achieve limited political aims. Among the objectives the US sought, the most important were the liberation of Kuwait and the restoration of its sovereignty. Achieving these required destroying or expelling the Iraqi force occupying the small state. The US applied overwhelming military force to the problem and scored one of the most lopsided victories in military history. It is true that the US forces possessed many advantages, including a stunning technological edge, but the US did not understand the scale of this before the war and elected to do all it could to ensure military success. The US was fortunate to have the freedom and ability to bring the desired units to the theater, but it also *chose* to do so. When JCS Chairman Colin Powell approached President Bush for essentially a doubling of the US forces to mount an offensive against the Iraqis, Bush quickly signed off on Powell's request because he wanted to provide the forces the military insisted it needed.[109] The US was fortunate here in many ways. Not only did it have leaders willing to ensure sufficient force for the task at hand, but the US also benefited from the end of the Cold War and the fact it faced no other significant threat, no danger of third-party intervention, and no geographic constraints upon operations against the enemy and their forces. Bush had not only the willingness to act here, but also the freedom to do so.

An important but complex part of the means issue is the potential use of nuclear weapons. We begin with a properly frightening thought: "The increasing number of nuclear players is leading to the greater probability that nuclear weapons will be used in anger at some time in the future."[110] The possibility that this is true should weigh heavily on every political and military leader who might have to face this issue. They are weapons the use of which would certainly have more political impact than any other military tool, but they are tools nonetheless. The failure to understand this simple (though horrifying) truth about atomic and nuclear weapons helped produce an entire body of literature related to so-called "limited nuclear war."[111] It is a literature standing on a means-based foundation that collapses under the weight of the simple question: what is the political aim? But we cannot ignore the fact that atomic weapons were *the* key catalyst in the development of post-Second World War limited war theory, beginning with Liddell Hart's 1946 *Harper's* article, "War, Limited." Henry Kissinger helped make a name for himself in strategy circles by writing on so-called "limited nuclear war" and had his critics.[112] But Kissinger, along with Brodie and many others, formed only part of a large and ever lengthening list of writers tackling the subject.[113] Unfortunately, the results brought confusion, not clarity.

Physicist Edward Teller gives us an example of how "limited nuclear war" is generally depicted. Teller believed American traditions and historical principles constrained US aggression, while the Russians had no such scruples and were thus willing to seize any advantage if given the chance. He worried that in the event of a Soviet attack, their forces could establish a strong position before US forces could arrive to stop them. To counter this, he argued that the US could fight a "limited nuclear war" by hitting military targets. This would be cheaper in manpower and also create the worst possible time for the Soviets to embark upon a nuclear war or launch a general attack on the US.[114] Here, as in most such examples, in a "limited nuclear war" one uses nuclear weapons but constrains the targeting in some fashion. Thus, the nuclear war is a "limited" one.

Many Cold War theorists understandably fixated upon how to use atomic and nuclear weapons, and what this would mean. This is not the place to examine the evolution of nuclear strategy, as it has been done well in many other places.[115] The issue for us surrounds the notion of "tacit" – meaning implied or unspoken – restraint regarding their use. What this meant during the Cold War was this: how did one reach an understanding with the Soviet Union regarding the parameters under which atomic and then nuclear weapons could be used without nuclear Armageddon being the result?[116] The answer (though not one many limited war theorists would agree with): one cannot, because you cannot know the enemy's mind. Brodie was among those who were skeptical about arriving at some kind of "tacit" understanding with the Soviets on rules for waging a "limited nuclear war."[117] He said, of a war between the Soviet Union and the West fought in Europe, "It is almost equally difficult to imagine both sides adopting *meaningful limitations* on the use of nuclear weapons, such as would prevent the complete devastation of the Continent."[118]

The problem with countries possessing nuclear weapons going to war – especially with another nation that has them – is that they might use them. Many Cold War-era authors insisted that some restraint would be exercised by both sides. One hopes. Unfortunately, the downside of being wrong is too great to bank upon this. In two Cold War US wargames that included the use of simulated battlefield nuclear weapons (one in Europe and the other in the US), both the quantity of weapons used as well as their tonnage grew quickly. The exercises ended with much of Western Europe and the South Central US destroyed and irradiated.[119] An Indian observer offers the following: "Those who still argue that war-fighting with nuclear weapons is feasible, with each side directing its weapons strictly on the adversary's military targets, appear to envisage an ability to impose such a rule on the adversary ... Such an expectation does not appear to be wholly realistic."[120] When two nuclear-armed states are at war, there is no forecasting what may occur when the machine of war is loosed. The risks of a nuclear exchange have just increased drastically. How great will be determined by Thucydides' "trinity" of fear, honor, and interest.[121]

The use of a single nuclear weapon by a combatant – even a so-called "tactical" one – could very likely lead to wider use and constitute a breaking of the so-called "nuclear taboo." The victim of the attack might well conclude the war is now being pursued for an unlimited political aim and see the threat as existential. The value of the object will then have changed, and one can expect an effort to escalate toward the extremes of force and violence by the regime that has suffered the nuclear blow – unless its leadership is weak or has been destroyed. Indeed, the Soviets believed that any use of such weapons by the Americans gave them the right to use whatever they wished however they wished, believing "American planning for *tactical* nuclear weapons is merely a stratagem to hobble the Soviets in case of war."[122] This also could lead to third-party intervention in the conflict in a conventional as well as a nuclear guise.

One might be inclined to consider such arguments over the fears of a nuclear exchange obsolete as we no longer live under the omnipresent threat of war between the Cold War superpowers. But the argument remains one worth having, because the world has no shortage of states possessing nuclear weapons, and not a few others trying to develop them. It is increasingly likely that there will be wars – even wars fought for limited aims – *between* nations possessing nuclear arsenals, though this does not mean nuclear weapons will be used. One could be applauded for arguing that this is simply ridiculous, but then one has to consider remarks such as these by a retired Indian Army general: "Most Indian analysts are convinced that the advent of nuclear weapons has not ruled out the feasibility of limited war."[123]

If one of the states involved in the war possesses nuclear arms, the decision to use them will be influenced by the level of threat to their vital interests. This was discussed clearly as early as the 1950s.[124] Since the end of the Second World War, we've seen no use of atomic or nuclear weapons, but there is nothing to say that this will remain true. The Second World War is the obvious only example, though one should remember the Allies sought unlimited political aims not limited ones. The US wars in Korea, Vietnam, and the Gulf, and Israel's in 1973 and 1982 – all fought for limited political aims (at least initially) by an atomic or nuclear-armed state against non-nuclear-armed enemies – saw no use of such weapons, even though the US bordered on defeat in Korea in late 1950 and failed in Vietnam. If the nuclear state is the defender, and the war remains politically limited – for both sides – the taboo will likely hold, though the aggressor would be foolish to bank upon this, especially if the defender has particularly strong or particularly unstable leaders. US President Dwight Eisenhower's threat to use atomic weapons (and planning for it) in an effort to hasten an end to the Korean War should be kept in mind.

Some of the political issues involved in the *potential* use of atomic weapons are illustrated by an event during the Korean War. In the wake of the Chinese intervention, Truman said at a November 30, 1950 press conference that the use of atomic weapons was on the table. This produced overwhelming international criticism, and the White House began issuing "clarifications." British Prime Minister Clement Attlee immediately flew to Washington to meet with Truman. Attlee worried the US was being distracted from strengthening NATO, and Truman promised to consult the British about any use of atomic weapons.[125] The British opposed their use in Korea, and local commanders said there were no proper targets, while the military saw the war as a Soviet feint, so the stockpiled weapons needed to be saved in case the Soviets moved on Europe.[126] What is important to point out here is that before the advent of hydrogen weaponry and intercontinental ballistic missiles (ICBMs), atomic devices were seen by many policymakers and military leaders as just much larger bombs. The Eisenhower-era strategy of "massive retaliation" depended upon a willingness to use atomic weapons. This point is illustrated by a March 16, 1955 remark by Eisenhower where he said that if suitable military targets presented themselves, he saw "no reason why they should not be used exactly as you would use a bullet or anything else."[127]

Countries possessing nuclear weapons are perfectly *capable* of waging wars with one another for limited political aims, and have also proved perfectly *willing* to do so.[128] Ideological and political disagreements between the Soviet Union and China produced a border war between these two nuclear-armed powers. They engaged in over 400 armed clashes in 1969 alone, eventually had large units in combat, and even launched amphibious landings against islands in the Ussuri River. Certainly, there was no formal declaration of war, but both fought like there was. No nuclear exchange resulted, but the danger of escalation was certainly there. The US became aware of the depths of the problem because a Soviet diplomat inquired regarding the American attitude if the Soviet Union preemptively attacked China's nuclear program. American refusal to countenance this seems to have acted as a constraint.[129]

The more dangerous problem is the long-running conflict between India and Pakistan. In 1999, using regular forces and Kashmiri guerrillas, Pakistan invaded Indian Kashmir in Kargil with the objective of redrawing the Line of Control and taking as much of the unoccupied territory as possible.[130] India responded militarily, but its initial attacks stumbled on rough terrain and poor execution. Artillery and air support were added, and the Indians threw back the Pakistanis. Pakistan did not commit more troops but did put its nuclear arsenal on alert and threatened its use. India responded by moving up more forces and preparing to broaden the war beyond Kargil if it could not eject the Pakistani forces. Pakistani leaders began fearing an Indian invasion. Fortunately, American diplomacy helped ratchet back the tensions.[131]

The use of other so-called "weapons of mass destruction" such as chemical and biological weapons are also certainly elements of means to be considered. Their use will also produce political effects, but these will be less dramatic. Indeed, when one looks at the use of chemical weapons by Saddam Hussein against the Kurdish citizens of his own nation and during the Iran–Iraq War of 1980–89, as well as Bashar Assad's use against his own people in Syria during the Syrian Civil War, one could argue that other nations will condemn their use but do very little about it. The George W. Bush administration certainly used Saddam's past use and perceived continued possession of chemical weapons to build their case for war against Iraq in 2003, but this was also a means of selling regime change.[132] The use of nuclear weapons is different, because of the level of their destructive force and the fears related to them. Using them is considered to potentially unleash Armageddon, because nuclear attacks by other powers could then ensue.

Moreover, one should not assume nuclear weapons will never be used because their destructive power is so great that no rational power would ever use them. Basing one's foreign relations and defense strategy upon a statement that cannot be proven is unwise. In 2018, there were fears that the threshold for the use of nuclear weapons was breaking down. Russia developed low-yield nukes to thwart any possible conventional Chinese and NATO attacks, and some suggested Pakistan was developing them to use in a future war with India. Some argue that overwhelming US conventional power is driving states such as Iran to develop nuclear weapons so they can thwart any US effort to do to them what the US did to Saddam Hussein in 2003.[133] But states like Iran also seek such weapons because they believe it will give them the freedom to pursue their political aims without interference. This could also easily prove a mistaken view.

There are certainly many obvious internal and external constraints that will bear upon the question of how much force can be used – other commitments, for example. But this is true in any war, and the fact that the aim is a limited one should not be used as an excuse to tie one's hands and reduce the chances of victory by bending an ear to bad theory.

7   Unknowns Not Considered or Envisioned

There are obviously other things that act as constraints, many of which can be lumped under the topics discussed above.[134] We have addressed only those most crucial to understanding our subject. In theory, the constraints one faces could be infinite. Leaders can act as constraints, intentionally or not. In general, but especially in the means realm, technology and its effects can act as constraints.[135] Most of the time, though, technology has its greatest impact in the tactical arena. Nuclear weapons are an obvious exception.

One should also consider money. Jomini wrote that "The financial condition of a nation is to be weighed among the chances of a war." He went on to say: "A power might be overrunning with gold and still defend itself very badly." He also wrote: "Iron weighs as much as gold in the scales of military strength. Still, we must admit that a happy combination of wise military institutions, of patriotism, of well-regulated finances, of internal wealth and public credit, imparts a nation the greatest strength and makes it capable of sustaining a long war."[136] Machiavelli noted "that it is not gold, as is vulgarly supposed, that is the sinews of war, but good soldiers, good soldiers may readily get you gold."[137] There will be, of course, many other things. The situation will determine them.

Conclusion

Early twentieth-century American journalist John Reed noted Pancho Villa's reaction upon receiving a copy of the 1907 Hague Rules on warfare, one sent to him by the US forces opposing him in Mexico: "He spent hours poring over it. It interested and amused him hugely," Reed noted. Villa said: "What is the Hague Conference? Was there a representative of Mexico there? . . . it seems to me a funny thing to make rules about war. It is not a game. What is the difference between civilized war and any other kind of war?"[138] Historian Quincy Wright wrote: "Proposals frequently made by military men and international lawyers for limiting methods of war or for localizing war seem to have little chance of success. Modern nations at war will use all their resources for victory and will pay little attention to the rules of good faith, honor, or humanity."[139]

Should there be constraints? The reality is that there are constraints and always will be. To pretend there aren't is to fail to understand war's nature and the truth of what one faces. The challenge – one with infinite complexity – is to understand how these affect the war you are fighting and overcome them. Imagination. Creativity. Study of the past. A flexible mind. These are what the leader needs here – and everywhere. Understanding the constraints and their respective effects upon the war you are fighting for a limited aim is the important second step. This is particularly pivotal for developing an understanding of the nature of the war. But this doesn't tell you how to fight it, which must be designed. The constraints exert enormous influence here. The development of appropriate strategy is the next step.

5 STRATEGY: HOW TO THINK ABOUT FIGHTING FOR A LIMITED POLITICAL AIM

> Strategy is harder than tactics because you have more time to act and
> thus more time to doubt. Also, in tactics you can see what is going on,
> in strategy you have to guess.[1]
>   Carl von Clausewitz

Introduction

In the aftermath of the October 1962 Cuban Missile Crisis,
Secretary of Defense Robert McNamara said: "There is no longer any
such thing as strategy, only crisis management."[2] Later, when the US
entered the war in Vietnam, McNamara wanted to ensure the civilians
managed the conflict (they weren't really fighting a war) as a way of
overcoming his distaste for the military leaders.[3] The civilians running the
White House and Pentagon didn't think the military had much useful advice
to offer.[4]

Later, after the US entered the Vietnam War in force,
McNamara apparently came to a different conclusion, at least about
the existence of strategy. Upon his return from an October 1966 trip to
Vietnam, he told President Johnson that "the enemy's strategy
remained 'keeping us busy and wait[ing] us out (a strategy of attriting
our national will.).'" Additionally, the failure of the Rolling Thunder
bombing campaign was also now becoming readily apparent as the
North continued its infiltration of men and material into South
Vietnam. US pacification efforts had also demonstrated little progress

against the Viet Cong's infrastructure, as the Communists kept their hold on most of South Vietnam's rural areas.[5] McNamara now believed in strategy's existence, but this, though, isn't the same as developing one that can achieve your political aims. That is critically important.

What Is Strategy?

There are many discussions in the literature regarding "a limited-war strategy."[6] There is no such thing. A particular strategy might be suited to wars fought both for limited and unlimited aims. It is the unique conditions under which strategy is implemented that generates the peculiarities. To have a comprehensive discussion of strategy – even in regard to wars fought for limited political aims – would require far more space than is available here. Our focus is upon how to *think* about strategy, discussing some of the misconceptions around strategy and so-called "limited wars," and the most important strategic approaches used historically in wars fought for limited aims.

As always, we must establish the basis for our analysis. The term "strategy" is used in myriad ways, but a good, general definition for military strategy given in Chapter 2 is: the larger use of military power in pursuit of political aims. Here, we are generally concerned with how military *force* is used in wartime, but military *power* is certainly useful in peacetime as a tool for pressuring an opponent, to back diplomacy, and many other things.

A good strategy has many requirements and elements we have discussed previously. First, it should be connected to a clear, obtainable political aim. This should include a vision of the post-war situation and how this will be arrived at. Second, it should be informed by a rational assessment of the situation. This should encompass analysis of one's own strengths and weaknesses (all the while considering the risks involved in the undertaking), while also trying to develop a complete picture of the enemy's capabilities, situation, and intent, and should include an understanding of the effects of your actions upon third-party states, as well as the constraints. This assessment should yield an understanding of your own centers of gravity (sources of strength) as well as the opponent's. This would be the point or points against which one's effort should be directed. Third, a good strategy includes a clear relationship between the ends (or political aims) sought, the ways one is trying to obtain these aims (generally strategy and operations), and the allocation of means sufficient for achieving the end. Fourth, there should be an awareness among the leaders regarding the limits of military force, as this is not always the correct tool, and usually not the only one needed to do the job. Fifth, the leaders must understand how to use force to achieve the political aim and have the ability to do so. Sixth, informed, rational strategic and operational planning must be informed by and support the elements mentioned above. Finally, there must be a plan for how to end the war and secure the peace based upon the political aim and the vision of this. This should include preparation for the inevitable negotiations.

The Stages of the Struggle

Regardless of the specific political aim being sought, all wars fought for limited political aims have two stages: the coercive or combat stage and the negotiation stage.[7] These can occur sequentially, intermittently, and even *simultaneously*, as fighting does not necessarily stop just because negotiations have begun. If you are fighting an offensive war for a limited political aim, you are attempting to coerce the opponent into giving you what you want, or, in other words, to bend them to your will without overthrowing the other regime, a fact that makes it less likely that you will impose a peace. If you are fighting a defensive war, you are trying to prevent yourself from being coerced. This is also extremely unlikely to allow you to impose a peace (though one might be forced upon you). Generally, once the combatant has achieved the ain (or not), or one side or both are no longer willing to continue the fight, negotiations for a ceasefire and (hopefully) a peace agreement will then ensue. But one should not take this as an absolute.

The Coercive or Combat Stage

As we've seen, the political aim sets the aim for the war, and everything flows from this. It will "thus determine both the military objective to be reached and the amount of effort it requires." With this established, "[t]he strategist," Clausewitz advises, must then

> define an aim for the entire operational side of the war that will be in accordance with its purpose. In other words, he will draft the plan of the war, and the [political] aim will determine the series of actions intended to achieve it: he will, in fact, shape

the individual campaigns and, within these, decide on the individual engagements.

This military effort should be directed at the enemy's means and will to wage the war: "If you want to overcome your enemy you must match your effort against his power of resistance, which can be expressed as the product of two inseparable factors, viz. *the total means at his disposal and the strength of his will.*"[8] In a strategic sense, the states are matching their strengths.

Critics will immediately say that the real answer is to fight "asymmetrically." But they forget that all wars are inherently asymmetrical, because no two powers possess equivalent strength or capabilities. Moreover, it is usually not clear whether this criticism is being directed at the tactical, operational, or strategic level of war. This argument is too often indicative of another logical flaw in the way Americans do strategic analysis.

Some might object to branding the first stage the coercive stage, as the concept of coercion of an opponent is often associated with actions that take place before fighting begins. At other times coercion is depicted as the end, and not as one of the ways for achieving the end.[9] Coercion is commonly defined as using force or threatening to use instruments of state power to bend another state or entity to do your will. Coercion is then generally divided into compellence and deterrence.[10] The literature is wracked with confusion and differing views over the use of these terms.[11]

The basic problem is this: *the authors writing on these subjects usually fail to draw the line between peace and war in their analysis.* This is the decisive analytical break. Coercion should be interpreted as acts of force: each state is trying to force the other to bend. Compellence and deterrence should be understood as strategies implemented to shape the actions of a state with which one is at peace. Compellence is the effort to make an opponent do something, to convince them to stop what they're doing, or reverse something they've done.[12] One compels a rival without actually fighting – the Nazi destruction of Czechoslovakia provides an example – and threats of violence are a big part of this. But when the violence begins, you have moved to coercion.

You are practicing deterrence when you seek to prevent an action.[13] The immediate response is to suggest that in wars one tries to deter enemy actions. Yes. But the situation has changed, because you are using violence to do so and not trying to prevent the outbreak of a conflict. Deterrence is a classic security method depicted in the Roman adage: "If you want peace, prepare for war."[14] Political scientist Nordal Åkerman notes that "The concept of deterrence is particularly elusive, in that it opens the door for so many speculations as to the reactions of the parties concerned, assumptions that can be conveniently altered as the analysis demands."[15]

Historically, deterring an aggressor has been exceedingly difficult, something clearly demonstrated by the number of wars since the Middle Ages.[16] The threat of even greater force in reply, as well as a demonstrated willingness to use it, does not always succeed.[17] Deterrence arises from physical and psychological factors, but has no validity if the opponent doesn't believe a reaction is coming. One must also have sufficient strength to deter an opponent.[18] Having allies strong enough to present their own deterrence is also obviously useful.[19] Finally, one should not confuse the capacity for deterring an opponent with the ability to win against the same or another opponent.[20] A journalist noted this geopolitical truth: "Any country that believes it will never be made to pay the price for the risks it takes will take ever-greater risks."[21]

Coercion can take many forms. Every element of national power can be used in support of the coercive act – and indeed, theory urges their use – to bring the conflict to an acceptable end as quickly as possible, and thus at a lower cost in blood and treasure. Moreover, as one author writes: "The decisive use of force requires the right balance between means and ends, based on an understanding of the dynamics of coercion."[22]

In a war for a defensive limited aim, the coercive phase is obviously the most dangerous for the defender (unless one is a particularly bad or unfortunate peacemaker). One must hope the means and will available are up to the task, or that fortune smiles, but it is better to trust in one's self and one's own actions than chance. Toughness and tenacity are sometimes enough. The Finns proved this by hard fighting against the Soviets in 1939–40. They lacked the strength to completely defeat their opponent, but their resistance raised the enemy's cost and bought enough time for the international situation to change and their opponent to worry about other things. Then came the time to make peace.

Negotiating the peace is the second phase of a war fought for limited political aim. Perhaps the attacker has what they want, or the defender is reaching the end of their strength, or one or both see an opportunity to end the struggle on acceptable, though not preferred, terms, or fear the war's continuation may lead to their complete destruction; any of these reasons – and others – may lead to a call for negotiating an end. This is the subject of the last chapter.

Assessment

Commenting on the North Vietnamese, US Secretary of Defense Robert McNamara said in 1966: "I never thought [the war] would go like this. I didn't think these people had the capacity to fight this way. If I had thought they could take this punishment and fight this well, could enjoy fighting like this, I would have thought differently from the start." Secretary of State Dean Rusk and General William Westmoreland also agreed that US leaders had underestimated the toughness of the North Vietnamese.[23] They were hardly alone in their failure to understand beforehand the enormous complexity of the task facing them, and US leaders have made the same error on other occasions. Thucydides observed that "It is a common mistake in going to war to begin at the wrong end, to act first, and wait for disaster to discuss the matter."[24] Similarly, Sun Tzu advised: "Know your enemy and know yourself."[25]

In order to avoid such problems, one should do a proper assessment (or net assessment, as it is sometimes called) of the enemy and yourself. An assessment is an analysis of the factors affecting the waging of the war; this includes probable responses by the opponent or potential opponents. Ideally, this is done before the war, but sometimes one is not given the choice. As Napoleon said, even Isaac Newton would shudder in the face of this equation.[26] We have neither Napoleon nor Newton, so we must instead struggle to be thorough and systematic.

Clausewitz gives us a road map for assessment:

> To discover how much of our resources must be mobilized for war, we must first examine our own political aim and that of the enemy. We must gauge the strength and situation of the opposing state. We must gauge the character and abilities of its government and people, and do the same in regard to our own. Finally, we must evaluate the political sympathies of other states and the effect the war may have on them. To assess

these things in all their ramifications and diversity is plainly a colossal task.[27]

We examined the importance and value of the political aim in the previous chapter. The potential effects of this are understood and should be kept in mind. Following Clausewitz's next admonition to gauge the relative and comparative strength of the opponents helps reveal whether one has the military means to achieve the desired political end. To arrive at clarity on this point demands development of as thorough as possible an understanding of one's own and the enemy's capabilities. This requires not only understanding their military, but also their government and people. We see here the link to what is generally referred to as Clausewitz's "Trinity," which serves as an assessment tool:

> As a total phenomenon its dominant tendencies always make war a paradoxical trinity – composed of primordial violence, hatred, and enmity, which are to be regarded as a blind natural force; of the play of chance and probability within which the creative spirit is free to roam; and of its element of subordination, as an instrument of policy, which makes it subject to reason alone.
>
> The first of these three aspects mainly concerns the people; the second the commander and his army; the third the government.[28]

Examining these factors provides the nuts and bolts of troops and equipment numbers and quality, but also indications of the important intangibles, such as the competence of the government and the will of the people, as well as the strengths and weaknesses of the enemy and ourselves. Machiavelli advised: "When one sets out to judge if anybody is going to do a thing, it is necessary first to see if he wishes to do it, then what assistance he may have, and what hindrance in doing it."[29]

Attempting a comprehensive assessment will help us avoid the mistake of assuming numbers and technological superiority equate to victory. It is risky to predict the outcome of a war based just on the supposedly known balance and characteristics of the forces involved. Quantification here is certainly useful, as it can provide an objective measure of relative strength, though one that can encourage the formulation of simplistic views. Calculating the dead and equipment losses also yields data demonstrating tactical and local success, but provides "little indication as to the overall effect on the ability of any military force to either apply or resist an opponent's force." The US war in Vietnam and the Franco-Prussian War provide examples of conflicts where the safe money would have been on the loser.[30] Kissinger warned that "while underestimating an adversary can be disastrous, overestimating his resources may lead to a dangerous paralysis of policy. Absolute numbers are important, but only the part of them that can be utilized effectively is strategically significant."[31]

The moral forces – such as fear, patriotism, courage, and so on – are critically important. These are impossible to quantify and exceedingly difficult to grasp, but examining them is indispensable for gaining an understanding of the nation with which you are at war. Napoleon is credited with saying, "The moral is to the physical as three to one." General Rupert Smith observed that one of the key problems in modern wars is that "we do not respect the enemy." We forget that he is a thinking, reasoning being, with ends of his own for which he is willing to fight and die and who has people willing to support him.[32]

Sun Tzu's advice on assessment is still valid: "With many calculations, one can win; with few one cannot. How much less chance of victory has one who makes none at all! By this means I examine the situation and the outcome will be clearly apparent."[33] We cannot consider everything, so we should do as Clausewitz advised and consider what is most probable. *The constraints discussed in the previous chapter also bear upon the assessment and the possible strategy. Their effects must be kept in mind.*

Intelligence

To do a correct assessment, one must have solid intelligence – or information – on the enemy. Clausewitz defined intelligence and told us why it is important: "By 'intelligence' we mean every sort of information about the enemy and his country – the basis, in short, of our own plans and operations."[34] Sun Tzu stresses the importance of information dominance: "Now the reason the enlightened prince and the wise general conquer the enemy whenever they move and their achievements surpass those of ordinary men is foreknowledge." He also insists that information on the enemy is so important that the wise general should go to virtually any lengths to obtain it.[35] Jomini's opinion was not far from his: "There are no fixed rules on such subjects, except that the government should neglect nothing in obtaining a knowledge of these details, and that it is indispensable to take them into consideration in the arrangement of all plans."[36]

But there is the very real problem that sometimes the intelligence is wrong, that it has been misinterpreted, or that we might fall victim to the enemy's deception. Clausewitz realized the importance of intelligence, but also had a deep skepticism toward it, deeming much of it "unreliable and transient," "contradictory," "false," something that serves to "multiply lies and inaccuracies," while often making "things seem grotesque and larger than they really are."[37]

Our assessment should reveal to us where we should focus our efforts against the enemy and protect ourselves. It should reveal critical vulnerabilities – gaps in the armor of the combatants – as well as what are known in Clausewitzian terms as centers of gravity – or sources of strength – upon which the enemy depends. These are the enemy's army, capital city, allies, leader, and public opinion. Everything should be focused upon destroying whichever of these points will bring about the enemy's collapse. The only exception is "when secondary operations look exceptionally rewarding." But even then, only the possession of "decisive superiority can justify diverting strength without risking too much in the principle theater."[38]

A counterargument is that a war for a limited aim should not demand the effort required to reach one of these centers of gravity. But this forgets the value of the object and that wars are not defined by the size of the forces used. A second counterargument is that one should aim at enemy critical vulnerabilities – or weaknesses – as a skilled assessment will reveal these on both sides, and those of the enemy should be exploited. This generally identifies operational problems, not strategic ones, which should indeed be exploited. But this distracts from Clausewitz's larger point. One is trying to end the war as quickly as possible, and destruction of the key element or elements ensuring the enemy's continued will or ability to resist is the most direct means of doing this. Sometimes merely threatening these is sufficient to bring about a change in the enemy's political aim. Exploiting a critical vulnerability may provide a path to attacking a center of gravity.

Another obvious counter to Clausewitz's argument is that one may not have the ability or power to attack the necessary center or centers of gravity, or has perhaps failed the test of creativity so important for the strategist and proved unable to develop a plan for achieving victory. At this point one should question whether or not the war should be continued.

Reassessment

Something recommended by all good strategic studies courses and works is reassessment. The law of interaction is in play in war, because the situation is in constant flux. Nothing is static. One acts. The other reacts. And vice versa. Wisdom demands reexamining the situation to understand the changing nature of the war. Ideally, this should be ongoing. The reality is that this is not so easy, as people are overwhelmed by present concerns. There are many events that should trigger reassessment, theoretically an infinite number, but sometimes these become apparent only when facing them. But there are also specific moments when reassessment is imperative. When should one reassess? *Whenever there is a big change in the situation.* Some examples include:

I   **A Change in the Political Aim**
As we've seen, when the Truman administration changed its political aim and decided to conquer North Korea, a deeper reassessment was needed. The decision-makers in the Truman administration simply did not grasp the depths of the importance of this.

2   **After a Defeat**
This seems simple and obvious to say – and it is – but that does not mean that combatants do it. It takes clarity of vision, the courage to take responsibility for one's actions, and the strength of character to look at a situation and say: "We screwed up. How do we fix it?" In September 1776, George Washington's Continental Army suffered a series of severe defeats in their defense of New York City. Washington had attempted to fight what he called a "war of posts," a defensive war fought from fortified positions in an effort to bleed the British sufficiently to bring them to terms. But General Sir William Howe, the British commander, refused to play by Washington's rules and inflicted crushing blows upon the American forces. Faced with the threat

of annihilation – both of his army and the cause – Washington and his commanders reassessed and changed their strategy. They launched a Fabian strategy of protraction.[39] Some leaders lack the necessary temperament, character, and wisdom to do as Washington did.

3   After a Victory

This is any significant battlefield or operational success. This can change the equation – on both sides – militarily and politically. One must try to determine the effects, which is easy to say but difficult in practice, a fact that does not excuse us from trying. Is the victory merely tactical, and in that case is it only a single throw? Or is it operational? In this case one must plan the next offensive, or prepare for the enemy's response. If it is strategic, then you must decide if it is time to secure the hard-won peace, if the opportunity is there and if your political aim has been achieved, or if it is beyond your reach. Sometimes leaders and commanders do not grasp this. One of the great failures on the part of the Truman administration is that after the success of the Inchon landings and the breakout of the UN forces from the Pusan Perimeter, the administration failed to reexamine the situation and seize the political opportunity that operational and tactical victory had delivered. The decision had already been made to fight another war.

Mao's Chinese repeated the mistake. Upon reaching the 38th parallel in Korea, Mao could have halted his forces and sought peace. Indeed, some of his generals urged him to stop because of the state of their army. But Mao wanted US forces off the peninsula, so the offensive continued. The Chinese, though, lacked the strength to achieve this.[40]

4   After the Entry or Exit of Third-Party Actors

The entry of a new combatant is an obvious time, as this adds the spin of another trinity into the struggle. An infinite number of new possibilities emerges. Again, think about what is most probable, but also remember to think imaginatively. Creativity is one of a leader's most potent weapons, because it allows them to see what others do not and adapt to the new situation. This should be done as quickly as possible, because of the potentially extensive effects. As we saw in the previous chapter, after the October 1950 entry of the Chinese into the Korean War, it took the Truman administration until May 1951 to issue to the

US military commander in the theater a clear revision of the political aim.

5   When You Discover Your Intelligence Is Wrong

In 1780, the British embarked upon what is known as their Southern Campaign, an effort to reconquer the rebellious American southern colonies. This failed, for many reasons, not the least of which was the American response, but critical to its failure was the mistaken belief that there existed in the South deep wells of support for the British that could be tapped to add to British strength. There was indeed significant Loyalist support, but not on the scale expected. This undermined the plan from the beginning.[41]

6   When the Enemy Has Changed Strategy

General William Westmoreland, the US ground force commander in Vietnam, realized in 1965 that the North Vietnamese had changed their strategy. Prior to this, the Communists had relied upon subversion and guerrilla war to overthrow the government of South Vietnam, but they now added conventional invasion to their repertoire of aggression. Westmoreland realized that because of this the US strategy of relying purely upon counterinsurgency was dead and a more vigorous response was required. Westmoreland was correct that a change was needed.[42] What this also shows is that an accurate reassessment of the situation does not necessarily translate into victory, because of your future actions and the enemy's.

7   When the Political or Military Leader or Leaders Change

The appearance of new political leaders can force dramatic change in the political aims. In January 1762, during the Seven Years War, Empress Elizabeth of Russia died. At the time, Russia was part of a coalition of powers fighting Frederick the Great's Prussia. Elizabeth's successor was a German prince who admired Frederick and decided upon peace instead of war. Russia's political aim changed because the leader changed.[43] Sometimes, though, the death of the leader does not produce a change in aim. When US president Franklin Delano Roosevelt died in April 1945, the US political aim remained the unconditional surrender of Germany and Japan.

The change of military leaders can mean a change in strategy. When Ulysses S. Grant became general-in-chief of the Union Army in 1864, this marked the end of a piecemeal and sporadic approach that had become the North's prosecution of the war. Grant instituted a strategy of simultaneous advances, attrition, and raids against Confederate resources that broke the South's will and ability to resist.[44]

8 When the Threat Has Changed

During the Vietnam War, when the North escalated its attacks against South Vietnam, Westmoreland realized that the threat was no longer just Viet Cong guerrillas, but also regular units of the North Vietnamese Army. A different threat necessitates a different response.[45]

9 When the Strategy of Either Side Appears to Be Failing

When one is failing, one usually looks for a way to change the situation. This will produce action, which can sometimes be unexpected. During the 1990–91 Gulf War, Saddam Hussein attempted to implement a strategy of attrition, meaning he planned to fight a defensive war and inflict enough casualties on the Americans that they would quit; he failed miserably. The Americans successfully attacked his strategy by relying upon an air campaign in the early phase of the war. There were lessons here for both sides. Saddam should have learned how outmatched his forces were. The US should have learned that the Iraqis were not as tough as assumed.[46] This sometimes becomes readily apparent after defeat in battle or the failure of a campaign, but not always.

10 When the Constraints Have Changed

During the Vietnam War, the Johnson administration gradually loosened the constraints on the use of force against North Vietnam. This led to extensive debate on how to use military force in Vietnam, particularly how to use air power.[47] These constraints changed again when Richard Nixon became the US president. The constraints were relaxed as Nixon allowed much heavier bombing of North Vietnam.[48]

11   **Whenever One Has the Opportunity**

Ideally, as mentioned above, reassessment should be ongoing. But, again, this is something easy to say but very difficult in practice. The press of events often overwhelms political and military leaders involved in a war, leaving them too little time to reexamine the infinitely complex problem they face. But when the opportunity to reexamine the situation occurs, it should be grasped, because new solutions or dangers might present themselves.

The next obvious question is this: what does one reassess? Everything relevant to the new situation. One may now want to change the aim or may need to increase or shrink the means required. Or perhaps it is now time to negotiate. The impulse is to look only at oneself, but this must be resisted. The war affects the enemy, coalition partners, and neutrals.

Sometimes a reassessment can be faulty and produce disastrous decisions. During the First World War, the Germans reassessed and predicted that they could force Britain to sue for peace in five months via a submarine campaign against merchant shipping. This was treated as an "unchallengeable assumption," but one that proved completely wrong, and is an example of confirmation bias as it proved what everyone involved wanted to hear. Simultaneously, German leaders argued that this change had to be made because they had no other viable option. Moreover, frustrations can drive leaders to open another front (which may or may not be the best way of prosecuting the war) because they believe it their only hope.[49]

Strategy and the Use of Military Force

Using military force to coerce an opponent to do your will has a tradition nearly as long as man's history. Ideally, what you are doing militarily should affect the enemy's material ability to wage war as well as their will. Sun Tzu notes: "He who intimidates his neighbors does so by inflicting injury upon them."[50] Similarly, Clausewitz says: "If the enemy is to be coerced you must put him in a situation that is even more unpleasant than the sacrifice you call on him to make."[51]

A potential problem here is that "Capturing enemy territory will reduce the strength of our forces in varying degrees, which are determined by the location of the occupied territory. If it adjoins our own – either as an enclave within our territory or adjoining it – the more directly it lies on the line of our main advance, the less our strength will suffer." Clausewitz goes on to say:

> The question whether one should aim at such a conquest, then, turns on whether one can be sure of holding it or, if not, whether a temporary occupation (by way of invasion or diversion) will really be worth the cost of the operation and, especially, whether there is any risk of being strongly counter-attacked and thrown off balance. In the chapter on the culminating point, we emphasized how many factors need to be considered in each particular case.[52]

One can also decisively defeat the enemy's forces. This raises eyebrows among some experts on "limited war" because they insist one cannot use overwhelming force. Decisively defeating the enemy works for both the attacker and the defender. If one destroys the enemy's ability to fight the war, they are more likely to give you what you want, whether you are demanding part of their territory or insisting they leave yours.[53]

The First Gulf War provides a clear example of this. The George H. W. Bush administration placed almost no constraints on the use of conventional military force against the opponent. This is one of the many factors that produced the overwhelming Iraqi military defeat.[54] There was no piecemeal increase in the level of force used for offensive operations, nor was there an effort to do anything other than use overwhelming air and ground power.

Ideally, the military action is executed as quickly as possible. French general and theorist André Beaufre insists that "Once the action has been initiated it should as a rule be rapid and brutal in order to reach the military objectives as quickly as possible and so *produce an international fait accompli*. This is increasingly essential because of the greater and greater interdependence between nations and their public opinions." If the war goes on, this gives the opponent time to gather support and perhaps convert what might have been a quick war into a long one.[55]

Fighting Beaufre's way would help reduce what General Rupert Smith has identified as the problem of timelessness in conflicts waged by Western states today. Among the reasons he gives for this affliction is the general confusion among leaders regarding what they are doing with their military forces. They don't send their forces to fight wars but to do "peacekeeping" or "stabilization operations," terms which describe the mission being undertaken rather than the political aim sought (perhaps one could see this as the tacticization of the political aim?). Moreover, General Smith continues, modern states don't fight to win but emphasize preservation of the committed military forces, out of fears that casualties will weaken public support and due to the fact that, since their forces are so small, it's difficult to replace both personnel and equipment losses.[56]

Surprise and Deception

Theorists have identified numerous factors that can provide an edge in the prosecution of a war. Surprise can give many advantages and sometimes turns "the weak into the strong" and "the strong into the unchallengeable."[57] Sun Tzu emphasizes the importance of deception as a means of shaping and manipulating the perceptions of the enemy.[58] General Rupert Smith thinks it "better to practice illusion rather than deception. In the latter one attempts to lie and deceive, in the former one seeks to have the opponent deceive himself."[59] There are, of course, innumerable other factors that should also be considered.

Timing

Deciding when to start a war is critical. Obviously, one aims to launch the struggle at the optimal moment for scoring success. But this applies to offensive limited wars, as those fighting a defensive war generally lack the luxury of choosing. But how does one know the optimum time? How do you know you've waited too long? What are the problems and dangers in waiting?

In the American Civil War, the Confederacy displayed a poor sense of timing. On April 6, 1861, Lincoln dispatched a messenger to inform South Carolina's governor, Francis W. Pickens, that the Union would resupply Fort Sumter but not reinforce it with men or material. Fearing lack of action would revive Union support in the South, Confederate President Jefferson Davis consulted with his cabinet and decided the Union presence had to go. Major Robert Anderson, Sumter's commander, refused the initial demand to surrender, but remarked to the men negotiating with him that he had food for only a few days. Confederate leaders, though, worried about a Union resupply effort. On April 12, 1861, at 4:30am, the Confederates fired on

Sumter, igniting the war. The South went to war too early. It should have endured the North holding a shard of South Carolina for a little longer, shipped their cotton through blockade-free ports, and imported needed weapons and supplies. The Confederates started the war before they were prepared, while simultaneously enraging the Union. The South did initially benefit from launching the war because of the secession of four states that joined the Confederacy. But seven states had already seceded. Given time, others were likely to follow.[60]

In February 1904, Japan launched what became known as the Russo–Japanese War (1904–05). After a very thorough assessment and meticulous planning, the Japanese concluded that an early war was better. General Iguchi Shogo wrote on June 8, 1903: "The present is the most favorable time for this purpose, bearing in mind the superiority of our forces over Russia, the fact that the Trans-Siberian [Railroad] is incomplete, the existence of the Anglo-Japanese Alliance, the hostility of the Chinese people etc. If we let today's favorable opportunity slip by, it will never come again."[61] The Japanese military believed February the optimal time because the Trans-Siberian Railroad had a bottleneck at Lake Baikal. In the summer, the Russians ferried men and material across. In winter, they relied on sledges. Moreover, Japan had finished its naval building program in 1903; Russia's would not be complete until 1905. In January 1904, after the failure of a fourth round of negotiations, Japanese leaders concluded that waiting now favored the Russians. They also knew Japan possessed temporary military superiority in the theater. On February 1, 1904, the request for war went to the emperor. The Japanese chose very well.[62]

Coalitions

One of the things too often forgotten in regard to America's wars – even its wars for limited aims – is that they are usually coalitional struggles, usually on both sides. Since the end of the Second World War, the US has carried the heaviest part of the military burden, but this doesn't mean the participation of other coalition members is unimportant. In the Korean, Vietnam, and Gulf Wars, US participation would have been impossible without a host-nation coalition partner. Moreover, despite the cry of unilateralism regarding US foreign policy, it is very unlikely (though not impossible) that the US will go to war alone. This applies as much to wars for limited aims as unlimited.

Coalitions have advantages: more strength, more capabilities, etc., but they also complicate the situation because the various partners might have different political aims, different constraints, different things they want to protect, or different views on how to fight the war. Henry Kissinger argues that three things have historically kept together coalitions: 1) joining for collective security; 2) ensuring the assistance of an ally in the event of conflict; and 3) lending legitimacy to foreign assistance in the form of troops or if intervening in another country.[63] These certainly apply to the US experience. Clear agreements on burden-sharing can also help strengthen the bonds and reduce suspicions.

The impact of coalitions upon the creation of strategy in the wars the US fought in Korea, Vietnam, and the Gulf was small. The US carried most of the military burden in all of these wars and thus essentially dictated strategy. But successful implementation of the strategy is nearly impossible to decree, as coalition partners are still independent actors even if their survival is completely dependent upon the US presence and US aid. As we see in the next chapter, coalitions also complicate war termination and peacemaking.

Wars for Limited Aims: The Most Likely Strategies Encountered

The above has detoured somewhat from an analysis dedicated solely to wars for limited aims. This was necessary to lay the foundation for the discussion that follows.

Protracted War Strategy

The United States has been on both sides of a protracted war strategy in its wars for limited aims. Protraction helped the US succeed in its war for independence; it helped produce the US failure in Vietnam. Sun Tzu, as we've seen, argues against this, but one may be forced to a fight a protracted war – as a path to victory or because the enemy has elected to try to win through this strategy. The decision by one side to protract the war is not uncommon in wars fought for limited political aims, particularly among insurrectionists, as this is a strategy sometimes chosen by the weak. One critic argues that, unfortunately for the US in the modern era, it has been "extremely difficult to carry on a protracted limited war," especially if the people aren't directly involved. They lack interest in foreign affairs, question the value and costs of US involvements overseas, and are "emotionally detached" from the wars.[64]

A strategy of protraction can take many forms. Those fighting a defensive war against an insurrection must understand this, because rebel groups often choose to protract a war. One of these is the Fabian strategy attributed to the Roman general Quintus Fabius Maximus Verrucosus, better known as Fabius the Delayer. He opposed the Carthaginian forces invading Italy by refusing to fight their superior army directly because this could lead to a decisive defeat. Instead, he harried their detachments, bleeding them over time.

To execute a Fabian strategy, the weaker side, fearing decisive defeat of its forces, chooses to avoid any battle that might result in the destruction of their army. Instead, they carefully pick places to fight where they have the advantage, while also wearing down the enemy's will and resources with many small attacks and carefully chosen battles. The one executing this strategy has to have space into which to flee in the face of enemy pursuit. This means the existence of internal or external sanctuary. The delayer also must have significant support among his people, because he is betting that the will of his side will last longer than the will of the opponent. He must produce successes from time to time to keep the support of the people while bleeding the enemy. The Fabian hopes to win – eventually – perhaps by weakening the foe enough to inflict a final, decisive defeat, by exhausting their will via the protraction of the conflict, or raising the cost of the war beyond what the enemy is willing or able to pay.

To Americans, the better-known practitioner of a Fabian strategy is George Washington. He and his commanders adopted the Fabian version of protraction. They avoided battle against superior British forces while simultaneously bleeding the enemy via partisan warfare. The Americans were slow to make a full shift to a strategy of protraction, and had some bumps along the way, but the new strategy was the cornerstone of victory.[65]

Another form of protracted war was developed by Mao Tse-Tung.[66] In 1938, Mao published "On Protracted War," his strategy for China to succeed against Japan. He insisted that China could win only through a strategy of protraction that combined the use of regular and irregular military forces. Mao urged "mobile warfare" with regular forces against the Japanese. Making use of the vastness of China, regular units could make quick advances and withdrawals, concentrations, and "dispersals." He insisted that the Chinese avoid "major decisive battles" and instead focus upon attrition of the enemy's morale and military strength. The guerrilla struggle would supplement mobile warfare. Recruited in large numbers from the peasants, the bulk of the Chinese population, Mao believed that, properly organized, they could "keep the Japanese army busy twenty-four hours a day and worry it to death."

From his experience fighting the Japanese, as well as the Nationalists, Mao proposed a three-phased theory of protracted war that contributed the modern model for rebel or guerrilla struggle. Phase one was the strategic defensive, or the "organization, consolidation, and preservation" phase. The Communists would be much weaker than their opponents, and thus had to act primarily on the defensive. They would build up their party organization and the basic structures they would need later, recruit and train their cadres, and expand support for the party while educating the people on the cause. They would adopt popular measures such as land reform but also use terror against opponents, and any element of authority to create instability and unrest.[67] This would undermine support for the Chinese Nationalist government.

Political preparation of the peasants was considered key. The Communists had to have peasant support, especially the guerrillas who depended upon them for everything. Mao said, "the guerrilla must be in the population as little fishes in the ocean."[68] The Communists would use force and coercion, but they stressed gaining the good will of the peasants and issued rules for dealing with them in January 1928. Securing and building a base area, along with recruiting and indoctrinating (or coercing) the people to win them to the Communist cause, were the core elements of phase one.[69]

Phase two was the strategic stalemate, the "progressive expansion," or "equilibrium" phase. It was time to move to phase two when the Communists possessed sufficient support among the people to enable the insurgents to fight with strength roughly equal to that of their enemy. The guerrillas would establish bases, increase their recruiting, and begin the training of regular forces for future use. They would also establish a government in controlled areas to present the people with an alternative.[70] Violence, sabotage, and terrorism increase. They would attack police and small military units in order to get equipment, arms, etc. As the guerrilla force grows, its political wing indoctrinates the local populace, expanding the area of guerrilla control. The struggle is attritional, and one of the primary objectives during the first two phases is winning as many converts to the cause as possible, to give the movement mass.

Phase three was the strategic offensive, "decision," or "destruction of the enemy" phase. Here, the guerrillas consider themselves strong enough to fight the enemy conventionally and achieve victory. Much of the guerrilla force is transformed into a regular army, but guerrilla warfare might still be carried on at the same time. This phase is intended to be shorter than the others. Ideally, the preparation proves so good that it is unnecessary to go to phase three to win.[71] The guerrillas might protract this phase by negotiating with their enemy to gain time in order to strengthen their military, political, social, or economic position, and to irritate their foe while eroding his strength. Mao believed his form of warfare could be particularly dangerous to countries with legislative governments because they were less capable of enduring financial and psychological burdens over a long period of time. Criticism of the war that arises will undermine the strength of the government's troops.[72]

This model of protracted war became the template for subsequent insurgencies in many places such as Vietnam, Algeria, and Malaysia. It is also the primary typology for how insurgencies are evaluated in regard to their progress.

Punitive and Cost-Imposing Strategies

C. E. Callwell, the author of the classic *Small Wars*, describes what today we would call a punitive expedition: "Hostilities entered upon to punish an insult or to chastise a people who have inflicted some injury."[73] Punitive expeditions today are commonly referred to as "drone strikes," or are done with cruise missiles, air strikes, and special operations forces. US President Donald Trump's 2018 firing of cruise missiles at Syria's Bashar Assad regime exemplifies a modern punitive expedition, a punishment for unacceptable behavior not unlike the British or French would have mounted against a foreign warlord in the nineteenth century.[74] Nations are doing as they did in the past, only they use something other than infantry and cavalry. This is one of the current forms of fighting a war for a limited aim.

There is also the option of "cost-imposing strategies," a concept rooted in defense expert Andrew Marshall's 1972 proposal for the US to take actions to impose costs on the USSR. This, though, is not always the answer, as "Cost imposing strategies are most effective against imperial powers, such as Japan in the Second World War and the Soviet Union in the Cold War, who have expansive political ambitions that outrun their economic or financial base and who, unlike North Vietnam in the Vietnam War, have no allies able to share the material burden." Eventually, such powers can face the financial or logistical problems related to being overstretched.[75]

One can also seek to convince the enemy to move its strategy in particular directions. This, though, generally only produces small but potentially cumulative effects, especially in comparison to conventional uses of force.[76]

Proportional Response, Surgical Strikes, and Minimum Force

In the post-modern era, a term one often hears from political leaders to describe their reactions to attacks of various kinds is "proportional response." For example, in response to what was initially viewed as a North Korean hacker attack against the Sony Corporation in 2014, President Obama promised to respond "proportionally."[77]

Defenders of acting in this manner argue that it demonstrates restraint, thoughtfulness, and caution, and can keep situations from getting out of hand. Detractors deem the term vacuous and argue that insisting you are responding "proportionally" merely gives the appearance of cautious reflection while broadcasting weakness and revealing a desire to do nothing. "Surgical strike" is a similar term.

Sometimes leaders who feel they have no choice but to act – perhaps from domestic political concerns, fear of being viewed as weak at home or abroad, or giving political opponents room to attack – will choose a "proportional response." Unfortunately, too often the so-called "proportional response" is delivered in a politcal vacuum, meaning that the executing power doesn't have a clear intent for it. At best, it is meant as a punitive action, but even this should have a clear aim driving it. When states are killing people, they should know *why*. A proper "proportional response" is doing what is needed to achieve the aim sought.

Related to this is what is sometimes called "the doctrine of minimum force." The desire to use as little force as is necessary is understandable, especially in the event of a civil disturbance. But this sentiment can be dangerous when fighting a war. It can place forces in danger and leave them in a weak position vis-à-vis an enemy. Using insufficient force to solve the problem one has decided to use force to resolve can extend the problem and produce more losses and bloodshed than if one had allocated sufficient force when the decision was made.[78]

For the defenders, it is very risky to present a so-called "proportional response," because they are often not certain of the attacker's intent. If defenders don't respond immediately, they "may well lose the chance of putting up an effective defense." Moreover, they cannot "be expected to be in a state of mind in which a cool and impartial appreciation of the situation can be rapidly and accurately made." Additionally, if the attacker thinks the intended victim is trying to use the bare minimum of force, they might succeed in putting themselves in such an advantageous position that "the final assault could be accomplished with little risk of failure."[79]

"Disproportionality" is a similar term, but one used to criticize the military response of someone with whose aim one disagrees. An example is the reproach cast upon Israel for its 2006 attacks against Hezbollah in Lebanon and Palestinian militant groups in Gaza. (This would be better classified as an old-fashioned punitive expedition like those mounted by Western Powers before the First World War. The Israelis were ensuring their neighbors realized the cost for attacks on Israel's civilian population.) Historian Hew Strachan points out that Israel no longer enjoys international sympathy when it is fighting wars for the same reasons it had waged its other conflicts between 1948 and 1967. In 2006, Israel was not seen as fighting for its survival. Moreover, many Europeans no longer see the utility of war, while others approached this conspiratorially, seeing a war for Israeli expansion or a neoconservative plot.[80]

Arguably, a "disproportional response" could lead to escalation of the level of violence involved (aims change, they do not escalate). It might, though this is war's natural tendency the longer the conflict goes on. But the increased use of force also sends a message that can lessen the chances of a future similar breach of the peace.

Signaling, Bargaining, and the Vietnam War

As we saw in Chapter 2, Thomas Schelling's theoretical ideas had significant effects upon limited war theory and directly contributed to the construction of US strategy for fighting the Vietnam War. This produced perhaps the greatest failure of limited war theorizing.

Secretary of Defense McNamara and the other leaders in the Johnson administration bought into limited war theories that stressed signaling to an enemy. Force was an element of signaling that would demonstrate resolve. This would, in turn, either deter an enemy or convince them to negotiate a settlement. To the Johnson administration, this offered a way to fight the war on the cheap without risking war with China or the Soviet Union.[81] But they dramatically underestimated how much pain the North Vietnamese regime was willing to endure.[82]

Johnson and his civilian and military advisors believed that a bombing campaign against the North was the solution. The military wanted a heavy bombing campaign with attacks on the military, industrial, and infrastructure elements of the North, including the mining of Haiphong Harbor. It was argued that this would force Hanoi to quit the war or face the destruction of their nation.[83] Walt Rostow, director of policy and planning and later National Security Advisor, expressed a concern that "too much thought is being given to the actual damage we do in the North, not enough to the signal we wish to send." He believed that as little force should be used as possible, and this should be done to signal and as a deterrence.[84]

Johnson's national security advisor McGeorge Bundy wanted "a gradual escalation strategy." His assistant, John McNaughton, was unsure what type of campaign would suffice, but also wanted to be sure the enemy received the proper signals and so approached his old Harvard colleague, Thomas Schelling, for ideas. Schelling, who saw war as a form of bargaining, argued for a bombing campaign that he insisted would succeed in a matter of weeks.[85] Signaling was an element of this, and an example of Schelling's thinking here was thus: "This strange, momentous dialogue may illustrate two principles for the kind of noncommittal bargaining we are forever engaged in with the potential enemy. First, don't speak directly at him, but speak seriously to some serious audience and let him overhear. Second, to get his ear, listen."[86] This misses the great problem with signaling: the enemy might misunderstand what you are saying or trying to signal.[87]

After the November 1, 1964, Communist attack on the US air base at Bien Hoa, Vietnam, the US examined three approaches to bombing: "A" – the status quo (essentially a punitive response); "B" – a heavy attack à la Curtis LeMay; and "C" – Rostow's "graduated response." They chose Rostow's approach, which became Rolling Thunder.[88] To McNamara and other Department of Defense civilians, "Rolling Thunder was a complicated game of signals with the North, as much psychological as military." There was, of course, resistance to the proposal, and a signaling strategy was something the JCS members never accepted as feasible.[89]

Rolling Thunder lasted from March 2, 1965 to October 31, 1968, and had two primary objectives: forcing the North Vietnamese to stop feeding men and material into the South, and convincing the North Vietnamese to enter into peace negotiations. There were four parts to this strategy that emphasized the idea of "graduated pressure": 1) coercing North Vietnam by threatening to destroy its industrial base; 2) controlling the level of force used, because using too much would destroy the hostage, i.e. North Vietnam's industry; 3) escalating the bombing gradually, thus convincing North Vietnam of America's willingness to go farther and – in Maxwell Taylor's words – "convey signals" that their destruction was nigh; 4) finally, tying diplomacy to the bombing, which to the civilians meant that they needed to keep the military on a tight leash. One of the great flaws in this plan was that there were fewer than thirty industrial sites in North Vietnam.[90]

The US embarked upon Rolling Thunder despite the fact that Johnson did not believe air power could deliver victory. There also seems to have been little confidence in government circles – beyond Rostow – that Rolling Thunder could actually work. The analysis by McNamara's Defense Department concluded that Rostow's approach was very unlikely to succeed, because the economy was 88 percent agricultural, the country was not dependent upon maritime trade, and the bombing didn't address the insurgency. But they also concluded that it might be the best available option. Johnson told McNamara in a June 21, 1965 telephone conversation: "I see no program from either Defense or State that gives us much hope of doing anything, except just praying . . . they'll quit. I don't believe they're ever going to quit. And I don't see any plan for victory – militarily or diplomatically."[91]

The first phase of Rolling Thunder was in the spring and summer of 1965, from March to August. The bombing attacks were designed to move progressively further north. For example, the attacks launched in March 1965 struck targets south of the 19th parallel. In May 1965, Rolling Thunder hit targets up to the 20th parallel. In July, the US struck a small number of targets above the 20th parallel.[92]

As the campaign continued, the constraints began to go away, a normal reaction when a strategy proves ineffective, but they never disappeared. In a March 8, 1965 report, Army Chief of Staff Harold K. Johnson recommended dropping various self-imposed constraints on the use of air power that had made it less effective. These were eventually removed, but demonstrate the exceedingly tight control exercised by the Johnson administration. The constraints included requirements that South Vietnamese aircraft participate in the attacks; that attacks hit only the primary target; that the use of classified ordnance be forbidden; that tight geographical limits on the targets available be imposed; and that approval be obtained from Washington to strike alternative targets when weather or other factors prevented an attack on the primary one. Johnson resisted changing only the expansion of the targeted areas.[93]

The second phase of Rolling Thunder lasted from August 1965 through May 1967. Its main purpose was interdiction against North Vietnamese efforts to move men and supplies into the South, which included attacks on the Ho Chi Minh Trail running through Laos. But as the campaign went on, the target list expanded, and the US began striking petroleum-related facilities and, later, electrical power generation.[94]

There were pauses in the campaign, a total of eight between March 1965 and March 1968.[95] For example, McNamara suggested the US stop bombing over Christmas 1965 to open the door for negotiations. Johnson agreed, even though he expected nothing from this. The bombing ceased for thirty-seven days, beginning on December 24. Johnson's skepticism proved correct. Neither Admiral U. S. Grant Sharp nor General William Westmoreland, the two key military commanders in Vietnam, were aware of the plan for a pause.[96]

May 1967 through March 1968 saw the third phase. Since there had been no success from the bombing, and feeling pressure from public opinion and Congress, Johnson removed more of the self-imposed constraints on bombing, and the US began hitting the industrial and transportation sites while maintaining the bombing's intensity. The bombing still failed to deliver the desired objectives. Moreover, it was no longer possible to ratchet up the pressure on the North because the industrial sites had been destroyed.[97] So much for theory.

April to November 1968 brought the final phase of Rolling Thunder. During this period the US gradually reduced the bombing. US public opinion was turning against the war, and Johnson was bowing to public pressure. The "bombing was rolled back from the Hanoi–Haiphong area, first to the twentieth parallel, then to the nineteenth." (We could call this "Unrolling Thunder.") After November 1968, Johnson halted bombing of the North except for interdiction raids along the demilitarized zone (DMZ) that marked the border between South and North Vietnam.[98]

The Johnson administration did coordinate diplomacy with the bombing. In June 1964, through Blair Seaborn, a Canadian official acting as the US intermediary with North Vietnam, the US promised escalation and destruction if the North didn't stop giving support to the Viet Cong. It was a hollow threat. Bombing North Vietnamese industry couldn't destroy the North's ability to wage the war because most of their military equipment came from their Communist brethren.[99] Walt Rostow (and some other members of the administration) fell victim to what is known as "mirror imaging," assuming that the enemy – and in this case Ho Chi Minh – saw things as the Americans did and thus had the same priorities, specifically that Ho valued economic growth above all else, just like Rostow.[100]

Rolling Thunder produced the opposite result of what was intended. General Maxwell Taylor, who served as US Ambassador to South Vietnam, drew the mistaken conclusion that bombing had helped end the Korean War and thus could do the same in Vietnam.[101] He termed Rolling Thunder "a strategy of gradualism" because of "the piecemeal employment of military forces at slowly mounting levels of intensity." A strategy he later admitted was wrong: "While this carefully controlled violence may have had some justification at the start," he wrote, "it ended by defeating its own purposes. Designed to limit the dangers of expanded war, it ended by assuring a prolonged war which carried with it dangers of expansion. The restrained use of air power suggested to the enemy a lack of decisiveness."[102] As Rolling Thunder heated up, Alexei Kosygin and some other Soviet diplomats feared the escalation of force in Vietnam and the Johnson administration's simultaneous intervention in the Dominican Republic could fuel action against Cuba and produce a war between the Soviets and the West. Most others, though, did not see things this way, and found their suggestions for mobilization and other actions beyond the pale.[103] The generation of such fears was one thing the Johnson administration had hoped to avoid.

The US could not achieve its aims via bombing because Rolling Thunder as implemented could neither decisively affect North Vietnam's will to prosecute the war nor its material ability. By early 1968, the US had lost over 900 aircraft and over 1,000 aircrew, half of them killed. McNamara's people calculated that it cost the US $10 to inflict $1 worth of damage, and none of this stopped the flow of men and supplies from the North to the South.[104] Between 1965 and 1968, the North "received approximately $600 million in economic aid and $1 billion in military assistance, while sustaining a cost of $370 million in measurable physical damage from bombing."[105] The US could not stop the infiltration because – as General Ridgway pointed out in his study of the Korean War – air interdiction is not nearly as effective as people hope.[106] Air war commander Admiral Grant Sharp wrote: "I had made the point many times that air attacks on lines of communication have never been able to stop infiltration, only hinder it. The primary objectives of using air power should not be to try to stop infiltration, but rather to destroy the sources of the material being infiltrated."[107] Schelling's and Rostow's version of limited war theory *ignored the importance of national will,* both in the opponent and the nation prosecuting the war. Theory (both for the use of air power and signaling) also failed to match reality.

Salami-Slicing

Another term that pops up in limited war discussions is "salami-slicing," meaning carving off small pieces of an adversary's territory in a way that does not provoke a dramatic enemy reply and whereby repetition leads to significant territorial gains. Some Indian authors insist China attempted this via incursions along the Indian border in the 1950s. Putin sliced off the Crimea, then moved on to the heavily ethnic Russian areas of Eastern Ukraine.[108]

This term, though, simply depicts a limited war in practice. One uses military force to seize the territory, which is the operational as well as the political aim (they can be the same). This is war being waged – successfully in Putin's case – for a limited political aim, an objective less than regime change.

Attrition and Limited War

The reaction of some is that attrition is not a suitable strategy for a war fought for a limited political aim, but that is to forget that the correct strategy is the one that delivers the political aim, and since wars are of infinite character, one cannot discount the fact that attrition may be correct. Henry Kissinger argued that "By its very nature war is a process of attrition. The problem for strategy is not to avoid attrition, but to determine which kind of attrition is strategically most significant."[109] Sometimes, an attrition strategy is considered a form of a strategy of exhaustion.[110]

But how do we define attrition? It is generally associated with the wearing down of the enemy's military forces with the intent that those forces either will be destroyed or their ability (or will) to resist will collapse. Physical attrition of forces attacks both the ability and the will of the opponent to resist. The 1916 German offensive against French forces at Verdun is a famous example of this. The Germans planned to kill enough Frenchmen to win the war. This, as is well known, failed. Critical to remember here is that one runs the risk of suffering just as much as the enemy.[111]

The US has often pursued an attrition strategy, even in wars fought for limited political aims. In Korea, Ridgway, who took command of 8th Army on December 26, 1950, adopted an attrition strategy. He said at a February 8, 1951 corps commanders meeting that the job was to kill the enemy – not hold territory – while preserving their own forces.[112] General Lawton Collins wrote that after the change in political aim in 1951, "The purpose of US and UN forces from this point was to put enough pressure on the enemy and kill enough of them to make them sign an agreement that would end the war."[113]

Their Chinese enemy eventually pursued essentially the same strategy. But here is an example where technological superiority, especially at the tactical level, gave the US a superiority in a situation that might seem counterintuitive. The US had a much greater ability to inflict casualties upon the Chinese than the Communists had to hurt the UN.[114]

The more famous American use of an attrition strategy occurred during the Vietnam War, though deeming this the sum total of US strategy here is a common oversimplification. The 1965 North Vietnamese conventional military offensive, combined with the failure of Rolling Thunder, shaped the construction of US strategy for the ground war in Vietnam. The head of the US Military Assistance Command, Vietnam, General William Westmoreland, did not think the destruction of enemy forces would be quick and "believed that this would entail a protracted war of attrition."[115]

In July 1965, Westmoreland proposed his plan for the war. In phase one, the US would put in enough troops to keep South Vietnam from collapsing. This would be done by the end of 1965. In phase two, the US and its allies would go on the offensive in the most important areas, destroying enemy units and doing pacification. There was no time limit offered for this. In phase three, if the enemy was still a problem, the US would spend a year to a year-and-a-half after the completion of phase two to defeat his forces and destroy them and their base areas.[116] Westmoreland's strategy comprised three planks: attrition, pacification (or counterinsurgency), which was coupled with "rural construction," and training of the South Vietnamese forces, or ARVN. Westmoreland noted on January 7, 1966: "It is abundantly clear that all political, military, economic, and security (police) programs must be completely integrated in order to attain any kind of success in a country which has been greatly weakened by prolonged conflict and is under increasing pressure by large military and subversive forces."[117]

What is also forgotten is a key factor contributing to the creation of strategy: the assessment of the threat. Westmoreland chose his approach – and his focus upon attrition – because he saw that the threat to South Vietnam's survival was not the Viet Cong (VC) guerrillas, but the North Vietnamese Army (NVA) and Main Force VC units. The latter were former guerrilla units that were now essentially regular, light infantry units. Westmoreland accurately assessed the situation in 1964 and 1965 because the North Vietnamese had changed how they were fighting the war and were ardently trying to topple the South Vietnamese regime.[118]

From the first large-scale commitment of US troops in 1965 until January 1968, Westmoreland pursued big unit operations against the enemy. The attritional element of the strategy was implemented via "search-and-destroy" operations that sought out enemy forces. Westmoreland believed he could inflict enough casualties on the enemy to drive them past a "crossover point" where they were losing more men than they could replace. A controversial and easily manipulated "body count" of enemy killed was one of the measures of effectiveness. Westmoreland paid less attention to pacification of the countryside or the development of South Vietnamese forces (which under his strategy were supposed to be dealing with the guerrillas by conducting pacification). Westmoreland argued that he didn't have the troops to do both pacification and search-and-destroy operations.[119]

Westmoreland was supported in his approach by his superiors. Secretary of Defense McNamara explained to President Johnson that Westmoreland's strategy would wear down the enemy and bring them to agree "to terms favorable to South Vietnam and the United States." McNamara also said: "Our object in Vietnam is to create conditions for a favorable outcome by demonstrating to the VC/DRV that the odds are against their winning. We want to create these conditions, if possible, without causing the war to expand." When Westmoreland formally presented his strategy to the president and other administration officials at a February 1966 conference in Honolulu, he made it clear that the war would be long and require a number of campaigns.[120]

Westmoreland had some success with his strategy. He inflicted a severe defeat on the North Vietnamese Army (NVA) at Ia Drang in November 1965. Between early 1967 and March 1969, the Viet Cong was virtually destroyed (the North's failed Tet Offensive contributed greatly to this), and the US made much progress toward pacification. Moreover, Westmoreland succeeded in propping up South Vietnam and forcing the North Vietnamese over to the defensive and to operate from their bases in Cambodia and Laos.[121]

But the strategy for the ground war had some basic flaws. The first of these was the assumption that attrition would work. Forcing the enemy over the "crossover point" was essentially impossible – unless the enemy cooperated. The North Vietnamese had deep wells of manpower in the North but could also count on support from China, which sent more than 320,000 troops to aid the North from 1965 to 1968, and had 130,000 troops in North Vietnam in 1968.[122] This allowed the North to send more troops to the South, which they supplemented with South Vietnamese sympathizers and people conscripted into the Viet Cong. The North could also choose when to decrease its force commitment, which it did after the defeat of its 1968–69 Tet Offensive.[123] The US failed to deliver success within the time its people would stomach a large commitment to the war. It also could not solve the weaknesses of the South Vietnamese regime.

Annihilation or Total Defeat of the Enemy

As we've seen, one can totally defeat – or annihilate – the enemy's military forces (we are not suggesting the annihilation of an enemy's population) in a war fought for a limited political aim. Sometimes this is required to achieve victory, and one must commit the necessary forces. The US Army's Chief of Intelligence, General Stephen J. Chamberlin, after visiting the US advisory mission supporting Greece's war against a Communist insurgency, argued in September 1947 that US advisors should boost Greek offensive-mindedness by advising and planning operations. He added that "The United States has only two alternatives – they [sic] should get out of Greece or stay and be prepared to commit the means to win."[124]

Many observers have noted the aforementioned US failure during the Korean War to defeat the Chinese Army in the spring of 1951 when it had the chance. Bernard Brodie wrote: "The cardinal error as we see it today was the halting of our offensive at the moment that the Communists first indicated an interest in opening armistice negotiations ... We paid bitterly for that error in the great prolongation of negotiations, in the unsatisfactory terms of settlement."[125] Raymond Aron echoed his sentiment, noting that "With a more successful conduct of the campaign, the United States would have been able to negotiate on the basis of a more favorable military situation."[126] MacArthur insisted in his famous farewell address: "But once war is forced upon us, there is no other alternative than to apply every available means to bring it to a swift end."[127]

The longer the war goes on, the longer the dying goes on, and greater the risks of the war's expansion. *If* defeating the enemy's military forces is the best way to bring the war to an end, this should be the military objective. The US did this in the First Gulf War. There will undoubtedly be future cases where this is again the answer to the problem.

Strategy, Nuclear Weapons, and Wars for Limited Political Aims

It is a blatant statement of the obvious that the possession of nuclear weapons by one or more combatants alters the nature of the war and the risks. We properly addressed nuclear weapons as an element of military means in the previous chapter, but that does not relieve us from examining them here.

The possession of such weapons has not made war nor the existence of conventional forces obsolete and has not always served successfully as a deterrent. American atomic weapons did not deter Chinese entry into the Korean War. In 1956, one Soviet general argued that these weapons necessitated larger forces because of expected heavy losses of troops. Moreover, past studies do not assume that their use will automatically bring a war to an end, as some might think. Western leaders in the 1950s proposed "broken-back" warfare, which examined the problems of continuing to fight a war against the Communists in Europe after a nuclear exchange.[128]

The potential use of atomic and nuclear weapons has consumed many scholars and policymakers since 1945, and this possibility has been a factor in the war-planning of nations that have them or fear they could be on their receiving end. Unfortunately, the traditional deterrence strategies developed during the Cold War do not necessarily now apply, as the situation is different. There is certainly the possibility that these weapons could be used by a state seeking to preserve itself (North Korea), or one seeking to punish an enemy (North Korea).[129]

In 2022, at the time of this revision, what is generally considered the most likely arena for the use of nuclear weapons is a war between India and Pakistan. Some authors from the region believe their potential use in a future conflict is very real.[130] Some Indian leaders believe nuclear weapons only "deter nuclear weapons and not war."[131] A war between India and Pakistan also has the distinct possibility of bringing in a third party.[132] China is the obvious state here.

India has spent an enormous amount of effort studying wars fought for limited aims between nuclear-armed powers, something very relevant to our discussion. In April 2004, the Indian Army publicly revealed its new doctrine, Cold Start. It is designed to allow India to quickly and decisively bring military force to bear against Pakistani proxy forces in Kashmir and win the war before international pressure can stop them.[133] This was a response in particular to the 1999 Kargil War that India fought against Pakistani incursion, as well as the terrorist attacks India suffered in 2001 and 2002.[134]

India had traditionally pursued a generally defensive strategy driven by the Sundarji Doctrine, which rested upon seven army "holding corps" in a defensive posture along the frontier with Pakistan. They were to hold ground in the event of attack and would be supported by three "strike corps." After the December 2001 terrorist attack in New

Delhi by Pakistani-backed militants, India wanted to demonstrate its willingness to fight unless Pakistan stopped such infiltrations by mobilizing and moving forces to the border. But it took an unexpectedly long three weeks to actually bring the "strike corps" to the frontier. The long lag-time gave the Pakistanis space to prepare and foreign powers such as the US the opportunity to bring diplomatic pressure. Moreover, the Pakistanis did not actually stop sponsoring incursions and attacks, despite public statements to the contrary.[135]

The Indians began rethinking their doctrine. They needed something that allowed them to use military force to achieve limited aims much more quickly and that also did not require full mobilization of the military. They also wanted the "holding corps" to have more offensive capability and wanted more ability to strike with surprise; Pakistan watched the "strike corps" constantly and thus always knew the offensive weapon's location. In theory, Cold Start allows India to quickly bring enormous force to bear against Pakistani forces. The three "strike corps" became eight division-strength "integrated battle groups" supported by air and naval units where appropriate. All units were to conduct continuous operations until India's political aims were achieved. The operational objective was no longer to cut Pakistan in half but to seize 50–80 kilometers of territory to use as a bargaining chip in negotiations.[136]

In the eyes of Indian planners, one of Cold Start's many advantages was stopping Pakistan from using the "regime survival" argument as an excuse for launching a nuclear strike in response to an Indian conventional attack. But this assumes that Pakistan won't see a penetration of Pakistani territory as a larger threat than India intends.[137]

Cold Start has its critics. A 2014 work doubts its wisdom in the nuclear era because of its offensive nature.[138] One author argued in 2013 that at that time India lacked the capability to do what its doctrine said, while also failing to give sufficient thought to the problem of balancing against China.[139]

All of this supports the general argument of this book for analyzing wars based upon the political aim – and making the latter clear. In theory, understanding the nature of an offensive war fought for a limited political aim is useful in the India–Pakistan case for lessening the risk of a nuclear exchange, because such a war would not be existential. When potentially facing such a literally explosive situation as the one between India and Pakistan, political leaders should know

what they want to achieve and make it clear, possibly even publicly – though don't expect the enemy to believe you.

Insurrection, Insurgency, Counterinsurgency, and Wars for Limited Political Aims

The literature on insurgency and counterinsurgency is voluminous,
and this is certainly not the place to discuss it, and wars in which insurgency
is the dominant factor are invariably described as "limited." What we must
point out is that much of the writing on these topics is tactical and thus not
directly related to our discussion. The literature suffers from a nearly
endemic lack of self-awareness on this point and does not deal with the
reality that tactical fixes often cannot address the larger strategic challenges.
This failing can lead to simplistic recommendations for addressing one of
the most complicated of military problems. Unfortunately, space requires
us to risk the same error.

As with all conflicts, we must begin the analysis by understanding the aim sought. Insurrections are invariably classified as limited wars
because the insurgents – tactically – fight using traditional guerrilla
warfare methods with forces that are usually small, weak, and poorly
armed – at least initially. It is the political aim that provides the basis for
analysis, not the size of the force, or the means and methods of warfare.
Insurrections can pursue limited or unlimited political aims, which will
depend upon the situation at hand. Do the insurgents want the overthrow of the regime (an unlimited political aim) or do they want something less – say, for example, thirteen colonies in an imperial
backwater? Mao Tse-Tung's Communists sought an unlimited political
aim – the overthrow of the Chinese Nationalist regime. The insurgents
may also have different aims against different opponents. The North
Vietnamese sought the destruction of the South Vietnamese regime, but
also the ousting of the US from South Vietnam. In either case, the
primacy of politics reigns supreme. This is also true even if the political
aim is clothed in religious rhetoric.

As always, the value of the object is key. If the insurgents want
the overthrow of the regime, this implies a high value on the political
aim for the insurgents as well as the leaders and supporters of the regime
that is now protecting itself. It is the counterinsurgent who is fighting the
war for a limited political aim. Indeed, the counterinsurgent – or

counter-insurrectionist (a term taken from historian Jeremy Black) – is always seeking a limited political aim, because they wish to preserve the regime and its control. Understandably, some will see this as counterintuitive. The political aim of maintaining control should not be confused with the fact that the government might be forced to completely destroy the enemy to achieve its limited aim. Do not confuse the aim with the means and methods used.

If the aim of the insurgents is not regime change but the redress of some grievances, the regime is wise to try to settle this via negotiations, which is historically one of the ways of ending an insurrection or insurgency and should not be balked at, except under very unusual circumstances. Sometimes the counterinsurgent surrenders to impatience here when they should not, denies the legitimacy of any grievances, and fights when talking might be the answer. The counterinsurgent also sometimes wants to fight with the tools and methods they possess without having to incur much in the way of political or social costs, while failing to realize when they need to adjust to the situation at hand.[140] The classic 1940 US Marine Corps *Small Wars Manual* offers some excellent advice here:

> The application of purely military measures may not, by itself, restore peace and orderly government because the fundamental causes of the conditions of unrest may be economic, political, or social. These conditions may have originated years ago and in many cases have been permitted to develop freely without any attempt to apply corrective measures. An acute situation finally develops when conditions have reached a stage that is beyond control of the civil authorities and it is too late for diplomatic adjustment. The solution of such matters being basically a political adjustment, the military measures to be applied must be of secondary importance and should only be applied to such an extent as to permit the continuation of peaceful corrective measures.[141]

Negotiations can be even more useful if this can lead to a quick achievement of the political aim desired, though one should be cautious about ceasing to apply military pressure during negotiations, as this can be interpreted as weakness. This is dealt with in more detail in the next chapter.

Insurgent or insurrectionist groups can be broken into two types: patriotic partisan resistance movements and revolutionary

movements. Patriotic partisan resistance groups usually begin spontan-
eously in the wake of an enemy invasion and then become more
organized. The Free French Resistance against the Nazis during the
Second World War is a famous example. Resistance doesn't end until
the invaders are expelled or the insurgents are convinced they can't
achieve their aims. Because they are usually directed at an invader,
such movements can have larger bases of support than revolutionary
movements because their appeal is broader.[142] Clausewitz studied and
planned such efforts and offers what he calls "Conditions Under Which
a General Uprising Can Succeed":

1 The war must be fought in the interior of the country.
2 It must not be decided by a single stroke.
3 The theater of operations must be fairly large.
4 The national character must be suited to that type of war.
5 The country must be rough and inaccessible, because of mountains,
   or forests, marshes, or the local methods of cultivation.[143]

   The second type of insurrectionist group – revolutionary
movements – have ideological or religious foundations. In the modern
era, they have most often been Marxist in character, though Islamic
State and other similar groups represent religiously driven
cousins. Mao Tse-Tung's Communists are the most famous and
among the most successful. These movements usually last until the
enemy government is toppled or the rebels killed.

   Though the motivations of these groups differ, they have many
things in common. But one must remember that no two insurgency
conflicts are alike, because no two wars are alike.[144] Indeed, one of
the errors in counterinsurgency can be taking lessons from one conflict
and applying them to another when they don't fit.

   Guerrillas sometimes have decentralized organizations, and local
leaders can have great control over the operations in their areas. The
leaders of the *wilayas*, or zones, of the FLN insurgency in Algeria possessed immense autonomy.[145] This is an advantage for the guerrillas if the
local leader is both good and aggressive. But if the insurgency is leader-
driven, this can be fatal if the leader or leaders are killed. The destruction
of the Sri Lankan insurgency demonstrates this.[146]

   The rebels (or guerrillas) depend heavily upon intelligence
because their survival often hinges upon having an information edge.
They make use of every man, woman, and child in areas under their

control, and often pressure citizens to produce useful information on the enemy while controlling information about themselves. The result is that the guerrillas generally have information superiority, allowing them to choose their points of attack. These attacks tend to be quick, especially in the early stages, and they tend to fight only when things are heavily in their favor. If they're losing an engagement, they usually withdraw. Their war is one of striking quick and hard, then disappearing. Their objective is not necessarily the enemy's armed forces, but his will and the mind of his leaders.

What most term "guerrilla warfare" and "terrorism" are the primary violence tools that insurgent groups use to get what they want. Terrorism is considered a tool of the weak, though it is conceptually flawed and limiting to view it this way. The North Vietnamese Communists commonly used terror against South Vietnam, but they were not weak in comparison to their South Vietnamese opponent. Some groups (such as the early Russian anarchists) went so far as to believe that terror alone would be enough to incite the masses and bring down the hated regime, though most realized this very unlikely.[147]

There are many definitions of terrorism, but one of the best is this: "terrorism is the intentional use of, or threat to use, violence against civilians or against civilian targets, in order to attain political aims."[148] Terror is used to obtain a political aim, but the point is not the death and destruction it generates: this is the visual result that is part of an effort to attack the target's spirit while simultaneously creating fear, thus driving the target to make political changes.[149]

Terrorism is also often mistakenly called a tactic. One of the reasons for this is a failure to understand the differences between tactics and strategy. For the Algerians who launched the 1954 uprising against France, terrorism was a strategy, not a tactic. Terror against civilians was intended to provoke a heavy French reaction which would drive people into the rebel camp.[150] Terrorism was a plank of North Vietnam's strategy against South Vietnam. It helped undermine and destabilize the South Vietnamese government while driving people to support the Communist cause or face the murder of themselves or their families. It was a primary element of Islamic State's warfighting strategy. The confusion here is that observers see the tactical application of violence in the form of car bombings or assassinations and then insist that terrorism is a tactic. This overlooks the concepts driving the tactical execution.

This brings us to one of the problems of countering groups using terrorism: this is not a job that should automatically be given to police forces, as some insist. Terrorism is a tool of insurgent organizations – for insurgent *armed* forces – and police often are not prepared and equipped to deal with them. Indeed, police are usually the target and victim, because, to the often better-armed, -trained, and -equipped insurgents, they are soft targets and representatives of the regime the insurgents oppose that can be easily killed and injured, thus demonstrating the reach of the insurgent forces, discrediting the state, and undermining its authority in the eyes of the people. Indeed, if the police cannot even protect themselves from insurgent terror attacks, how can they protect the local farmer, teacher, or businessman? Sometimes terrorism is indeed a policing problem, and one cannot deny the utility of effective policing and skilled intelligence-gathering by police forces in a fight against groups using terrorism. But leaders should be careful that they are using the right tool for the right job.[151]

Terror also doesn't always work. During the Malayan Emergency (1948–60), it drove people away from the insurgency.[152] Islamic State gained much through the use of terror, but this also helped bring the US, France, and other nations into the war. Also, the counterinsurgents must work to ensure that they are not blamed for enemy acts. This can be difficult. The FLN successfully pinned one of their 1957 massacres on the French, and US forces in Iraq unfairly received the blame for a 2004 Baghdad bombing.[153]

Successful insurrectionist movements make great use of distraction and deception. They seek to draw the enemy to one thing while attacking another. Deception, maneuver, flexibility, concealment of their true purpose – these are the attributes of successful guerilla operations. Counterinsurgency theorist John J. McCuen argues that for the revolutionary to win they must take Mao's advice and wage a "strategically protracted war" and 1) wear down the enemy's strength through the cumulative effects of combat; 2) get stronger by gaining the support of the people while establishing base areas and taking needed material from the enemy; and 3) obtain outside support – political and especially military.[154]

Dispersion of insurgent forces is necessary because of their weakness. If they concentrate, they easily can be destroyed. Moreover, because they usually work in small packets, they are difficult to eliminate and can operate in the enemy's rear. This also makes the guerrillas seem more numerous than they really are. The insurgents build a shadow government, sometimes behind a puppet leader. They also seek to "win converts from the restless youth whom they bombard with propaganda, train, and add to their political agents or guerrillas."[155]

The counterinsurgent always wants a quick war and is too often surprised by the reality that counterinsurgency takes a long time and is almost always protracted. Scholars differ on how long insurgencies last, as there are so many different variables involved in calculating this, most of which are very difficult to control. Six to eleven years is not unusual.[156] Counterinsurgency expert Robert Thompson wrote: "If one tries to talk about speed in pacification, it must be remembered that it will take as long to get back to the preferred status quo ante as it took the other side to get to the new position."[157]

There are many factors that contribute to the length of an insurgency – material and psychological – on both sides. Sometimes the counterinsurgent simply doesn't understand the task facing them. Theorist John McCuen wrote: "Winning a revolutionary war will take massive organisation, dedication, sacrifice and time. The government must decide early if it is willing to pay the price. Half-measures lead only to protracted, costly defeats."[158] Insurgency theorist David Galula believed that one of France's greatest problems in suppressing the rebellion in Algeria was "The political instability in France and the absence of a firm, continuing, clear-cut policy on the part of the various French governments all through the war." The counterinsurgent must have a clear aim that it keeps in sight and a coherent program that impresses upon the opponent that the counterinsurgent is "acting according to a well thought-out plan that leaves them no room for maneuvering." The French, despite the experience of their wars in Indochina and Algeria, never possessed a coherent counterinsurgency doctrine.[159] Historian Jeffrey Record aptly observed that, for the counterinsurgent, "the combination of a weaker political will and an inferior strategy can be a recipe for defeat."[160]

A Typology of Insurgency and Counterinsurgency

Critically, when there is an insurrection or an insurgency *both sides* must strive to control the following three key factors: 1) the support of the people; 2) the control of internal or external sanctuary by the insurgents; and 3) whether or not the insurgent has outside support. If the insurgent secures all three of these, this will likely mean victory for the rebels. If the counterinsurgent force controls these factors, it will probably win.

I   The Support of the People
        Winning the support of the people is crucial for the results of the insurrection. They are "the key to the entire struggle," and their alienation from their rulers can be a source of insurrection.[161] This is not always the case, though, as groups such as the Chinese and North Vietnamese Communists worked to alienate the people from their regimes, but the people are still the key. Mao Tse-Tung wrote: "Because guerrilla warfare basically derives from the masses and is supported by them, it can neither exist nor flourish if it separates itself from their sympathies and cooperation."[162] The challenge for both sides lies in determining how to win them to your camp while keeping them from the other side, or at least ensuring their neutrality.

        The means issue in wars of this type is often a sticking point. One of the great mistakes made by counterinsurgents is to believe that they can win cheaply and use minimal force to do so. One must always use a level of means *sufficient* to obtain the political aim. Sometimes a small force is the answer. The level and intensity of the insurgency will reveal this. But one of the most common errors of counterinsurgents is to not send sufficient force quickly enough. McCuen writes: "The sooner the governing power reacts, the less will be the resources required and the shorter will be the period in which they have to be applied ... Remember, that the most serious – and the most common – error in counter-insurgency warfare is to do too little too late."[163] The *Small Wars Manual* advises that "when forced to resort to arms to carry out the object of the intervention, the operation must be pursued energetically and expeditiously in order to overcome the resistance as quickly as possible."[164]

        Unfortunately, this is often easier said than done, and sometimes it's not the whole answer. In an effort to quell the 1954 Algerian revolt, the French eventually put large numbers of troops on the ground. They mobilized reservists, extended the mandatory service time of conscripts, and committed elite units such as the paratroopers and the Foreign Legion, all to try to ensure they had sufficient forces to provide security as well as hunt down the insurgents. The French eventually destroyed the bulk of the insurgent force in Algeria, but this did not ultimately deliver victory. Numerous other factors, such as the existence of external sanctuary and support, succored the Algerian cause.[165]

When the insurgency began in Iraq in 2003 against the US and allied forces, the US had insufficient troops on the ground to exert control over Iraq and hunt down insurgents. Indeed, the US never got a handle on the situation in Iraq until it increased its own troop numbers, stood up large numbers of Iraqi police and army units, and armed anti-Al Qaeda Sunni tribesmen. Quickly dispatching larger numbers of troops earlier – and better military and civilian planning and leadership – might have prevented some of these problems, or at least made it possible to stabilize Iraq sooner.[166] The US should have remembered the advice of its hard-won past experience. The *Small Wars Manual* advised: "The occupying force must be strong enough to hold all of the strategical points of the country, protect its communications, and at the same time furnish an operating force sufficient to overcome the opposition wherever it appears."[167]

Gaining an understanding of the depths of the insurgency is also critical. One reason the British initially suffered failure in Malaya was that the Communist insurgency had already metastasized. It had begun during Japanese occupation in the Second World War and had been supported by the British. By the end of the war in 1945, it was well developed and had deep roots in the countryside. By 1951, the insurgency reached its peak strength of 10,000 active members, but also had more than 100,000 supporters.[168] A similar thing occurred in South Vietnam. The famous soldier and writer Bernard Fall determined that in South Vietnam the evidence of Communist penetration could be seen in the assassination of village chieftains, the failure of the South to collect taxes in a district, and the success of the Viet Cong in taxing the area. Six months before the 1963 murder of South Vietnam's president, Ngo Dinh Diem, between March and May 1963 the Communists were collecting taxes in forty-two of forty-five South Vietnamese provinces.[169] The insurgency had metastasized *before* the US escalation. This makes the counterinsurgent's job much more difficult, though not impossible. More time, effort, and sacrifice will inevitably be required.

Winning back a population under insurgent control can be difficult. In *Small Wars*, Callwell advises keeping the enemy under constant pressure, but this can only be done by first properly preparing. To do this, he essentially argues for a version of what the French called *quadrillage*. The theater is divided into sections that include outposts for defense; these are supported with fast columns pursuing the insurgents. The size of the sections is based upon the geography and terrain. These zones are further subdivided so as to systematically strip them of the food supplies necessary to the enemy and methodically clear them of guerrillas. Troops should be moved from less troublesome to more difficult zones, a decision made based upon local conditions. The concept dates at least to the French Revolutionaries' efforts to suppress the 1793 uprising in the Vendée.[170]

There are many similar ideas that seek to restore government control and separate the insurgents from the people. One is population resettlement. This famously worked wonders in Malaysia, where the primary source of the insurgency's manpower – the ethnic Chinese minority – could be resettled in protected villages. The US and South Vietnamese launched a similar plan, known as the strategic hamlet program. The results were mixed, partly because of South Vietnamese failures in implementation of the program, and partly because the majority Buddhist South Vietnamese had ancestral ties to their land and resented being moved.[171]

Totalitarian states also do clearing operations and remove populations sympathetic to or susceptible to insurgent influence, but democratic states generally intend to co-opt the people, while the authoritarians usually punish them. Stalin's forced population removal of minorities that might prove disloyal, as well as his wholesale murder of the population in places like the Ukraine, made it exceedingly difficult for an insurgency to emerge. Displacing the population by mass deportations, or mass importation of sympathetic populations, such as the Chinese Communist practice of moving Han Chinese into Tibet, is another way of controlling the situation.[172] This, though, can produce resentments that create problems.

A related point is that one of the factors upon which the guerrillas can sometimes count is the self-restraint of the counterinsurgent when dealing with the civilian population. One cannot make a blanket statement here, but this is generally a rule of behavior among democratic states conducting counterinsurgency.[173] This does not apply to totalitarian states. The Russians used essentially unrestrained military power to prevent the insurgents from establishing themselves among the population in Ukraine in the post-Second World War era and Chechnya in 1999. The Syrians acted similarly against the Muslim Brotherhood in the 1980s. In Chechnya, the Russian response convinced many Chechen leaders that it was impossible to resist. This allowed the Russians to co-opt them and shift the burden to local security forces. Such brutality can have effects that are, to some, counterintuitive: "Paradoxically, collective punishment has at times turned the population against the rebels, who are blamed for the devastation." This has sometimes been the reaction of civilians in the Syrian Civil War who blame the rebels for Assad bombing them.[174] It is not so easy to predict the reaction of the population to violence in such circumstances. It seems to boil down to the harsh issue of whom the people fear the most.

How counterinsurgents should use force is a critical issue and will directly affect the direction in which the population sways. Killing the leaders of insurgent groups often increases the chances of a government victory and reduces the level of insurgent violence. The government rarely suffers any negative effects as a result of this, and it's "likely to be more effective than capturing them." The more the group is dependent upon the leader, the greater the effect. Killing insurgent leaders, though, does not guarantee success. This is particularly true if the group has a developed bureaucracy and popular support. Some studies have found that killing the leaders of terrorist organizations becomes less effective if the group has existed for more than twenty-five years.[175] As is so often the case, the result depends upon the circumstances.

One question is whether the counterinsurgent should concentrate on killing the insurgents or winning over the population through other means. The answer is usually both. But what is also critical is establishing the rule of law, which is especially important for underpinning the credibility of the counterinsurgent. Insurgents exploit the contradictions in governance, law, land ownership, minority rights, or whatever else gives them an edge.

Insurgency expert Otto Heilbrunn boils down the counterinsurgent's use of force:

> To sum up: security operations will produce dividends only if the police and members of the population co-operate; the terrorists' hold over the population is thus broken, and the security forces have a good chance to win the hearts and minds campaign. If this co-operation cannot be obtained, the security forces are unlikely to win. Military operations can only immobilise the terrorists, and their hold over the population will probably

continue; while counter-terror can lead to the terrorists' arrest but strengthens the people's allegiance to the terrorists' cause.[176]

If one is a foreign state conducting counterinsurgency in another land, this adds another layer of difficulty, especially if the uprising is fueled by nationalism.[177] The Algerian War provides an example. The French viewed themselves as protecting part of France, but the bulk of native Algerians saw them as an alien force.

The quality of governance can sway the people and is critical to consider, especially if one is conducting counterinsurgency in another state. If the host nation suffers from bad government, the counterinsurgency effort is less likely to succeed. This doesn't mean it can't, but one must assume the difficulty increases by an order of magnitude. American diplomat George F. Kennan wrote in February 1948: "You can help any government but one which does not know how to govern." One reason George Marshall refused to allow the post-Second World War US mission to China to expand and assume the same roles as the advisory mission to Greece – meaning allowing US advisors to give tactical and strategic advice – was because Marshall believed US advisors could exert influence over Greek leaders more readily than they could China's head, Chiang Kai-Shek. Rightly or wrongly, many of Truman's advisors believed the Nationalists lost their civil war because of Chiang's "inability to govern."[178] If the decision is made to provide assistance, it must be appropriate. When advising, it is wise to remember Lawrence of Arabia's Article 15: that it is better they "do it tolerably than that you do it perfectly."[179]

It is critically important to find the source of the governing problem. Is it internal to the government itself, or external? Internal problems run to the obvious: weak, oppressive, or corrupt leaders are common, as are problems in the system itself. Sometimes the need for reform is obvious, and there is a general failure to address this. Here, it is important to determine whether or not the problems are self-generated, and if the regime has a willingness to address them. Unfortunately, it is too often the case that governments simply fail to understand the conditions in their own country. This can make them weak and susceptible to internal attacks.[180] Addressing political, economic, and other grievances can be a useful tool for ending an insurgency, as rebel groups often exploit these. Doing so removes points around which insurrectionists can rally support.

What is sometimes forgotten here is that at least some of the governing problem may be external, because the country is suffering from subversion or the effects of the insurgency. For example, during the Vietnam War there were obvious problems of corruption and incompetence in the South Vietnamese government that dramatically reduced its effectiveness. But the South's governance capability was seriously undermined by the North Vietnamese insurgency's constant propaganda and physical attacks upon the Southern regime as the Communist North conducted an extensive campaign of assassination and kidnapping against Southern officials. This drastically increases the problem of governance while discrediting the regime, which is the point of the activity as the insurgents establish a shadow government to replace the state's rulers. Counterinsurgency theorist Bernard Fall observed in regard to Vietnam: "When a country is being subverted it is not being outfought: it is being out-administered."[181]

The counterinsurgent should remember to treat prisoners well. If not, this can have negative effects upon their relations with the people. Don't be afraid to treat them under the rules of the Geneva Convention if this is necessary to maintain internal or foreign support. One can certainly add the caveat that this does not mean recognition of the political legitimacy of the opponent, but that this is being done for administrative reasons and to demonstrate integrity to the international community. Exert public pressure upon the insurgents to do the same, though this will undoubtedly fail, because the insurgents, especially smaller groups, usually lack the willingness or ability to act according to any international norms. Mao argued for the good treatment of prisoners as a way to win them to his cause. But the Communists also never shrunk from using any form of violence they believed useful. Another option is to treat counterinsurgents as criminals. One then faces the problems of criminal prosecution and all this entails. Sometimes though, this might be the best solution. This will be determined by the circumstances. Don't be afraid to give amnesty to insurgents if this will end the war on acceptable terms, and if you can bear the domestic and international political costs of doing so.

A harsh truth is that the counterinsurgent cannot fight as the insurgent fights. Their aims are different, which dictates what each side can and must do to achieve its goals. The guerrilla often holds the initiative, and often "has the freedom of his poverty."[182] Robert Taber writes:

By contrast, the purpose of the counter-revolutionary is negative and defensive. It is to restore order, to protect property, to preserve existing forms and interests by force of arms, *where persuasion has already failed*. His means may be political in so far as they involve the use of still more persuasion – the promise of social and economic reforms, bribes of a more localized sort, counter-propaganda of various kinds. But primarily the counter-insurgent's task must be *to destroy the revolution by destroying its promise* – that means by proving, militarily, that it cannot and will not succeed.[183]

One problem is that counterinsurgents become so concerned with the tactical issues that they do not see the larger picture. Indeed, some examinations of counterinsurgency argue that counterinsurgency is largely a form of tactics.[184] David Galula observed that it was hard to alter the way the French Army defined success. Leaders were judged upon their results, meaning the number of enemy "killed or captured, not by the number of schools opened by the Army in his zone." Thus, they were more interested in military operations.[185]

Critically, both sides will try to win over the people through propaganda or information operations. This is an arena where the counterinsurgent is often weak. Galula criticized the French effort in Algeria by noting: "If there was a field in which we were definitely and infinitely more stupid than our opponents, it was propaganda."[186] This same argument has been made regarding US information operations against Islamic State.[187]

2 Controlling Sanctuary

This was, of course, addressed in the previous chapter. But it is critical to touch upon it here in a minor way. For the insurgent, who is usually weaker than the regime he opposes, or, in the case of the North Vietnamese, weaker than the primary ally of its opponent, possession of sanctuary for its government and its military forces is a vital component for building toward success. For the counterinsurgent, removing insurgent sanctuary, both foreign and internal, is critical. One of the primary reasons the Afghan Taliban could continue its war against the US after 2003 was its possession of sanctuary in Pakistan.

The political aims will, of course, affect sanctuaries, as well as where the war will be fought.[188] This acts as a constraint upon military activity, particularly on the part of the counterinsurgent, who historically restricts where its military forces will fight by placing sanctuary countries off limits, or, such as in the case of the British in the War for American Independence, simply lacks sufficient forces to control enough territory to effectively remove the sanctuary. One observer notes this post-Second World War truth: "The respect for sanctuary has been carried to an extraordinary extent in twentieth-century limited war."[189]

The loss of sanctuary can be fatal to insurgents. The post-Second World War Greek Communist insurgents lost bases and support from Yugoslavia's Tito after his 1948 rift with the Soviet Union. Moreover, the Greeks learned to do counterinsurgency, addressed economic issues, and had much US support.[190] With UN help, South Korea isolated the battlespace, and, in Operation Ratkiller (the South Korean anti-guerrilla operation), killed 20,000 insurgents and bandits by the end of January 1952.[191] Mao's "Long March" allowed him to construct a sanctuary in the Chinese hinterland, and though the Japanese invasion also contributed to the survival of Chinese Communism, the ability to create and preserve a safe base also proved instrumental. The possession of sanctuary in China – and Chinese aid – proved critical to North Vietnamese success against the French. Sanctuaries in Tunisia and Morocco did not prevent the French from essentially destroying FLN forces inside Algeria, but it did permit the FLN to build an army as an international symbol of resistance. The Tamil Tiger rebels in Sri Lanka had no sanctuary and no external ally. When the Sri Lankan forces penetrated into their heartland and killed the rebel leader, the movement was destroyed.

One of the great benefits enjoyed consistently by the North Vietnamese Communist forces was sanctuary. As rebels against France, they had external sanctuary in China when needed, as well as internal sanctuary in many parts of what is now northern Vietnam. When the US began fighting the North Vietnamese conquest of South Vietnam, the Communist forces benefited from external sanctuary in North Vietnam, Laos, Cambodia, and parts of South Vietnam. This gave the North the ability to dictate the momentum of the war, the timing of their attacks, a relatively secure line of supply via Laos, and safe areas for refit and resupply in Cambodia.[192] The US inability to control the battlespace under such constraints meant that it could not protect pacification efforts from North Vietnamese attacks, which was important for ensuring their success, especially against a deep-rooted insurgency.[193]

3   Controlling Outside Support

Something that most successful insurgencies have in common is external assistance.[194] Mao agreed.[195] This can be material and political, with material usually, but not always, being the more important. The insurgents generally strive to secure this, and with good reason. They are almost always weak in comparison with their enemies, and external assistance can give them arms, money, critical diplomatic recognition, and so many other things they need to succeed. The counterinsurgents must separate the insurgents from outside support. This can be as critical as separating the insurgents from the people, which also must be done.

Insurgent movements can win without outside support, but it's difficult. The Bolsheviks fought their way to success without external help, securing their victory in 1921. In their 1919–21 war, the Irish Republican insurrectionists succeeded in gaining most of what they wanted from Britain without significant outside support. Mao Tse-Tung's Chinese Communists received outside support from the Soviet Union near the end of their struggle against the Nationalists, but this, arguably, speeded up rather than determined their success. Their possession of capable, resolute leaders, their ability to successfully appeal ideologically to the Chinese people, and the weaknesses of their opponent contributed greatly to the Communists winning.

Without external support, defeat is the more likely result for the insurgent. The Confederacy failed to achieve its independence partially because Abraham Lincoln helped ensure Great Britain and France didn't join the war on the side of the rebel South. The Malaysian Communist insurgents (1954–62) had no outside help and did not succeed. The West Papuan Independence movement against Indonesia has not succeeded, despite many years of resistance; it has no outside support. The mid nineteenth-century Taiping rebels had no foreign support, while the Chinese government received Anglo-French aid that helped it achieve victory. The failed 1857 Indian revolt also had no foreign support. The 1967 Biafran revolt in Nigeria was quickly crushed because the Biafrans' sea links were cut. This made foreign aid impossible.[196] The American colonists triumphed over Great Britain, but the intervention of France and Spain – particularly the former – proved decisive. The Vietnamese Communists won against France in 1954. Chinese aid (and sanctuary) proved critical. Soviet and Chinese support also contributed greatly to the North Vietnamese victory over the US and South Vietnam. The Algerian insurgents triumphed even after suffering the near total destruction of their forces in Algeria because of international political support.

Defining Victory in Insurgency and Counterinsurgency

Defining victory here depends upon what one is seeking. The political aims of the insurgents differ from those of the counterinsurgents. Usually, for the rebels, the control of their own state counts as victory. This was certainly the view of the Algerians and Mao's Communists. For the counterinsurgent it's not so simple. Galula points out that "counterinsurgency seldom ends with a ceasefire and a triumphal parade."[197] He also observed:

> What constitutes victory in this sort of war? When does pacification end? My personal answer can be stated this way: victory is won and pacification ends when most of the counterinsurgent forces can safely be withdrawn, leaving the population to take care of itself with the help of a normal contingent of police and Army forces. It is therefore necessary to make the population participate actively in the counterinsurgent effort, to mobilize it in the struggle.[198]

The bottom line in counterinsurgency: will the people support the government? If not – one should consider quitting.

Conclusion

The above has touched on a large number of issues often in only a cursory manner. It presents only a framework for beginning an examination of strategy and should be considered an introduction to the topic. A knowledge of history and a creative mind are among the most important things that political leaders and soldiers can bring to the construction of strategy. And they should not think themselves beyond repeating the mistakes of their predecessors.

But they must also consider how to end the war and secure the peace. If the strategy developed has produced success, or the opposite has been the result, it will be time to end the war. This is the final step, and perhaps intellectually the most difficult.

6 AND YOU THOUGHT THE WAR WAS HARD: ENDING THE WAR AND SECURING THE PEACE

There is only one result that counts: *final victory*.[1]
Carl von Clausewitz

Introduction

Perhaps the most difficult part of waging a war for a limited political aim is ending it. During the First Iraq War, a number of the Bush administration's members realized they needed a plan for ending the war.[2] President Bush himself had thought about this and was not unaware of the potential difficulties:

> We've got to find a clean end, and I keep saying, how do we end this thing? ... You can't use the word surrender – the Arabs don't like that apparently. How do we quit? How do we get them to lay down their arms? How do we safeguard civilians? And how do we get on with our role with credibility, hoping to bring security to the Gulf?"[3]

General Colin Powell had read Iklé's *Every War Must End*, the premier book on this subject, which someone gave him right before the war began. He was so impressed by Iklé's ideas, particularly his discussion of how little thought leaders give to actually ending wars, that he had pieces of the book photocopied and given to Cheney, Scowcroft, and the members of the JCS. Powell wrote: "We were fighting a limited war under a limited mandate for a limited purpose, which was soon going to be achieved. I thought that the people responsible ought to start thinking about how it would end."[4] Representatives from the State Department discussed this with their opposite numbers in Britain, and Schwarzkopf's staff included an expert in war termination. Bush's Special Assistant, Richard Haas, supplied Bush and Scowcroft with a memo on the subject. Despite all of this, in the end the administration failed to prepare for what they knew was coming.[5]

Entering a war can be quite easy, especially if one is attacked. Getting out – particularly for the United States since the end of the Second World War – can prove far more difficult. Ending wars is something the US has forgotten how to do, a failure for which it has paid a heavy price, especially since 2003. Iklé observed in 2005: "It is crucial, therefore, that the United States and its friends relearn the rules for ending a war with strategic foresight and skill so that the hard-won military victories will purchase a lasting political success."[6] Iklé understands the point of it all: winning the war and securing the peace. Critically, he denotes the difference between a military or battlefield victory and victory in the war itself, meaning the achievement of one's political aim. Battlefield success in a war fought for a limited aim has no meaning unless one secures it via a formal agreement.[7] It is rare that writers or politicians make this deadly and important distinction. Moreover, Liddell Hart warns us: "If you concentrate exclusively on victory, with no thought for the after effect, you may be too exhausted to profit by the peace, while it is almost certain that the peace will be a bad one, containing the germs of another war."[8] We must win the war. But we must also win the peace.

The failure to understand all of this and to pursue wars to a clear end has thrust the US into an era of seemingly permanent war.[9] At the time of the revision of this book in 2022, the US had been at war in at least one country since 2001. The fact that it suffers from permanent war makes it even more critical to relearn how to terminate a conflict – preferably with a victorious result.

We begin with this foundational point: *wars fought for limited political aims are almost always ended via a negotiated settlement.*[10] This is not an absolute, because you can never be sure what the enemy will do, but it is close. Since the war won't end in regime change and thus the imposition of your will upon the opponent, negotiations will undoubtedly ensue. Also, if you find you can't achieve your aims, negotiations can provide a path out of the war. Nevertheless, historically almost no one plans for this before entering the conflict and usually during it. Why is one issue examined below.

We must also remember that the war's ending will be disorderly, chaotic, violent, and that there could be as many different endings as there are combatants.[11] The Treaty of Versailles that followed the First World War is well known, but most are not as familiar with the fact that there were many other agreements signed between the various combatant powers.[12] Moreover, this disordered process can produce problems that lead to future wars.[13]

War Termination: What It Is – And What It Is Not

As always, we first must define the terms of our discussion. In regard to war termination, the late Michael Handel concluded: "All that it can logically imply is that war has been stopped – it does not inevitably entail conflict reduction or resolution. We must therefore conclude that war termination is a necessary but not sufficient condition for peace, since the discontinuation of hostilities does not necessarily include positive progress towards peace."[14] Analyst William Flavin speaks of "the formal end of fighting, not the end of conflict," which is both clear and succinct.[15] We must remember that ending the fighting (though it might end the war) is not the same as codifying a secure peace.

In the nineteenth century, there were certain internationally understood terms related to ending a war. A temporary stay in the fighting of a day or so in order to exchange prisoners, bury casualties, and even negotiate a more extended pause was known as a "ceasefire" or a "suspension of arms." When combatants agreed to an "armistice" or "truce," such agreements might cover the theater or the war itself. They could have a time limit, or not, and were often a step toward negotiations to end the war. The one-sided laying down of arms by fortresses, armies, or even regions could be classified as "capitulations" or "surrenders," but any agreement made by and between the military leaders directly involved could be rejected by the political leaders if they felt these crossed beyond the military commanders' purview. US President Andrew Johnson famously overrode Union General William Tecumseh Sherman's May 1865 agreement with his Confederate counterpart, Joseph E. Johnston.[16]

The term "war termination" should not be used interchangeably with the misbegotten "exit strategy."[17] The latter implies getting out of the war – usually in defeat – and usually because the side searching for an exit is no longer willing to continue the struggle. This also does not mean that the war has ended in a clear way, though it likely will, as the side not choosing to "exit" might be in a position to achieve victory.

With the above as a starting point, we can equate the use of the term "war termination" with an armistice (or a ceasefire), which is intended generally as a temporary agreement to stop the fighting. None of these is a synonym for a peace agreement, though sometimes it can end up substituting for one, usually unintentionally. It is not always possible to bring the warring parties to formally conclude the war (most likely because of the costs involved or the intransigence of an ideologically driven totalitarian state). In these cases, an armistice that ends the fighting might be the best result one can achieve. The US signed an armistice in the Korean War in 1953 and one with Saddam Hussein's Iraq in 1991. These ended the fighting but did not lead to formal peace settlements.

Ideally, what "peace" means is defined in a written agreement signed by representatives of the various warring parties or states. This is not necessarily a peace that both sides *like* (an ideal rarely achieved), but the best peace both sides can *accept*, and – hopefully – that lasts. This often proves difficult, which is part of the reason we number our world wars and the US wars in Iraq. Why is addressed below.

Clearing the Deck

Before discussing the difficulties involved in concluding wars for limited political aims, we must first resolve some ancillary issues that in more thoughtful eras were self-evident: 1) that victory is important, and 2) that wars should end.

The Issue of Victory

General Douglas MacArthur is sometimes ridiculed for having said "There is no substitute for victory." But he was indeed correct. People and states fight to achieve something or to defend themselves. One must not ignore the critical moral effects of the importance of seeking *military* victory, as well as victory in the war itself, upon the soldiers tasked with obtaining it and the people at home who must labor and suffer in support of the war. One author notes: "To ask a man to risk his life and the lives of his men in order to take a hill on the way to 'victory' is one thing; to ask him to do so in a conflict where he is constrained from pursuing clear-cut victory is a very different thing."[18] Peoples fight to win as well. Their support becomes increasingly critical if the war becomes protracted. Losing this can bring defeat just as quickly as losing a battle. Moreover, people do not like to sacrifice if there is no prospect of victory – in battle or in the war itself. Military victory – properly utilized – can deliver political victory. In wars fought for limited political aims it is only possible to achieve a political victory in the absence of military victory when the opponent is weak or naïve. *Victory matters.*

Why is this important? Victory – and its opposite, defeat – are clarifying.[19] Victory, as French author Raymond Aron reminds us, is only one step on the road to peace.[20] Moreover, victory in the war itself – not just on the battlefield – is also a political act.[21] Whether one wins or loses is the critical factor in determining the war's political effects.[22] We must not forget that we should go to war to win – not to lose or achieve a stalemate. Victory costs. Defeat costs more.

How should we define *victory*? The sixth-century Byzantine general Belisarius said: "The most complete and happy victory is this: to compel one's enemy to give up his purpose, while suffering no harm oneself."[23] This is a thought with which Sun Tzu would agree, as his ideal is to "take all under heaven" (preferably intact), and to do so without fighting.[24] These are certainly ideal types one should strive to reach, but returning to basic principles is the most practical for our purposes. Victory is achieving the political aim or aims for which one is fighting, whether these are offensive or defensive, and hopefully at an acceptable cost. Unfortunately, too often since the Korean War US and Western political and military leaders and intellectuals have forgotten that victory matters when one goes to war. Victory – winning – is the point of the war.[25]

Despite the obviousness of this, the foreign relations and limited war literature is rife with examples of an insistence upon not winning. A 2006 book notes: "Again and again over a half century, events have belied American statesmen, who believe that victory is an archaic concept, and that military pressure must be carefully graduated to 'send signals' for securing specific objectives."[26] The more uninformed discussions even stress the danger of pursuing victory,[27] a bizarre insistence one won't find among those against whom the US has fought wars. If you aren't trying to win, you're trying to lose, and you're killing people while doing so. The enemy *wants* to win. One hopes that Putin's actions in Ukraine after 2014, Bashar al-Assad's in Syria since 2011, and the Taliban's 2021 victory proved this to Western leaders and intellectuals who think otherwise.

The earliest example of this sentiment I've discovered appeared in 1951 during the Korean War. What makes this particularly surprising is that the author, a US Navy Captain, US Naval Academy graduate, and veteran of the Pacific War, was at the time working at the office of the Chief of Naval Operations and had a connection with the National War College. Moreover, his work was published by *Proceedings*, the official journal of the US Navy. He wrote: "The subject of this essay is an unpopular one: *not winning*. This is not the same as losing. It means fighting a limited war to a draw. In limited war circumstances, victory can no longer be cast in the traditional mold. We cannot aspire to 'win' in the historical sense of annihilating the enemy." The author failed to realize that, in war, not winning is the same as losing. Nor does he realize that one can indeed decisively defeat (or annihilate) the enemy to achieve limited political aims. He then insists that "[i]n practical terms, it [a limited war] can mean fighting to a draw. It can mean fighting with one hand tied behind our back. It implies indecisive fighting, sparring, uneasy truces with the issues still unresolved."[28] As we've seen in the preceding chapters, such problems are generally self-imposed and the result of poor leadership. This author is hardly alone.[29]

The flawed thinking of the 1950s remains with us. This 2013 example of the depths to which US thinking on war has fallen comes from a veteran of more than two decades in the US foreign service. He not only discounts the idea of "victory," but also criticizes US leaders for attempting to achieve it. He insists that "studies of American warfare are too 'victory centric.'" It is better, he essentially insists, while confusing the tactical and the strategic, to lose the war than to try to win it.[30]

Why do we have common propagation of views that conflict so intensely with the history of human and state behavior? The Cold War is certainly part of the problem, especially its related and not unfounded terror of a nuclear war. The muddled thinking surrounding these fears (which we addressed earlier), produced such advice as: "In limited war 'winning' is an inappropriate and dangerous goal, and a state which finds itself close to it should immediately begin to practise restraint."[31] Political scientist Robert McClintock wrote that because of nuclear weapons, "The question of military 'victory' enters the equation with increasing reservations. The emphasis becomes one of survival. A peace without victory might be tolerable, but a peace without survival would be meaningless."[32] Liddell Hart gave us something similar.[33]

The concern is understandable, but these theorists allowed their fears of a possible future to undermine their coherency of thought in regard to their current military challenges. The unintended effect of their flawed theorizing was to infect Western strategic thinking with a fear of victory, one that has continued into the post-Cold War era. Others see here a manifestation of post-modern self-loathing, one driven by fears of being seen as triumphal in regard to one's own nation and people. In the US one can add to this the fear of being seen as traditionally patriotic. Theorist Edward Luttwak writes: "The West has become comfortably habituated to defeat. Victory is viewed with great suspicion, if not outright hostility. After all, if the right-thinking are to achieve their great aim of abolishing war they must first persuade us that victory is futile or, better still, actually harmful."[34]

The most grievous passage I've discovered along this line serves as the perfect transition, as it reveals the result of the cumulative intellectual errors in Western limited war theorizing. This author – political scientist John C. Garnett – uses as a starting point an inaccurate critique of General Douglas MacArthur's views that demonstrates a misunderstanding of the difference between the end sought and the means and methods being used to achieve it. He wrote that MacArthur:

> was one of many soldiers who have found it very difficult to get used to the idea that the object of limited war is not to destroy the armed forces of the enemy, but to communicate with their political masters, to bargain with them by means of a violent, physical dialogue, to engage in what Schelling calls "coercive diplomacy" and "tough bargaining." In an important sense, conventional limited wars are not about winning at all. They are about not losing, and fighting in such a way that the enemy will prefer either a compromise peace or a continuation of the fighting to escalation to the nuclear level.
>
> Because winning is a dangerous goal for both sides, one might expect limited wars either to drag on for many years, or

to end in a compromise peace which was satisfactory for neither side but bearable to both.[35]

This quote encapsulates the many problems examined earlier in this text: not understanding the reality of war; the confusion of ends and means; not understanding the underlying dominance of the political end being sought; the use of force as "signaling"; the failure to understand that victory matters; all viewed through a nuclear lens that is often irrelevant. The last paragraph explicitly reveals the result of the accumulated bent concepts in our "limited war" ideas: permanent war.

Why Ending a War Matters

We are forced to discuss the seemingly obvious good of bringing a war to an end because Western leaders (and US leaders rank among the worst offenders) no longer understand that wars should end – successfully. If a state is willing to fight a war but not willing to try to win it, what can arise is a state of permanent or protracted war. We have forgotten a basic truth that Alexander the Great attributed to Aristotle: "The ultimate object of war is a stable peace."[36] Similarly, Liddell Hart observed that "no nation engages in war, offensive or defensive, without the idea that it will end in a better state of peace."[37] Generally, both sides want a more secure position than they possessed before the conflict.[38]

Why do we have permanent wars? And what are the results of this? The first reason these occur we have discussed above: US leaders no longer value or understand victory. Second, the fact that modern, liberal democracies use very small forces generally composed of volunteers means that the conflict directly affects a tiny percentage of the population. This means that the costs of the war are generally born by those most willing to sacrifice and to serve. Public support for these wars is thus easier to preserve. It does not mean that America's wars are not without political risks for its leaders. George W. Bush's Republican party was pummeled in the 2006 mid-term elections because of the failures of his administration in Iraq. This gave his Democratic Party political opponents an issue to use against him.

There are also many other unfortunate results arising from permanent and protracted wars. Sun Tzu defined them succinctly and warned of war's potential to fatally weaken the state: "When your weapons are dulled and your ardor damped, your strength exhausted and treasure spent, neighboring rulers will take advantage of your distress to act. And even though you have wise counsellors, none will be able to lay good plans for the future." He insisted that "there has never been a protracted war from which a country has benefited."[39]

The counterargument, of course, is that you may be a weak power, usually an insurrectionist one, and may need to protract the war in order to win. The Americans in the Revolutionary War, Mao Tse-Tung's Communists in China's civil war, and the Vietnamese Communists are three successful examples of this. But all of these powers eventually made peace and waged their wars with clear political aims in mind.

International relations expert Audrey Kurth Cronin identifies one of the many problems that emerge as wars prolong: "means become ends, tactics become strategy, boundaries are blurred, and the search for a perfect peace replaces reality." Her example of the Obama administration's increased use of drones perfectly illustrates this point. President Obama extended his tactical control even further by personally selecting the individuals being targeted for assassination.[40] This is the Vietnam War's failed Rolling Thunder bombing campaign *redux*, a lesser version of McNamara and Johnson picking bombing targets.[41] President Obama noted the problem of perpetual war in a May 23, 2013 speech, and even called for the repeal of the 2001 Authorization for Use of Military Force (AUMF) under which many post-9/11 US military actions have been conducted. Neither President Obama nor the Republican-controlled Congress made a serious effort to address this issue.[42]

It is obvious that new thinking is needed on how to end wars and secure the peace, particularly in wars for limited political aims, as they do not generally end with the enemy prostrate. The examination of the complex issues surrounding ending wars for limited aims in the next section is followed by a methodological approach for tackling the problems.

Ending a War for Limited Political Aims: The Nature of the Problem

The most important fact to remember here is that wars fought for limited political aims are nearly always ended by negotiations rather than the complete defeat of the enemy. *Every piece of the war-termination puzzle flows from this*. As we've seen, inflicting a complete defeat on the enemy can indeed be a viable method for winning a war fought for limited aims, but this is not the norm. Moreover, these wars can be harder to terminate because there may be no clear winner, and they are dominated by the constraints discussed earlier.[43]

Ending the War: Some Effects of a Failure to Prepare

The ending of a war is something for which combatants almost never plan – even if they are aware of the need to do so. Before attacking the US and Great Britain in December 1941, the Japanese discussed the necessity of ending the war, but never came to a clear answer regarding how. The Japanese military hoped a change in American public opinion would somehow bring an end, but they lacked the strength to force this.[44] Clausewitz speaks of the importance of this issue, especially when a war is becoming increasingly bloody and intense. The last sentence of the relevant passage is the key one:

> Theory, therefore, demands that at the outset of a war its character and scope should be determined on the basis of the political probabilities. The closer these political probabilities drive war toward the absolute, the more the belligerent states are involved and drawn in to its vortex, the clearer appear the connections between its separate actions, and *the more imperative the need not to take the first step without considering the last*.[45]

The 1990–91 Gulf War shows us what can happen in the endgame when one has not heeded this advice. When the time came to negotiate a ceasefire, Schwarzkopf and Powell discussed having the talks on the deck of the battleship *Missouri*. "I wanted to make it obvious that this meeting was a surrender ceremony in everything but name," Schwarzkopf wrote later. But this they ruled out because they had too little time to prepare and bring the delegates from the various nations to a ship in the Gulf.[46]

Instead, Schwarzkopf chose the Iraqi air base at Jalibah, 95 miles inside Iraq, because having it on Iraqi ground symbolized their defeat. It was also easy for the Iraqi delegates to reach. But the site proved too dangerous, because of unexploded ordnance, and Schwarzkopf then chose Iraq's Safwan airfield near the Kuwait border. Schwarzkopf had ordered the nearby crossroads taken the day before and had been told it had been done, but was then informed the US did not hold the airfield and had no forces nearby. He ordered VII Corps to get to the site. A show of overwhelming American force convinced the Iraqi commander holding Safwan that discretion was the better part of valor, and Schwarzkopf ordered a horde of combat vehicles to be deployed in fighting positions to show the Iraqi representatives what they faced.[47]

The Iraqi delegation chosen to negotiate the ceasefire had problems getting through areas already controlled by the growing rebellion and had to be escorted by Republican Guard tanks. One member of the security detail was wounded on the way. Saddam had instructed them to go to the negotiations "with the feeling and spirit of the victorious."[48] The Iraqis were represented by a pair of three-star generals that Schwarzkopf had never heard of. There was concern in Washington about the Iraqi representatives, but it was decided that if Lieutenant General Sultan Hashid Ahmad headed the Iraqi delegation and also held sufficient authority from his government, he was acceptable. Schwarzkopf and Saudi Prince Khalid bin Sultan, the commander of the Arab coalition forces, sat across from the Iraqis. A number of representatives from various coalition nations observed.[49]

Earlier, Powell had had Schwarzkopf work up the terms of the ceasefire. He sent these to Powell, who told him they had to be reviewed by the Departments of Defense and State, as well as the White House. Approval and transmission to the Iraqis via Moscow followed. The terms included: the return of POWs and the remains of those killed in action; the location of Weapons of Mass Destruction (WMD) sites; a demarcation line between the forces so there were no accidents; and a Saudi request for confirmation of Kuwaiti and Saudi sovereignty and other issues, such as the return of around 3,000 Kuwaiti men whom the Iraqis had taken hostage.[50]

The meeting began at 11am, March 3, 1991. Schwarzkopf orchestrated the scene, and the Iraqis essentially accepted the US terms and a version of what the Saudis wanted. The ceasefire line was the only initial sticking point. This was inside Iraq, and the Iraqi generals only bent on this when they were assured it was temporary and did not mean a change of the borders. At the end, Schwarzkopf asked if the Iraqis had any matters to raise. The Iraqis asked to fly helicopters to move their officials inside Iraq. Schwarzkopf wrote in his memoirs: "It appeared to me a legitimate request. And given that the Iraqis had agreed to all our requests, I didn't feel it was unreasonable to grant one of theirs." (One should never feel obligated to grant an enemy's request.) Ahmad then asked if this included armed helicopters. Schwarzkopf told him it did. This became one of the most controversial issues to come out of the conference, and Schwarzkopf tells us why: "In the following weeks, we discovered what the son of a bitch had really had in mind: using helicopter gunships to suppress rebellions in Basra and other cities."[51] Schwarzkopf and others later argued that the twenty to twenty-four intact divisions that Saddam possessed in Iraq were more important.[52]

First – and critically – the Bush administration had no plan for ending the war.[53] As we saw above, this had been discussed but no one acted on the concern. Second, Schwarzkopf received very little guidance from his political superiors before he went into the ceasefire meetings. He also made very little effort to obtain any.[54] The following from Schwarzkopf's memoir is interesting:

> If need be, I would go to Safwan and wing it. For one thing, the talks would be limited to military matters, and I understood what needed to be done; for another, our side had *won*, so we were in a position to dictate terms. Even so, I knew I'd feel better walking into that meeting tent with the full authority to speak for the United States. If I had to take a hard line, I'd be much more convincing if I could say, "the United States insists" rather than "Schwarzkopf insists."[55]

Yes. The US had "won" – on the battlefield. But Schwarzkopf forgot that the war was still going on. Negotiations are a part of the struggle. They are not detached from it. Going in unprepared is not helpful. Moreover, dictating terms is not so easy if you are not willing to continue using force or if the leaders of the enemy regime are not particularly sensitive to the effects upon their people and nation of their refusal to agree. It is unfortunate that Schwarzkopf was not aware of this caution from Clausewitz: "To bring a war, or one of its campaigns, to a successful close requires a thorough grasp of national policy. On that level strategy and policy coalesce: the commander-in-chief is simultaneously a statesman."[56] Ending the fighting, and ending the war itself, are simultaneously political *and* military issues.

Conversely, the Russo–Japanese War of 1904–05 offers a rare glimpse of an effort at planning the war's end. Before launching their struggle, the Japanese decided they would ask the US to mediate its conclusion. They dispatched to Washington Kaneko Kentaro, who had attended Harvard University with President Theodore Roosevelt, with the mission of convincing Roosevelt to negotiate the war's end at the right time. He had also been sent to cultivate American popular support for Japan.[57]

But even such forethought does not guarantee success. The Japanese pre-war plan to have Roosevelt mediate worked perfectly. But the Japanese negotiating position at the talks to end the Russo–Japanese War was weakened by the fact that they did not continue to make military gains after their victory at Mukden. Very aware of earlier Japanese aggressiveness, Russian officials read the lack of this as a sign of Japanese exhaustion and thus inability to push any further. The Japanese could not keep the Russians from seeing Tokyo's weakness. Japanese civilians rioted after the terms of the treaty were revealed, as they expected more and were particularly upset by the absence of an indemnity.[58]

In some respects, this nearly universal historical failure to prepare for the end of a war is understandable. The overwhelming pressure of fighting a war inhibits nations from seriously considering how to end it.[59] Sometimes the policymakers realize that they need to decide how to end the war, but then don't act on this. In the 1990–91 Gulf War, President Bush pondered this on a number of occasions, noting on January 15, 1990: "I have trouble with how this ends. Say the air attack is devastating and Saddam gets done in by his own people. How do they stop? How do we keep from having overkill?"[60]

There is also the reality that sometimes war is thrust upon you with no chance to plan for its termination before it begins, or you are simply too weak to see a way out. This is especially true for small powers forced to defend themselves from bigger ones. In such cases tough resistance can provide time for the situation to change and open routes out of the conflict. Such was Finland's case in the face of the 1939 Soviet invasion. Hard fighting preserved Finland's independence.[61] But this did not mean they got the peace they wanted. In 1940, the Finns journeyed to Moscow hoping to negotiate, but received no choice but to sign – unchanged – a treaty drafted by the Soviets.[62]

The Decision to End the War: Timing and Negotiations

The decision to end the war is driven by myriad factors, not all of which are necessarily rational.[63] If you convey to the enemy your fear that the cost of victory is too high, the enemy can conclude you're not willing to do what is necessary to stave off defeat.[64] Related to this is the key issue of whose side time is on in the negotiations. In other words, whom will delay help the most?[65]

In all of this one must be careful to understand the issue of the timing of the end of the war and the inevitable negotiations that will ensue regarding the cessation of combat as well as the war itself. The decision regarding when to open negotiations is exceedingly complex and depends upon innumerable factors being weighed by both sides: military success – or the lack thereof; whether or not one combatant, or both, feels that the moment for talks has arrived; a fear that this moment may pass;[66] and any other factor related to the current situation.

Critical to the timing of negotiations is awareness of the motivations and conditions of the opponent. One author reminds us that "[i]n an era when limited wars fought to secure limited goals are the norm, a vital component of any strategic vision is a clear idea of the conditions that will cause the enemy to abandon the fight and reluctantly accept a new status quo on our terms."[67] Information on this, of course, is often very difficult to obtain, and we should be careful in being overly harsh with criticism of those handed the difficult negotiating task. One should make the utmost effort to try to understand the opponent's political aims, ideology, motivations, and the myriad other factors driving their decision to negotiate. One must always ask: why are they here? What do they want? What is their psychological and physical state? Sun Tzu provides us some excellent advice:

> When the enemy's envoys speak in humble terms, but he continues his preparations, he will advance. When their language is deceptive but the enemy pretentiously advances, he will retreat. When the envoys speak in apologetic terms, he wishes a respite. When without a previous understanding the enemy asks for a truce he is plotting.[68]

Sun Tzu's comment reveals that negotiations are a weapon.[69] This is something the Communists always understood, and they used negotiations as a propaganda tool and a sword as early as the 1917 Bolshevik Revolution. During the Korean War, Li Kenong, the leader of the Communist delegation, instructed his colleagues to remember that negotiations were a form of fighting and that they were "political battle." Li also pointed out that "the truce talks could not be separated for even one second from the situation on the battleground," and ensured that the Communist negotiators were kept closely apprised regarding the military situation because they could not make truce terms if they did not understand the military situation.[70] A North Vietnamese general explained their approach in 1965: "Fighting while negotiating is aimed at opening another front, at making the puppet [South Vietnamese] army more disintegrated, at stimulating and developing the enemy's contradictions and thereby depriving him of propaganda weapons, isolating him further, and making those who misunderstand the Americans clearly see their nature."[71] When negotiating with the enemy, Saint Augustine suggests something worth remembering here: "it is not that they love peace less, but that they love their kind of peace more."[72]

The decision to negotiate is fraught with dangers and problems. Sometimes one must overcome the resistance of one's own government, people, or military forces to negotiate. During the French–Algerian War, there were secret contacts between French Socialist Party representatives and the Algerian rebels, the FLN. This was not unusual, as other governments, those of Ireland and South Africa for example, had avenues of communication with groups they branded "terrorists." The French government's approach was predicated on the belief that when the war ended negotiations would follow, but the government of Guy Mollet and its predecessors wanted to negotiate only from a position of strength.[73] Negotiating – even unofficially – with the FLN, though, caused problems for France. When this became public knowledge, it strengthened the leaders of the FLN forces in Algeria, made its Muslim population reticent to support France, and angered French military and political figures striving to win over Algeria's Muslim inhabitants.[74] Negotiating in such a situation can forecast weakness, even if one knows that such talks are inevitable. Some may feel betrayed by secret talks, while others have to be brought along. The negotiators, as representatives of the people, and thus their will or opinions, must keep this in mind. This is especially true in liberal democracies, as public opinion can have more effect than in non-democratic states where it is tightly controlled.

Some oppose any negotiations while the fighting continues, and there can be good reasons for this. Leaders may fear this undermines the morale of their forces or encourages their people to lessen their effort, because they believe the war could end soon. The enemy might see weakness in negotiating or offer terms difficult to reject that do not deliver the desired aim. They also might fear tensions with coalition partners over even the idea of negotiating. The Second World War agreement of the Allies to accept only unconditional surrender from members of the Axis coalition was intended to help forestall alliance problems.[75] One should also consider the role of outside pressure.[76]

The reluctance of the population or the military to support negotiations can be overcome partially by the continual portrayal of this as normal and desired. The Finns constantly negotiated with the Soviets during the 1939–40 Russo–Finnish War, as well as what the Finns call "the Continuation War" of 1941–44. India and Pakistan carried out talks in Tashkent during their 1965 conflict without injuring their war efforts or support from their respective populations. It is not wise to condemn all negotiations when you are fighting a war that will likely be ended by them. Iklé notes that "[t]he very stubbornness with which government leaders sometimes oppose negotiating while fighting induces an adverse reaction at home and among the troops, once talks with the enemy have become unavoidable."[77]

Public opinion certainly plays a role in negotiating the peace. In the First World War, the French and British governments had promised their people Germany would bear the cost of the struggle. This made their peacemaking efforts more difficult. Public pressure helped drive the US to terminate its struggle in Vietnam. The absence of pressure from public opinion enabled the North Korean and North Vietnamese governments to ignore the suffering of their respective peoples while negotiating.[78]

There are, of course, many approaches to take to negotiations, and whether one is a combatant or a third party seeking to resolve the conflict will influence what you should or should not do. An experienced third-party conflict negotiator once commented that two things can be particularly toxic in negotiations. First, never give or inflict upon the opponent a sense of or the experience of humiliation. Humiliating them can contribute to making the peace unstable. Second, the negotiator insisted, never ask: "What is your solution to the problem?" Patience is important, and linked to this is giving the parties a chance to say everything they believe is important.[79] The exception to this rule is when it is apparent that the parties are merely stalling for time, or they are simply using the negotiations for propaganda. The Chinese example during the Korean War springs immediately to mind.

One can also certainly wait too long to negotiate a peace. Such was the German situation in the First World War. By the time Berlin decided it could stomach a negotiated settlement, their military and strategic position had deteriorated so much that they had no leverage over their opponents.[80]

Imposing time limits for the length of the negotiations can be worthwhile – particularly if the opponent is obviously stalling – as sometimes this can be useful for bringing matters to an end. Kissinger suggested this as something that might have broken the negotiation stalemate in Korea.[81] French Premier Pierre Mendès-France successfully imposed a time limit on the negotiations for ending the French Indochina War. He took office on June 17, 1954, and promised the resignation of his government if there was no deal reached by July 20, 1954. This worked because Mendès-France prepared for a successor to send more troops to Indochina, and the Vietnamese knew that any government that followed his would be more hawkish.[82] Former US Senator George Mitchell, when helping negotiate what became known as the 1999 Good Friday Agreement as part of the peace process in Northern Ireland, eventually gave the sides a date by which he needed to end his involvement in the talks.[83] But one must be careful doing this. Mitchell had earned the trust of both sides and was a neutral party. When one is directly negotiating and there is no interlocutor, the situation is completely different. A time limit can still be useful as a demonstration of seriousness and a counter to obvious stalling and dishonesty, but it can also be a catalyst or excuse for walking away from the table. Also, what if the other side won't agree? Can you then unilaterally declare a time limit without suffering the collapse of the negotiations? As in so many instances, the answer is: "It depends."

The issue of timing of negotiations must be considered from the flipside as well. If you are winning and the operational momentum is on your side and the picture improving, stopping to negotiate might be a bad decision, because it can rob you of the chance to put the enemy into a position where they have no choice but to make peace. The Korean War gives us an excellent example of this.

As we mentioned briefly at the beginning of our story, one of the most contentious decisions of the Korean War was the US agreement to negotiate with the Communist forces in the early summer of 1951. As we've seen, the US and UN forces had successfully repulsed the various Chinese offensives, inflicting heavy losses upon their opponents and severely weakening the Communist forces. The operational commander, Lieutenant General James Van Fleet, believed the Communist forces were ripe for destruction, an assessment supported by other high-ranking US officers, such as Chief of Naval Operations Admiral Forrest Sherman, and important commanders in Korea, such as X Corps commander Major General Edward M. Almond, 1st Marine Division head Major General Gerald C. Thomas, and the naval forces chief and later head of the US negotiating team Vice Admiral C. Turner Joy.[84]

Van Fleet saw an opportunity. He believed that combining a land offensive with an amphibious invasion behind the Communist lines at Tongchon, south of Wonsan on the eastern shore of the Korean peninsula, would allow the encirclement and destruction of the retreating Chinese forces. Moreover, it would allow UN forces to establish a defensive line across the narrowest part of the peninsula stretching approximately from Pyongyang to Wonsan. His commander, General Matthew Ridgway, would not allow the operation and restricted Van Fleet to seizure of what the US command designated as the Wyoming and Kansas lines, which lay about 20 miles beyond the 38th parallel.[85]

Ridgway objected for several reasons. First, the offensive went against the guidance he had received from the Joint Chiefs of Staff (JCS) on May 1 because it was beyond the Kansas–Wyoming line limit. This meant he needed to consult the JCS, and that would likely lead to other important administration figures being brought into the process. This would take much effort and time. Second, rumors of an impending ceasefire seemed to make it unnecessary, especially as they might have to give back any ground taken: a slow, steady advance would be sufficient to provide a defensible line during the UN negotiations. Third, the move would stretch some forces too thin, and he believed all of them were tired and needed a rest. Their discussion of the issue ended on May 25.[86]

Van Fleet believed that from May 22 to June 10, 1951 the UN had the opportunity to crush the Chinese forces. "We had him beaten and could have destroyed his armies," he insisted in a 1953 article. But the US failed to act and thus squandered its immense advantage. After June 10, Van Fleet believed, the Chinese were too well dug in.[87]

Van Fleet was indeed correct about the weakness of his opponent. At the end of May and in early June 1951, their eroding military position began frightening the Chinese. They feared they would be pushed back to the Pyongyang–Wonsan line, and also fretted about another amphibious invasion behind their lines. Mao adopted a strategy of limited attacks and seeking a ceasefire via negotiations. Talks between Kim, Mao, and Stalin ensued during the first two weeks of June, and Stalin gave his permission to seek an armistice. Moreover, by this time the US had stopped its advance and made it clear that its leaders also wanted talks.[88]

Truman first announced his desire to negotiate in an April 11, 1951 radio address.[89] American diplomat George F. Kennan met with Jacob Malik, the Soviet representative to the United Nations, on Long Island on May 31 and again on June 5. Ridgway was told that negotiations were in the wind.[90] The first public call for an armistice came from Malik on June 23 and was followed by a statement from Soviet Deputy Foreign Minister Andrei Gromyko on June 27. On June 26, Secretary of State Dean Acheson had said before the House Military Affairs Committee that the US "military objectives in Korea would be satisfied if the Communists withdrew north of the 38th Parallel and gave adequate guarantees against renewal of aggression."[91] The UN ruled that the US could negotiate an armistice without further UN approval. An agreement was also made to negotiate via the military commanders. The US military leaders were reluctant to take the job, but Truman told them to do so. Ridgway was instructed "that the chief interest of the United States was to end the fighting and to obtain assurances that it would not be renewed." He was to stick to military matters aimed at doing this, not political matters that dealt with the fate of Korea (this is an important distinction). Truman then authorized Ridgway to broadcast to the Communists that word had been received that the Communists wanted an armistice. Ridgway did so on June 30, telling the Chinese that if they were interested in negotiations for a ceasefire or an armistice, he was willing to begin talks. They replied to Ridgway on July 1, and eventually agreed to meet at Kaesong on July 8.[92]

Not everyone was happy with this decision. South Korean President Syngman Rhee resisted the talks (he still wanted unification). Van Fleet remembered him saying: "When the truce talks began in July of 1951, he warned they were a trick to save a defeated enemy. That has turned out to be precisely true."[93] The head of the UN armistice delegation, US Vice Admiral C. Turner Joy, had this firmly demonstrated to him on July 12, 1951, when Ridgway forbade the UN delegates to return to the talks at Kaesong until the Communists agreed to honor their commitment to remove military forces from the meeting area and stop interfering with the movements of the delegates. Joy wrote: "Their urgent need for a breathing spell left the Communists no choice except that of acceding to General Ridgway's just demands for equity at Kaesong."[94]

There was also resistance in Washington to the US initiating a truce. In a June 28, 1951 meeting, General Hoyt Vandenberg, the Air Force Chief of Staff, opposed Ridgway, sending a message along these lines to the enemy command. Vandenberg said "that the drain of hostilities was now beginning to tell on the Communist forces and that we should in no sense be put in the position of suing for peace at this point or stopping the fighting just when it was beginning to hurt the other side." The White House supported a truce approach, and the State Department had been working for this diplomatically for a number of months. General Omar Bradley, the JCS chair, believed that the US public's support for the war and that of its allies would be weakened by a failure to take what looked like a chance to end the war by not taking up the Soviet proposal. He said that this did not mean the US was suing for peace.[95]

Criticism of the decision to halt and negotiate has been intense: Henry Kissinger, Bernard Brodie, Raymond Aron – all insist this was a mistake.[96] The Chinese force was certainly ripe for destruction, as Van Fleet insisted. Mao recognized this and wanted a two-month pause (June and July) in order to prepare for the renewal of offensive operations in August. Mao, in a note to Kim Il-Sung, wrote: "If the enemy does not make large-scale amphibious landings in our rear, then our goal can be achieved. If the enemy does not send new reinforcements and does not make an amphibious landing, then in August we will be significantly stronger than now."[97]

Bernard Brodie observed: "We paid bitterly for that error in the great prolongation of negotiations, in the unsatisfactory terms of settlement, and, above all, in the disillusionment and distaste which [the] American people developed as the main emotional residue of their experience with limited war."[98] Moreover, as political scientist Fred Iklé pointed out, "More Americans were killed during the two years of truce negotiations than during the first year of the war before negotiations started. Among all the United Nations forces, fatalities during the negotiating period were about double those suffered previously."[99] The US would have benefited from heeding Sun Tzu's aforementioned advice to be suspicious of your enemy's motivations for agreeing to talk.[100]

The above demonstrated the importance and difficulty of planning for the ending of the war, as well as various issues surrounding negotiations and their timing. The next section puts us on a path toward a better understanding of what to consider when preparing for this difficult task, and gives us some guidance on how to tackle the challenge.

The Key Questions

Those facing the difficult task of ending any war – especially a war fought for limited political aims – must keep in the forefront of their minds these three critical questions:

1 What is being sought politically?
2 How far must or should one go militarily to achieve this?
3 Who will maintain the peace settlement, and how?[101]

The variety of factors in play around each of these is simply overwhelming, but that is part of the reason for making the effort to address them systematically. Moreover, *these issues are inextricably intertwined*. This is not a checklist where one crosses off each completed task sequentially. The forces related to all three are at work *simultaneously*.

1   What Is Being Sought Politically?

We start here because this is what the war is about, the why of the war. Clausewitz tells us: "The ultimate object is the preservation of one's own state and the defeat of the enemy's; again in brief, the intended peace treaty, which will resolve the conflict and result in a common settlement."[102] Remember the value of the object. The nation has gone to war to defend its threatened interests or to achieve something deemed politically necessary. The war will eventually arrive at a point where one or both sides wish to end it. Ideally, your aim has been achieved. But this is not always the case. It may have become apparent that one cannot achieve it. Perhaps its cost has exceeded its value, or maybe one is facing defeat and *needs* to end the war. If one combatant does not want an end, they must be convinced to change their mind. Force, threats, and promises are the primary means. Some of these must sometimes be applied to allies because they may have different views about ending the war and the myriad issues involved.

Combatants must not only know their own political aim, *they must also have fixed in their mind what victory looks like.* Or, in other words, how they believe the post-war situation should appear. The existence of coalitions complicates this, because it can be difficult to have all the "victors" on the same page not only in regard to what the settlement should be, but also in how it should be enforced and maintained. If at all possible, settle your respective political aims before the fighting is over. Things are in flux during the war, and you may have allies different from those when the war began. Plan the peace as well as you planned the war. British and American experts devoted a lot of time in 1942 and 1943 to studying Germany and considering the post-war settlement, but the US did nothing to plan for the end of the 1990–91 Gulf War and its aftermath.[103]

Sometimes it is suggested that one declare victory and leave, and indeed this is an option. But the problem with doing so is that you might fail to achieve or secure your political aim, or you might leave a worse situation both for your interests and in humanitarian terms. For example, on January 2, 1933, the US Marines departed Nicaragua. The US terminated its six-year intervention by declaring that it had left the foundations of a democratic government (which had been determined via elections), and a National Guard force that was non-political and that thus would ensure further elections would also be free. The US had failed to completely eliminate Augusto César Sandino's guerrillas, but with the onset of "the Great Depression," the US was in a cost-cutting mindset and simply decided "to declare its intervention to have been successful." A year later, General Anastasio Somoza, the head of the National Guard, took over Nicaragua and ruled it until his assassination in 1956.[104] On a similar note, after previously rejecting the Versailles Treaty signed with Germany after the First World War, the US Congress unilaterally declared it was at peace with Germany in July 1921.[105]

Another element affecting the issue of what to ask for politically is that one's coalition partners may have different political aims or have no desire to end the war. This complicates the issue for both sides, and you may have to coerce multiple opponents into making peace while also compelling your own allies to agree. One of the factors contributing to the prolongation of the Korean War was that North Korea's allies and benefactors – Stalin's Soviet Union and Mao's China – saw benefit in continuing the struggle. Stalin found the war a cheap distraction for the Americans that also allowed him to keep the Chinese on a tight leash; Mao found it useful for foreign prestige and to get developmental aid from the Soviet Union for modernization of both his civilian and military structures.[106] Stalin's death likely proved one of the keys to breaking the stalemate in Korea. After a March 18, 1953 resolution, the new Soviet chiefs told Kim Il-Sung that they wanted the war ended. Kim and Mao agreed. It is possible that the war might have soon ended without Stalin's death, as he had decided to make the necessary concessions to do so before his debilitating stroke on March 1 1953.[107]

The Americans faced problems with their allies in both the Korean and Vietnam Wars. South Korea's Syngman Rhee resisted US efforts to negotiate an armistice in 1953 because he did not want the war to stop until the Korean peninsula was fully under the South Korean flag. He went so far as to sabotage the negotiations in an effort to keep the war going. The US brought Rhee into line with promises of support and threats of abandonment.[108] Similarly, in 1972 when the US was struggling to end its involvement in Vietnam, South Vietnam's President Nguyen Van Thieu resisted signing the agreement because it allowed North Vietnam to keep the areas of South Vietnam it occupied and to leave its forces in the South. This essentially meant the surrender of large tracts of South Vietnam to Communist control. Nixon threatened Thieu with abandonment if he did not sign and sweetened the deal with promises of military and economic aid, and a commitment to support South Vietnam against future Northern aggression.[109] The first promise was partially kept, the second was not.

The two Koreas and South Vietnam suffered from the fact that they were smaller and thus weaker powers. Such states involved in negotiating an end to a war are more often than not dependent upon their powerful coalition partner or partners, who may prove willing to sacrifice the interests and even the existence of the lesser powers to make peace. One can see this clearly in the Peace of Nicias during the Peloponnesian War, when Sparta made peace with Athens without consulting its coalition partners and bargained away the freedom of other states. One work advises that "Any small power drawn into peace negotiations with a big-power sponsor is well advised to keep its hands firmly on its weapons. However small its armaments, they are nevertheless more real than any promise could ever be."[110]

In the 1990–91 Gulf War, the primary US political aim was the liberation of Kuwait. There were some others as well, such as protecting US citizens overseas and promoting "the security and the stability of the Persian Gulf," and the expulsion of Iraqi forces from Kuwait was also included.[111] The liberation of Kuwait mattered most. The problem was that once it began to appear that the primary political aim had been achieved, the Bush administration became a bit fuzzy in regard to what it truly sought to obtain politically, as well as how it should obtain it. As America's Korean War experience demonstrated, US policymakers sometimes have trouble keeping their eye on the political aim. In the First Gulf War, US leaders did not repeat the mistake of changing the political aim without sufficiently considering the effects – at least not quite. But their thoughts and actions begin running toward moving from a limited political aim – liberating Kuwait – to an unlimited political aim of overthrowing Saddam Hussein.

After the war, Secretary of State James Baker said in regard to removing Saddam and thus changing the regime that the Bush administration was "careful not to embrace it as a war aim or political aim." But during the war the coalition certainly bombed targets in the hope Saddam was there, which is perfectly understandable, as his death would likely have brought an immediate end to the war. National Security Advisor Brent Scowcroft worried that if Saddam fell, the US would be stuck with a massive nation-building effort and an Iraq that would end up being ruled by "another, perhaps less problematic, strongman."[112] They had certainly considered the possibility of Saddam's removal, and during a January 9, 1991 meeting with Iraqi Foreign Minister Tariq Aziz, Baker delivered a letter from President Bush that made it clear that if Saddam used chemical or biological weapons or destroyed Kuwait's oil fields or related infrastructure, Iraq would "pay a terrible price." Baker also told Aziz: "If there is any use of weapons like that, our objective won't be the liberation of Kuwait, but the elimination of the current Iraq regime and anyone responsible for using those weapons would be held accountable."[113] This commitment even found its way into the document outlining the administration's aims.[114]

On February 15, 1991, before the Iraqis agreed to a ceasefire, and even before the beginning of the coalition ground offensive, President Bush said in a speech that another way to avoid bloodshed

was for the Iraqis to overthrow Saddam. He said later this was something he added "impulsively." This sparked an immediate press frenzy
regarding whether or not the US had added another aim: overthrowing
Saddam. Bush replied that it had not.[115] He repeated his call for the
Iraqis to rebel when announcing the ceasefire talks at Safwan.[116] This
raises a key point: had the US political aim changed? National Security
Advisor Brent Scowcroft later called the first mention of revolt
an "impulsive ad lib" which he believed resulted in President Bush
facing unfair charges that he "had encouraged the Iraqi people to rise
against Saddam and then failed to come to their aid when they did, at the
end of the conflict." A presidential speech is never routine, especially
one concerning a war. Repeating the call, as Bush did later, arguably
demonstrated a deeper commitment to or consideration of the idea.
Scowcroft went on to say:

> It is true that we hoped Saddam would be toppled. But we never
> thought that could be done by anyone outside the military and
> never tried to incite the general population. It is stretching the
> point to imagine that a routine speech in Washington would
> have gotten to the Iraqi malcontents and have been the motiv-
> ation for the subsequent actions of the Shiites and Kurds.[117]

After the war, the Bush administration temporarily insisted that the US
would not agree to the lifting of economic sanctions as long as Saddam
remained in power. This constituted a *de facto* switch to a political aim
of regime change.[118]

So, had the war's aim changed? Or had it become unclear? The
fact that it is difficult to answer this question makes one lean toward
a lack of clarity in the minds of the political leaders. As we've seen before,
this is a problem. If you don't know what you want, how do you make
a peace that will help you get it? Having a clearer vision of what they
wished the end of the war to look like might not have prevented the many
problems ending the war that we see below, because this is such an
exceedingly difficult task, even for a combatant who has been so spectacu-
larly successful on the battlefield, but it certainly wouldn't have hurt.

2   How Far Must or Should One Go Militarily?

When trying to deduce the proper usage of military power for
ending a war one must – as always – keep the political aim or aims being

sought firmly rooted in one's mind. There are, of course, many routes to victory, and Clausewitz gives us a useful list of options for using military force to end a war:

a destruction of the enemy's forces
b the conquest of his territory
c a temporary occupation or invasion
d projects with an immediate political purpose
e passively awaiting the enemy's attacks.

"Any one of these," he insists, "may be used to overcome the enemy's will: the choice depends on circumstances." Moreover, the personalities of leaders and their personal relations add infinite other possibilities for achieving the policy objective.[119]

a   First, the "Destruction of the Enemy's Forces"

We will take Clausewitz's options as he presents them, the first being "the destruction of the enemy's forces." As we have seen, some limited war literature argues against this; some authors even forbid it.[120] But as we've also seen, this is a self-imposed constraint that ignores the reality of warfare, history, and human nature. Destroying the enemy's forces is indeed an option in wars fought for limited political aims, and may be the quickest and least costly means of achieving the political aim. One of the problems with many members of recent generations of US political and military leaders is that they have not understood this. The counterargument is Sun Tzu's insistence that one should not put the enemy on death ground because they will fight harder. What is forgotten here is that Sun Tzu is speaking about a tactical situation. A close reading of Sun Tzu's text clearly reveals that he had no qualms about destroying the enemy's ability to resist if that was what one had to do to win the war.[121]

When do you end the fighting? It can end too soon. Theorist Edward Luttwak insists that "an unpleasant truth often overlooked is that although war is a great evil, it does have a great virtue: it can resolve political conflicts and lead to peace. This can happen when all belligerents become exhausted or when one wins decisively. Either way the key is that fighting must continue until a resolution is reached." He goes on to note that in our present era conflicts among less powerful states are often stopped "before they could burn themselves out and establish the preconditions for lasting settlement."[122] The problem, of course, is what this may mean.

Clausewitz also points out the reality that when using military force, it may not be possible to completely overthrow the enemy. In his discussion of the "culminating point" he reminds us that one can go too far: "Thus the superiority one has or gains in war is only the means and not the end; it must be risked for the sake of the end. But one must know the point to which it can be carried in order not to overshoot the target; otherwise instead of gaining new advantages, one will disgrace oneself." He sums up the potential problem thusly: "Even if one tries to destroy the enemy completely, one must accept the fact that every step gained may weaken one's superiority."[123] Moreover, if you go too far "it would not merely be a *useless* effort which could not add to success. It would in fact be a *damaging* one, which would lead to a reaction; and experience goes to show that such reactions have completely disproportionate effects."[124]

After the success of MacArthur's Inchon landing and breakout from the Pusan Perimeter, the UN forces in Korea pushed to the 38th parallel and stopped. They had – arguably – reached their culminating point. They could hold what they had against any potential counterattack and had decisively defeated the enemy's armed forces. Critically, they had achieved the political aim: securing an independent South Korea. They had won the war. Instead of now securing the peace, and despite a deep – and justified – fear of the conflict's expansion, Truman elected to seize North Korea and ordered MacArthur and his forces north. South Korean forces crossed the 38th on October 1, 1950. US forces followed on October 9.[125] Truman had now passed the culminating point, as he could only hope to hold what he was taking if none of the war's circumstances changed. He also received a form of the potential reaction against which Clausewitz warned in the shape of Chinese intervention.

The First Iraq War presents an example of the counter-problem of a combatant not doing enough militarily to ensure achievement of the political aims. On February 25, 1991, at 9 pm Eastern Standard Time, President Bush made a speech in which he included the ceasefire terms: Iraqi compliance with relevant UN resolutions; restitution for damages caused; the release of all POWs and detainees; and that the Iraqis meet with Schwarzkopf within the next 48 hours. Meanwhile, the coalition forces kept military pressure on the Iraqi forces. On February 27, 1991, in Riyadh, the Central Command (CENTCOM) commander and coalition forces chief, General Schwarzkopf, gave what became known as "the Mother of All Briefings." In his presentation he discussed the ground war and announced that the coalition had accomplished its assigned mission.[126]

Powell and Schwarzkopf had started thinking the end was near and discussed this on February 27. The Iraqis were in full retreat, and the media had begun talking about "the Highway of Death," which was the wreckage of large elements of the Iraqi Army on the highway leading from Kuwait to Iraq. Scowcroft and other administration officials also worried about the international impression created by this. After four days of the ground war, though, Schwarzkopf said he needed a fifth day to ensure that Iraq's military was so degraded that Saddam could no longer threaten his neighbors. When Powell briefed President Bush on the military situation, he said the Iraqi Army was broken and fleeing, and said that he would probably bring a recommendation to stop the fighting the next day. Bush surprised Powell by asking him that, if that was so, why couldn't they end it immediately? Conversations between Powell and Schwarzkopf and Schwarzkopf and his commanders followed. No one objected. The JCS members also supported the president's desire. Bush ordered a stop to the war, but this led to a discussion of the timing.[127]

White House Chief of Staff John Sununu suggested midnight Washington time, because this would make it "the Hundred Hour War." This would be Thursday, February 28, 8am Riyadh time, which gave Schwarzkopf almost the day he had wanted earlier.[128] Calling it "the Hundred Hour War" also had a nice ring to it.[129] Scowcroft later deemed this "probably too cute by half."[130] Many observers have pointed out that this forgets the previous six weeks of intensive bombing.

The bigger issue is the unilateral nature of the US decision, meaning that the enemy was not involved. President Bush wrote: "Eventually I decided it was our choice, not Saddam's; we would declare an end once I was sure we had met all our military objectives and fulfilled the UN resolutions."[131] Moreover, Colin Powell tells us, the US decided to brand it a "suspension of hostilities" in order "to make clear that this was not a cease-fire negotiated with the Iraqis, but a halt taken on our own initiative."[132] The decision to end the war in this manner proved a mistake.

On February 28, the very day of the ceasefire, Saddam said that Bush's unilateral decision proved that the Iraqis had won, a move Bush made because the Iraqi Army was still resisting the coalition. An Iraqi general claimed Bush acted because the coalition started taking casualties and saw it could not achieve its goal of destroying Iraq's military forces and enforcing partition or regime change. That the coalition quit because it was now taking casualties in the ground war found its way into the Iraqi official history.[133] Bush's reaction is worth recounting in full:

> It's now early Thursday morning on the 28th. Still no feeling of euphoria. I think I know why it is. After my speech last night, Baghdad radio started broadcasting that we've been forced to capitulate. I see on the television that public opinion in Jordan and in the streets of Baghdad is that they have won. It is such a canard, so little, but it's what concerns me. It hasn't been a clean end – there is no battleship *Missouri* surrender. This is what's missing to make this akin to WWII, to separate Kuwait from Korea and Vietnam.[134]

Moreover, after the decision to stop the war was made, Schwarzkopf informed Powell that, if they stopped, some of the Republican Guard units and T-72 tanks might get away. Powell wrote: "I told him to keep hitting them, and I would get back to him. I passed Norm's report to the President and the others. Although we were all taken slightly aback, no one felt that what we had heard changed the basic equation." They believed they would have to absorb some criticism for not extending the fight, but Bush stuck to his decision to end it.[135]

Should the US have continued the fighting? The question that immediately follows is: to what end? What do you want the fighting to achieve? Driving to Baghdad and overthrowing Saddam's regime was not an option in the eyes of the Bush administration. The UN resolutions under which the war was being fought did not support it, the coalition would not have survived it, and the administration had no desire to engage in a massive nation-building effort they felt sure would be their task. But continuing the fighting until Saddam's forces were shattered even more was an option that would have helped make possible the Bush administration's desire for the overthrow of Saddam – but it would not have guaranteed it, a fact that is sometimes ignored in this discussion. Continuing the destruction of Saddam's forces would certainly have helped achieve the objective of increasing security in the Gulf, because it would have lessened Saddam's ability to attack or threaten his neighbors. Powell certainly thought this a good idea, something he made clear earlier by his insistence that he wanted to see Saddam's tanks as "smoking kilometer fence posts all the way to Baghdad."[136]

Other critics insist that Bush should have allowed the war to go on until Iraq surrendered unconditionally. But, they argue, since Bush instituted a unilateral ceasefire, it allowed Saddam to maintain his hold on Iraq, because enough of his military machine remained intact. Saddam then claimed victory; he should have never been left in a position to do so.[137] However, the argument for continuing the war ignores the impossibility of achieving Saddam's surrender without – at the minimum – the invasion of Iraq, one that would probably have had to include a drive on Baghdad. The events of the 2003 Iraq War make Saddam's agreement to an unconditional surrender unlikely under any imaginable circumstances.

Others argue that continuing the war would have forced Saddam to admit defeat and possibly sign the ceasefire himself. This is possible. But the Bush administration feared that they could not force him to appear and sign an agreement. They could have been correct, but a push into southern Iraq combined with promises to halt as soon as Saddam signed a ceasefire – or better yet an actual peace treaty – might have encouraged the Iraqi dictator to bend. The terms of the agreement with the coalition did not support a drive into Iraq, but the US forces were already there when Bush called for the ceasefire. The response of Bush and Scowcroft to such arguments was this: "Trying to eliminate Saddam, extending the ground war into an occupation of Iraq, would have violated our guideline about not changing objectives in midstream, engaging in 'mission creep,' and would have incurred incalculable human and political costs."[138]

After the war, Iraq continued to threaten neighboring states, but US National Security Directive 54 of January 15, 1991, declared that one of the US political aims was increasing security and stability in the Persian Gulf. To the then JCS chairman, Powell, accomplishing this required the Republican Guard's destruction. The operational – or military – objectives of the US in the conflict thus included the destruction of Iraq's Republican Guard, Iraqi dictator Saddam Hussein's most important – and most loyal – military force, and one of the props holding him in power. But the US unilaterally stopped the fighting before doing so. Another day of fighting with this in mind could have seen its destruction.[139] One could argue that the US failed to reach the culminating point of victory because it did not destroy Saddam's ability to threaten his neighbors and had to surge troops into the region twice in the next decade.[140] But there were also risks and costs in continuing the fighting, and this should never be forgotten.

In 1968–69, the North Vietnamese fought a number of campaigns against South Vietnamese and US forces that are collectively known as the Tet Offensive. The Communists suffered enormous casualties, including more than 50,000 killed. This saw the gutting of the Vietcong guerrilla force, particularly its critical cadre. The North Vietnamese Army also took a heavy beating, and the North Vietnamese had to reduce their operational tempo.[141] Militarily, the US now had an opportunity to capitalize on the enemy's military defeat and intensify its pacification efforts (which it did), as well as its conventional operations against both the VC and the North Vietnamese Army. But the US soon began unilaterally reducing its troop strength when – arguably – it should have committed more heavily. Now was the best chance the US had of breaking the insurgency, but weakening US public opinion and US President Richard Nixon's desire to extricate the nation from the war meant that the US could not (or perhaps would not) capitalize on the enemy having gone too far.[142]

Sometimes combatants realize they have reached the culminating point even though they are not applying any knowledge of Clausewitz's theory. During the Russo–Japanese War, the Japanese knew after their victory over the Russian Army at Mukden in early 1905 that they could no longer launch significant ground attacks against the main Russian force. The Japanese leaders refused to advance farther into Manchuria and thus suffer more casualties and also assume more risk. Their manpower was exhausted, and the army could at best put another one or one-and-a-half divisions in the field. Japan also now had a war debt of £52 million, and it might become harder to borrow needed funds. General Gentarō Kodama told his superiors that it was time to stop the war, and that, since Japan was in a position to negotiate from strength, it should do so. On April 21, 1905, Japan decided to ask the US to mediate.[143] If the political aim has been achieved, one should make

203 / The Key Questions

peace – if this can be done under acceptable terms – or at least try to, because there is usually no longer any reason to continue the war.[144]

Related to this is a concept known as "the principle of continuity," which means keeping the enemy under pressure until they are ready to make an agreement. As mentioned above, during the Korean War Ridgway rejected Van Fleet's proposal for an offensive against a weakened and withdrawing enemy. Historian Brad Lee notes: "Despite the approach of negotiations with the Communists, he overlooked the urgent need for getting the maximum possible leverage from US military courses of action." It is here that the principle of continuity applied to Van Fleet's situation vis-à-vis the Chinese 1951. Shortly after this, Ridgway did receive permission from Washington to apply more pressure to the Chinese by using his forces, but by then the opportunity had passed and the Chinese were in much better positions.[145] Van Fleet himself balked at launching some operations because the casualties would now be too high.[146] Brad Lee wisely observes:

> Going further may well be necessary to achieve enough leverage to compel the losing side to do the winning side's political will in full measure and for a long time to come; in other cases, it is necessary for the winning side also to get leverage over allies who have a different vision of "a better state of peace." But in all cases going further involves costs and risks. The challenge of political rationality is to weight accurately the possible benefits against the probable costs.[147]

US leaders once had a better understanding of the use of force, even in wars fought for limited political aims. In the Mexican War (1846–48), one could argue that the US "conquered a peace."[148] This war also presents an example of a war for a limited political aim where sufficient force was used to make the enemy prostrate – which had been necessary because Mexico had proven reluctant to quit – and where the victor then presented terms that did not include the complete eradication of the nation. The American Civil War provides another example of a war for a limited political aim where the US destroyed the insurrectionists using overwhelming force while imposing their will on the enemy. There are, of course, immediate reactions to defining the American Civil War as one fought for limited aims, but this is certainly the case, as the Union sought to reclaim its pre-war possessions, while the Confederacy only wanted to rip-off a few states and – in Jefferson Davis' words – "to be left alone."[149]

A drastic increase in the number of forces committed to the fight can affect the enemy politically by giving political space or opportunities to enemy leaders who want peace, or to convince the enemy leaders to opt for peace. A gradual build-up or gradual escalation of force or forces does not usually produce a shift toward peace, because gradual increases are more easily absorbed or countered. However, a small increase in military force might – indirectly – produce change over time via battlefield victory or the implementation of a military stalemate that convinces the enemy to make peace.[150]

b   Second, "the Conquest of His Territory"

Clausewitz advised:

> Even when we cannot hope to defeat the enemy totally, a direct and positive aim still is possible: the occupation of part of his territory.
>
> The point of such a conquest is to reduce his national resources. We thus reduce his fighting strength and increase our own. As a result we fight the war partly at his expense. At the peace negotiations, moreover, we will have a concrete asset in hand, which we can either keep or trade for other advantages.
>
> This is a very natural view to take of conquered territory, the only drawback being the necessity of defending that territory once we have occupied it, which might be a source of some anxiety.[151]

One may not always be able to immediately make newly captured territory reduce the costs of waging the war, but it certainly provides a bargaining chip for peace negotiations. During the Russo–Japanese War, Tokyo seized the Russian island of Sakhalin with this in mind. It was the only Russian territory taken during the war, and its fate played a part in the peacemaking.[152]

c   Third, "a Temporary Occupation or Invasion"

The US temporarily occupied Mexico City in 1848 in order to force an end to the war. Mexico, after its initial battlefield defeats, had refused to fold. Mexican leaders rebuffed negotiation attempts and united around General Antonio López de Santa Anna when he returned from exile. Santa Anna expanded the army and prepared to fight. US President James K. Polk replied with an offensive led by General Winfield Scott. Scott was chosen over Zachary Taylor, who had emerged as a hero because of his victories and was thus a possible political rival to Polk. Scott was given half of Taylor's army and some other forces and told to seize Veracruz and march on Mexico City, winning battles and forcing a peace. Scott's capture of Mexico City resulted in negotiations with a new government that delivered America's political aims.[153]

Some critics of US actions in the First Iraq War suggest that the US should have kept its forces in the areas of southern Iraq that it controlled. During the ceasefire negotiations at Safwan, the Iraqis brought up the presence of these coalition forces. Schwarzkopf promised to evacuate them as soon as possible. He (and his superiors) could have used this as leverage, as the Iraqis so obviously wanted them out of Iraq. This territory also provided a bargaining chip for inducing Saddam to sign a formal peace treaty. The fact that the Iraqi generals resisted a ceasefire line based upon where the forces stood, because they feared it meant surrendering territory, indicates the importance of Iraq's territorial integrity in at least their eyes and probably in Saddam's. Additionally, British Prime Minister Margaret Thatcher had suggested before the war the seizure of the Rumaila oil field and holding it until the coalition recovered the cost of the war and the Iraqis agreed to its other demands.[154]

During the Korean War, US Chief of Naval Operations Admiral Forrest Sherman advised occupying North Korea up to the narrow neck. This would allow the establishment of the shortest defensive line while giving the US and UN forces the southern part of North Korea – including the capital of Pyongyang. This could have been used as a bargaining chip in negotiations with the Communists in exchange for US forces withdrawing below the 38th. Sherman believed holding this ground might even allow the US to dictate terms in order to secure a US withdrawal. This, though, was never tried.[155]

d   Fourth, "Projects with an Immediate Political Purpose"

During the War of 1812, the international environment changed dramatically with the abdication of Napoleon in April 1814. When they were still at war with France, the British fought "to control the American war and the Americans' trade with France." Now they wanted a quick end to the war that came with some territorial gains – especially in Maine – and a western Indian state. Meanwhile, for the US, the maritime issues that had helped produce the war suddenly evaporated with Napoleon's fall. They also abandoned the desire for territorial gains at Britain's expense, meaning Canada. This had never been an official political aim, but it had been the hope and intent of many. Now, both sides fought for chips to play at the peace table. President James Madison needed some means of satisfying the people's sense of national honor. The defensive victory at Plattsburgh demonstrated at least some success after a string of military defeats and failures crowned by the British burning of the White House. The American defensive victory at Baltimore gave Madison another gain.[156]

e   **Fifth, "Passively Awaiting the Enemy's Attacks"**

Here, we are talking about a defensive war, one fought to hold on to what we have. At the end of the Russo–Japanese War, there developed a situation where both sides were essentially awaiting the attacks of the other. Japan had exhausted its army, and its military leaders saw any further advance into Manchuria as disastrous. They were also approaching bankruptcy. The Russians were pouring in reinforcements and soon had 800,000 troops in the region, and many Russian leaders still wanted to fight. But the Russians were also suffering from the outbreak of what became the failed 1905 Revolution and needed their forces for internal security.[157] Tough negotiations for peace followed.

One could also potentially face a situation where it is impossible to secure a peace even after winning militarily. In his recent examination of the problems of terminating a possible future war in the Baltic States between Russia and NATO, one investigating a scenario in which NATO succeeds in driving out the Russians, Lukas Milevski shows that NATO would have almost no ability to convince nuclear-armed Russia to make peace. He points out that "Russia would be thwarted but not defeated and there would be no politically acceptable way of using military force to coerce Russia into acquiescing to defeat."[158]

3   **Who Will Maintain the Peace Settlement, and How?**

The problem with some agreements is that they are seen as temporary expedients and not taken seriously by their signatories. Clausewitz cautions: "Lastly, even the ultimate outcome of war is not always to be regarded as final. The defeated state often considers the outcome merely as a transitory evil, for which a remedy may still be found in political conditions at some later date."[159] The 1954 Geneva Accords and the 1961 agreement to neutralize Laos are great examples of this. The North Vietnamese Communists signed them but never had any intention of abiding by the terms.[160]

One must think about the differences in ending wars fought for limited and unlimited aims. Some argue it is easier to enforce terms such as disarmament with the complete overthrow of the regime and an occupation, and thus this tends to create a more stable post-war environment.[161] Liddell Hart, though, argued that a negotiated peace to which the combatants have not been forced to conform because their power has been destroyed and in which they freely participate (he sees something along the eighteenth-century model) is easier to maintain, and the signatories are more likely to keep the terms because they have agreed to them. If terms are forced upon them, he continues, they are more likely to feel no obligation to maintain them.[162] The truth is that both of these observations are correct. Every peacemaking situation is as unique as every warmaking situation. The variables and their weights are unique to each event. Successful peacemaking may very well require as much creativity as successful warfighting.

There seem to be two key things critical to making a peace work: 1) a formal treaty; and 2) clear and enforceable terms. It would be foolish, though, to assume that these are silver bullets for the problem and the only things one must consider. This is obviously the ideal, but peacemaking is more difficult in a war fought for a limited political aim, because usually one has not completely disarmed the opponent; nor is the opponent necessarily prostrate and forced to accept whatever peace is dictated.

A Formal Treaty: Problems and Promises

One the most famous peace agreements was negotiated at Versailles after the Great War, or, as we now call it, the First World War, which perhaps demonstrates its level of success. French Marshal Ferdinand Foch said of the Versailles Treaty: "This is not a peace. It is an armistice for 20 years."[163] Ideally, one of the things a peace agreement should do is resolve the problems that led to the war (if possible). This is considered by some scholars as the most likely route to a lasting peace but has also been rare since the end of the Second World War.[164] One of the great tragedies of the Versailles settlement is that even the victorious parties did not agree on what issues caused the war. To France, the problem was German aggression; to Britain, it was the collapse of the European balance of power; to the US, it was secret treaties. This was exacerbated by disagreements between the various Allied political and military leaders. This fundamental difference in views multiplied the problems in making peace.[165] It also forces us to recall the previous admonition to coalition partners to have their differences sorted before they have reached this stage.

Obviously, one hopes to make a better peace than the one forged at Versailles. Machiavelli wrote: "If one wants to find out if a peace settlement is stable or secure, one has among other things to figure out who is dissatisfied with that settlement, and what can grow out of such dissatisfaction."[166] Historian Michael Howard insisted that "a war, fought for whatever reason, that does not aim at a solution which takes into account the fears, the interests and, not least, the honour of the defeated peoples is unlikely to decide anything for very long."[167] Peace, though, does not usually satisfy all the winners, and sometimes the terms agreed upon are ambiguous.[168] These are problems one must struggle to overcome.

One critical key to securing a lasting peace is a formal settlement that includes official documents of surrender or peace, whatever the case may be. Done properly, this removes much ambiguity about where power and authority will lie. The victorious Allied powers waged the Second World War for unlimited political aims and not limited ones, but one of the strengths of the conflict's settlement was the Allied insistence on formal acts of surrender from the Italians, Germans, and Japanese, agreements arranged by official representatives from both sides. The US failed to do this in Iraq in 2003, despite the fact that important officials such as Iraqi Foreign Minister Tariq Aziz had surrendered to the Americans.[169] This, though, still might not have prevented the insurgency that followed, particularly that waged by Al Qaeda.

Part of the problem is a historical one. Between 1480 and 1970, wars were as likely to be ended by a formal treaty as not.[170] One result of the decline of formal declarations of war, as well as formal peace treaties to end them, is ambiguity in regard to whether nations are legally at war with one another.[171] This is the situation one hopes a formal peace agreement resolves. But one has to negotiate with the enemy, both to stop the fighting and to make the final treaty. As we've seen, these are different, though clearly related, tasks. Michael Handel suggested that "different types of leaders are needed for the various stages of war termination." The person who negotiates the termination of the fighting is not necessarily the best person to negotiate the war's formal end.[172]

Peace treaties obviously do not mean permanent peace. The vast scope of human history screams against this despite its obvious value. One work insisted "no peace is permanent, and nothing so surely guarantees war as dissatisfaction with contingency and the attempt to establish perpetual peace."[173] Another text argued that there cannot be permanent peace, because there are so many in the world who do not see war as evil – and who will never be convinced that it is – and see in it a positive good. Nietzsche and Homer were among the latter.[174] The ancient Greeks saw war as glorious. The Japanese warrior culture before the Second World War didn't view it as evil. Muslim jihadists believe in war as the means of achieving their dream of a restoration of the ancient Islamic caliphate. One cannot help but argue that the war against Nazism was a definite good. And sometimes nations fight because refusing to do so means annihilation.

It can be to the weaker power's advantage to seek a clear, final peace treaty because it can constrain future actions by its adversaries, particularly democratic ones, since they are more likely to adhere to such agreements. At the end of the 1990–91 Gulf War, the Iraqis could have pushed for an agreement that would have tied the hands of the US in regard to future action. A permanent peace could have made it much more difficult for President George W. Bush to win approval from the US Congress to go to war against Iraq in 2003.

Often, insurrections are not terminated formally, as the sides usually don't recognize one another's legitimacy.[175] This though, is not an absolute, and states often negotiate with insurgent forces to bring about the end of hostilities. The 1919–21 Irish rebellion against Britain, for example, was ended by negotiations.

Ending wars with several powers usually means concluding several treaties. Two treaties signed at Westphalia in 1648 ended most of the hostilities of the Thirty Years War, but there were eleven other treaties made during and after, and the fighting continued another eight years. As we've seen, ending the First World War – a conflict that included seventy-nine bilateral wars – required five treaties signed between 1919 and 1920, but the Kemalist revolution in Turkey prevented the ratification of the Treaty of Sèvres. Peace with Turkey was only concluded in 1924. The Russians concluded a number of separate peace treaties with their various antagonists.[176]

As mentioned above, one must keep in mind that an armistice or ceasefire that stops the fighting is not the same as a settlement concluding the war. Unless the agreement to stop the fighting has a time limit, an armistice can end up being the *de facto* settlement. Moreover, such agreements can mean that it is easy to restart hostilities and almost always lack official political acceptance of their permanence by either side, even if they go on for decades.[177] The 1953 agreement ending the Korean War is an example of an enduring armistice, if not an enduring peace agreement. The First Iraq War concluded in 1991 with a ceasefire but not a treaty. The fighting in the First World War was ended by an armistice, but peace was concluded by a series of treaties. One must remember this distinction when analyzing the conclusion of conflicts.

An armistice (or ceasefire) is not the preferred ending to a war, as it can leave open too many doors for restarting the conflict. The combatants may have different motives for agreeing to the ceasefire, and these motives might not include an actual willingness to make peace. One or both of the combatants may simply view the ceasefire as a means of gaining a pause for rebuilding their strength and preparing for the next round. For example, the Chinese sought, but did not receive, an armistice in Korea in the early summer of 1951 because their army teetered on the brink of destruction. Ceasefires and other provisional endings to wars also generally fail to address what will happen after the fighting ends. They address the fighting, not the political problems. A ceasefire might lead to a political settlement, but it also might not.[178] A question one should consider here is this: has either side decided to abandon their earlier political aim or aims? If so, what now do they want?

Some argue that the losing side should quickly sign an internationally recognized peace treaty so it can be reintegrated quickly into the body of nations. If your domestic political or economic situation is particularly dire, this could very well be the case. But if you are the losing side and there is an armistice in place that has halted the fighting, and you aren't occupied, you should consider delaying as long as possible. "Time," as Clausewitz says, "accrues to the defender. He reaps where he did not sow." He meant the defender in war, but if your military and domestic political situations are firm enough to support it, the loser can delay in an effort to weaken the terms and lower the costs they will incur. Delay may also allow the loser to exploit differences among his coalition enemies.[179] Delay can be more fruitful and have less risk and cost for the loser in a war fought for a limited political aim than an unlimited one – *if* they are not risking their complete destruction, which might be the case if they are fighting a defensive war. There are always exceptions, of course. The risk here is that the terms you get might be worse. But that is why you must understand the situation clearly to weigh the danger of delay in relation to the rewards. An armistice can be an extremely valuable tool if properly exploited.

Another key to establishing a lasting peace is signing an official agreement (or agreements) with *all* of the combatants that include verifiable enforcement mechanisms. This is very easy to say, but exceedingly difficult to do, especially if you are not imposing your will upon the enemy. Formal agreements, though, are critically important for helping establish a lasting peace "in part because they provide an opportunity to specify various enforcement mechanisms that foster trust and increase the costs of defection. More significantly, they are important because they specify who gets what and thereby determine the benefits of peace and the incentives to return to war."[180] Historians Gordon Craig and Alexander George warn of some of the problems here:

> Elements of a peace agreement often lack clarity, suffer from ambiguity, and permit of contradictory interpretations. Sometimes acceptance of such flaws may be necessary if any agreement at all is to be achieved. Some matters dealt with in the peace settlement, therefore, may in fact be in the nature of pseudo-agreements that merely paper over fundamental disagreement and pave the way for future conflict. Or enforcement provisions for key components of the agreement may be so inadequate as to create the likelihood that the settlement will crumble and perhaps entirely collapse at some later point.[181]

Political scientist Paul Kecskemeti argued that "The fullest measure of rationality, however, is represented by those terminal settlements that are mutually acceptable to the parties regardless of the costs and risks involved in rejecting or repudiating them."[182]

Enforcing the Terms

One analyst notes in regard to treaties that nations sign: "If either belligerent expected that the other would not honor the agreement, it is improbable that they would accept the agreement in the first place."[183] This gives us some room for hope. But it does not remove the reality that, for a number of reasons, enforcing treaty terms can be more difficult than actually arriving at them. Strategic analyst Anthony Cordesmann cautions (though one can argue with this) that the US and its allies "need to understand that they cannot control the end state, that conflict termination agreements almost never shape the aftermath of a conflict even when it actually ends, and that the real-world challenges of moving from conflict to stability are far greater and involve far longer time periods."[184]

Among the many problems with enforcing peace terms is that the defeated often don't accept the articles of the agreement they have just signed. When Prussia made peace with Napoleon in 1807, it wasted little time in ignoring the military restrictions placed upon it and conducted a partially clandestine effort to improve its military condition, one in which Clausewitz happily participated.[185] Famously, the Germans cheated extensively on the military restrictions of the Versailles Treaty of 1919. The army developed its armored warfare concepts partially based on clandestine, illegal work with the Soviets, while the German navy secretly built submarines in Finland, Sweden, and Japan.[186]

The arms limitation agreements placed upon Iraq after 1991 and Germany post-1919 were constantly violated by the defeated powers. The authors of one study note: "The absence of a specified tripwire and time frame for compliance in both the 1920s and 1990s is what produced hesitation, muddle, international disagreement and ultimately the withdrawal of both inspection commissions." The authors also found that "Indeed, though a necessary condition for any effective policing of arms-limitation regimes, monitoring and verification mechanisms are by themselves insufficient. They must be accompanied by enforcement mechanisms, and by the political will to use them and keep them in place."[187]

Another problem is that you only have so much time to enforce the disarmament clauses and other terms of the treaty, because states may start to wriggle out of the provisions. As we've just seen, in the post-First World War period Germany began immediately violating the terms of Versailles. After the 1990–91 Gulf War, Saddam Hussein had no qualms in manipulating UN weapons inspections. Moreover, the victors and the international community can quickly lose interest, and the international community can become a block to enforcement, because its members begin to see the victor in a bad light.[188]

This produces another enforcement problem: the victor's insistence upon enforcing the peace can lead to their being deemed the problem in the international arena and the true threat to peace and stability.[189] Such has at times been the fate of the United States and Israel in recent decades, and France in the aftermath of the First World War. This strange dichotomy creates an argument for the victor making a quick peace and the defeated pursuing delay, again, depending upon the military, political, and diplomatic situations. The victor, especially if a great power, might have to stiffen its spine and take the criticism to get what it wants. A strong leader will also not so easily bend to media and international criticism. This is usually short-lived and is always fickle, because some other thing will come along to divert the focus of both.

There is also the opposite enforcement problem, in that those who sign up for the job later refuse to bear the burden. This is sometimes a result of being portrayed as an international bully or a malcontented international actor. Such fears led to only four of the twenty-seven signatories of the 1919 Versailles agreements doing their part as enforcers during the occupation of the Ruhr in 1923. It is also hard to hold the interest of nations in enforcement as other problems arise that seem more pressing – and indeed sometimes are. After the 1990–91 Gulf War, enforcement of United Nations Special Commission (UNSCOM) inspections of Iraq became less important in the face of the collapse of Yugoslavia and the wars that followed. The US and Britain were criticized for the enforcement of the "no-fly zones" in Iraq after the 1990–91 Gulf War.[190] The US also received increasing international criticism for its enforcement of UN-mandated sanctions.

Other problems abound. Geography can affect the enforcement of terms just as it does the waging of the war because of the proximity of the defeated to the victors. After the First World War, distance and the Atlantic Ocean allowed the US to ignore a revisionist and revanchist Germany; France had no such luxury.[191] Disputes over post-war territorial control also weaken settlements. One scholar insists that "Territory is the only variable that significantly affects the risk of recurrent conflict."[192] History certainly seems to support this. Bismarck's annexation of Alsace and Lorraine after the 1870–71 Franco–Prussian War caused long-term bitterness between France and Germany. The question of the possession of Kashmir feeds conflict between India and Pakistan today, as do the results of the various Arab–Israeli wars. Geography can at times make terms self-enforcing, where the location of the new border or its particular terrain can make launching a war more difficult.[193]

There are other problems arising from the enforcement of the terms: "If a government does not intend permanently to occupy and administer a territory but merely to make a treaty in which the people agree that they will trade on favorable terms or concede other intangible advantages, what assurances can there be that they will continue to carry out these obligations after the armies are gone?"[194] This is arguably easier to do in a war fought for limited political aims, because you have not asked for much. But it is also arguably more difficult because, after the peace, you may lack the leverage to compel the enemy into keeping their end of the bargain.

The April 3, 1991 United Nations Security Council Resolution 687, referred to as "the Mother of All Resolutions" because at that time it was the Security Council's lengthiest ever, formalized the cease-fire conditions of the First Gulf War. One could argue that this was as close to a peace treaty as one could get. The Resolution also added other sanctions and inspections, and mandated Baghdad disclose all of its WMD and ballistic missiles to UN-supervised destruction. Iraq was ordered to pay for damages committed in Kuwait, as well as the environmental damage done to the Gulf via its purposefully pumping oil into the sea in an effort to hinder the coalition's war effort. All revenue that Iraq derived from the sale of oil was supposed to go to a fund to pay for these damages; the remainder could be used for food or reconstruction. The "Oil for Food Program" evolved from this.[195]

After the war, the US implemented a form of containment against Saddam with the aims of preventing a new burst of Iraqi aggression and keeping Saddam from rebuilding his military capability. Containment had four primary elements: 1) disarmament via the UN program, particularly in regard to WMD and ballistic missiles; 2) UN monitoring; 3) the presence of US military forces, particularly via what began as the No-Fly Zones protecting the Shia and Kurds; and 4) maintaining sanctions put in place during the war to prevent Saddam from re-arming. Interestingly, no one had expected these sanctions to drive Saddam out of Kuwait, but now expected them to effect a change in Iraqi behavior. Over the long term, the sanctions system began to breakdown via corruption in the UN-backed "Oil for Food Program" and the willingness of nations such as China to simply ignore them when it suited their needs.[196] Publicly, Saddam complied, but cheated at every opportunity and began rebuilding his chemical and biological weapons programs. He particularly masked efforts to rebuild his shattered nuclear program.[197]

There are a number of ways to enforce the terms of a treaty. But unfortunately, historian Quincy Wright argued, most of the things statesmen have done historically when trying to resolve issues of both war and peace have made the world less stable and produced war, not peace.[198] Structures need to be built to protect everyone's rights.[199] This, of course, can be difficult. Monitoring with external groups is a common practice but deciding who these organizations or nations should be is difficult because of suspicions on all sides as to who is an honest actor. Occupation or peacekeeping forces are certainly an option, but these come with their own problems.

Achieving some kind of reconciliation is of course ideal. Iklé argues that "not only can reconciliation be an alternative route toward a more lasting peace, but today's enemy may become a future ally, while today's ally may pose a future threat."[200] But, again, the history and emotions behind the problem can make this difficult to achieve.

Moreover, victory does not always mean peace. Israel's victories in its wars kept the state alive but did not bring peace. Some in the liberal West have even come to resent its success as well as its survival.[201] Israel was once seen as the underdog, but some now brand it a bully and deem it oppressive (tingeing some of this criticism is the traditional anti-Semitism of Western elites).

One of the things that may be necessary in order to maintain the peace is the rebuilding of the other state, which can include all or some of its administrative or security arms. This will very likely be the case during and in the aftermath of a counterinsurgency situation. Historically, this has proven very difficult. One author writing in 2013 noted that in cases since 1898 where the mission was completed or ended, the US and UN succeeded only 48 percent of the time. Policymakers simply do not understand or agree upon how to produce success. How one should approach this is certainly in dispute, and the massive literature suggests different approaches: liberalization first, or building institutions first, or providing security first. Some argue for finding the right sequence. One author believes sequencing to be a myth, and that one can't do this because every situation is different.[202] Analyst Anthony Cordesmann observed that since the Second World War, achieving security and stability in a nation has only been possible in states capable of doing it themselves.[203]

Demilitarized zones can be helpful guarantors of peace, especially if they are big enough to keep forces separated, such as the ones established after the war between El Salvador and Honduras (the Soccer or Football War), between Israel and Syria in the Golan Heights, and between North and South Korea.[204] Some argue that "mechanisms such as demilitarized zones, monitoring, and arms-control limitations are not merely effective in mitigating security fears arising from commitment problems; because such mechanisms increase the costs of returning to war, they generally increase the contact zone and thereby enhance the robustness of the settlement."[205] But it is impossible to prove this is a maker of peace.

Third-party guarantors of the peace can add to stability. The presence of peacekeepers and external monitors can also help keep the peace.[206] Third-party peacekeeping forces became more available after 1945, but the evidence for the success of such measures is mixed, and some studies doubt their utility for establishing a lasting peace. But they can be a tool for creating peace, because the promise of their commitment by a third party can help induce states to make an agreement, if not necessarily a lasting one.[207] Sometimes the UN backs interventions, but many find UN efforts lack credibility because of their failure in places such as Sudan, Rwanda, and Srebrenica, and the fact that there seems to be no coherency in regard to decisions to intervene.[208]

There can be problems securing the peace if one does not make it clear to the population of a defeated state that its leaders have indeed lost the war and led their nation to defeat. This can have unfortunate consequences, especially if the defeated state is a revanchist power. After the First World War, German Socialist Chancellor Friedrich Ebert greeted returning troops who marched through Berlin's Brandenburg Gate by remarking that no one had defeated them on the battlefield. The German leaders knew the truth, but the people did not have to accept the fact that their military forces had been defeated. The victorious Allies failed to make this clear.[209]

In 1991, Iraq's Saddam Hussein broadcast loudly that his forces had not been defeated militarily. As we've seen, the Iraqi official history of the war branded the military defeat a military victory, and Saddam and his regime publicly proclaimed a victory over the Americans. Neither the Iraqi people nor Saddam had to accept that their military forces had been defeated, as well as their nation.[210]

Sometimes the loser's defeat needs to be made clear to prevent the rise of myths and lies that allow groups to undermine the peace. The Nazi "stab in the back" myth is perhaps the best-known example of this. Hitler and the Nazi party perpetuated the lie that the German Army had not been defeated in 1918 but had been "stabbed in the back" on the home front, particularly by Socialists and Jews. The failure of the Allies to force recognition of this by the German government, people, and especially the military commanders, such as Field Marshals Paul von Hindenburg and Erich Ludendorff who had led Germany to defeat, gave the Nazis a powerful propaganda tool.

But the victor must also be careful in the manner in which the defeat is made apparent. Sometimes, as in the case of Germany after the First World War, making defeat plain might have defused future problems. But there may be times when one needs to be sure to not humiliate the defeated opponent, because it can cause bitterness and resentment and make it more difficult to achieve a lasting peace. Clausewitz understood this on a very personal level. He is best known as a theorist, but he was also a professional soldier. After the fall of Napoleon in 1815, he was part of the Prussian occupation force in France. He observed (and indeed participated in) Prussian forced requisitions of goods and material, and criticized punitive efforts directed at the French, such as Marshal Gebhard von Blücher's efforts to blow up Paris' Jena Bridge. Clausewitz believed the British were more intelligent in their peacemaking, because they behaved with generosity. He considered the Prussians bad winners.[211]

Avoiding the above-mentioned issue of humiliating your opponent (accompanied by subterfuge) was part of the equation for successfully ending the 1932 Chaco War between Bolivia and Paraguay. The Paraguayans insisted that Bolivia accept their victory and that the boundary line fall near the extent of their advance. The Bolivians were unwilling to accept this, but also unable to throw back the enemy force.

The warring powers eventually concluded a three-phased settlement. Secretly, Paraguay and Bolivia agreed on the new border. Then, the international tribunal that had been created to negotiate peace announced that they had decided the boundary line would be what had already been secretly agreed. Then the agreement had to be ratified in each state. Paraguay did so in a national plebiscite, whereas Bolivia gave approval via a vote in its congress. This allowed Bolivia to save face and gave Paraguay what it wanted. The settlement has held.[212]

The famous Prussian statesman Otto von Bismarck insisted that peace be made quickly and moderately. On Prussia's 1866 victory over Austria-Hungary he noted that "In positions such as ours was then, it is a political maxim after a victory not to inquire how much you can squeeze out of your opponent, but only to consider what is politically necessary."[213] But Bismarck went too far in 1871 by taking Alsace and agreeing to annex the areas of Lorraine populated by French-speakers. This was done to eliminate a French route of attack against southern reaches of Germany over the Rhine, but Bismarck miscalculated in regard to French nationalist feelings. The French saw the annexations as humiliation, and this sparked a deep French desire for vengeance against Germany.[214]

Some consider the Versailles Treaty of 1919 the ultimate example of a punitive peace, particularly because of the reparations it forced upon Germany. Its defenders will argue – rightfully – that the reparations were not definitively harsher than those Germany put upon Russia at Brest-Litovsk in 1918 and France in 1871. The first of these never held, and the second, as we've seen, helped cause enormous and long-term animosity among the French.

One must also remember the effects of defeat. Obviously, everything here depends upon whether or not you are the defeated. One of the first things one should do (at least in a liberal democracy) is to accept its reality when it occurs. But one should not use euphemisms to describe it; this can destroy your credibility with your own people. For example, one author says that the point of his work is to get leaders to focus on "the loss-cutting skill set."[215] It would be better for them to realize that they have lost or failed – failure meaning they have not achieved their political aim – and that it is time to put the conflict to rest. This, of course, is easier said than done, and can require more moral and political courage than starting the war because of the domestic and international costs in prestige, money, and so on, but also because it is simply heart-rending to lose. Defeat is deeply humiliating psychologically, and some find it easier to continue than to accept the unacceptable. As with so many of the factors in war – indeed, everything – the value of the object will be critical, and one must never forget the views and role of the nation's people. It is easier to accept the loss of something of less value, but that does not make it *easy* to accept. The obvious counterargument is that sometimes leaders and states simply refuse to accept defeat even when it has occurred and see the result as temporary.

Some argue that in the larger context of the Cold War that it was good for the US to leave Vietnam in defeat, because this freed resources to fight the longer, unlimited Cold War. This idea is intellectually bankrupt. The costs of defeat – even in a war fought for a limited political aim – cannot be predicted before the disaster occurs. Defeat in Vietnam cost the US greatly in reputation and prestige. After 1975, the US paid a heavy price for defeat because some of its enemies – real and potential – viewed it as a paper tiger. Saddam Hussein, Osama Bin Laden, and others drew the lesson that the US lacked staying power and would not endure casualties. This is a foolish conclusion to have reached, but this did not stop them from doing so. The lesson they should have drawn is that the US can and will fight for a limited aim in support of an ally for a very, very long time (the US was in Vietnam in some capacity from 1954 to 1975), and that if the US population is not properly informed and led by its leaders that it will eventually demand a lowering of the cost.

Finally, Michael Howard offers this caution: "Also, it is important that war should not be conducted in such a manner as to subvert the prospects for lasting peace."[216] Unfortunately, this, despite its wisdom and like everything else related to war, is easier to advise than to ensure.

Conclusion

We must keep in mind that victory matters. In war, the costs of defeat are too high, even in wars not fought for the survival of the state. Defeat in Vietnam proved devastating to US interests and credibility in the decades afterwards. Your enemies draw lessons from defeat, often the wrong ones. Saddam Hussein and Osama Bin Laden looked at the US failure in Vietnam and concluded the US was feckless and weak and thus not a credible threat.

In a 2014 speech, Chairman of the Joint Chiefs of Staff General Martin Dempsey said that we don't spend enough time studying war termination.[217] This is certainly the case. Once the leaders have a view of what victory looks like, they should seek to bring it about as quickly as possible. It is also important for them to have a vision of the peace they hope to get, and a plan for how to maintain it. As we've seen above, this is an extremely difficult and complex subject (one whose surface we have barely scratched), but also an exceedingly important one.[218] An ancient Chinese strategist once noted this relevant truth: "To win victory is easy; to preserve its fruits difficult."[219]

CONCLUSION: IS HISTORY RHYMING?

> I have been told in conversation that this is an absurd war and an absurd strategy. And so, no doubt, it is.[1]
>
> Klaus Knorr

The More Things Change . . .

On April 14, 2021, President Joseph Biden announced the US would withdraw its forces from Afghanistan by September 11, 2011, the twentieth anniversary of the September 11 terrorist attacks that caused America's war in Afghanistan. Biden inherited a Trump administration commitment to depart by May 1, 2021 but announced this would instead begin on May 1. Biden promised continued support for Afghanistan, including its security forces, and promised an "over the horizon" counterterrorism strategy to counter any emerging threat in Afghanistan. He also told the Taliban to expect American retribution if they interfered with the American withdrawal.[2]

Biden insisted he was bound by the February 2020 Doha agreement the Trump administration signed with the Taliban, one the Taliban had broken by refusing to separate from Al Qaeda and failing to seriously negotiate with Kabul's democratically elected government. Biden insisted the US couldn't stay in Afghanistan, where the US had only 2,500 troops, and needed to withdraw to meet the challenge from China. Biden had long wanted a withdrawal and promised this during his presidential campaign. This desire remained despite the US implementing a version of the light-footprint counterterrorism strategy he had advocated at the beginning of the Obama administration. It was "highly unlikely," Biden insisted, that the Taliban would take over Afghanistan.[3]

American military commanders argued against withdrawal, insisting the US needed to maintain 2,500 troops there to keep the Taliban at bay and prevent Afghanistan from again becoming a terror group haven. Biden overrode them. Both JCS chair General Mark Milley and CENTCOM's commander, General Kenneth McKenzie, wanted a continued presence.[4] On July 13, two dozen US diplomats at the Kabul embassy warned in a memo to Secretary of State Tony Blinken that the US withdrawal would mean Afghanistan's collapse. Neither Biden's White House nor Jake Sullivan and his NSC saw the memo; Sullivan read about it in the *Wall Street Journal* a month after its dispatch. The cable also offered advice (unheeded) for speeding evacuation.[5]

On July 8, 2021 Biden announced a new withdrawal date: August 31. The reason for the change isn't immediately clear, but many remarked that it stepped away from September 11. Biden noted that staying in Afghanistan longer meant the Taliban would renew attacks on US forces and that this would force the US to dispatch additional troops. Milley revealed later that if the US didn't leave by August 31, the Taliban might renew fighting against the Americans, which would require committing 30,000 more US troops. Milley still advised keeping 2,500 troops in Afghanistan.[6]

The US began withdrawing in May, and the situation deteriorated far more quickly than the administration expected.[7] Afghanistan's army and police had a paper strength of 300,000. But this number was inflated by "ghost soldiers" carried on the books. Undermining the force was extensive corruption and leadership incompetence. Additionally, as America transitioned to Afghan control over the last decade, Afghan leaders in Kabul focused on personal enrichment and not good governance.[8]

The Taliban, meanwhile, slowly increased its strength in the countryside, established shadow governments in areas they controlled, undermining the authority and credibility of the Kabul government. They established ties with provincial elders and Kabul officials, building a strong position for negotiating with enemy forces and leaders when they thought it time, and filling the ruling and security vacuum they created.[9] Moreover, the Taliban had long laid the foundation for the

Kabul government's collapse by undermining the will of the Afghan forces and government. The Doha Agreement had disillusioned an already weak army and police, and the American announcement of withdrawal "shattered the confidence" of the Kabul government and its forces. Even the Taliban was shocked by the speed and ease of their advance.[10]

Without its American backstop, the Afghans' will to fight collapsed under Taliban pressure. It was a force designed to fight with American backing, particularly air support, intelligence, and logistics. When the US removed the contractors providing maintenance and intelligence, the Afghan security forces began coming apart. The Afghans could no longer support their 400 positions throughout the country, many of which required resupply by air.[11]

Biden said in the press conference following his July 8 speech that he trusted the Afghan forces to hold up against the Taliban and didn't see Afghanistan's fall as inevitable.[12] CIA Director William Burns said in a July 22, 2021 interview that "The Taliban are making significant military advances; they're probably in the strongest military position that they've been in since 2001."[13] The administration stayed the course. Biden insisted the collapse came much sooner than anticipated, but some intelligence assessments given to both the Trump and Biden administrations predicted collapse could come in days.[14]

The first Afghan provincial capital, Zaranj, fell to the Taliban on August 6.[15] For much of August 7, as Afghanistan collapsed into Taliban hands, its president, Ashraf Ghani, sat on the lawn at the presidential palace reading a book. President Joe Biden played golf in Delaware. On August 8, the US embassy advised Americans to leave as soon as possible. There was no sense of urgency anywhere. The Taliban offensive unrolled with a stunning rapidity as Kabul's forces fled, surrendered, or switched sides. By August 10, Afghan officials were resigning and fleeing the country. Ghazni surrendered without a fight on August 12, opening the Taliban's path to Kabul from the south. Afghan officials saw this as a turning point. The State Department had already ordered the destruction of "sensitive" documents. August 12 also saw the defenses of both Herat and Kandahar evaporate. On August 13, panic hit Kabul. Ghani and key members of his government fled on August 15 as Taliban forces entered the capital. Afghanistan's democratically elected government was dead.[16]

The collapse of the Afghan army and the Taliban's quick final campaign destroyed America's evacuation plans. The administration had intended to leave 650 troops to guard the embassy. This meant there were insufficient troops to also hold Bagram's key airport. Biden approved its closure, which meant operating out of Kabul. Biden's push for a rapid withdrawal put the Departments of Defense and State on different paths, and Milley accused State of waiting too long to order an evacuation. This, combined with the quick collapse of Kabul's army, forced the administration to launch an evacuation mission entailing the dispatch of 6,000 US troops to Kabul to secure its airport. An August 26 suicide bombing killed thirteen American service members supporting the evacuation. The administration had received abundant intelligence that such an attack might occur.[17]

The US and others evacuated 124,000 people by August 31, but left behind perhaps 200 Americans and most of the tens of thousands of Afghans who had helped the Americans.[18] France's Emmanuel Macron, Germany's Angela Merkel, and Great Britain's Boris Johnson all pressed Biden to extend the August 31 deadline. He refused.[19]

In total, 2,461 American military personnel were killed in the Afghan War. Perhaps 69,000 Afghan soldiers and police also died, as did perhaps 47,000 civilians. The US spent $824.9 billion, an average of $3.4 billion per month.[20] Comparisons with America's 1975 evacuation of Hanoi quickly emerged, but instead of the image of helicopters departing the roof of the US embassy, the picture was of Afghans falling to their deaths from American aircraft fleeing Kabul. CNN journalist Peter Bergen wrote: "Biden is presiding over a debacle entirely of his own making in Afghanistan."[21]

A Path Forward?

One task of future American leaders is to prevent this from happening again. How then should we *think* about a war like Afghanistan?

Ideally, the US should first determine what victory looks like. Its leaders should adopt the political aim or aims it wishes to achieve or can accept, and then determine whether or not achievement is possible. US leaders need to understand their political aim – and the complexity it generates – and understand the effects this continuously exerts upon whether or not the aim can be achieved.

The next step is developing a strategy for achieving this aim that takes into consideration the numerous and complex relevant constraints, identifies – among other things – the political aims of opponents and the centers of gravity (or sources of strength) for both sides, and provides the necessary means to implement the strategy and achieve the political aim sought. This must include a plan for ending the war and securing the peace.

Obviously, there will be innumerable internal and external constraints strewn across America's path. For example, the internal problems in Afghanistan dominated: corrupt governance, tribal fractiousness, weak though growing security forces, a country broken in innumerable ways by almost forty years of war – the list goes on. The primary external constraint – an interested third-party actor in the form of Pakistan – is also well known. Another key external issue was the level of willingness of the US and its allies to continue fighting in Afghanistan and the size of the forces they were ready to commit.

If we look back at our typology of insurrection, we recall the three keys to succeeding in a war with an active insurgency: 1) support of the people; 2) control of internal or external sanctuary for the insurgents; and 3) the insurgent's possession of outside support. Could the Afghan government have kept and grown its support from the Afghan people on its own, meaning without US and external support, while denying this to the Taliban? This is doubtful. It could have maintained sufficient support with US backing (though for how long will remain an unanswered question), but it couldn't fund or keep in the field its security forces without foreign and especially American assistance, or maintain its government, and couldn't continue the fight without US military support. Relatedly, could the US have maintained sufficient support from its own people and its allies for this war? It did so for twenty years (though some allies fell away) and could have continued if it kept low its casualties and those of its Western partners.

US leaders during the Obama, Trump, and Biden administrations tried to negotiate an end to the Afghan War, which is an acceptable path to ending a conflict, and one the Bush administration failed to seize when offered in December 2001.[22] But this must be approached with a deep understanding of the fact that the enemy doesn't end the war just because you want to or think it's in their interests to do so. They invariably must be coerced into stopping, something neither administration succeeded in doing. The Trump administration succeeded in concluding the Doha Agreement but this lacked any enforcement provision, was never kept by the Taliban, and undermined the Afghan government by demoralizing its security forces. Moreover, Trump's last defense secretary, Christopher Miller, said the administration hoped to convince Ghani to quit or accept a "power-sharing agreement with the Taliban" that permitted an American counterterrorism presence of around 800 troops to go after groups like Islamic State. Trump's reelection defeat killed any such idea.[23]

To have a chance of achieving what the US needed most in Afghanistan – an Afghan government that could stand largely on its own – the US had to control the other two planks of our insurgency typology: the insurgent's possession of sanctuary and access to outside support. They are joined at the hip and reveal the Taliban's dominant center of gravity – the source of its strength – its ally. The Taliban certainly enjoyed support among segments of the Afghan population, particularly the Pashtu, but eliminating the Taliban's external sanctuary and external support would have made it possible – theoretically – to reduce its internal support to a manageable level, because Taliban internal sanctuaries could then be eliminated with sufficient numbers of Afghan and coalition forces. It is also possible that the removal of its Pakistani sanctuaries would convince the Taliban to negotiate seriously.

The Bush and Obama administrations made no serious effort to address Taliban sanctuary. The Trump administration began pressuring Pakistan to stop supporting the Taliban and Al Qaeda, as these groups undermined Afghanistan's government and eliminated any chance of stability in this unfortunate state. These efforts produced no significant change in Pakistan's behavior.[24]

Considering all the above, particularly Taliban sanctuary in Pakistan and America's failure to address it, the small number of US troops, and the weaknesses of the Afghan forces and government, US strategy had little hope of delivering victory barring some chance event. US leaders needed to change what they wanted to achieve in Afghanistan or alter American strategy in a manner that would allow it to achieve the desired political aim, and then commit sufficient means for doing this for as long as needed. But the failure to eliminate Taliban sanctuary in Pakistan meant the US could only hope to achieve any desired political aim with an enormous commitment of troops or by building an Afghan army large enough to prevent Taliban incursions from Pakistan while also securing the nation against internal Taliban supporters. The first was politically unacceptable to American leaders. Internal Afghan weaknesses probably made the later impossible.

All of this, of course, is exceedingly easy to say, and trying to offer a resolution for a problem as complex as Afghanistan isn't possible in a few thousand words. Approaching such situations in a clear manner helps.

How We Think about War Matters

The Biden administration chose defeat in Afghanistan but had ample help getting here. The big problems – identified earlier – are that Americans understand neither the importance and effects of the political aims (the ends) nor the meaning of their value, poorly understand the use of force (the ways) and the problems entailed, and fail to commit sufficient forces (the means), all while US political leaders fail to demand or value victory. This has produced lost, badly waged, perpetual, and protracted wars.

Why is this important? Because, this is how Americans currently *think* about fighting wars. American and Western leaders send men and women into wars that they won't call wars, don't understand, and don't expect or even intend to win. Indeed, they don't even acknowledge the value and necessity of winning. They spend lives with no hope or sometimes even intent of making things better for the people of their own nations or the people in the states who suffer the harsh effects of Western military power. Western elites and leaders lack the intellectual foundation to discuss war in a rational and logical manner, and they generally do not study war, or even history. Political decision-makers and their staffs are considered among the least informed.[25] Some media figures and the experts they consult are just as muddled in their thinking. We need an intellectual preparation for war, but US and other Western leaders now lack this.[26]

General James M. Dubik points out the danger of US leaders not thinking clearly about war and failing to call it what it is: "We set ourselves up for failure when we convince ourselves that a particular use of force requires less upfront thinking, planning, preparation or organization because it's 'not war'; that our aims need not be as clear as they would be in 'real war'; or that we need not think through the ends-ways-means or the tactical-operational-strategic relationships as completely as we would if we were waging a 'war.'"[27]

We see a dangerous example of the lack of clarity in US thinking in regard to war and strategic issues in the propagation of such terms as "hybrid war." Supposedly, this depicts the most recent incarnation of so-called limited war. What its use actually demonstrates is that too many defense and security intellectuals do not understand the differences between tactics, operations, strategy, and the political aim. The term's popularity is largely a result of Vladimir Putin's forces being branded as conducting so-called hybrid war against Ukraine because of Russia's deceptive and unconventional methods. Supposedly, *"Hybrid Wars incorporate a range of different modes of warfare, including conventional capabilities, irregular tactics and formations, terrorist acts including indiscriminate violence and coercion, and criminal disorder.* These multi-modal activities can be conducted by separate units, or even by the same unit, but are generally operationally and tactically directed and coordinated within the main battlespace to achieve synergistic effects" (italics in original).[28]

At first glance, this definition seems workable, but it is simply a depiction of tactical means and methods supplemented by subversion and criminality, two activities carried out both in peace and war.[29] The hybrid war literature and the term's recent popularity reveal a common failure on the part of analysts and leaders to understand the differences between war and peace, and to call things as they are. War entails the use of militarized violence, generally for a political aim, but it does not preclude the use of subversion, which states practice against other states whether they are at war with them or not. German scholar Thomas Rid brilliantly dissects this issue in relation to so-called "cyberwar" in an article appropriately titled "Why Cyberwar Will Not Take Place." Cyber attacks in peacetime are examples of subversion, but they will also occur during a war. But cyber attacks can also be criminal acts. One of the strengths of Rid's analysis is to remind us of the necessary existence of violence as a political instrument as an act of war.[30]

Recalling the relationship between the pursuit of the political aim and the elements of grand strategy presented earlier – meaning how we use all the elements of national power in pursuit of a political aim – easily clarifies this issue. For example, what Russia did beginning in 2014 in Ukraine was to conduct a war for a limited political aim using both violent and non-violent subversive means. Many political leaders and commentators fail to brand this war a war despite the facts and honest analysis saying otherwise. But one must remember that the abovementioned analytical tool applies to both peace and war. If a state is not at war, this does not mean that it is not attempting to subvert a rival state. The Cold War epitomized this, and reexamining the myriad ways in which the US used its military and non-military elements of national power in this era holds many lessons for today.

But it also provides pitfalls, as "hybrid war" proponents repeat a Cold War intellectual error. In 1951, US Navy Captain Harvey B. Seim wrote about what he called "Fringe War." This, he noted in the context of the Cold War, "is localized, yet global; it consists primarily of a series of minor engagements for limited objectives; it is carried out by relatively small forces; it utilizes puppet or satellite groups as a smokescreen to mask the single coordinated Communist effort; it is waged in many different manners, both military and non-military."[31] These are the characteristics often attributed to hybrid war. Moreover, Putin's Russians have nothing on the North Vietnamese Communists, whose strategy in their war against South Vietnam included subversion of the enemy government, terrorism, assassination, propaganda, clandestine operations, guerrilla warfare, and conventional invasion.[32] The supposed distinctions attributed to hybrid war are the result of falsely extrapolating from tactical innovation the birth of a new creation.

The unfortunate result of the penetration of bad ideas is the construction of elements of US strategy on myth and misunderstanding – just as occurred so often during the Cold War – in this case producing an example of what the late Michael Handel branded the tacticization of strategy.[33] In 2015, hybrid war made its way into the US *National Military Strategy* where it sat on an equally intellectually bankrupt "Continuum of Conflict" consisting of "State Conflict," "Hybrid Conflict," and "Non-State Conflict." This document insists that a hybrid conflict "[b]lends conventional and irregular forces to create ambiguity, seize the initiative, and paralyze the adversary. May [sic] include use of both traditional military and asymmetric systems."[34]

The first problem with this definition – and this criticism fits the document's descriptions for state and non-state conflict – is that this is an expression of the means and methods used to wage war, and thus provides no foundation for constructive analysis. All warfare blends conventional and irregular forces and traditional and "asymmetric systems," war's very nature creates ambiguity, and seizing the initiative is part of the job, as is paralyzing the enemy. There is nothing here that has not been practiced since ancient times. Thucydides would have defined this as "war."

The "gray zone" and its myriad versions emerged into general usage in 2015 as a broken way of examining Russia's actions during its war against Ukraine. It combined an ignorance of history and theory with the false notion that there exists a gray zone between peace and war and a lack of awareness that subversion has always been a tool of state action during both war and peace. Gray zone proponents were actually describing what some of these same people branded "great power competition," while conflating war and peace and failing to call wars wars.[35] Those pushing "political warfare" are making the same mistake of confusing peace and war.

The Gerasimov Doctrine or Russian New Generation Warfare myth arose after the Libya War, when Russian Chief of the General Staff Valery Gerasimov penned his incoherent assessment of the modern operational environment. Western analysts falsely spun his ramblings into a supposed new Russian approach to war after Putin's subsequent and unconnected Crimea invasion. This generated mountains of flawed analysis, particularly on Russian strategy and the key question of whether or not a nation is at war or at peace.[36]

The result of all of this was that an ahistorical *tactical* idea (hybrid war) and *two things that don't exist* (the gray zone and the Gerasimov Doctrine) became underpinnings for American strategic thinking and that of Washington's allies.

Second, the potential enemies of the US think quite differently about these matters. Historian Hew Strachan noted in 2013 that "For Americans, limited war is now associated with failure."[37] This is largely because of the US experience in Vietnam, but this should not be the case, because the most likely form of a future war for the US and its allies is a war fought for a limited political aim as well as in other hotspots such as the Asian subcontinent. It is unlikely (though not impossible) that either Pakistan or India will seek to overthrow the other in any possible future war because of the very real risk of a nuclear exchange.

One must, of course, qualify the statement above about wars for limited aims being the most likely ones faced by the US and its friends.

The current Iranian regime would gladly topple the Israeli government if it had the power to do so. China is certainly able, and undoubtedly willing, to overthrow the government of Taiwan when it thinks it can do so at an acceptable political and physical cost. Some states around the periphery of Putin's Russia should also not take lightly the potential of Russian aggression. Putin's war in Ukraine has made this abundantly clear to anyone willing to see. Soviet writers understood the use of force, and there is no reason to think Russia's current rulers don't recall advice such as this:

> The ruling classes of every state, resorting to war as an instrument of policy, must have clearly in mind the forms which hostilities will take and the conditions necessary for victory, and at least the basic outlines of post-war perspectives in the event of victory or defeat. Any neglect of this theoretical and practical problem has always been severely dealt with by history.[38]

Force was for getting what you wanted, and it was laughable to see it any other way. Nothing seems to have changed.

The Chinese have spent significant time thinking about how to wage a future limited war. In 1985, Chinese leaders decided that the Soviet Union was no longer the most likely opponent. The biggest threat was now "local limited war (*jubu zhanzheng*) around China's borders." This change came before Mikhail Gorbachev's ascension to power in the Soviet Union and was a response to what Beijing saw as a shift in the global power balance and the evolution of the international environment. The Chinese believed that such future conflicts would be fought for limited political aims and "require the swift and effective application of military force." The Maoist warfare three phases of defense, stalemate, and offensive were deemed invalid. Technology allowed the aggressor to quickly seize the initiative. Because of this, mobilizing the entire nation for war was no longer the correct strategy. China needed a standing force that could act quickly in a highly lethal manner. The Chinese forces in each of their different geographical "Military Regions" began training to fight based upon the conditions of their respective "war zones," in the expectation that the forces in each zone would have to act independently. Nuclear forces were seen "as preventing a major power from threatening the People's Republic with nuclear war in order to deter

Beijing from a chosen course of action." The Chinese put more emphasis on mobility, lethality, quickness in command, control, communications, and intelligence action, and a combined-arms approach integrating land, sea, and air forces. But they also realized that they must have advanced technology to have any chance of "stopping and winning a modern war."[39]

The Chinese have continued to re-evaluate their ideas on war. The 2013 edition of *The Science of Military Strategy*, which reveals the thinking of the heads of the People's Liberation Army (PLA), "stresses the importance of new domains in conventional warfighting, calling for a more equal focus on the ground, air, sea, space and cyber domains." It also details the four ways Chinese leaders believe they might have to use the nation's military tools: 1) repelling an invasion of China; 2) fighting a war for Taiwan; 3) wars with neighbors over disputed lands and volatility in border states; and 4) uses of military power that aren't necessarily part of a war, such as protection of sea lanes and counterterrorism.[40]

Maritime action has exerted increasing power over Chinese military ideas, which helps drive Chinese thinking in *The Science of Military Strategy* toward limited war: "given ongoing disputes in the South and East China Seas, the book assesses that the most likely kind of war for China is 'a limited military conflict in the maritime domain,' while the most important war to prepare to wage 'is a relatively larger and high intensity local war under nuclear conditions in the maritime direction.'" It also insists upon ending wars "in a controlled manner."[41]

A Final Word

At an October 2017 conference at the Austrian Defence Academy in Vienna, Austria, one largely devoted to so-called hybrid war, the closing speech was given by an Austrian general. Though the attendees were a global cast of important strategic-studies analysts and scholars, the general by far gave the wisest advice: that Austria should not pay too much attention to everything that comes out of American think-tanks.

I do not pretend I have presented *the* way of thinking about wars fought for limited political aims, but I have presented *a* way, one better than what we have and that I hope will aid American leaders.

I end with a quotation from Clausewitz, who would have never tired of being quoted: "One can, after all, not condemn a method without being able to suggest a better alternative."[42] If you can do so, please write loudly, because one thing is abundantly clear: US leaders and the people who guide them are in enormous need of instruction.

ACKNOWLEDGMENTS

As always, I have incurred numerous debts, some of which I will undoubtedly forget to mention, and for which I sincerely apologize. Much of the research was made possible by the extraordinary interlibrary loan labors of the Naval Postgraduate School's Irma Fink and Zooey Lober. Hal Blanton, Fred Drake, Michael Jones, Lukas Milevski, Bob Tomlinson, Jonathan Ward, Craig Whiteside, Thomas-Durrell Young, and three anonymous reviewers read parts or all of the manuscript, pointed me toward sources, and provided ideas and advice. Hew Strachan read early drafts of the first chapters and introduced me to Cambridge University Press. There, Michael Watson acted as an excellent editor. I am particularly indebted to Samuël Kruizinga of the University of Amsterdam for reading and commenting upon the entire manuscript.

I am also beholden to Robert Johnson, the director of the Changing Character of War Programme at the University of Oxford's Pembroke College. Some of the research and initial writing was done during my time in his program in 2016. I am also grateful to Lonnie Johnson and the dedicated staff of Fulbright Austria. The grant I was awarded in 2017 to do research and to teach at the Diplomatic Academy in Vienna made completing the manuscript possible. Markus Kornprobst, the Diplomatic Academy's chair of political science, kindly opened the door for me to spend the 2017–18 academic year in Vienna. Most of the manuscript was written during this time.

I also benefited from my many years teaching various versions of the US Naval War College's *Strategy and Policy* course at the

Naval Postgraduate School in Monterey, California. This course forces those who take it (and those who teach it) to evaluate and re-evaluate ideas.

The book is dedicated to two of my former colleagues and current friends: Hal Blanton and Mike Jones. Thanks for teaching me so much. *SDG*

* * *

Author's note: this work, published in 2022, is an updated version of the 2019 publication.

NOTES

1   Are We at War? What Do We Want? And Do We Want to Win?

1. "Leaving Afghanistan, US General's Ghostly Image Books Place in History," *Reuters*, August 31, 2021, https://www.reuters.com/world/asia-pacific/leaving-afghanistan-us-generals-ghostly-image-books-place-history-2021-08-31/; Nancy A. Youssef and Gordon Lubold, "Last U.S. Troops Leave Afghanistan after Nearly 20 Years," *Wall Street Journal* (August 30, 2021), https://www.wsj.com/articles/last-u-s-troops-leave-afghanistan-after-nearly-20-years-11630355853
2. Joe Biden, Remarks by President Biden on the Way Forward in Afghanistan, April 14, 2021, https://www.whitehouse.gov/briefing-room/speeches-remarks/2021/04/14/remarks-by-president-biden-on-the-way-forward-in-afghanistan/
3. Gary R. Hess, *Presidential Decisions for War: Korea, Vietnam, and the Persian Gulf* (Baltimore, MD: Johns Hopkins University Press, 2001), 20–27.
4. Leo Shane III, "DoD to Deploy 'Targeting Force' to Hunt Down ISIS Leaders," *Military Times* (December 1, 2015), www.militarytimes.com/story/military/capitol-hill/2015/12/01/carter-isil-hasc-war/76609562/
5. Caroline Holmqvist, *Policing Wars: On Military Intervention in the Twenty-First Century* (Houndsmill, UK: Palgrave Macmillan, 2014), 50.
6. Audrey Kurth Cronin, "The 'War on Terrorism': What Does It Mean to Win?" *Journal of Strategic Studies*, Vol. 37, No. 2 (2014), 175.
7. Franklin D. Roosevelt, "State of the Union Address" (January 6, 1942), in Gerhard Peters and John T. Woolley, *The American Presidency Project*, www.presidency.ucsb.edu/documents/state-the-union-address-1
8. John Garnett, "Limited War," in John Baylis, Ken Booth, John Garnett, and Phil Williams, *Contemporary Strategy: Theories and Policies* (New York: Holmes & Meier, 1982), 123.
9. Robert McClintock, *The Meaning of Limited War* (Boston: Houghton Miffin, 1967), 5.
10. Robert E. Osgood, *Limited War: The Challenge to American Strategy* (Chicago University Press, 1957), 1–2.
11. Brig. Gen. Gurmeet Kanwal, Indian Army (retired), July 1, 2010, in G. D. Bakshi, *Limited Wars in South Asia: Need for an Indian Doctrine* (Delhi: Centre for Land Warfare Studies, 2010), vii–viii.

12. Carl von Clausewitz, *On War*, Michael Howard and Peter Paret, trans. and eds. (Princeton University Press, 1984), 69; Carl von Clausewitz, *Strategie*, Marc Guarin, trans., (unpublished manuscript); Sir Julian Corbett, *Some Principles of Maritime Strategy*, Eric Grove, introduction and notes (Annapolis, MD: Naval Institute Press, 1988 [1911]), 44–46.

13. Some examples: Ian Bertram, "The Return of Limited War," *The Strategy Bridge* (September 13, 2016), www.thestrategybridge.org/the-bridge/2016/9/13/the-return-of-limited-war; Taylor Dinerman, "The Limits of Limited War," *Gatestone Institute* (October 27, 2011), www.gatestoneinstitute.org/2539/limits-of-limited-war; David Ignatius, "The Problem with America's Limited Wars," *Washington Post* (October 9, 2014), www.washingtonpost.com/opinions/david-ignatius-reality-check-on-limited-war/2014/10/09/19c8c95e-4ff2-11e4-babe-e91da079cb8a_story.html.

14. Seymour J. Deitchman, *Limited War and American Defense Policy* (Cambridge, MA: MIT Press, 1964), 16–18, 24–26. The author calls the Huk Rebellion the Philippine Civil War, which is not an inaccurate depiction. See also this list: Robert H. Gormley, "Limited War and the Striking Fleets," *US Naval Institute Proceedings*, Vol. 89, No. 2 (February 1963), 55.

15. Hew Strachan, *The Direction of War: Contemporary Strategy in Historical Perspective* (Cambridge University Press, 2013), 112–113.

16. Ignatius, "The Problem with America's Limited Wars." For a better but still fuzzy approach, see Ted Galen Carpenter, "A Really Bad Idea: A 'Limited' War with Iran," *The National Interest* (April 14, 2015), http://nationalinterest.org/feature/really-bad-idea-limited-war-iran-12623

17. Barack Obama, "President Obama's Speech on Combating ISIS and Terrorism" (September 10, 2014), www.cnn.com/2014/09/10/politics/transcript-obama-syria-isis-speech/

18. Some examples: Carpenter, "A Really Bad Idea: A 'Limited' War with Iran"; Sydney J. Freedberg Jr., "No Longer Unthinkable: Should the US Ready for 'Limited' Nuclear War?" *Breaking Defense* (May 30, 2013), http://breakingdefense.com/2013/05/no-longer-unthinkable-should-us-ready-for-limited-nuclear-war/; Ignatius, "The Problem with America's Limited Wars."

19. Some examples: Spencer D. Bakich, *Success and Failure in Limited War: Information and Strategy in the Korean, Vietnam, Persian Gulf, and Iraq Wars* (University of Chicago Press, 2014); Adam Elkus, "The Shadow of Limited War," *Red Team Journal* (July 15, 2010), http://redteamjournal.com/2010/07/the-shadow-of-limited-war/; Lawrence Freedman, "Ukraine and the Art of Limited War," *War on the Rocks* (October 2014), http://warontherocks.com/2014/10/ukraine-and-the-art-of-limited-war/#_; Jacob Grygiel and A. Wess Mitchell, "Limited War Is Back," *The National Interest* (August 28, 2014), 37, http://nationalinterest.org/feature/limited-war-back-11128; Taewoo Kim, "Limited War, Unlimited Targets: US Air Force Bombing of North Korea during the Korean War, 1950–1953," *Critical Asian Studies*, Vol. 44, No. 3 (2012), 467; Kori Schake, "The Perils of Limiting Our Wars," *War on the Rocks* (October 16, 2014), http://warontherocks.com/2014/10/the-perils-of-limiting-our-wars/

20. Garnett, "Limited War," 126.

21. Michael R. Gordon, "Powell Delivers a Resounding No on Using Limited Force in Bosnia," *The New York Times* (September 28, 1992), www.nytimes.com/1992/09/28/world/powell-delivers-a-resounding-no-on-using-limited-force-in-bosnia.html?pagewanted=all

22. David C. Brooks, "Lessons from Limited Wars. Cutting Losses: Ending Limited Interventions," *Parameters*, Vol. 43, No. 3 (2013), 99–100.

23. Thomas C. Greenwood, "The Elusive Quest for Victory in War," *Proceedings*, Vol. 147, No. 10 (October 2021), https://www.usni.org/magazines/proceedings/2021/october/elusive-quest-victory-war

24. Edward Luttwak, *On the Meaning of Victory: Essays on Strategy* (New York: Simon and Schuster, 1986), 289, quoted in Colin S. Gray, *Defining and Achieving Decisive Victory* (Carlisle, PA: Strategic Studies Institute, US Army War College, 2002), 3.

25. Everett Carl Dolman, *Pure Strategy: Power and Principle in the Space and Information Age* (Abingdon, UK: Frank Cass, 2005), see 1–17, esp. 5–6.

26. Holmqvist, *Policing Wars*, 37, 44, 48–49.

27. Rupert Smith, *The Utility of Force: The Art of War in the Modern World* (New York: Knopf, 2007), 13.

28. D. Clayton James, with Anne Sharp Wells, *Refighting the Last War: Command and Crisis in Korea* (New York: Free Press, 1993), 204–214.

29. Louis Morton, "The Twin Essentials of Limited War," *Survival: Global Politics and Strategy*, Vol. 3, No. 3 (1961), 136.

30. Colin F. Jackson, "Lost Chance or Lost Horizon? Strategic Opportunity and Escalation Risk in the Korean War, April–July 1951," *Journal of Strategic Studies*, Vol. 33, No. 2 (2010), 283; Report to the National Security Council by the Executives Secretary, NSC 48/5, May 17, 1951, in United States, Department of State, *Foreign Relations of the United States* (hereafter *FRUS*), *1951, Asia and the Pacific* (Washington, DC: USGPO, 1977), Vol. I, Part 1, 33–34, https://history.state.gov/historicaldocuments/frus1951v06p1/pg_33

31. National Security Council Report, NSC 81/1, "United States Courses of Action with Respect to Korea" (September 9, 1950), History and Public Policy Program Digital Archive, Truman Presidential Museum and Library, http://digitalarchive.wilsoncenter.org/document/116194.pdf?v=b5f4cbf0ae773fe6970014edb854029e

32. Colin F. Jackson, "Lost Chance or Lost Horizon?" 256–274.

33. James, *Refighting the Last War*, 99.

34. Douglas MacArthur, "Farewell Address to Congress, April 19, 1951," www.americanrhetoric.com/speeches/douglasmacarthurfarewelladdress.htm

35. James, *Refighting the Last War*, 112.

36. Hugh G. Wood, "American Reaction to Limited War in Asia: Korea and Vietnam, 1950–1968" (Ph.D. thesis, University of Colorado, 1974), 57.

37. James, *Refighting the Last War*, 25, 116.

38. Rob de Wijk, *The Art of Military Coercion: Why the West's Military Superiority Scarcely Matters* (Amsterdam: Mets & Schilt, 2005), 9.

39. Jim Puzzanghera, "Feinstein Criticizes Obama's Islamic State Strategy, Urges More US Special Forces in Syria," *Los Angeles Times* (November 22, 2015), www.latimes.com/world/la-fg-obama-isis-criticism-20151122-story.html

40. Barack Obama, "Press Conference by President Barack Obama – Antalya, Turkey" (November 16, 2015), www.whitehouse.gov/the-press-office/2015/11/16/press-conference-president-obama-antalya-turkey; Robert Tracinski, "Barack Obama: Worst. President. Ever," *The Federalist* (November 19, 2015), http://thefederalist.com/2015/11/19/barack-obama-worst-president-ever/

41. Obama, "Press Conference by President Obama – Antalya, Turkey"; Obama, "President Obama's Speech on Combating ISIS and Terrorism."

42. Clausewitz, *On War*, 88–89.

43. Obama, "Press Conference by President Obama – Antalya, Turkey."

44. Tracinski, "Barack Obama: Worst. President. Ever."

45. Matthew Yglesias, "Obama's Biggest Terrorism Struggle: How to Sell 'Don't do stupid shit' as a Strategy" (November 18, 2015), www.vox.com/2015/11/18/9751340/paris-attack-dont-do-stupid-shit

46. Bernard-Henri Lévy, "Thinking the Unthinkable: This Is War," Steven B. Kennedy, trans., Globe and Mail (November 16, 2015), www.theglobeandmail.com/globe-debate/thinking-the-unthinkable-this-is-war/article27284617/

47. Obama, "President Obama's Speech on Combating ISIS and Terrorism."

48. Julian Robinson, "'ISIS to Outlast Obama's Presidency': Military Campaign to Destroy Terror Group Could Take THREE Years, Senior US Officials Warn," The Daily Mail (September 8, 2014), www.dailymail.co.uk/news/article-2747640/ISIS-outlast-Obama-s-presidency-Military-campaign-destroy-terror-group-years-senior-U-S-officials-warn.html; Mark Landler, "Obama, in Speech on ISIS, Promises Sustained Effort to Rout Militants," The New York Times (September 10, 2014), www.nytimes.com/2014/09/11/world/middleeast/obama-speech-isis.html

49. See Barack Obama, "Remarks by the President in Address to the Nation on the Way forward in Afghanistan and Pakistan" (December 1, 2009), www.whitehouse.gov/the-press-office/remarks-president-address-nation-way-forward-afghanistan-and-pakistan

50. Scott Wilson and Al Kamen, "'Global War on Terror' Is Given New Name," Washington Post (March 25, 2009), www.washingtonpost.com/wp-dyn/content/article/2009/03/24/AR2009032402818.html

51. The Daily Beast (September 11, 2014), www.thedailybeast.com/cheats/2014/09/11/kerry-u-s-is-not-at-war-with-isis.html

52. I am indebted to Samuël Kruizinga and Tom Young for making this point.

53. For a succinct discussion of the historical legal issues regarding US non-declarations of war, see Gregory E. Fehling, "America's First Limited War," Naval War College Review, Vol. 53, No. 3 (summer 2000), 101–143, esp. 113–128.

54. Chiara Libiseller and Lukas Milevski, "War and Peace: Reaffirming the Distinction," Survival, Vol. 63, No. 1 (2021), 106–107.

55. Anthony Codevilla and Paul Seabury, War: Ends and Means, 2nd edn. (Dulles, VA: Potomac Books, 2006), 5.

56. Strachan, The Direction of War, 10–12, 108, 110–111; Terry Jones, "Why Grammar Is the First Casualty of War," The Daily Telegraph (December 1, 2001), www.telegraph.co.uk/news/uknews/1364012/Why-grammar-is-the-first-casualty-of-war.html; Codevilla and Seabury, War, 5.

57. Clausewitz, On War, 582.

58. Sun Tzu, The Art of War, Samuel B. Griffith, trans. (London: Oxford University Press, 1971), 100.

59. Luttwak, On the Meaning of Victory, 289, quoted in Gray, Defining and Achieving Decisive Victory, 3.

60. Dominic Tierney, The Right Way to Lose a War: America in an Age of Unwinnable Conflicts (New York: Little, Brown, 2015), 5–6.

61. Beatrice Heuser, The Evolution of Strategy: Thinking about War from Antiquity to the Present (Cambridge University Press, 2010), 45.

62. Quoted in Hoffman Nickerson, Can We Limit War? (Port Washington, NY: Kennikat Press, 1977 [1933]), 34.

63. I am indebted to Tom Young for this point.

64. Strachan, The Direction of War, 117.

65. Rupert Smith, The Utility of Force, 11–12.

2 The Way We Think about War (Particularly So-Called Limited War) Is Broken: Here Is How We Fix It

1. Urs Schwarz, *American Strategy: A New Perspective. The Growth of Politico-Military Thinking in the United States* (Garden City, NY: Anchor/Doubleday, 1967), 94.
2. Robert E. Osgood, "The Reappraisal of Limited War," *The Adelphi Papers*, Vol. 9, No. 54 (1969), 54.
3. Clausewitz, *On War*, 132.
4. Corbett, *Some Principles of Maritime Strategy*, 3–7.
5. Clausewitz, *On War*, 141, 144.
6. Peter Paret, *Understanding War: Essays on Clausewitz and the History of Military Power* (Princeton University Press, 1992), 103.
7. Clausewitz, *On War*, 69.
8. Email from Lukas Milevski, April 10, 2019.
9. This is sometimes expressed as DIMEFIL (Diplomatic, Information, Military, Economic, Financial, Intelligence, Law Enforcement). But in my view "intelli- gence" is subsumed in "information," "financial" in "economic," and "law enforcement" pushes us below the level of grand strategy. On DIMEFIL and the "Whole-of-Government Approach," see Jeffrey W. Meiser, "Ends + Ways + Means = (Bad) Strategy," *Parameters*, Vol. 46, No. 4 (winter 2016–17), 84–85.
10. For a history of the concept of grand strategy, see Lukas Milevski, *The Evolution of Modern Grand Strategic Thought* (Oxford University Press, 2016).
11. US Government, Department of the Army, *ADP 3–0: Unified Land Operations* (Washington, DC: Dept. of the Army, October 2011), 35, www.army.mil/e2/rv5_downloads/info/references/ADP_3-0_ULO_Oct_2011_APD.pdf. I am indebted to Bob Tomlinson for this definition.
12. For a succinct discussion of the differences, see Donald Stoker, *Clausewitz: His Life and Work* (Oxford University Press, 2014), 16.
13. Peter Paret, "A Total Weapon of Limited War," *Royal United Services Institute*, Vol. 105, No. 617 (1960), 34. This also appears as Paret's "Eine totale Waffe in begrenzten Krieg," *Wehrwissenschaftliche Rundschau: Zeitschrift für die europäische Sicherheit*, Vol. 9, No. 10 (1959), 555–564.
14. John Horne, "Introduction: Mobilizing for 'Total War', 1914–1918," in John Horne, ed., *State, Society, and Mobilization in Europe during the First World War* (Cambridge University Press, 1997), 4.
15. Hew Strachan, *Clausewitz's On War: A Biography* (New York: Atlantic Monthly Press, 2007), 19.
16. See John Horne, "Introduction," 3–5, and Ian F. W. Beckett, "Total War," in Clive Emsley, et al., eds., *War and Peace and Social Change in Twentieth Century Europe* (Milton Keynes, UK: Open University Press, 1989), esp. 28, 31–32.
17. Jan Willem Honig, "Problems of Text and Translation," in Hew Strachan and Andreas Herberg-Rothe, eds., *Clausewitz in the Twenty-First Century* (Oxford University Press, 2007), 64–65. I am among those who have made the mistake of linking absolute war with total war in Clausewitz's work: Donald Stoker, "The Myth of Total War," *The Strategy Bridge* (December 17, 2006), https://thestrategybridge.org/the-bridge/2016/12/17/the-myth-of-total-war
18. Clausewitz, *On War*, 80–89, esp. 85, 579–581. Clausewitz does contradict himself in his unfinished text by saying Napoleon waged absolute war, but the full text clearly reveals the intent of his methodology.

19. The editors of a four-volume study of "Total War" never arrived at a definition. See the introductions in Stig Förster and Jörg Nagler, eds., *On the Road to Total War: The American Civil War and the German Wars of Unification, 1861–1871*, German Historical Institute (Cambridge University Press, 1997); Manfred F. Boemke, Roger Chickering, and Stig Förster, eds., *Anticipating Total War: The German and American Experiences, 1871–1914* (Cambridge University Press, 1999); Roger Chickering and Stig Förster, eds., *Great War, Total War: Combat and Mobilization on the Western Front, 1914–1918* (Cambridge University Press, 2000); Roger Chickering and Stig Förster, eds., *The Shadows of Total War: Europe, East Asia, and the United States, 1919–1939*, German Historical Institute (Cambridge University Press, 2003); Roger Chickering, Stig Förster, and Bernd Greinder, eds., *A World at Total War: Global Conflict and the Politics of Destruction, 1937–1945* (Cambridge University Press, 2010).

20. Brian Bond, *War and Society in Europe, 1870–1970* (Montreal: McGill-Queens University Press, 1998), 168. Problems with the term "total war" are dealt with at length in Donald Stoker, "What's in a Name II: 'Total War' and Other Terms that Mean Nothing," *Infinity Journal*, Vol. 5, No. 3 (fall 2016), 21–23.

21. Eugenia C. Kiesling, "'Total War, Total Nonsense' or 'The Military Historian's Fetish,'" in Michael S. Neiberg, ed., *Arms and the Man: Military History Essays in Honor of Dennis Showalter* (Leiden: Brill, 2011), 220.

22. Tierney, *The Right Way to Lose a War*, 7. The author notes that the term "major war" is problematic because it could be major for one side and not the other. But the real reason is that "major war," like "total war," has no concrete meaning, 317 fn. 12.

23. Osgood, *Limited War*, 3.

24. Donald Stoker, *The Grand Design: Strategy and the US Civil War* (Oxford University Press, 2010), 24.

25. Ephraim M. Hampton, "Unlimited Confusion over Limited War," *Air University Quarterly Review*, Vol. 9 (spring 1957), 31. For an overview of French thinking on "limited" and "total war," see Vincent Desportes, *Comprendre la guerre*, 2nd edn. (Paris: Economica, 2001), 139–168.

26. Kiesling, "'Total War,' Total Nonsense,'" 216.

27. I am indebted to Lukas Milevski for this last point.

28. Strachan, *The Direction of War*, 17.

29. McClintock, *The Meaning of Limited War*, cover, 5.

30. Lukas Milevski, "The Modern Evolution of Grand Strategic Thought" (Ph.D. thesis, University of Reading), 202–203.

31. William Olson, "The Concept of Small Wars," *Small Wars & Insurgencies*, Vol. 1, No. 1 (1990), 44.

32. Osgood, "The Reappraisal of Limited War," 41–42.

33. Morton H. Halperin, "Limited War: An Essay on the Development of the Theory and an Annotated Bibliography," *Occasional Papers in International Affairs*, No. 3 (May 1962), 1; B. H. Liddell Hart, "War, Limited," *Harper's*, Vol. 192, No. 1150 (March 1946), 193–203.

34. Arthur E. Brown, "The Strategy of Limited War," in Arthur F. Lykke Jr., ed., *Military Strategy: Theory and Application* (Carlisle Barracks, PA: United States Army War College, 1993), 221.

35. Schwarz, *American Strategy*, 95.

36. Bernard Brodie, *Strategy in the Missile Age* (Santa Monica, CA: RAND, 1959), vi. Some works incorrectly claim that current limited war thinking is a reaction to John Foster Dulles' 1954 "massive retaliation speech." See, for example, Nordal Åkerman, *On the Doctrine of Limited War* (Lund: Berlingska Boktryckeriet, 1972), 119. Much

modern limited war writing was inspired by Dulles' speech, but the foundation came earlier.

37. Milevski, "The Modern Evolution of Grand Strategic Thought," 201–202; Bernard Brodie, review essay, "More about Limited War," *World Politics*, Vol. 10, No. 1 (October 1957), 114.

38. B. H. Liddell Hart, *The Revolution in Warfare* (New Haven, CT: Yale University Press, 1947), 36. The previously mentioned article, Liddell Hart, "War, Limited," 193–203, was drawn from this book.

39. Brodie, *Strategy in the Missile Age*. See also Bernard Brodie's other related works: *Escalation and the Nuclear Option* (Princeton University Press, 1966); *The Meaning of Limited War* (Santa Monica CA: RAND, 1958); "Politique de dissuasion et guerre limitée," *Politique étrangère*, No. 6 (1990), 543–552; *Strategy in the Nuclear Age* (Princeton University Press, 1965); "Unlimited Weapons and Limited War," *The Reporter*, Vol. 8 (November 18, 1954), 16–21; and "Learning to Fight a Limited War," in William P. Gerbering and Bernard Brodie, *The Political Dimension in Strategy: Five Papers* (Los Angeles, CA: UCLA Press, 1968), 26–32, reprinted from the *Los Angeles Times* (December 3, 1967).

40. Brodie, *Strategy in the Missile Age*, 310–311. Brodie insists upon the necessity of restraint in other places as well, Brodie, *The Meaning of Limited War*, 3–4.

41. Osgood, *Limited War*, 1–2.

42. Ibid., 2, 4, 238.

43. Hampton, "Unlimited Confusion over Limited War," 32.

44. Robert B. Johnson, "Tactical Warfare and the Limited War Dilemma," *TEMPO Review Paper* (Santa Barbara, CA: General Electric Company, 1961), 11.

45. Some examples: Brodie, *Strategy in the Missile Age*, 310–311; Garnett, "Limited War," 128; McClintock, *The Meaning of Limited War*, 5; D. K. Palit, *War in the Deterrent Age* (London: Macdonald, 1966), 168; Swaran Singh, "Indian Debate on Limited War Doctrine," *Strategic Analysis*, Vol. 23, No. 12 (2000), 2181–2182.

46. Henry A. Kissinger, *Nuclear Weapons and Foreign Policy* (New York: Harper and Brothers, 1957), 174–202. See also Henry A. Kissinger, "Limited War: Conventional or Nuclear?" *Survival: Global Politics and Strategy*, Vol. 3, No. 1 (1961), 2–11.

47. Brodie, *Strategy in the Missile Age*, 330–331. Schelling has an appendix in his *The Strategy of Conflict* (Cambridge, MA: Harvard University Press, 1963 [1960]), "Nuclear Weapons and Limited War," 258–266.

48. An example: Arm-San Kim, "A Note on Sunzi's Art of War and Limited War: A Modern Interpretation," *Korean Journal of Defense Analysis*, Vol. 6, No. 1 (1994), 251–252.

49. Åkerman, *On the Doctrine of Limited War*, 16.

50. Hampton, "Unlimited Confusion over Limited War," 28.

51. C. E. Callwell, *Small Wars: Their Principles and Practice*, 3rd edn., introduction by Douglas Porch (Lincoln, NE: University of Nebraska Press, 1996 [1906]), 21.

52. Thomas C. Schelling, *Arms and Influence* (New Haven, CT: Yale University Press, 1966), 33.

53. Stephen Peter Rosen, "Vietnam and the American Theory of Limited War," *International Security*, Vol. 7, No. 2 (fall 1982), 85–86.

54. Jack S. Levy, "Big Wars, Little Wars, and Theory Construction," *International Relations*, Vol. 16, No. 3 (1990), 216.

55. Robert B. Johnson, "Tactical Warfare," 11.

56. For a discussion of many of the efforts at classifying wars, see Errol A. Henderson and J. David Singer, "'New Wars' and Rumors of 'New Wars,'" in Paul F. Diehl, ed., *War* (London: Sage Publications, 2005), Vol. I, 398–425.

57. See Hew Strachan, "Strategy and the Limitation of War," *Survival: Global Politics and Strategy*, Vol. 50, No. 1 (2008), 51.

58. Thomas K. Finletter, *Power and Policy: US Foreign and Military Policy in the Hydrogen Age* (San Diego: Harcourt, Brace and Co., 1954), 81–192, especially 84–85.

59. Osgood, *Limited War*, 267–274, 307; Henry Kissinger, "Military Policy and the Defense of the 'Grey Areas,'" *Foreign Affairs*, Vol. 33, No. 3 (April 1958), 416–428. See also E. Biörklund, "Can War Be Limited? (in General or Local Wars)," *Air Power*, Vol. 6 (summer 1959), 287–293.

60. For a debate that Adam Elkus conclusively wins, see: Adam Elkus, "50 Shades of Gray: Why the Gray Wars Concept Lacks Strategic Sense," *War on the Rocks* (December 15, 2015), http://warontherocks.com/2015/12/50-shades-of-gray-why-the-gray-wars-concept-lacks-strategic-sense/; Michael J. Mazarr, "Struggle in the Gray Zone and World Order," *War on the Rocks* (December 22, 2015), http://warontherocks.com /2015/12/struggle-in-the-gray-zone-and-world-order/; Adam Elkus, "Abandon All Hope, Ye Who Enter Here: You Cannot Save the Gray Zone Concept," *War on the Rocks* (December 30, 2015), http://warontherocks.com/2015/12/abandon-all-hope-ye-who-enter-here-you-cannot-save-the-gray-zone-concept/; Michael J. Mazarr, "The Strange Debates of Strategy," *War on the Rocks* (January 14, 2016), http://waronther ocks.com/2016/01/the-strange-debates-of-strategy/.

61. Other examples: Osgood, *Limited War*, 62; D. Suba Chandran, *Limited War: Revisiting Kargil in the Indo-Pak Conflict* (Safdarjung Enclave, India: India Research Press, 2005), 3–4.

62. Another example: Bakich, *Success and Failure in Limited War*, 20.

63. For examples see: Garnett, "Limited War," 124, 128; Chandran, *Limited War*, 3–4.

64. Chandran, *Limited War*, 3–4.

65. Antoine-Henri Jomini, *The Art of War*, G. H. Mendell and W. P. Craighill, trans. (Westport, CT: Greenwood, 1971 [1862]), 13–34.

66. For an example, see Frank G. Hoffman, "The Contemporary Spectrum of Conflict: Protracted, Gray Zone, Ambiguous, and Hybrid Modes of Warfare," *The Heritage Foundation: 2016 Index of US Military Strength*, 25–36, http://index.heritage.org /military/2016/essays/contemporary-spectrum-of-conflict/

67. Harry G. Summers Jr., *On Strategy: A Critical Analysis of the Vietnam War* (Novato, CA: Presidio Press, 1984), 104–105.

68. James M. Dubik, "By Any Other Name, War Is Still War," *Army Magazine*, Vol. 66, No. 6 (June 2016), www.armymagazine.org/2016/05/13/by-any-other-name-war-is -still-war/. Another, not as harsh critique: Michael W. Cannon, "The Development of the American Theory of Limited War, 1945–1963" (MA thesis, School of Advanced Military Studies, 1989), 37.

69. Some disagree but make the errors recorded above: Mary Kaldor, "In Defence of New Wars," *Stability*, Vol. 2, No. 1 (2013), 1–16; Mary Kaldor, *New and Old Wars: Organized Violence in a Global Era*, 3rd edn. (Cambridge: Polity Press, 2012). For the definitive dissection of this issue, see Mats Berdal, "The 'New Wars' Thesis Revisited," in Hew Strachan and Sibylle Scheipers, eds., *The Changing Character of War* (Oxford University Press, 2011), 108–133.

70. Milevski, "The Modern Evolution of Grand Strategic Thought," 221; Ian Clark, *Waging War: A Philosophical Introduction* (Oxford: Clarendon Press, 1990), 62; Olson, "The Concept of Small Wars," 40. See also Maxwell D. Taylor, "Improving

Our Capabilities for Limited War," *Army Information Digest*, Vol. 14 (February 1959), 6.

71. Examples include: Allen Guttmann, ed., *Korea and the Theory of Limited War* (Boston: D. C. Heath, 1967); Trumbull Higgins, *Korea and the Fall of MacArthur: A Précis in Limited War* (New York: Oxford University Press, 1960); David Rees, *Korea: The Limited War* (New York: St. Martin's Press, 1964); Edmund Traverso, ed., *Korea and the Limits of Limited War* (Menlo Park, CA: Addison-Wesley Publishing, 1970).

72. National Security Council Report, NSC 81/1, "United States Courses of Action with Respect to Korea," September 9, 1950, History and Public Policy Program Digital Archive, Truman Presidential Museum and Library, http://digitalarchive .wilsoncenter.org/document/116194.pdf?v=b5f4cbf0ae773fe6970014edb854029e

73. Some examples: Bernard Brodie, *War and Politics* (New York: Macmillan, 1973), 70–71; George C. Herring, *From Colony to Superpower: US Foreign Relations since 1776* (New York: Oxford University Press, 2008), 641.

74. Chen Jian, *China's Road to the Korean War: The Making of the Sino–American Confrontation* (New York: Columbia University Press, 1994), 179–80; Xiaobing Li, *China's Battle for Korea: The 1951 Spring Offensive* (Bloomington, IN: Indiana University Press, 2014).

75. Truman approved NSC 48/5 on May 17, 1951; see Christopher M. Gacek, *The Logic of Force: The Dilemma of Limited War in American Foreign Policy* (New York: Columbia University Press, 1994), 61.

76. Schelling, *Arms and Influence*, 136.

77. For criticism of Schelling's ideas, see also: Richard Ned LeBow, "Thomas Schelling and Strategic Bargaining," *International Journal*, Vol. 51, No. 3 (summer 1996), 555–576; Ned Richard Lebow, "Reason Divorced from Reality: Thomas Schelling and Strategic Bargaining, "*International Politics*, Vol. 43 (2006), 429–452.

78. Schelling, *Arms and Influence*, 129–130.

79. Li, *China's Battle for Korea*, xvii.

80. Alan R. Millett, *The Korean War: The Essential Bibliography Series* (Washington, DC: Potomac Books, 2007), 49, 80.

81. Morton, "The Twin Essentials of Limited War," 137.

82. See Conrad C. Crane, "To Avert Impending Disaster: American Military Plans to Use Atomic Weapons during the Korean War," *Journal of Strategic Studies*, Vol. 23, No. 2 (June 2000), 72–88.

83. James, *Refighting the Last War*, 237.

84. Morton, "The Twin Essentials of Limited War," 135.

85. Åkerman, *On the Doctrine of Limited War*, 184–185.

86. Schelling, *The Strategy of Conflict*, 6, 16.

87. Olson, "The Concept of Small Wars," 44.

88. Schelling, *The Strategy of Conflict*, 53, 102.

89. Mark Clodfelter, *The Limits of Air Power: The American Bombing of North Vietnam* (New York: Free Press, 1989), 157–158.

90. Schelling, *The Strategy of Conflict*, 16–19. See also Thomas C. Schelling, "Bargaining, Communication, and Limited War," *Conflict Resolution*, Vol. 1, No. 1 (March 1957), 19–36.

91. Leon Gouré, *Soviet Limited War Doctrine* (Santa Monica, CA: RAND, 1963), 1–3. See also the editors' discussion in V. D. Sokolovskii, *Soviet Military Strategy*, H. Dinerstein, L. Gouré, and T. Wolfe, eds. (Santa Monica, CA: RAND, 1963), 289–293, and Jean-Christophe Romer, "L'URSS et la guerre limitée," *Stratégique*, Vol. 54, No. 2 (1992), www.institut-strategie.fr/strat_054_ROMER.html. For a Soviet look at various Western limited war definitions, see also: T. Kondratov,

"What Is 'Limited War'?" *Soviet Military Review*, No. 1 (August 1973), 48–49. For an East German piece on limited war, see Rudolph Hellborn, "Die bonner Theses des begrenzten Krieges," *Deutsche Aussenpolitik* (June 1960), 602–617.

92. Jonathan Samuel Lockwood, *The Soviet View of US Strategic Doctrine: Implications for Decision Making*, foreword by Leon Gouré (New Brunswick: Transaction Books, 1983), 71–74.

93. Ibid., 67.

94. Gouré, *Soviet Limited War Doctrine*, 4–12.

95. Honoré M. Catudal, *Soviet Nuclear Strategy from Stalin to Gorbachev: A Revolution in Soviet Military and Political Thinking* (Berlin: Arno Spitz, 1988), 128.

96. Rosen, "Vietnam and the American Theory of Limited War," 89–90.

97. Rosen, "Vietnam and the American Theory of Limited War," 89–90.

98. Fred Kaplan, quoted in Esther-Mirjam Sent, "Some Like It Cold: Thomas Schelling as a Cold Warrior," *Journal of Economic Methodology*, Vol. 14, No. 4 (December 2007), 467.

99. V. R. Raghavan, "Limited War and Nuclear Escalation in South Asia," *The Nonproliferation Review*, Vol. 8, No. 3 (2001), 88.

3   The Political Aim: Why Nations Fight (Limited) Wars

1. Robert Saundby, "War – Limited or Unlimited?" *Air Power*, Vol. 2 (1955), 100.

2. Gordon and Trainor, *The Generals' War: The Inside Story of the Conflict in the Gulf* (New York: Back Bay Books, 1995), 33–34.

3. Clausewitz, *On War*, 69. Sir Julian Corbett imposes "unlimited" and "limited" on Clausewitz in Corbett, *Some Principles of Maritime Strategy*, 41–52.

4. Clausewitz, *On War*, 81, 88–89, 579.

5. J. W. Ellis Jr. and T. E. Greene, "The Contextual Study: A Structured Approach to the Study of Political and Military Aspects of Limited War," *Operations Research*, Vol. 8, No. 5 (September–October 1960), 640.

6. Codevilla and Seabury, *War*, 40.

7. Joseph G. Dawson III, "The US War with Mexico: The Difficulties of Concluding a Victorious War," in Matthew Moten, ed., *Between War and Peace: How America Ends Its Wars* (New York: Free Press, 2011), 85.

8. Rupert Smith, *The Utility of Force*, 217–218.

9. See the discussion of this point in William Flavin, "Planning for Conflict Termination and Post-Conflict Success," *Parameters* (autumn 2003), 97–98.

10. William W. Kaufmann, *Policy Objectives and Military Action in the Korean War* (Santa Monica, CA: RAND, 1956), 16 fn. 12.

11. Crane, "To Avert Impending Disaster," 75–76.

12. J. Lawton Collins, *War in Peacetime: The History and Lessons of Korea* (Boston: Houghton Mifflin, 1969), 246–248.

13. Ibid., 246–248, 252; Matthew Ridgway, *The Korean War* (New York: Da Capo, 1967), 82.

14. J. Lawton Collins, *War in Peacetime*, 262–263.

15. Ibid., 264–265.

16. Gacek, *The Logic of Force*, 66; Memorandum for the Record of a Department of State – Joint Chiefs of Staff Meeting (February 13, 1951), *FRUS, 1951, Korea and China*, February 13, 1951, Vol. VII, Part 1, 174–175.

17. J. Lawton Collins, *War in Peacetime*, 298, 300; James F. Schnabel, *Policy and Direction: The First Year* (Washington, DC: Center of Military History, 1992), 383–387, 395–396.

18. J. Lawton Collins, *War in Peacetime*, 303–305; NSC 48/5, May 17, 1951, *FRUS, 1951, Asia and the Pacific*, Vol. I, Part 1, 33–34.
19. J. Lawton Collins, *War in Peacetime*, 301; Schnabel, *Policy and Direction*, 395–396.
20. Kaufmann, *Policy Objectives*, 16.
21. Summers, *On Strategy*, 140, 149.
22. Memorandum from the Secretary of Defense, March 16, 1964, and NSAM 288, March 17, 1964, *FRUS, Vietnam, 1964*, Vol. I, 153–154, 172–173.
23. Martin Dempsey, "Keynote Speech on Civil–Military Relations at the Center for a New American Security" (December 1, 2014), minutes 5–7:25, www.youtube.com/watch?v=8ORRt-lSRwU
24. Carl von Clausewitz, *Carl von Clausewitz: Two Letters on Strategy*, Peter Paret and Dan Moran, trans. and eds. (Fort Leavenworth, KS: Combat Studies Institute, US Army Command and General Staff College, 1984), 1–3.
25. Clausewitz, *On War*, 92.
26. Ibid., 81.
27. Clausewitz, *On War*, 89.
28. Denis Warner and Peggy Warner, *The Tide at Sunrise: A History of the Russo-Japanese War, 1904–1905* (Abingdon, UK: Routledge, 2004), 174.
29. Ian Nish, *The Origins of the Russo-Japanese War* (Abingdon, UK: Routledge, 1985), 159.
30. For the value of the object to Japan, see Warner and Warner, *The Tide at Sunrise*, 175.
31. Steven William Nerheim, "NSC-81/1 and the Evolution of US War Aims in Korea, June–October 1950," *Strategy Research Project* (Carlisle, PA: US Army War College, 2000), 5–6.
32. Alan R. Millett, *The War for Korea, 1950–1951: They Came from the North* (Lawrence, KS: University Press of Kansas, 2010), 116.
33. Harry S. Truman, *Memoirs by Harry S. Truman* (New York: Doubleday, 1955), Vol. II, 335, 337.
34. Millett, *The War for Korea, 1950–1951*, 118–119.
35. Truman, *Memoirs*, Vol. II, 340.
36. John Mueller, *Retreat from Doomsday: The Obsolescence of Major War* (New York: Basic Books, 1989), 122.
37. George B. Herring, *America's Longest War: The United States and Vietnam, 1950–1975*, 3rd edn. (New York: McGraw-Hill, 1996), 126.
38. Lawrence Freedman and Efraim Karsh, *The Gulf Conflict, 1990–1991: Diplomacy and War in the New World Order* (Princeton University Press, 1995), 73, 75–76.
39. Hess, *Presidential Decisions for War*, 221.
40. George Bush and Brent Scowcroft, *A World Transformed* (New York: Vintage Books, 1999), 435, 446.
41. Brodie, *The Meaning of Limited War*, 8.
42. Strachan, *The Direction of War*, 109–110.
43. Henry Kissinger, *Diplomacy* (New York: Simon and Schuster, 1994), 674.
44. Gideon Rose, *How Wars End: Why We Always Fight the Last Battle* (New York: Simon and Schuster, 2010), 192–194.
45. Example inspired by Raymond G. O'Connor, "Victory in Modern War," *Journal of Peace Research*, Vol. 6, No. 4 (1969), 368.
46. Li, *China's Battle for Korea*, xix.
47. Barack H. Obama, "Transcript of Obama Speech on Afghanistan" (December 2, 2009), http://edition.cnn.com/2009/POLITICS/12/01/obama.afghanistan.speech.transcript/index.html

48. Christopher Griffin, "From Limited War to Limited Victory: Clausewitz and Allied Strategy in Afghanistan," *Contemporary Security Policy*, Vol. 35, No. 3 (2014), 457; Matt Millham, "Obama Refocuses the Mission with Drawdown," *Stars & Stripes* (June 23, 2011), www.stripes.com/news/obama-refocuses-the-mission-with-drawdown-1.147315

49. Ben Rhodes, *The World As It Is: A Memoir of the Obama White House* (New York: Random House, 2018), 79; Obama, "Transcript of Obama Speech on Afghanistan."

50. Thomas Jocelyn, "Losing a War," *The Weekly Standard* (August 27, 2018), www.weeklystandard.com/thomas-joscelyn/losing-a-war Jocelyn argues that this is proven by Trump's willingness to negotiate with the Taliban. I think a better argument is that Trump said he preferred pulling out of Afghanistan.

51. Dean Acheson, *The Korean War* (New York: W. W. Norton, 1971), 57–59. In his memoirs, Paul Nitze, who ran the State Department's Policy and Planning Staff, disingenuously argues that MacArthur went beyond his orders by moving large forces to the Manchurian border that might provoke Chinese or Soviet intervention, but he doesn't mention that MacArthur was advancing north under orders from Washington. Paul. H. Nitze, with Ann M. Smith and Steven L. Rearden, *From Hiroshima to Glasnost: At the Center of Decision – A Memoir* (New York: Grove Weidenfeld, 1989), 108.

52. UN Resolution, July 7, 1950, https://documents-dds-ny.un.org/doc/RESOLUTION/GEN/NR0/059/74/IMG/NR005974.pdf?OpenElement

53. Truman, *Memoirs*, Vol. II, 359.

54. Some examples include: Ridgway, *The Korean War*, 44; Douglas MacArthur, *Reminiscences* (New York: McGraw-Hill, 1964), 358; Hess, *Presidential Decisions for War*, 45. Acheson titled his memoir *Present at the Creation: My Years in the State Department* (New York: W. W. Norton, 1969).

55. J. Lawton Collins, *War in Peacetime*, 149.

56. See especially *FRUS, 1950, Korea*, Vol. VII, 393–395, 458–461, 502–510, 600–603, 712–721, 781–782.

57. Hess, *Presidential Decisions for War*, 38, 44; John M. Pruitt Jr., "Limited War: A Model for Entry, Conduct, and Termination" (MA thesis, Naval Postgraduate School, 1984), 124; *FRUS, 1951, Korea and China*, Vol. VII, and fn. 3, https://history.state.gov/historicaldocuments/frus1950v07/d188

58. Dan Reiter, *How Wars End* (Princeton University Press, 2009), 67, 79.

59. Ibid., 66–67; Nerheim, "NSC-81/1," 11.

60. Hess, *Presidential Decisions for War*, 45.

61. Nerheim, "NSC-81/1," 13; William Stueck, *Rethinking the Korean War: A New Diplomatic and Strategic History* (Princeton University Press, 2002), 94–96, 98; Bradford A. Lee, "Strategic Interaction: Theory and History for Practitioners," in Thomas Mahnken, ed., *Competitive Strategies for the 21st Century* (Palo Alto, CA: Stanford University Press, 2012), 44 fn. 19.

62. Reiter, *How Wars End*, 63, 76.

63. Ibid., 67–68; Nerheim, "NSC-81/1," 16, 20–21; NSC-81/1, September 9, 1950, http://digitalarchive.wilsoncenter.org/document/116194.pdf

64. J. Lawton Collins, *War in Peacetime*, 147.

65. NSC-81/1, September 9, 1950. For the Truman administration and containment, see John Lewis Gaddis, *Strategies of Containment*, 2nd edn. (Oxford University Press, 2005), 3–124.

66. Truman, *Memoirs*, Vol. II, 345.

67. Michael R. Gordon and Bernard E. Trainor, *Endgame: The Inside Story of the Struggle for Iraq, from George W. Bush to Barack Obama* (New York: Pantheon, 2012), 8–10;

Condoleezza Rice, "Iraq: Goals, Objectives, and Strategy," October 29, 2002, Rumsfeld Papers, http://library.rumsfeld.com/doclib/sp/4136/2002-10-29%20From %20Condoleezza%20Rice%20re%20Principals'%20Committee%20Review%20of %20Iraq%20Policy%20Paper.pdf; George W. Bush, "President Discusses the Future of Iraq," February 26, 2003, https://georgewbush-whitehouse.archives.gov/news/ releases/2003/02/20030226-11.html

68. Gordon and Trainor, *Endgame*, 11–12.
69. Ibid., 12, 28.
70. Ibid., 13–15.
71. Ibid., 14–15.
72. Ibid., 18.
73. One expert identified nineteen different groups: Ahmed S. Hashim, *Insurgency and Counterinsurgency in Iraq* (Ithaca, NY: Cornell University Press, 2006), 170–176. Globalsecurity.org identified thirty groups at one point in 2005.
74. Millett, *The War for Korea, 1950–1951*, 14.
75. Clausewitz, *On War*, 632.
76. Manpreet Sethi, "Conventional War in the Presence of Nuclear Weapons," *Strategic Analysis*, Vol. 33, No. 3 (2009), 419. The author goes on to say:

> In fact, for this reason, it may be said that in the presence of nuclear weapons, Pakistan can never hope to militarily resolve the issue of Kashmir with India. It will have to ultimately find a political solution. It is a different matter, though, whether Pakistan is really interested in resolving the issue of Kashmir or whether it only uses this to further its military strategy of bleeding India through proxy war. See also Ignatius, "The Problem with America's Limited Wars."

See also Ignatius, "The Problem with America's Limited Wars."

77. Hess, *Presidential Decisions for War*, 220.
78. Saundby, "War – Limited or Unlimited?" 101.
79. The quotation is constructed from those of John D. Hayes, *Peripheral Strategy . . . Littoral Tactics . . . Military Policy: Strategic Aspects of World Political Geography* (New York: Rinehart and Co., 1957), 409, quoted in Wayne Richard Martin, "An Analysis of United States International Relations before and during Limited War" (Ph.D. thesis, University of Southern California, 1970), 10, and Thomas L. Fisher, "Limited War – What Is It?" *Air University Quarterly Review*, Vol. 9 (winter 1957–58), 141.
80. Strachan, *The Direction of War*, 130–133.
81. I am indebted to my old colleague Michael W. Jones for this point.
82. Lawrence Freedman, "On War and Choice," *The National Interest* (May–June 2010), 12–13. For an opposing view, one based upon the standard unclear definitions of war, see Richard N. Haass, *War of Necessity, War of Choice: A Memoir of Two Iraq Wars* (New York: Simon & Schuster, 2009), 9–11.
83. An example: Strobe Talbot, "Unilateralism: Anatomy of a Foreign Policy Disaster," *Brookings Institute* (February 21, 2007), www.brookings.edu/opin ions/unilateralism-anatomy-of-a-foreign-policy-disaster/
84. Lionel Beehner, "The 'Coalition of the Willing,'" *The Council on Foreign Relations* (February 22, 2007), www.cfr.org/backgrounder/coalition-willing
85. Harry G. Summers Jr., "Full Circle – World War II to the Persian Gulf," *Military Review* (February 1992), 40.
86. William O'Brien, *The Conduct of Just and Limited War* (New York: Praeger, 1981), 231.

87. Philip Gourevitch, "What Obama Didn't Say," *The New Yorker* (September 11, 2014), www.newyorker.com/news/daily-comment/obama-didnt-say

88. George Will, "Obama is Defying the Constitution on War," *The Washington Post* (September 17, 2014), www.washingtonpost.com/opinions/george-will-obama-needs-congress-to-approve-this-war/2014/09/17/26de9d3e-3dc9-11e4-boea-8141703bbf6f_story.html?noredirect=on&utm_term=.4c0e4073c2ba

89. Thomas M. Nichols, *Eve of Destruction: The Coming Age of Preventive War* (Philadelphia: University of Pennsylvania Press, 2008), 4–6.

90. Brodie, *Strategy in the Missile Age*, 227 fn. 2.

91. Nichols, *Eve of Destruction*, 4–6.

92. Quoted in Brodie, *Strategy in the Missile Age*, 234–235.

93. Nichols, *Eve of Destruction*, 4–6.

94. Brodie, "Unlimited Weapons and Limited War," 17.

95. Brodie, *Strategy in the Missile Age*, 235.

96. "NSC 68: A Report to the National Security Council, 14 April 1950," *Naval War College Review*, Vol. 27, No. 6 (May–June 1975), 51–108.

97. Paul Seabury, "Provisionality and Finality," *The Annals of the American Academy of Political and Social Science*, Vol. 392 (November 1970): 98.

98. Quincy Wright, "How Hostilities Have Ended: Peace Treaties and Alternatives," *The Annals of the American Academy of Political and Social Science*, Vol. 392 (November 1970), 53–54.

99. Gregory E. Fehling, "America's First Limited War," *Naval War College Review*, Vol. 53, No. 3 (summer 2000): 118, 121–127.

100. Mariah Zeisberg, *War Powers: The Politics of Constitutional Authority* (Princeton University Press, 2013), 1.

101. The War Powers Act of 1973, http://avalon.law.yale.edu/20th_century/warpower.asp

102. Fehling, "America's First Limited War," 118.

103. Summers, *On Strategy*, 46.

104. Seabury, "Provisionality and Finality," 98–99; Fehling, "America's First Limited War," 118.

105. Foreword in Hess, *Presidential Decisions for War*, ix.

106. Mark Clodfelter, "Nixon and the Air Weapon," in Dennis E. Showalter and John G. Albert, eds., *An American Dilemma: Vietnam, 1964–1973* (Chicago: Imprint Publications, 1993), 174.

107. Hess, *Presidential Decisions for War*, 225.

108. Charlie Savage, "Barack Obama's Q&A," *Boston Globe* (December 20, 2007), http://archive.boston.com/news/politics/2008/specials/CandidateQA/ObamaQA/

109. Hess, *Presidential Decisions for War*, 23, 25.

110. J. Lawton Collins, *War in Peacetime*, vii.

111. Hess, *Presidential Decisions for War*, 34.

112. Ibid., 34, 36.

113. Millett, *The War for Korea, 1950–1951*, 121.

114. Ibid., 122.

115. Acheson, *The Korean War*, 26.

116. Hess, *Presidential Decisions for War*, 34–35, 116.

117. Ibid., 35.

118. Acheson, *The Korean War*, 32–34.

119. US Government, Department of State, "Authority of the President to Repel the Attack in Korea," Department of State Memorandum of July 3, 1950, *Department of State Bulletin*, Vol. 23 (July 31, 1950), 173–177.

120. Ibid., 174–177.
121. Hess, *Presidential Decisions for War*, 36–37.
122. Ibid., 35.
123. J. Lawton Collins, *War in Peacetime*, 32.
124. Marilyn B. Young. "Historian Marilyn B. Young Discusses 'Limited War, Unlimited,'" webcast, Library of Congress, Washington, DC (July 8, 2009), www.loc.gov/today/cyberlc/feature_wdesc.php?rec=4683, minute 23:00.
125. Millett, *The War for Korea, 1950–1951*, 124.
126. Truman, *Memoirs*, Vol. II, 331–464. The only example I found in Truman's memoir where he calls the Korean War a war is when he recounts a meeting with British Prime Minister Clement Atlee: "Atlee also had doubts about a limited war in Korea. He said he saw the reason behind it and certainly considered it, rationally, the thing to do. But he foresaw trouble because, he believed, we would find people clamoring for total victory—and that meant unlimited war." Ibid., Vol. II, 406. Among the many interesting things about this statement is the failure of both leaders to under- stand that at that moment they were pursuing an unlimited objective against North Korea, as well as the fact that they could achieve victory in Korea without pursuing the added unlimited objective of overthrowing the Chinese regime.
127. Hess, *Presidential Decisions for War*, 38.
128. Ibid., 225–226.
129. Gacek, *The Logic of Force*, 195.
130. Herring, *America's Longest War*, 133–135.
131. Bruce Kuklick, *Blind Oracles: Intellectuals and War from Kennan to Kissinger* (Princeton University Press, 2006), 140.
132. Herring, *America's Longest War*, 136–137.
133. Hess, *Presidential Decisions for War*, 87–88.
134. Ibid., 86.
135. Kuklick, *Blind Oracles*, 139.
136. George C. Herring, "'In Cold Blood': LBJ's Conduct of Limited War in Vietnam," *The Harmon Memorial Lectures*, No. 93 (Colorado Springs, CO: US Air Force Academy, 1990), 11.
137. Hess, *Presidential Decisions for War*, 84.
138. Herring, "'In Cold Blood,'" 2.
139. Dale Walton, *The Myth of Inevitable US Defeat in Vietnam* (Abingdon, UK: Routledge, 2002), 22.
140. Kuklick, *Blind Oracles*, 140.
141. Bush and Scowcroft, *A World Transformed*, 417–418.
142. Freedman and Karsh, *The Gulf Conflict*, 294.
143. Ibid., 79–81, 83, 111.
144. Kevin M. Woods, *The Mother of All Battles: Saddam Hussein's Strategic Plan for the Persian Gulf War* (Annapolis, MD: Naval Institute Press, 2008), 159.
145. Statement by Secretary of Defense Weinberger at National Press Club, "The Uses of Military Power," November 28, 1984, http://insidethecoldwar.org/sites/default/files/documents/Statement%20by%20Secretary%20of%20Defense%20Weinberger%20at%20National%20Press%20Club,%20November%2028,%201984.pdf
146. "Powell's Doctrine, in Powell's Words," Washington Post (October 7, 2001), https://www.washingtonpost.com/archive/opinions/2001/10/07/powells-doctrine-in-powells-words/e8fd25c5-a97f-4550-8cbd-0588eb4a9d8e/

4   Constraints: Or Why Wars for Limited Political Aims are So Difficult

1. Clausewitz, *On War*, 637.
2. Tolstoy quoted in Michael Howard, "*Temperamenta Belli*: Can War be Controlled?" in Michael Howard, ed., *Restraints on War: Studies in the Limitation of Armed Conflict* (Oxford University Press, 1979), 7.
3. Raymond Aron quoted in Marilyn B. Young, "Limited War, Unlimited," minute 10:16.
4. See most famously Schelling, *The Strategy of Conflict*, especially 53.
5. Åkerman, *On the Doctrine of Limited War*, 16.
6. Michael Howard quoted in Ian Clark, *Limited Nuclear War: Political Theory and Conventions* (Princeton University Press, 1982), 27.
7. Some examples: G. Teitler, "Oorlogvoering: Eenvormigheid en Verscheidenheid," in G. Teitler, J. M. J. Bosch, and W. Klinkert, eds., *Militaire Stratégie* (Amsterdam: Mets & Schilt, 2002), 87–88; E lbridge Colby, "America Must Prepare for Limited War," *The National Interest* (November–December 2015), http://nationalinterest/.org/print/feature/america-must-prepare-limited-war-14104; Fisher, "Limited War – What Is It?", 127–142; Robert H. Scales Jr., *Firepower in Limited War*, revised edn. (Novato, CA: Presidion, 1995), x; Klaus Knorr, "Limited Strategic War," in Klaus Knorr and Thornton Read, eds., *Limited Strategic War* (New York: Praeger, 1962), 3–4, 20; Grygiel and Mitchell, "Limited War Is Back," 37–44, http://nationalinterest .org/feature/limited-war-back-11128
8. Clausewitz, *On War*, 594.
9. Corbett, *Some Principles of Maritime Strategy*, 59.
10. Richard Frank, "Ending the Pacific War: 'No Alternative to Annihilation,'" in Daniel Marston, ed., *The Pacific War Companion* (Oxford: Osprey Publishing, 2005), 227–245.
11. This argument is directly influenced by Robert Osgood's discussion of actual and self-imposed restraints.
12. Elkus, "The Shadow of Limited War."
13. Robert Saundby, "The Doctrine of Proportional Force," *Military Review*, Vol. 37 (October 1957), 88.
14. Pruitt, "Limited War," 30.
15. Joseph Lepgold and Brent L. Sterling, "When Do States Fight Limited Wars? Political Risk, Policy Risk, and Policy Choice," *Security Studies*, Vol. 9, No. 4 (2000), 130.
16. Clausewitz, *On War*, 77, 137.
17. Sun Tzu, *The Art of War*, 142–143.
18. Clausewitz, *On War*, 593.
19. Ibid., 260.
20. Ibid., 598.
21. Brodie, "Learning to Fight a Limited War," 31.
22. Summers, *On Strategy*, 34; Herring, "'In Cold Blood,'" 10–16.
23. Kissinger, *Diplomacy*, 674–677.
24. Sun Tzu, *The Art of War*, 73.
25. Kissinger, *Diplomacy*, 674–677.
26. Deitchman, *Limited War and American Defense Policy*, 88–89.
27. Bill Hayden, "Opening Address," in Peter R. Young, ed., *Defence and the Media in the Time of Limited War* (London: Frank Cass, 1992), 13.
28. Rupert Smith, *The Utility of Force*, 286–289, 400.

29. Richard C. Eichenberg, "Victory Has Many Friends: US Public Opinion and the Use of Military Force, 1981–2005," *International Security*, Vol. 30, No. 1 (summer 2005), 141; Christopher Gelpi, Peter D. Feaver, and Jason Reifler, "Success Matters: Casualty Sensitivity and the War in Iraq," *International Security*, Vol. 30, No. 3 (winter 2005–06), 45.
30. Eichenberg, "Victory Has Many Friends," 141; Freedman and Karsh, *The Gulf Conflict*, 227.
31. Steven Casey, *Selling the Korean War: Propaganda, Politics, and Public Opinion in the United States, 1950–1953* (Oxford University Press, 2008), 359.
32. Bruce A. Lesh, "Limited War or Rollback of Communism?: Truman, MacArthur, and the Korean Conflict," *OAH Magazine of History*, Vol. 22, No. 4 (October 2008), 50.
33. Steven Philip Gietschier, "Limited War and the Home Front: Ohio during the Korean War" (Ph.D. thesis, The Ohio State University, 1977),221.
34. Hess, *Presidential Decisions for War*, 70.
35. Lesh, "Limited War or Rollback of Communism," 50.
36. J. Lawton Collins, *War in Peacetime*, 303.
37. Hess, *Presidential Decisions for War*, 227.
38. James R. Kerin Jr., *Remembering Limited War: Reflections on the Korean War in Selected American Novels* (Carlisle Barracks, PA: US Army War College, 2000).
39. Herring, "'In Cold Blood,'" 10–14, 17–18.
40. W. Thomas Mallison Jr., *Studies in the Law of Naval Warfare: Submarines in General and Limited Wars* (Washington, DC: USGPO, 1968), 183.
41. Herring, "'In Cold Blood,'" 16–17.
42. Rosen, "Vietnam and the American Theory of Limited War," 134.
43. Hess, *Presidential Decisions for War*, x.
44. Kissinger, *Diplomacy*, 675–676.
45. William S. Turley, *The Second Indochina War: A Concise Political and Military History*, 2nd edn. (Lanham, MD: Rowan and Littlefield, 2009), 151–154.
46. Fred Charles Iklé, *Every War Must End* (New York: Columbia University Press, 1971), 24.
47. Jomini, *The Art of War*, 14.
48. Iklé, *Every War Must End*, 27.
49. Warner and Warner, *The Tide at Sunrise*, 176–177.
50. James, *Refighting the Last War*, 17.
51. Gacek, *The Logic of Force*, 55; Acheson, *The Korean War*, 55; Truman, *Memoirs*, Vol. II, 361–362.
52. Nitze, *From Hiroshima to Glasnost*, 108.
53. Osgood, *Limited War*, 172.
54. Hess, *Presidential Decisions for War*, 54.
55. Nathan Yu-jen Lai, "United States Policy and the Diplomacy of Limited War in Korea, 1950–1951" (Ph.D. thesis, University of Massachusetts, 1974), 147–148.
56. J. Lawton Collins, *War in Peacetime*, 175.
57. Hess, *Presidential Decisions for War*, 45.
58. Acheson, *The Korean War*, 58.
59. Carter Malkasian, "Toward a Better Understanding of Attrition: The Korean and Vietnam Wars," *The Journal of Military History*, Vol. 68, No. 3 (July 2004), 929.
60. Turley, *The Second Indochina War*, 96; Lien-Hang T. Nguyen, *Hanoi's War: An International History of the War for Peace in Vietnam* (Chapel Hill, NC: University of North Carolina Press, 2012), 116, 128.
61. This is explored in Gacek, *The Logic of Force*, 158–178.
62. Schnabel, *Policy and Direction*, 76.

63. Malkasian, "Toward a Better Understanding of Attrition," 929.
64. David Clayton, "British Foreign Economic Policy towards China, 1949–60," *Electronic Journal of International History*, Article 6, http://sas-space.sas.ac.uk /3393/1/Journal_of_International_History_2000_n6_Clayton.pdf
65. Mallison, *Studies in the Law of Naval Warfare*, v.
66. Howard, "*Temperamenta Belli*," 7.
67. On North Vietnamese Communist strategy, see Douglas Pike, *Viet Cong: The Organization and Techniques of the National Liberation Front of South Vietnam* (Cambridge, MA: MIT Press, 1966), 213–253.
68. John A. Thompson, *A Sense of Power: The Roots of America's Global Role* (Ithaca, NY: Cornell University Press, 2015), 6.
69. Corbett, *Some Principles of Maritime Strategy*, 59.
70. Deitchman, *Limited War and American Defense Policy*, 82–83.
71. Corbett, *Some Principles of Maritime Strategy*, 80.
72. This is inspired by a discussion in Robert Strausz-Hupé, "Nuclear Blackmail and Limited War," *Yale Review*, Vol. 48 (winter 1959), 179.
73. Iklé, *Every War Must End*, xii–xxiii.
74. Traverso, ed., *Korea and the Limits of Limited War*, 35.
75. Gacek, *The Logic of Force*, 58–60.
76. J. Lawton Collins, *War in Peacetime*, 264.
77. Kissinger, *Diplomacy*, 680–681; Nguyen, *Hanoi's War*, 163; Gregory Daddis, "'A Better War?' – The View from the Nixon White House," *Journal of Strategic Studies*, Vol. 36, No. 3 (2013), 365–372.
78. Schelling, *Arms and Influence*, 132–133.
79. Raghavan, "Limited War and Nuclear Escalation in South Asia," 87–89.
80. Saundby, "The Doctrine of Proportional Force," 87.
81. Clausewitz, *On War*, 81.
82. de Wijk, *The Art of Military Coercion*, 14.
83. Douglas MacArthur, "Farewell Address to Congress, April 19, 1951," www .americanrhetoric.com/speeches/douglasmacarthurfarewelladdress.htm
84. Elkus, "The Shadow of Limited War"; Eldon Carr, *The Role of the Military in Ending Limited War*, USAWC Research Paper (Carlisle Barracks, PA: US Army War College, 1973), 15.
85. Hampton, "Unlimited Confusion over Limited War," 28–29. Hampton realized the inherent escalatory danger, though his article is unclear on a definition of limited war.
86. General James Gavin, *War and Peace in the Space Age*, quoted in Robert C. Richardson III, "Do We Need Unlimited Forces for Limited War?" *Air Force*, Vol. 42 (March 1959), 53.
87. Clausewitz, *On War*, 585.
88. James, *Refighting the Last War*, 18–19.
89. Millett, *The War for Korea, 1950–1951*, 132–133.
90. Larry Elowitz, "Korea and Vietnam: Limited War and the American Political System" (Ph.D. thesis, The University of Florida, 1972), 214; Colin F. Jackson, "Lost Chance or Lost Horizon?" 276–277.
91. MacArthur, *Reminiscences*, 337.
92. J. Lawton Collins, *War in Peacetime*, 233–234.
93. Ibid., 205–206.
94. James M. Gavin, "Why Limited War?" *Ordnance*, Vol. 42 (April 1958), 809.
95. J. Lawton Collins, *War in Peacetime*, 18–19; Hess, *Presidential Decisions for War*, 8; Millett, *The War in Korea, 1950–1951*, 126.

96. Taewoo Kim, "Limited War, Unlimited Targets," 489.
97. Millett, *The War in Korea, 1950–1951*, 170.
98. Schnabel, *Policy and Direction*, 240–247.
99. MacArthur, *Reminiscences*, 372.
100. Taewoo Kim, "Limited War, Unlimited Targets," 489.
101. Elowitz, "Korea and Vietnam," 215.
102. MacArthur, *Reminiscences*, 331.
103. Stueck, *Rethinking the Korean War*, 165; Schnabel, *Policy and Direction*, 393.
104. Gacek, *The Logic of Force*, 70–71.
105. Taewoo Kim, "Limited War, Unlimited Targets," 487, 489–490.
106. Ridgway, *The Korean War*, 75–76.
107. Taewoo Kim, "Limited War, Unlimited Targets," 489.
108. Rosemary Foot, *A Substitute for Victory: The Politics of Peacemaking at the Korean Armistice Talks* (Ithaca, NY: Cornell University Press, 1990), 213–214.
109. Gordon and Trainor, *The Generals' War*, 153–154.
110. Polly M. Holdorf, "Limited Nuclear War in the 21st Century," in Mark Jansson, ed., *A Collection of Papers from the 2010 Nuclear Scholars Initiative* (Washington, DC: CSIS, 2010), 138.
111. For a brief overview of limited war theory development and nuclear war (though one suffering from the standard definitional issues), see Andrew L. Ross, "The Origins of Limited Nuclear War Theory," in Jeffrey A. Larsen and Kerry M. Kartchner, eds., *On Limited Nuclear War in the 21st Century* (Stanford University Press, 2014), 21–48.
112. Kissinger, "Limited War: Conventional or Nuclear?" 2–11. See also Henry A. Kissinger, *Nuclear Weapons and Foreign Policy* (New York: Harper & Brothers, 1957), 174–202; Henry A. Kissinger, *The Necessity for Choice: Prospects of American Foreign Policy* (New York: Harper, 1960), 55–98. For a critical review of one of his works, see Paul. H. Nitze, "Limited Wars or Massive Retaliation?" review of Henry A. Kissinger, *Nuclear Weapons and Foreign Policy, The Reporter* (September 5, 1957), 40–41.
113. Some examples: Anthony Buzzard, P. M. S. Blackett, Denis Healey, and Richard Goold-Adams, *On Limiting Atomic War* (London: Royal Institute of International Affairs, 1956); T. N. Dupuy, "Can America Fight a Limited Nuclear War?" *Survival: Global Politics and Strategy*, Vol. 3, No. 5 (1961), 220–234; Lawrence Martin, "Limited Nuclear War," in Howard, ed., *Restraints on War*, 103–122; Eric Mlyn, *The State, Society, and Limited Nuclear War* (Albany, NY: State University of New York Press, 1995); Osgood, *Limited War*, 251–259. The bibliography has many more.
114. Terence Check, "'Clean' Bombs and 'Limited' War: Edward Teller's Cold War Arguments," in James F. Klumpp, ed., *Argument in a Time of Change: Definitions, Frameworks, and Critiques* (Annandale, VA: National Communications Association, 1998), 306–307.
115. One of many examples: Lawrence Freedman, *The Evolution of Nuclear Strategy* (New York: St. Martin's Press, 1983).
116. For one of many discussions, see Brodie, *Strategy in the Missile Age*, 322–323.
117. Ibid., 322–323 fn. 9.
118. Brodie, *The Meaning of Limited War*, 21, see also 16–17.
119. Hanson W. Baldwin, "Limited War," *The Atlantic Monthly*, Vol. 203 (May 1959), 40.
120. Krishnaswamy Subrahmanyam, quoted in Ali Ahmed, *India's Doctrine Puzzle: Limiting War in South Asia* (New Delhi: Routledge, 2014), 31.

121. Robert B. Strassler, ed., *The Landmark Thucydides: A Comprehensive Guide to the Peloponnesian War* (New York: Touchstone, 1996), 43.
122. Deitchman, *Limited War and American Defense Policy*, 46. See also V. Mochalov and V. Dashichev, "The Smoke Screen of the American Imperialists," *Red Star* (December 17, 1957), Leon Gouré, trans., published as *Soviet Commentary on the Doctrine of Limited Nuclear War* (Santa Monica, CA: RAND, 1958); Lockwood, *The Soviet View of US Strategic Doctrine: Implications for Decision Making*, 65–66.
123. Kanwal in Bakshi, *Limited Wars in South Asia*, ix.
124. Hampton, "Unlimited Confusion over Limited War," 40.
125. Hess, *Presidential Decisions for War*, 60–62.
126. Brodie, *The Meaning of Limited War*, 13–14.
127. Saundby, "The Doctrine of Proportional Force," 88.
128. Quinn J. Rhodes, "Limited War under the Nuclear Umbrella: An Analysis of India's Cold Start Doctrine and Its Implications for Stability on the Subcontinent" (MA thesis, Naval Postgraduate School, 2010),67–68.
129. Jonathan Haslam, *Russia's Cold War: From the October Revolution to the Fall of the Wall* (New Haven, CT: Yale University Press, 2011), 257–259; Kerry R. Bolton, "Sino–Soviet–US Relations and the 1969 Nuclear Threat," *Foreign Policy Journal* (May 17, 2010), www.foreignpolicyjournal.com/2010/05/17/sino-soviet-us-relations-and-the-1969-nuclear-threat/3/
130. Feroz Hassan Khan, Peter R. Lavoy, and Christopher Clary, "Pakistan's Motivations and Calculations for the Kargil Conflict," in Peter R. Lavoy, *Asymmetric Warfare in South Asia: The Causes and Consequences of the Kargil Conflict* (Cambridge University Press, 2009), 64–65.
131. Manpreet Sethi, "Conventional War in the Presence of Nuclear Weapons," *Strategic Analysis*, 416–418.
132. This is, of course, a point much debated. On Saddam's simultaneous pre-2003 efforts to disarm, maintain his WMD manufacturing infrastructure, and bluff his enemies into believing he had WMD, see Kevin M. Woods, Michael R. Pease, Mark E. Stout, Williamson Murray, and James G. Lacey, *The Iraqi Perspectives Project: A View of Operation Iraqi Freedom from Saddam's Senior Leadership* (Washington, DC: Joint Center for Operational Analysis, 2013), 91–95. For amounts of chemical weapons and uranium found in Iraq after 2003, see Deroy Murdock, "Bush Didn't Lie: Then Why Did His Administration Sit on the Evidence of Saddam Hussein's WMDs?," *National Review* (October 16, 2014), www.nationalreview.com/2014/10/bush-didnt-lie-deroy-murdock/
133. Freedberg, "No Longer Unthinkable."
134. James Cable, "Limited War," *International Relations*, Vol. 11, No. 6 (1993), 561, suggests "Humanitarian Constraints," but is this violence or the level of violence?
135. Deitchman, *Limited War and American Defense Policy*, 132.
136. Jomini, *The Art of War*, 45–46.
137. Niccolò Machiavelli, *Discourses on Livy*, Ninnian Hill Thomson, trans. (Mineola, NY: Dover Publications, 2007), 175.
138. Geoffrey Best, "Restraints on War by Land before 1945," in Howard, ed., *Restraints on War*, 2.
139. Quincy Wright, *A Study of War*, 2nd edn. (University of Chicago Press, 1965), 1322.

5   Strategy: How to Think about Fighting for a Limited Political Aim

1. Clausewitz, *On War*, 178–179.
2. Quoted in Herring, "'In Cold Blood,'" 4.

3. Kuklick, *Blind Oracles*, 145.
4. Herring, "'In Cold Blood,'" 4.
5. Hess, *Presidential Decisions for War*, 125.
6. An example: Robert E. Osgood, "Limited War Strategy," *Army*, Vol. 9 (December 1958), 53–54.
7. In Corbett's view, limited wars have two stages: 1) the territorial stage, meaning occupying what you want; and 2) the coercive stage, meaning pressuring the enemy to agree to give you what you want; see *Some Principles of Maritime Strategy*, 46. His first stage is too restrictive, as not all limited wars are fought for territorial objectives, and coercion is the means of achieving what one wants.
8. Clausewitz, *On War*, 77, 81, 177.
9. In one example, coercion is defined as "the use of threatened force, and at times the limited use of actual force to back up the threat, to induce an adversary to change its behavior." Using force is not the same as threatening it. Its use changes everything. Daniel Byman and Matthew Waxman, *The Dynamics of Coercion: American Foreign Policy and the Limits of Military Might* (Cambridge University Press, 2002), 1.
10. Some examples: de Wijk, *The Art of Military Coercion*, 11–12; Patrick C. Bratton, "When Is Coercion Successful? And Why Can't We Agree on It?" *Naval War College Review*, Vol. 58, No. 3 (summer 2005), 101; Byman and Waxman, *The Dynamics of Coercion*, 1, 6–8; Schelling, *Arms and Influence*, 69–80; Robert J. Art, *A Grand Strategy for America* (Ithaca, NY: Cornell University Press, 2003), 4–5.
11. An analysis of part of the problem: Bratton, "When Is Coercion Successful?" 100.
12. Ibid., 101.
13. André Beaufre, *Strategy of Action*, R. H. Barry, trans. (London: Faber and Faber, 1967), 27.
14. Charles-Philippe David and Jean-Jacques Roche, *Théories de la sécurité: Définitions, approches, et concepts de la sécurité internationale* (Paris: Montchrestien, 2002), 50.
15. Åkerman, *On the Doctrine of Limited War*, 158–159.
16. Kissinger, "Limited War: Conventional or Nuclear?" 4–5.
17. Brodie, *Strategy in the Missile Age*, 272.
18. Kissinger, *Nuclear Weapons and Foreign Policy*, 132–134. For a good discus- sion of the psychological, see also Åkerman, *On the Doctrine of Limited War*, 152.
19. Maxwell D. Taylor, "On Limited War," *Army Information Digest*, Vol. 13 (June 1958), 5.
20. Brodie, *Strategy in the Missile Age*, 274, 397.
21. Brett Stephens, "Normalizing Iran" (January 18, 2016), *Wall Street Journal*, www.wsj.com/articles/normalizing-iran-1453162144
22. de Wijk, *The Art of Military Coercion*, 9–10.
23. Jeffrey Record, *Beating Goliath: Why Insurgencies Win* (Washington, DC: Potomac Books, 2007), 5.
24. Strassler, ed., *The Landmark Thucydides*, 44.
25. Sun Tzu, *The Art of War*, 84.
26. Clausewitz, *On War*, 85–586.
27. Ibid., 585–586.
28. Ibid., 89.
29. Letter to Giovanni Ridolfi, June 12, 1506, in Marco Cesa, ed., *Machiavelli on International Relations* (Oxford University Press, 2014), 127.
30. Rupert Smith, *The Utility of Force*, 240–241.

31. Kissinger, *Nuclear Weapons and Foreign Policy*, 151.
32. Rupert Smith, *The Utility of Force*, 244, 278.
33. Sun Tzu, *The Art of War*, 71.
34. Clausewitz, *On War*, 117.
35. Sun Tzu, *The Art of War*, 144–145.
36. Jomini, *The Art of War*, 34.
37. Clausewitz, *On War*, 117, 140.
38. Ibid., 595–596, 618.
39. Donald Stoker and Michael W. Jones, "Colonial Military Strategy," in Donald Stoker, Kenneth J. Hagan, and Michael T. McMaster, eds., *Strategy in the War of American Independence: A Global Approach* (London: Routledge, 2010), 5–14.
40. Li, *China's Battle for Korea*, 53–54.
41. See John Shy, *A People Numerous and Armed: Reflections on the Military Struggle for American Independence* (Ann Arbor: University of Michigan Press, 1990), 193–212.
42. Gregory Daddis, *Westmoreland's War: Reassessing American Strategy in Vietnam* (Oxford University Press, 2014), 60, 73.
43. Gerhard Ritter, *Frederick the Great: A Historical Profile*, Peter Paret, ed. and trans. (Berkeley: University of California Press, 1968), 125.
44. Stoker, *The Grand Design*, 351–353.
45. Daddis, *Westmoreland's War*, 60.
46. Woods, *The Mother of All Battles*, 14–21, 129, 137–139.
47. For an account of this by a critic and participant, see U. S. Grant Sharp, *Strategy for Defeat: Vietnam in Retrospect* (Novato, CA: Presidio, 1998).
48. Iklé, *Every War Must End*, 45–46, 49, 52.
49. Iklé, *Every War Must End*, 45–46, 49, 52.
50. Sun Tzu, *The Art of War*, 113.
51. Clausewitz, *On War*, 77.
52. Ibid., 611–612.
53. Corbett writes that "limited wars do not turn upon the armed strength of the belligerents, but upon the amount of that strength which they are able or willing to bring to bear at the decisive point." But this isn't always true. They *can* turn on strength. It is more likely to turn on the defender's strength – if both sides are seeking a limited objective – because of the natural strength of the defense. But this is sometimes not enough.
54. See Gordon and Trainor, *The Generals' War*, 153–154.
55. Beaufre, *Strategy of Action*, 110–111.
56. Rupert Smith, *The Utility of Force*, 272–273, 291, 294, 380–381.
57. Codevilla and Seabury, *War*, 11.
58. Sun Tzu, *The Art of War*, 66.
59. Rupert Smith, *The Utility of Force*, 289.
60. Stoker, *The Grand Design*, 32–33.
61. Nish, *The Origins of the Russo-Japanese War*, 157.
62. Warner and Warner, *The Tide at Sunrise*, 158, 162–166.
63. Kissinger, *Nuclear Weapons and Foreign Policy*, 237–238.
64. Ramon Λ. Ivey, "Limited War, National Will, and the All Volunteer Army," Study Project (Carlisle Barracks, PA: US Army War College, 1988), 5.
65. Stoker and Jones, "Colonial Military Strategy," 11–18, 29–30.
66. Mao Tse-Tung, "The Three Stages of Protracted War," in *Selected Military Writings* (Peking: Foreign Language Press, 1967), 210–219.

67. Ian F. W. Beckett, *Modern Insurgencies: Guerrillas and Their Opponents since 1750* (London: Routledge, 2001), 73–74.
68. Mao Tse-Tung, *On Guerrilla Warfare*, Samuel B. Griffith II, trans. (Urbana, IL: University of Illinois Press, 2002).
69. Beckett, *Modern Insurgencies*, 74.
70. Ibid., 75.
71. Ibid., 75–76.
72. Andrew Mack, "Why Big Nations Lose Small Wars: The Politics of Asymmetric Conflict," *World Politics*, Vol. 27, No. 2 (1975), 185.
73. Callwell, *Small Wars*, 27.
74. President Trump also said the US sought to achieve a number of political aims with this attack. See Michael C. Bender and Louise Radnofsky, "Trump Says Strikes Aimed at Ending Syria's Use of Chemical Weapons, Sending Message to Russia and Iran," *The Wall Street Journal* (April 13, 2018).
75. Bradford A. Lee, "Strategic Interaction," 35.
76. Ibid., 40.
77. *The New York Times* (December 19, 2014), www.nytimes.com/2014/12/20/world/fbi-accuses-north-korean-government-in-cyberattack-on-sony-pictures.html
78. This is influenced by Saundby, "The Doctrine of Proportional Force," 85.
79. Ibid., 85.
80. Strachan, "Strategy and the Limitation of War," 33.
81. Herring, "'In Cold Blood,'" 4, 23.
82. Walton, *The Myth of Inevitable US Defeat*, 109.
83. Allan R. Millett and Peter Maslowski, *For the Common Defense: A Military History of the United States of America*, 2nd edn. (New York: Free Press, 1994), 577.
84. Rosen, "Vietnam and the American Theory of Limited War," 91.
85. Sent, *Some Like It Cold*, 465.
86. Schelling, *Arms and Influence*, 286.
87. George H. Quester, "Wars Prolonged by Misunderstood Signals," *The Annals of the American Academy of Political and Social Science*, Vol. 392 (November 1970), 35.
88. David Milne, "'Our Equivalent of Guerrilla Warfare': Walt Rostow and the Bombing of Vietnam, 1961–1968," *The Journal of Military History*, Vol. 71, No. 1 (January 2007), 185.
89. Kuklick, *Blind Oracles*, 145.
90. Robert Pape, *Bombing to Win: Air Power and Coercion in War* (Ithaca, NY: Cornell University Press, 1996), 175, 178–180.
91. Milne, "'Our Equivalent of Guerrilla Warfare,'" 187, 184–185, 188.
92. Pape, *Bombing to Win*, 178–179.
93. Sharp, *Strategy for Defeat*, 65–66.
94. Pape, *Bombing to Win*, 178–179; Clodfelter, *The Limits of Air Power*, 92–107.
95. Clodfelter, *The Limits of Air Power*, 119.
96. Milne, "'Our Equivalent of Guerrilla Warfare,'" 190; Sharp, *Strategy for Defeat*, 107.
97. Pape, *Bombing to Win*, 183–184; Clodfelter, *The Limits of Air Power*, 107–112.
98. Pape, *Bombing to Win*, 184.
99. Ibid., 185, 192.
100. Milne, "'Our Equivalent of Guerrilla Warfare,'" 171.
101. Foot, *A Substitute for Victory*, 221.
102. Gacek, *The Logic of Force*, 400 fn. 19.

103. Haslam, *Russia's Cold War*, 225.
104. Millet and Maslowski, *For the Common Defense*, 585.
105. Pape, *Bombing to Win*, 193.
106. Ridgway, *The Korean War*, 75.
107. Sharp, *Strategy for Defeat*, 134.
108. Jasjit Singh, "Dynamics of Limited War," *Strategic Analysis*, Vol. 24, No. 7 (2000), 1209; Beaufre, *Strategy of Action*, 115–116; Freedman, "Ukraine and the Art of Limited War."
109. Kissinger, *Nuclear Weapons and Foreign Policy*, 155.
110. J. Boone Bartholomees Jr., "The Issue of Attrition," *Parameters*, Vol. 38, No. 2 (spring 2010), 9–10.
111. Ibid., 9–10, 14.
112. Malkasian, "Toward a Better Understanding of Attrition," 922.
113. J. Lawton Collins, *War in Peacetime*, 305–306.
114. Michael C. Hunt, "Beijing and the Korean Crisis, June 1950–June 1951," *Political Science Quarterly*, Vol. 107, No. 3 (autumn 1992), 465–468; Malkasian, "Toward a Better Understanding of Attrition," 922.
115. Malkasian, "Toward a Better Understanding of Attrition," 931–932.
116. Walton, *The Myth of Inevitable US Defeat*, 53.
117. Daddis, *Westmoreland's War*, 78.
118. Ibid., 60, 76–77.
119. Walton, *The Myth of Inevitable US Defeat*, 50, 54, 48–49; Millet and Maslowski, *For the Common Defense*, 580.
120. Malkasian, "Toward a Better Understanding of Attrition," 934, 937–938.
121. Walton, *The Myth of Inevitable US Defeat*, 50, 54, 58; Millet and Maslowski, *For the Common Defense*, 580–581.
122. Qiang Zhai, *China and the Vietnam Wars, 1950–1975* (Chapel Hill, NC: University of North Carolina Press, 2000), ix–x, 153.
123. On North Vietnamese strategy, see Nguyen, *Hanoi's War*; Turley, *The Second Indochina War*; Pike, *Viet Cong*.
124. Chester J. Pach, *Arming the Free World: The Origins of the United States Military Assistance Program, 1945–1950* (Chapel Hill, NC: University of North Carolina Press, 1991), 135.
125. Brodie, *The Meaning of Limited War*, 12.
126. Raymond Aron, "Can War in the Atomic Age Be Limited?" *Confluence*, Vol. 5 (July 1956), 104. This article also appears as: "A l'Âge atomique peut-on limiter la guerre?" *Preuves: Cahiers mensuels du congrès pour la liberté de la culture*, No. 58 (December 1958), 30–39.
127. MacArthur, "Farewell Address to Congress, April 19, 1951."
128. Freedman, *The Evolution of Nuclear Strategy*; Iklé, *Every War Must End*, 27.
129. Holdorf, "Limited Nuclear War in the 21st Century," 138, 142.
130. See the discussion in Ali Ahmed, *India's Doctrine Puzzle*, 32; Khurshid Khan, "Limited War under the Nuclear Umbrella and Its Implications for South Asia," http://sacw.pagesperso-orange.fr/saan/2005/khurshidkhan.pdf, 1, 9; Chandran, *Limited War*, 104.
131. Ali Ahmed, *India's Doctrine Puzzle*, 5. See also Rahul K. Bhonsle, "Kargil 1999: Limited War, Unlimited Consequences," *CLAWS Journal* (summer 2009), 81–82.
132. Khan, "Limited War under the Nuclear Umbrella," 5.
133. Walter C. Ladwig III, "A Cold Start for Hot Wars? The Indian Army's New Limited War Doctrine," *International Security*, Vol. 32, No. 3 (winter 2007–08), 158; Rhodes, "Limited War under the Nuclear Umbrella," 1, 19, 21.

134. Bhonsle, "Kargil 1999," 75–76, 83. On the Kargil War see also: Zafar Iqbal Cheema, "The Strategic Context of the Kargil Conflict: A Pakistani Perspective," in Lavoy, *Asymmetric Warfare in South Asia*, 41–63; Khan, Lavoy, and Clary, "Pakistan's Motivations and Calculations for the Kargil Conflict," 64–91.

135. Ladwig, "A Cold Start for Hot Wars?" 158–162.

136. Ibid., 162–166.

137. Ibid., 166, 172.

138. Ali Ahmed, *India's Doctrine Puzzle*, 3.

139. Shashank Joshi, "India's Military Instrument: A Doctrine Stillborn," *Journal of Strategic Studies*, Vol. 36, No. 4 (2013), 528–530.

140. Roger Darling, "A New Conceptual Scheme for Analyzing Insurgency," *Military Review*, Vol. 54, No. 2 (February 1974), 27.

141. United States, Department of the Navy, USMC, *Small Wars Manual* (Washington, DC: USGPO, 1987 [1940]), 15–16.

142. Based upon Mao, *On Guerrilla Warfare*, 47–48.

143. Clausewitz, *On War*, 480.

144. Mao, *On Guerrilla Warfare*, 49.

145. Douglas Porch, *The French Secret Services: A History of French Intelligence from the Dreyfus Affair to the Gulf War* (New York: Farrar, Straus, and Giroux, 2003), 362–363; Alistair Horne, *A Savage War of Peace: Algeria, 1954–1962* (New York Review of Books, 2006), 82.

146. Donald Stoker, "Six Reasons Insurgencies Lose: A Contrarian View," *Small Wars Journal* (July 4, 2009), http://smallwarsjournal.com/jrnl/art/six-reasons-insurgencies-lose, 5–6.

147. Peter R. Neumann and M. L. R. Smith, "Strategic Terrorism: The Framework and Its Fallacies," *Journal of Strategic Studies*, Vol. 28, No. 4 (2005), 573, 576–577.

148. Boaz Ganor, "Defining Terrorism – Is One Man's Terrorist Another Man's Freedom Fighter?" *International Institute for Counterterrorism* (January 1, 2010), www.ict.org.il/Article/1123/Defining-Terrorism-Is-One-Mans-Terrorist-Another-Mans-Freedom-Fighter#gsc.tab=0

149. Neumann and Smith, "Strategic Terrorism," 574, 576.

150. Porch, *The French Secret Services*, 362–363.

151. On the use of police here, see Donald Stoker and Edward B. Westermann, eds. *Expeditionary Police Advising and Militarization: Building Security in a Fractured World* (Solihull, UK: Helion & Co., 2018).

152. John J. McCuen, *The Art of Counter-Revolutionary Warfare: A Psycho-Politico-Military Strategy of Counter-Insurgency* (Harrisburg, PA: Stackpole, 1966), 31.

153. Neumann and Smith, "Strategic Terrorism," 578.

154. McCuen, *The Art of Counter-Revolutionary Warfare*, 30.

155. Ibid., 33.

156. Patrick B. Johnston and Brian R. Urlacher, "Explaining the Duration of Counterinsurgency Campaigns" (February 25, 2012), http://patrickjohnston/.info/materials/duration.pdf; Donald Stoker, "Insurgencies Rarely Win and Iraq Won't Be Any Different (Maybe)," *Foreign Policy* (January 15, 2007), http://foreignpolicy.com/2007/01/15/insurgencies-rarely-win-and-iraq-wont-be-any-different-maybe/

157. Robert Thompson quoted in Kevin Dougherty, *The United States Military in Limited War: Case Studies in Success and Failure* (Jefferson, NC: McFarland, 2012), 92–93.

158. John McCuen, quoted in Swaran Singh, *Limited War: The Challenge of US Military Strategy* (New Delhi: Lancers Books, 1995), 141–142.

159. David Galula, *Pacification in Algeria, 1956–1958* (Santa Monica, CA: Rand, 2006 [1963]), 208, 268, 177.
160. Record, *Beating Goliath*, 67.
161. Robert Taber, *The War of the Flea: Guerrilla Warfare Theory and Practice* (St. Albans, UK: Paladin, 1970), 22–23.
162. Mao, *On Guerrilla Warfare*, 44.
163. McCuen quoted in Swaran Singh, *Limited War*, 139.
164. USMC, *Small Wars Manual*, 13.
165. Anthony Clayton, *The Wars of French Decolonization* (London: Routledge, 1994), 156, 159; Porch, *The French Secret Services*, 372.
166. The authoritative studies are: Michael R. Gordon and Bernard E. Trainor, *Cobra II: The Inside Story of the Invasion and Occupation of Iraq* (New York: Vintage, 2007); Gordon and Trainor, *Endgame*.
167. USMC, *Small Wars Manual*, 15.
168. James S. Corum, "Building the Malayan Army and Police – Britain's Experience during the Malayan Emergency, 1948–1960," in Kendall D. Gott, ed., *Security Assistance: US and International Historical Perspectives* (Leavenworth, KS: Combat Studies Institute Press, 2006), 292–295.
169. Bernard B. Fall, "The Theory and Practice of Insurgency and Counter-Insurgency," *Military Review* (September–October 2015), 46.
170. Callwell, *Small Wars*, 130–135; Anthony Clayton, *The Wars of French Decolonization*, 121; Douglas Porch, *Counterinsurgency: Exposing the Myths of the New Way of War* (Cambridge University Press, 2013), 5–6.
171. Turley, *The Second Indochina War*, 70–71; Guenter Lewy, *America in Vietnam* (Oxford University Press, 1980), 25; Ian F. W. Beckett, "Robert Thompson and the British Advisory Mission to South Vietnam, 1961–1965," *Small Wars & Insurgencies*, Vol. 8, No. 3 (1997), 41–63.
172. David H. Ucko, "'The People are Revolting': An Anatomy of Authoritarian Counterinsurgency," *Journal of Strategic Studies*, Vol. 39, No. 1 (2016), 43, 44–45.
173. Edward N. Luttwak, *Strategy: The Logic of War and Peace* (Cambridge, MA: Belknap Press of Harvard, 1987), 132.
174. Ucko, "'The People Are Revolting,'" 43, 45, 48–49.
175. Patrick B. Johnston, "Does Decapitation Work? Assessing the Effectiveness of Leadership Targeting in Counterinsurgency Campaigns," *International Security*, Vol. 36, No. 4 (spring 2012), 62–65, 68–69, 75, 77; Jenna Jordan, "Attacking the Leader, Missing the Mark: Why Terrorist Groups Survive Decapitation Strikes," *International Security*, Vol. 38, No. 4 (spring 2014), 10–11 and fn. 15.
176. Otto Heilbrunn, "When the Counter-Insurgents Cannot Win," *Royal United Services Institution Journal*, Vol. 114, No. 653 (March 1969), 56–57.
177. Michael Howard, "The Classical Strategists," *The Adelphi Papers*, Vol. 9, No. 54 (1969), 31.
178. Pach, *Arming the Free World*, 160, 176, 195.
179. T. E. Lawrence, "The 27 Articles of T. E. Lawrence," *The Arab Bulletin* (August 20, 1917), https://wwi.lib.byu.edu/index.php/The_27_Articles_of_T.E._Lawrence
180. USMC, *Small Wars Manual*, 20–21.
181. Fall, "The Theory and Practice of Insurgency and Counter-Insurgency," 45–46.
182. Taber, *The War of the Flea*, 21–23.
183. Ibid., 23.
184. This is the major theme of Porch, *Counterinsurgency*.

185. Galula, *Pacification in Algeria*, 178–179.
186. Ibid., 104.
187. Haroro J. Ingram and Craig Whiteside, "Outshouting the Flea: Islamic State and Modern Asymmetric Strategic Communications," in Andrea Dew, Marc Genest, and S. C. M. Payne, eds., *From Quills to Tweets: How America Communicates War and Revolution* (Washington, DC: Georgetown University Press, 2019).
188. Hampton, "Unlimited Confusion over Limited War," 38.
189. McClintock, *The Meaning of Limited War*, 200.
190. Jeremy Black, *Insurgency and Counterinsurgency: A Global History* (Lanham, MD: Rowan and Littlefield, 2016), chapter 7.
191. Ridgway, *The Korean War*, 191.
192. Herring, *From Colony to Superpower*, 739.
193. Daddis, *Westmoreland's War*, 67–68.
194. Record, *Beating Goliath*, xi, 22, 132.
195. O'Connor, "Victory in Modern War," 382.
196. Black, *Insurgency and Counterinsurgency*, chapters 5, 7.
197. Galula, *Pacification in Algeria*, 244.
198. Ibid., 168.

6 And You Thought the War Was Hard: Ending the War and Securing the Peace

1. Clausewitz, *On War*, 582.
2. Rose, *How Wars End*, 222–223.
3. Bush and Scowcroft, *A World Transformed*, 235.
4. Colin L. Powell, *My American Journey* (New York: Random House Ballantine, 1996), 519.
5. Rose, *How Wars End*, 222–223.
6. Iklé, *Every War Must End*, xv.
7. Pruitt, "Limited War," 49–50.
8. B. H. Liddell Hart, *Strategy*, 2nd edn. (New York: Praeger, 1967), 366, quoted in Flavin, "Planning for Conflict Termination," 95.
9. For a view on this, see Tanisha M. Fazal and Sarah Kreps, "The United States' Perpetual War in Afghanistan: Why Long Wars No Longer Generate a Backlash at Home," *Foreign Affairs* (August 20, 2018), www.foreignaffairs.com/articles/north-america/2018–08–20/united-states-perpetual-war-afghanistan
10. I am indebted to George Baer for my first exposure to this observation.
11. Edward C. Luck and Stuart Albert, "Introduction," in Edward C. Luck and Stuart Albert, eds., *On the Ending of Wars* (Port Washington, NY: Kennikat Press, 1980), 3–4.
12. The additional treaties included the Treaty of Saint-Germain-en-Laye, the Treaty of Trianon, the Treaty of Sèvres, and the Treaty of Lausanne.
13. Luck and Albert, "Introduction," 3–4.
14. Michael Handel, "The Study of War Termination," *Journal of Strategic Studies*, Vol. 1, No. 1 (1978), 52.
15. Flavin, "Planning for Conflict Termination," 96.
16. Wright, "How Hostilities Have Ended," 55.
17. For a good, skeptical examination of "exit strategy," see Gideon Rose, "The Exit Strategy Delusion," *Foreign Affairs*, Vol. 77, No. 1 (January–February 1998), 56–67.
18. Malcolm W. Hoag, *On Local War Doctrine* (Santa Monica, CA: RAND, 1961), 3. This work is terribly flawed, but the author did understand this point.
19. Seabury, "Provisionality and Finality," 103.

20. See Martin S. Alexander and John F. V. Keiger, "Limiting Arms, Enforcing Limits: International Inspections and the Challenges of Compellance in Germany Post-1919, Iraq Post-1991," *Journal of Strategic Studies*, Vol. 29, No. 2 (2006), 345.

21. J. Boone Bartholomees, ed., "Theory of Victory," *Parameters*, Vol. 38, No. 2 (summer 2008), 26.

22. Codevilla and Seabury, *War*, 14.

23. Quoted in William Frank, Frank von Hippel, and Barbara G. Levi, "Army Operations in Limited War," *Army Information Digest*, Vol. 13 (June 1958), 44.

24. Sun Tzu, *The Art of War*, 79.

25. Clausewitz, *On War*, 582.

26. Codevilla and Seabury, *War*, 71.

27. One of many examples: Jennie Carignan, "Victory as a Strategic Objective: An Ambiguous and Counter-Productive Concept for the High Command," *Canadian Military Journal*, Vol. 7, No. 2 (spring 2017), 13.

28. Harvey B. Seim, "The Navy and the Fringe War," *US Naval Institute Proceedings*, Vol. 77 (August 1951), 27, 28.

29. James E. King Jr., "Deterrence and Limited War," *Army*, Vol. 8 (August 1957), 25.

30. Brooks, "Lessons from Limited Wars," 100.

31. Garnett, "Limited War," 126.

32. McClintock, *The Meaning of Limited War*, 1–2.

33. Liddell Hart, *Strategy*, xviii.

34. Luttwak, *On the Meaning of Victory*, 289.

35. Garnett, "Limited 'Conventional' War in the Nuclear Age," in Michael Howard, ed., *Restraints on War: Studies in the Limitation of Armed Conflict* (Oxford University Press, 1979), 86–87.

36. Quoted in Arkin, von Hippel, and Levi, "Army Operations in Limited War," 46.

37. Liddell Hart, *The Revolution in Warfare*, 109–110.

38. Cronin, "The 'War on Terrorism,'" 189.

39. Sun Tzu, *The Art of War*, 73.

40. Cronin, "The 'War on Terrorism,'" 174, 183, 185.

41. Lewy, *America in Vietnam*, 378.

42. Cronin, "The 'War on Terrorism,'" 185.

43. Pruitt, "Limited War," 45–46.

44. Iklé, *Every War Must End*, 3–4.

45. Emphasis added, Clausewitz, *On War*, 584.

46. Norman H. Schwarzkopf and Peter Petre, *It Doesn't Take a Hero* (New York: Bantam, 1992), 473.

47. Ibid., 476–478.

48. Woods, *The Mother of All Battles*, 244–245.

49. Schwarzkopf and Petre, *It Doesn't Take a Hero*, 479–480.

50. Ibid. William Thomas Allison, *The Gulf War, 1990–91* (New York: Palgrave, 2012), 141–142.

51. Allison, *The Gulf War*, 143; Schwarzkopf and Petre, *It Doesn't Take a Hero*, 488–489.

52. Schwarzkopf and Petre, *It Doesn't Take a Hero*, 488–489; Bush and Scowcroft, *A World Transformed*, 488; Robert M. Gates, *Duty: Memoirs of a Secretary of State* (New York: Knopf, 2014), 26.

53. Allison, *The Gulf War*, 146.

54. Gordon and Trainor, *The Generals' War*, 444.

55. Schwarzkopf and Petre, *It Doesn't Take a Hero*, 480.

56. Clausewitz, *On War*, 611.

57. Warner and Warner, *The Tide at Sunrise*, 175.

58. Paul R. Pillar, *Negotiating Peace: War Termination as a Bargaining Process* (Princeton University Press, 1983), 199–201; Andrew Gordon, "Social Protest in Imperial Japan: The Hibiya Riot of 1905," *The Asia-Pacific Journal*, Vol. 12, No. 3 (July 20, 2014), 3.

59. Iklé, *Every War Must End*, 2.

60. Bush and Scowcroft, *A World Transformed*, 447–448.

61. Iklé, *Every War Must End*, 5–6.

62. Pillar, *Negotiating Peace*, 18 fn. 6.

63. Iklé, *Every War Must End*, 9; Cronin, "The 'War on Terrorism,'" 174.

64. William R. Hawkins, "Imposing Peace: Total vs. Limited Wars, and the Need to Put Boots on the Ground," *Parameters* (summer 2000), 5.

65. Morton Halperin, "War Termination as a Problem in Civil–Military Relations," *Annals of the American Academy of Political and Social Science*, Vol. 392, No. 1 (1970), 93.

66. Pillar, *Negotiating Peace*, 53.

67. David J. Oberst, *Why Wars End: An Expected Utility War Termination Model* (Carlisle Barracks, PA: US Army War College, 1992), 58.

68. Sun Tzu, *The Art of War*, 120.

69. One of the few to make this observation, which he does in regard to revolutionary warfare, is Deitchman, *Limited War and American Defense Policy*, 38.

70. Chai Changwen, "The Korean Truce Negotiations," in Xiaobing Li, Allan R. Millett, and Bin Yu, trans. and eds., *Mao's Generals Remember Korea* (Lawrence, KS: University Press of Kansas, 2001), 187–188.

71. Pillar, *Negotiating Peace*, 52.

72. Quoted in Codevilla and Seabury, *War*, 23.

73. Martin Evans, *Algeria: France's Undeclared War* (Oxford University Press, 2012), 177.

74. Galula, *Pacification in Algeria*, 144.

75. Iklé, *Every War Must End*, 85–86.

76. See Suba Chandran, "Limited War with Pakistan: Will It Secure India's Interests?" *ACDIS Occasional Paper*, University of Illinois at Urbana-Champagne: Program in Arms Control, Disarmament, and International Security (August 2004).

77. Iklé, *Every War Must End*, 86.

78. Handel, "The Study of War Termination," 63.

79. Lecture delivered under Chatham House rules.

80. Rose, *How Wars End*, 21.

81. Kissinger, *Nuclear Weapons and Foreign Policy*, 152.

82. Pillar, *Negotiating Peace*, 206–208.

83. Lecture delivered under Chatham House rules.

84. Colin F. Jackson, "Lost Chance or Lost Horizon?" 256 and fn. 5, 257; C. Turner Joy, *How Communists Negotiate* (New York: Macmillan, 2013 [1955]), 166; Foot, *A Substitute for Victory*, 36.

85. Colin F. Jackson, "Lost Chance or Lost Horizon?" 259–260, 267–268.

86. Ibid., 269.

87. Ibid., 271; James A. Van Fleet, "The Truth about Korea: From a Man Now Free to Speak," Part 1, *Life*, Vol. 34, No. 19 (May 11, 1953), 127, 132; Colin F. Jackson, "Lost Chance or Lost Horizon?" 271–275, dissects the post-war arguments on this issue. See also on these events: Robert B. Bruce, "Tethered Eagle: Lt. General James

A. Van Fleet and the Quest for Military Victory in the Korean War," *Army History* (winter 2012), 6–29.

88. Stueck, *Rethinking the Korean War*, 138–139.
89. Pillar, *Negotiating Peace*, 55.
90. Acheson, *The Korean War*, 119–120.
91. J. Lawton Collins, *War in Peacetime*, 327; Stueck, *Rethinking the Korean War*, 149.
92. J. Lawton Collins, *War in Peacetime*, 327–328, 330; Acheson, *The Korean War*, 120–122; Ridgway, *The Korean War*, 182; Truman, *Memoirs*, Vol. II, 456, 458–459.
93. James A. Van Fleet, "The Truth about Korea: How We Can Win with What We Have," Part II, *Life* (May 8, 1953), 164.
94. Joy, *How Communists Negotiate*, 30–31.
95. Chuck Downs, "Limited War: The Initial Failures of Appeasement Policy toward North Korea," *The Heritage Foundation* (August 8, 2000), www.heritage.org/asia/report/limited-war-the-initial-failures-appeasement-policy-toward-north-korea; *FRUS, 1951, Korea and China*, Vol. VII, 566– 569.
96. Kissinger, *Nuclear Weapons and Foreign Policy*, 152; Kissinger, "Military Policy," 461; Brodie, *The Meaning of Limited War*, 12; Aron, "Can War in the Atomic Age Be Limited?" 104. This article also appears under his name as "A l'Âge atomique peut-on limiter la guerre?" 30–39.
97. Colin F. Jackson, "Lost Chance or Lost Horizon?" 273–274.
98. Brodie, *The Meaning of Limited War*, 12.
99. Iklé, *Every War Must End*, 90.
100. Sun Tzu, *The Art of War*, 120.
101. These three questions were developed over the years by the faculty of the US Naval War College's Strategy Department.
102. Clausewitz, *On War*, 484.
103. Alexander and Keiger, "Limiting Arms," 359, 386.
104. Bryce Wood, "How Wars End in Latin America," *The Annals of the American Academy of Political and Social Science*, Vol. 392 (November 1970), 47–49.
105. Wright, "How Hostilities Have Ended." 56.
106. Stueck, *Rethinking the Korean War*, 157–158, 171; Avram Agov, "North Korea's Alliances and the Unfinished Korean War," *The Journal of Korean Studies*, Vol. 18, No. 2 (fall 2013), 237–238.
107. Reiter, *How Wars End*, 89.
108. Stueck, *Rethinking the Korean War*, 176, 189–192.
109. Nguyen, *Hanoi's War*, 297. See also Robert Randle, "Peace in Vietnam and Laos: 1954, 1962, 1973," in David Smith and Robert Randle, eds., *From War to Peace: Essays in Peacemaking and War Termination* (New York: Trustees of Columbia University, 1974), 50–55.
110. Codevilla and Seabury, *War*, 258–259.
111. National Security Directive (NSD) 54 (January 15, 1991).
112. Rose, *How Wars End*, 217–218.
113. W. Andrew Terrill, *Escalation and Intrawar Deterrence during Limited Wars in the Middle East* (Carlisle, PA: Strategic Studies Institute, US Army War College, September 2009), 73–74.
114. NSD 54 (January 15, 1991).
115. Gordon and Trainor, *The Generals' War*, 435; Bush and Scowcroft, *A World Transformed*, 471–472.
116. Gordon and Trainor, *The Generals' War*, 443.

117. Bush and Scowcroft, *A World Transformed*, 472.

118. Gordon and Trainor, *The Generals' War*, 477.

119. The italics in the original have been removed. Clausewitz, *On War*, 94.

120. Garnett, "Limited War," 125–126.

121. Sun Tzu, *The Art of War*, 130–133.

122. Edward Luttwak quoted in Mazarr, "The Folly of 'Asymmetric' War," 43.

123. See Clausewitz's discussions of the culminating point of attack and the culminating point of victory, *On War*, 528, 566–573, esp. 570.

124. Ibid., 570.

125. Stueck, *Rethinking the Korean War*, 88–89.

126. Allison, *The Gulf War*, 139.

127. Colin L. Powell, *My American Journey*, 519–523; Bush and Scowcroft, *A World Transformed*, 485–486.

128. Colin L. Powell, *My American Journey*, 523.

129. Gordon and Trainor, *The Generals' War*, 422–423.

130. Bush and Scowcroft, *A World Transformed*. 486; Allison, *The Gulf War*, 139.

131. Bush and Scowcroft, *A World Transformed*, 484.

132. Colin L. Powell, *My American Journey*, 523.

133. Woods, *The Mother of All Battles*, 240–243.

134. Bush diary, February 28, 1991, in Bush and Scowcroft, *A World Transformed*, 486–487.

135. Colin L. Powell, *My American Journey*, 523.

136. NSD 54 (January 15, 1991); Gordon and Trainor, *The Generals' War*, 84.

137. See Allison, *The Gulf War*, 146.

138. Bush and Scowcroft, *A World Transformed*, 489.

139. NSD 54 (January 15, 1991); Gordon and Trainor, *The Generals' War*, 423–426.

140. Kenneth Pollack, *The Threatening Storm* (New York: Random House, 2002), 69–70, 88.

141. Daddis, *Westmoreland's War*, 141–142; Turley, *The Second Indochina War*, 178; Nguyen, *Hanoi's War*, 129–130.

142. Daddis, *Westmoreland's War*, 141–142; Kissinger, *Diplomacy*, 674–677, 681.

143. Warner and Warner, *The Tide at Sunrise*, 525.

144. Pruitt, "Limited War," 45.

145. Bradford A. Lee, "Winning the War but Losing the Peace? The United States and the Strategic Issues of War Termination," in Bradford A. Lee and Karl F. Walling, eds., *Strategic Logic and Political Rationality: Essays in Honor of Michael I. Handel* (London: Frank Cass, 2003), 260, 264.

146. Schnabel, *Policy and Direction*, 403.

147. Bradford A. Lee, "Winning the War," 265.

148. O'Connor, "Victory in Modern War," 369.

149. Stoker, *The Grand Design*, 20–21.

150. Iklé, *Every War Must End*, 55–56.

151. Clausewitz, *On War*, 611.

152. Warner and Warner, *The Tide at Sunrise*, 527.

153. Dawson, "The US War with Mexico," 89–90, 99.

154. Gordon and Trainor, *The Generals' War*, 447.

155. Colin F. Jackson, "Lost Chance or Lost Horizon?" 270.

156. Wayne E. Lee, "Plattsburgh 1814: Warring for Bargaining Chips," in Moten, ed., *Between War and Peace*, 57–58.

157. Warner and Warner, *The Tide at Sunrise*, 527; William C. Fuller Jr., *Strategy and Power in Russia, 1600–1914* (New York: The Free Press, 1992), 404.

158. Lukas Milevski, *The West's East: Contemporary Baltic Defense in Strategic Perspective* (Oxford University Press, 2018), Chapter 7. See also Lukas Milevski, "Prospective Strategy for Baltic Defense: The Russian Public and War Termination in the Baltic States," *Military Review* (January–February 2018), 58–70.
159. Clausewitz, *On War*, 80.
160. Seabury, "Provisionality and Finality," 100.
161. Alexander and Keiger, "Limiting Arms," 387; Suzanne Werner, "The Precarious Nature of Peace: Resolving the Issues, Enforcing the Settlement, and Renegotiating the Terms," *American Journal of Political Science*, Vol. 43, No. 3 (July 1999), 927–928.
162. Liddell Hart, *The Revolution in Warfare*, 44–45.
163. Michael S. Neiberg, "To End All Wars? A Case Study of Conflict Termination in World War I," in J. Boone Bartholomees Jr., ed., *US Army War College Guide to National Security Issues: National Security Policy and Strategy*, 5th edn. (Carlisle Barracks, PA: Strategic Studies Institute, US Army War College, 2012), Vol. II, 342–343.
164. Virginia Page Fortna, "Scraps of Paper? Agreements and the Durability of Peace," *International Organization*, No. 57 (spring 2003), 363.
165. Neiberg, "To End All Wars?" 344.
166. Letter to Francesco Vettori, August 10, 1513, in Marco Cesa, ed., *Machiavelli on International Relations* (Oxford University Press, 2014), 129.
167. Gray, *Defining and Achieving Decisive Victory*, 12.
168. Alexander and Keiger, "Limiting Arms, Enforcing Limits," 387.
169. Iklé, *Every War Must End*, xii–xiii.
170. Wright, "How Hostilities Have Ended," 52.
171. Seabury, "Provisionality and Finality," 98.
172. Handel, "The Study of War Termination," 58.
173. Codevilla and Seabury, *War*, 15.
174. Nickerson, *Can We Limit War?* 9.
175. Seabury, "Provisionality and Finality," 99.
176. Wright, "How Hostilities Have Ended," 56–57.
177. Ibid., 55–56.
178. Seabury, "Provisionality and Finality," 102.
179. Alexander and Keiger, "Limiting Arms," 359–360.
180. Suzanne Werner and Amy Yuen, "Making and Keeping Peace," *International Organization*, Vol. 59, No. 2 (spring 2005), 262.
181. Gordon A. Craig and Alexander L. George, *Force and Statecraft: Diplomatic Problems of Our Time* (Oxford University Press, 1983), 229, quoted in Alexander and Keiger, "Limiting Arms," 368.
182. Paul Kecskemeti, "Political Rationality in Ending War," *The Annals of the American Academy of Political and Social Science*, Vol. 392 (November 1970), 113.
183. Werner, "The Precarious Nature of Peace," 917.
184. Anthony Cordesmann, *The "End State" Fallacy: Setting the Wrong Goals for War Fighting* (Washington, DC: CSIS, 2016), 1.
185. Stoker, *Clausewitz*, 94.
186. Björn Forsén and Annette Forsén, "German Secret Submarine Exports, 1919–35," in Donald J. Stoker Jr. and Jonathan A. Grant, eds., *Girding for Battle: The Arms Trade in a Global Perspective* (Westport, CT: Praeger, 2003), 113–134.
187. Alexander and Keiger, "Limiting Arms," 383, 385.
188. Ibid., 386.

189. Ibid., 361.
190. Ibid., 361–364.
191. Ibid., 359.
192. Werner, "The Precarious Nature of Peace," 924.
193. H. E. Goemans, *War and Punishment: The Causes of War Termination and the First World War* (Princeton University Press, 2000), 33.
194. Wright, *A Study of War*, 858.
195. Allison, *The Gulf War*, 146.
196. Pollack, *The Threatening Storm*, xxiv–xxviii.
197. Allison, *The Gulf War*, 146.
198. Wright, *A Study of War*, 1332.
199. Lecture delivered under Chatham House rules.
200. Iklé, *Every War Must End*, 11.
201. For an example, see Luttwak, *On the Meaning of Victory*, 291.
202. Paul D. Miller, *Armed State Building: Confronting State Failure, 1898–2012* (Ithaca: Cornell University Press, 2013), 2, 8–9.
203. Anthony H. Cordesmann, *Creeping Incrementalism: US Strategy in Iraq and Syria from 2011 to 2015* (Washington, DC: CSIS, 2015), 4.
204. Fortna, "Scraps of Paper?" 357.
205. Werner and Yuen, "Making and Keeping Peace," 263.
206. Fortna, "Scraps of Paper?" 359–360.
207. Reiter, *How Wars End*, 41.
208. Feargal Cochrane, *Ending Wars* (Cambridge, UK: Polity Press, 2008), 53–55.
209. Alexander and Keiger, "Limiting Arms," 355.
210. Ibid.
211. Stoker, *Clausewitz*, 252–253.
212. Wood, "How Wars End in Latin America," 42, 49.
213. Bismarck quoted in Osgood, *Limited War*, 72.
214. Osgood, *Limited War*, 73.
215. Brooks, "Lessons from Limited Wars," 100.
216. Gray, *Defining and Achieving Decisive Victory*, 12.
217. Dempsey, "Keynote Speech on Civil–Military Relations," minute 8:20.
218. Other sources consulted for this topic include: Clark C. Abt, *A Strategy for Terminating a Nuclear War* (Boulder, CO: Westview Press, 1985); Sam Allotey, et al., *Planning and Execution of War Termination* (Maxwell Air Force Base, AL: Air Command and Staff College, 1997); John R. Boulé II, "Operational Planning and Conflict Termination," *JFQ (Joint Force Quarterly)*, (autumn–winter, 2001– 02), 97–102; H. A. Calahan, *What Makes a War End?* (New York: Vanguard Press, 1944); Berenice A. Carroll, "How Wars End: An Analysis of Some Current Hypotheses," *Journal of Peace Research*, Vol. 6, No. 4 (1969), 295–321; Berenice A. Carroll, "War Termination and Conflict Theory: Value Premises, Theories, and Policies," *The Annals of the American Academy of Political and Social Science*, Vol. 392 (November 1970), 14–29; Norman Cigar, "Croatia's War of Independence: The Parameters of War Termination," *The Journal of Slavic Military Studies*, Vol. 10, No. 2 (1997), 34–70; Stephen J. Cimbala, ed., *Strategic War Termination* (New York: Praeger, 1986); Bruce B. G. Clarke, "Conflict Termination: A Rational Model," *Studies in Conflict & Terrorism*, Vol. 16, No. 1 (1993), 25–60; Michael Clarke, "The Ending of Wars and the Ending of Eras," *The RUSI Journal*, Vol. 160, No. 4 (2015), 4–9; Lewis A. Coser, "The Termination of Conflict," *The Journal of Conflict Resolution*, Vol. 5, No. 4 (December 1961), 347–353; Cécile Fabre, "War Exit," *Ethics*, Vol. 125, No. 3 (April 2015), 631–652; James L. Foster and Garry D. Brewer,

"And the Clocks Were Striking Thirteen: The Termination of War," *Policy Sciences*, Vol. 7, No. 2 (June 1976), 225–243; Michael C. Griffith, *War Termination: Theory, Doctrine, and Practice* (Fort Leavenworth, KS: School of Advance Military Studies, 1992); Herman Kahn, "Issues of Thermonuclear War Termination," *The Annals of the American Academy of Political and Social Science*, Vol. 392 (November 1970), 133–172; Kecskemeti, "Political Rationality in Ending War," 105–115; Paul Kecskemeti, *Strategic Surrender: The Politics of Victory and Defeat* (Stanford University Press, 1958); Adam Lockyer, "How Democracies Exit Small Wars: The Role of Opposition Parties in War Termination," *The Australian Journal of International Affairs*, Vol. 66, No. 3 (2012), 381–396; Kristopher W. Ramsey, "Settling It on the Field: Battlefield Events and War Termination," *Journal of Conflict Resolution*, Vol. 52, No. 6 (December 2008), 850–879; Harry G. Summers Jr., "War: Deter, Fight, Terminate, the Purpose of War is a Better Peace," *Naval War College Review*, Vol. 39, No. 1 (1986), 18–29; Suzanne Werner, "Negotiating the Terms of Settlement: War Aims and Bargaining Leverage," *The Journal of Conflict Resolution*, Vol. 42, No. 3 (June 1998), 321–343; "Response to Suzanne Werner and Amy Yuen, 'Making and Keeping Peace,'" *Organization*, Vol. 59, No. 2 (Spring 2005), 261–292, 8 pages, www.columbia.edu/~vpf4/Response%20to%20Werner%20and%20Yuen.pdf; Donald Wittman, "How a War Ends: A Rational Model Approach," *The Journal of Conflict esolution*, Vol. 23, No. 4 (December 1979), 743–763.

219. Wu Ch'I in Appendix I, Sun Tzu, *The Art of War*, 152.

Conclusion: Is History Rhyming?

1. Klaus Knorr, "Limited Strategic War," in Knorr and Read, eds., *Limited Strategic War*, 30.
2. Joe Biden, "Remarks by President Biden on the Way forward in Afghanistan," April 14, 2021, https://www.whitehouse.gov/briefing-room/speeches-remarks/2021/04/14/remarks-by-president-biden-on-the-way-forward-in-afghanistan/
3. Lara Seligman et al., "How Biden's Team Overrode the Brass on Afghanistan," *Politico*, April 14, 2021, https://www.politico.com/news/2021/04/14/pentagon-biden-team-overrode-afghanistan-481556; Peter Bergen, "The Worst Speech of Biden's Presidency," CNN, July 9, 2001, https://www.cnn.com/profiles/peter-bergen
4. Seligman et al., "How Biden's Team Overrode the Brass on Afghanistan."
5. Ellie Kaufman, "Five Takeaways from Senior Military Leaders' Testimony on Afghanistan," CNN, September 28, 2021, https://www.cnn.com/2021/09/28/politics/five-takeaways-senate-afghanistan/index.html; Jonathan Guyer, "The Unheeded Dissent Cable," *American Prospect*, August 26, 2021, https://prospect.org/world/unheeded-dissent-cable-white-house-misses-afghanistan-warning/
6. Joe Biden, "Speech on the Drawdown of US Forces in Afghanistan," July 8, 2021, https://millercenter.org/the-presidency/presidential-speeches/july-8-2021-speech-drawdown-us-forces-afghanistan; Fred Kaplan, "We Now Know Why Biden Was in a Hurry to Exit Afghanistan," *Slate*, September 28, 2021, https://slate.com/news-and-politics/2021/09/biden-afghanistan-exit-troops-milley.html
7. Chas Danner, "Why Afghanistan's Security Forces Suddenly Collapsed," *New York Magazine* (August 17, 2021), https://nymag.com/intelligencer/2021/08/why-afghanistans-security-forces-suddenly-collapsed.html
8. Danner, "Why Afghanistan's Security Forces Suddenly Collapsed."

9. Douglas London, "CIA's Former Counterterrorism Chief for the Region: Afghanistan, Not an Intelligence Failure – Something Much Worse," *Just Security*, August 18, 2021, https://www.justsecurity.org/77801/cias-former-counterterrorism-chief-for-the-region-afghanistan-not-an-intelligence-failure-something-much-worse/

10. "How the Taliban Engineered 'Political Collapse' of Afghanistan," *Reuters*, August 17, 2021, https://www.reuters.com/world/asia-pacific/how-taliban-engineered-political-collapse-afghanistan-2021-08-17/; Kaufman, "Five Takeaways from Senior Military Leaders' Testimony on Afghanistan."

11. Danner, "Why Afghanistan's Security Forces Suddenly Collapsed."

12. Biden, "Speech on the Drawdown of US Forces in Afghanistan."

13. Guyer, "The Unheeded Dissent Cable."

14. London, "CIA's Former Counterterrorism Chief for the Region: Afghanistan, Not an Intelligence Failure – Something Much Worse."

15. Michael R. Gordon et al., "Inside Biden's Afghanistan Withdrawal Plan: Warnings, Doubts but Little Change," *WSJ*, September 5, 2021, https://www.wsj.com/articles/inside-the-biden-administrations-push-to-exit-afghanistan-11630855499

16. Yaroslav Trofimov et al., "'The Taliban Are Here': The Final Days before Kabul's Collapse," *Wall Street Journal*, August 20, 2021, https://www.wsj.com/articles/the-taliban-are-here-the-final-days-before-kabuls-collapse-11629505499

17. Kevin Liptak et al., "'A Direct Punch in the Gut';: Inside Biden's Biggest Crisis as He Races to Withdraw from Afghanistan," *CNN*, August 28, 2021, https://www.cnn.com/2021/08/28/politics/biden-behind-scenes-crisis-attack-kabul-afghanistan/index.html; Jonathan Swan and Zachary Basu, "Scoop: Milley's Blunt Private Blame for the State Department," *Axios*, September 29, 2021, https://www.axios.com/milley-state-department-afghanistan-evacuation-ebb00a6b-a59d-42b9-b5e0-348b0227b89b.html

18. Joe Biden, "Remarks on Situation in Afghanistan," August 16, 2021, https://millercenter.org/the-presidency/presidential-speeches/august-16-2021-remarks-situation-afghanistan; Gordon et al., "Inside Biden's Afghanistan Withdrawal Plan."

19. Liptak et al., "'A Direct Punch in the Gut': Inside Biden's Biggest Crisis as He Races to Withdraw from Afghanistan."

20. Nancy A. Youssef and Gordon Lubold, "Last U.S. Troops Leave Afghanistan after Nearly 20 Years," *Wall Street Journal*, August 30, 2021, https://www.wsj.com/articles/last-u-s-troops-leave-afghanistan-after-nearly-20-years-11630355853

21. Peter Bergen, "Biden Deserves Blame for the Debacle in Afghanistan," *CNN*, August 13, 2021, https://www.cnn.com/2021/08/12/opinions/afghanistan-president-biden-debacle-bergen/index.html

22. Jack Fairweather, *The Good War: Why We Couldn't Win the War or the Peace in Afghanistan* (New York: Basic Books, 2014), 41–45.

23. "Trump's Pledge to Exit Afghanistan Was a Ruse, His Final SecDef Says," *Defense One*, August 18, 2021, https://www.defenseone.com/policy/2021/08/trumps-pledge-exit-afghanistan-was-ruse-his-final-secdef-says/184660/

24. Jocelyn, "Losing a War."

25. de Wijk, *The Art of Military Coercion*, 11.

26. Codevilla and Seabury, *War*, 1–2, 7.

27. Dubik, "By Any Other Name, War Is Still War."

28. Frank G. Hoffman, *Conflict in the 21st Century: The Rise of Hybrid Wars* (Arlington, VA: Potomac Institute for Policy Studies, 2007), 7, 14, 37. See also: Frank G. Hoffman, "Hybrid vs. Compound War," *Armed Forces Journal* (October 1, 2009), http://armed/forcesjournal.com/hybrid-vs-compound-war/; Frank G. Hoffman, "Further Thoughts on Hybrid Threats," *Small Wars Journal*

(March 2, 2009), http://smallwarsjournal/.com/jrnl/art/further-thoughts-on-hybrid-threats; Frank G. Hoffman, "On Not-So-New Warfare: Political Warfare vs. Hybrid Threats," *War on the Rocks* (July 28, 2014), https://warontherocks.com/2014/07/on-not-so-new-warfare-political-warfare- vs-hybrid-threats/. The bibliography has additional sources.

29. For a critical assessment of hybrid war writing, see Robert Johnson, "Hybrid War and Its Countermeasures: A Critique of the Literature," *Small Wars & Insurgencies*, Vol. 29, No. 1 (2018), 141–163.

30. Thomas Rid, "Cyberwar Will Not Take Place," *Journal of Strategic Studies*, Vol. 35, No. 1 (2012), 5–32.

31. Seim, "The Navy and the Fringe War," 838.

32. On North Vietnam's war against South Vietnam, see Turley, *The Second Indochina War*; Nguyen, *Hanoi's War*; Pike, *Viet Cong*.

33. Michael I. Handel, *Masters of War: Classical Strategic Thought*, 3rd edn. (London: Frank Cass, 2001), 46, 353–360.

34. United States, Joint Chiefs of Staff, *The National Military Strategy of the United States of America 2015* (June 2015), 4.

35. Donald Stoker and Craig Whiteside, "Blurred Lines: Gray-Zone Conflict and Hybrid War – Two Failures of American Strategic Thinking," *Naval War College Review*, Vol. 73, No. 1 (2020), https://digital-commons.usnwc.edu/nwc-review/vol73/iss1/4

36. Ibid.; Charles K. Bartles, "Getting Gerasimov Right," *Military Review* (January–February 2016), 30–31; Mark Galeotti, "I'm Sorry for Creating the 'Gerasimov Doctrine,'" *Foreign Policy* (March 5, 2019), https://foreignpolicy.com/2018/03/05/im-sorry-for-creating-the-gerasimov-doctrine/; Valery Gerasimov, "The Value of Science in Prediction," *Military-Industrial Courier* (February 27, 2013), Rob Coalson, trans., in "The Gerasimov Doctrine and Russian Non-Linear War," *Moscow's Shadows*, https://inmoscowsshadows.wordpress.com/2014/07/06/the-gerasimov-doctrine-and-russian-non-linear-war/

37. Strachan, *The Direction of War*, 134.

38. N. Talensky, "On the Character of Modern Warfare," *International Affairs* (October 1969), 23.

39. Paul H. B. Godwin, "Chinese Military Strategy Revised: Local and Limited War," *The Annals of the American Academy of Political and Social Science*, Vol. 519 (January 1992), 193–198. See also Chu, Shulong, "The PRC Girds for Limited, High-Tech War," *Orbis* (spring 1994), 187–189.

40. M. Taylor Fravel, "China's Changing Approach to Military Strategy: The Science of Military Strategy from 2001 to 2013," in Joe McReynolds, ed., *China's Evolving Military Strategy* (Washington, DC: Brookings, 2016), 52–54.

41. Ibid., 52–53, 63.

42. Clausewitz, *On War*, 161.

BIBLIOGRAPHY

Abd al-Jabber, Faleh. "Why the Uprisings Failed." *Middle East Report*, No. 176 (May–June 1992): 2–14.

Abegglen, Christoph M. V. "Clausewitz and Beaufre – The Relationship of Politics and War." War Studies Program, King's College, London, circa 2000, www.military.ch/abegglen/papers/clausewitz_and_beaufre.pdf

Abt, Clark C. *A Strategy for Terminating a Nuclear War*. Boulder, CO: Westview Press, 1985.

Acheson, Dean. *The Korean War*. New York: W. W. Norton, 1971.

    Present at the Creation: My Years in the State Department. New York: W. W. Norton, 1969.

Ackerman, Bruce and Oona Hathaway. "Limited War and the Constitution: Iraq and the Crisis of Presidential Legality." *Michigan Law Review*, Vol. 109, No.4 (February 2011): 447–517.

Adamsky, Dmitry (Dima). "If War Comes Tomorrow: Russian Thinking about 'Regional Nuclear Deterrence.'" *The Journal of Slavic Military Studies*, Vol. 27, No. 1 (2014): 163–188.

Agov, Avram. "North Korea's Alliances and the Unfinished Korean War." *The Journal of Korean Studies*, Vol. 18, No. 2 (fall 2013): 237–238.

Ahmed, Ali. *India's Doctrine Puzzle: Limiting War in South Asia*. New Delhi: Routledge, 2014.

    India's Limited War Doctrine: The Structural Factor. New Delhi: Institute for Defence Studies and Analyses, 2012.

    "Political Dimensions of Limited War." *Institute for Defence Studies and Analyses* (March 29, 2010), www.idsa.in/idsacomments/PoliticalDimension sofLimitedWar_aahmed_290310

"Preparing for 'Limited Nuclear War.'" *Military and Defence Articles*, No. 982 (March 7, 2003).

"Towards a Proactive Military Strategy: 'Cold Start and Stop.'" *Strategic Analysis*, Vol. 35, No. 3 (2011): 401–416.

Ahmed, Firdaus. "The Impetus behind Limited War." *Institute of Peace and Conflict Studies* (July 24, 2002), http://scotomastudio.com/the-impetus-behind-limited-war/

Åkerman, Nordal. *On the Doctrine of Limited War*. Lund: Berlingska Boktryckeriet, 1972.

Akers, Joshua K. "Limited War, Limited Enthusiasm: Sexuality, Disillusionment, Survival, and the Changing Landscape of War Culture in Korean War-era Comic Books and Soldier Iconography." MA thesis, James Madison University, 2013.

Albert, Stuart and Edward C. Luck, eds. *On the Endings of Wars*. Port Washington, NY: Kennikat Press, 1980.

Alexander, Martin S. and John F. V. Keiger. "France and the Algerian War: Strategy, Operations, and Diplomacy." *Journal of Strategic Studies*, Vol. 25, No. 2 (2002): 1–32.

"Limiting Arms, Enforcing Limits: International Inspections and the Challenges of Compellance in Germany Post-1919, Iraq Post-1991." *Journal of Strategic Studies*, Vol. 29, No. 2 (2006): 345–394.

Allison, William Thomas. *The Gulf War, 1990–91*. New York: Palgrave, 2012.

Allotey, Sam, et al. *Planning and Execution of War Termination*. Maxwell Air Force Base, AL: Air Command and Staff College, 1997.

Arkin, William, Frank von Hippel, and Barbara G. Levi. "Addendum: The Consequences of a 'Limited' Nuclear War in East and West Germany." *Ambio*, Vol. 12, No. 1 (1983): 57.

"Army Operations in Limited War." *Army Information Digest*, Vol. 13 (June 1958): 41–48.

"The Consequences of a 'Limited' Nuclear War in East and West Germany." *Ambio*, Vol. 11, No. 2/3 (1982): 163–173.

Aron, Raymond. "A Half-Century of Limited War?" *Bulletin of Atomic Scientists*, Vol. 12, No. 4 (1956): 99–104.

"A L'âge atomique peut-on limiter la guerre?" *Preuves: Cahiers Mensuels du Congrès pour la Liberté de la Culture*, No. 58 (December 1958): 30–39.

"Can War in the Atomic Age Be Limited?" *Confluence*, Vol. 5 (July 1956): 99–114.

Paix et guerre entre les nations. 4th edn. Paris: Calmann-Lévy, 1962.

Arquilla, John and Ryan Nomura. "Three Wars of Ideas about the Idea of War." *Comparative Strategy*, Vol. 34, No. 2 (March 2015): 185–201.

Arreguin-Toft, Ivan. "How the Weak Win Wars: A Theory of Asymmetric Conflict." *International Security*, Vol. 26, No. 1 (summer 2001): 93–128.

Art, Robert J. *A Grand Strategy for America* (Ithaca, NY: Cornell University Press, 2003).
  "To What Ends Military Power." *International Security*, Vol. 4, No. 3 (spring 1980): 3–35.
Ayson, Robert. *Thomas Schelling and the Nuclear Age.* London: Frank Cass, 2004.
Baggs, Andrew Rayburn, Jr. "Bombing, Bargaining, and Limited War: North Vietnam, 1965–1968." Ph.D. dissertation, University of North Carolina Chapel Hill, 1972.
Bailey, Sydney D. *The Korean Armistice.* New York: St. Martin's Press, 1992.
Bakich, Spencer D. *Success and Failure in Limited War: Information and Strategy in the Korean, Vietnam, Persian Gulf, and Iraq Wars.* University of Chicago Press, 2014.
Bakshi, G.D. *Limited Wars in South Asia: Need for an Indian Doctrine.* Delhi: Centre for Land Warfare Studies, 2010.
Balaban, Constantin-Gheorghe. "Limited Negotiations but Unlimited War in the Middle East." *Strategic Impact*, Vol. 1, No. 1 (2009): 10–16.
Baldor, Lolita C. "US Commander: No Need for Major Change in Afghan War Plan as New General Takes Over." *Military Times* (August 8, 2018), www.militarytimes.com/news/your-military/2018/08/08/us-commander-no-%20need-for-major-change-in-afghan-war-plan-as-new-general-takes-over/
Baldwin, Hanson W. "The Case for Escalation." *New York Times Magazine* (February 27, 1966): 22, 79–82.
  "Limited War." *The Atlantic Monthly*, Vol. 203 (May 1959): 35–43.
Barnett, Frank R., William C. Mott, and John C. Neff, eds. *Peace and War in the Modern Age.* Garden City, NY: Anchor Books, 1965.
Bartholomees, J. Boone, Jr. "The Issue of Attrition." *Parameters*, Vol. 40, No. 1 (spring 2010): 5–19.
  "Theory of Victory." *Parameters*, Vol. 38, No. 2 (summer 2008): 25–36.
  ed., *US Army War College Guide to National Security Issues.* 5th edn. 2 vols. Carlisle, PA: Strategic Studies Institute, June 2012.
Bartles, Charles K. "Getting Gerasimov Right." *Military Review* (January–February 2016): 30–38.
Bassford, Christopher. "Clausewitz's Categories of War and the Suppression of 'Absolute War.'" *Clausewitz.com* (January 2017), www.clausewitz.com/bibl/Bassford-ClausewitzsCategoriesOfWar.pdf
Baumann, Paul Edward. "Limited War through Airpower and the Political Exploitation of POWs." MA thesis, Texas Tech University, December 1997.
Baylis, John, Ken Booth, John Garnett, and Phil Williams. *Contemporary Strategy: Theories and Policies.* New York: Holmes & Meier, 1975.
Beaufre, André. *Dissuasion et stratégie.* Paris: Armand Colin, 1964.

Introduction a la stratégie. Paris: Armand Colin, 1963.

An Introduction to Strategy. R. H. Barry, trans. London: Faber and Faber, 1965.

Stratégie de l'action. Paris: Armand Colin, 1964.

Strategy of Action. R. H. Barry, trans. London: Faber and Faber, 1967.

Strategy for Tomorrow. London: Macdonald and Jane's, 1974.

Beaumont, Roger A. "The Constabulary Function Dilemma." *Military Review*, Vol. 79, No. 1 (March–April 1999): 57–60.

"The Military Utility of Limited War." *Military Review*, Vol. 47, No. 5 (May 1967): 53–57.

Beckett, Ian F. W. *Modern Insurgencies: Guerrillas and Their Opponents since 1750*. London: Routledge, 2001.

"Robert Thompson and the British Advisory Mission to South Vietnam, 1961–1965," *Small Wars & Insurgencies*, Vol. 8, No. 3 (1997): 41–63.

"Total War." In Clive Emsley, et al., eds. *War and Peace and Social Change in Twentieth Century Europe*. Milton Keynes, UK: Open University Press, 1989.

Beehner, Lionel. "The 'Coalition of the Willing.'" *The Council on Foreign Relations* (February 22, 2007), www.cfr.org/backgrounder/coalition-willing

Bellamy, Ian. "More Arithmetic of Deterrence: Throw Weight, Radioactivity, and Limited Nuclear War." *Royal United Services Institute*, Vol. 14, No. 2 (June 1, 1979): 35–38.

Bem, Allen P. "Defeating Denial: Limited Nuclear War and the Small World Problem." *The Journal of Psychology*, Vol. 130, No. 5 (1990): 693–695.

Bender, Michael C. and Louise Radnofsky. "Trump Says Strikes Aimed at Ending Syria's Use of Chemical Weapons, Sending Message to Russia and Iran." *The Wall Street Journal* (April 13, 2018).

Bennett, Bruce W. *Fatality Uncertainties in Limited Nuclear War*. Santa Monica, CA: RAND, 1977.

"On Preparedness for Limited Nuclear War." In Larsen and Kartchner, eds. *On Limited Nuclear War in the 21st Century*, 211–243.

Berdal, Mats. "The 'New Wars' Thesis Revisited." In Hew Strachan and Sibylle Scheipers, eds. *The Changing Character of War*. Oxford University Press, 2011, 108–133.

Bernal, J. D. "Disarmament and Limited Nuclear War." *New World Review*, Vol. 26 (January 1958): 30–37.

Bertram, Ian. "The Return of Limited War." *The Strategy Bridge* (September 13, 2016), www.thestrategybridge.com/the-bridge/2016/9/13/the-return-of-limited-war

Best, Geoffrey. "Restraints on War by Land before 1945." In Howard, ed. *Restraints on War*, 17–38.

Bhonsle, Rahul K. "Kargil 1999: Limited War, Unlimited Consequences." *CLAWS Journal* (summer 2009): 73–87.

Biddle, Tami Davis. *Strategy and Grand Strategy: What Students and Practitioners Need to Know*. Carlisle Barracks, PA: United States Army War College Press, 2015.

Biörklund, E. "Can War Be Limited? (in General or Local Wars)." *Air Power*, Vol. 6 (summer 1959): 287–293.

Black, Jeremy. *Insurgency and Counterinsurgency: A Global History*. Lanham, MD: Rowan and Littlefield, 2016.

"The Problems of a Great Power." *The RUSI Journal*, Vol. 157, No. 4 (2012): 80–84.

Blamey, Geoffrey. *The Causes of War*. New York: The Free Press, 1973.

Blight, James G. "'Limited' Nuclear War?: The Unmet Psychological Challenge of the American Catholic Bishops." *Science, Technology, & Human Values*, Vol. 10, No. 4 (autumn 1985): 3–16.

Boemke, Manfred F., Roger Chickering, and Stig Förster, eds. *Anticipating Total War: The German and American Experiences, 1871–1914*. German Historical Institute. Cambridge University Press, 1999.

Boesche, Roger. "Kautilya's *Arthaśāstra* on War and Diplomacy in Ancient India." *The Journal of Military History*, Vol. 67, No. 1 (January 2003): 9–37.

Bolger, Daniel. *Why We Lost: A General's Inside Account of the Iraq and Afghanistan Wars*. Boston: Houghton Mifflin Harcourt, 2014.

Bolton, John. "America's Unimportant, Unserious Wars." *Small Wars Journal* (February 7, 2018), http://smallwarsjournal.com/jrnl/art/america%E2% 80%99s-unimportant-unserious-wars

Bolton, Kerry R. "Sino–Soviet–US Relations and the 1969 Nuclear Threat." *Foreign Policy Journal* (May 17, 2010), www.foreignpolicyjournal.com/ 2010/05/17/sino-soviet-us-relations-and-the-1969-nuclear-threat/3/

Bond, Brian. *War and Society in Europe, 1870–1970*. Montreal: McGill-Queens University Press, 1998.

Boulé II, John R. "Operational Planning and Conflict Termination." *JFQ (Joint Force Quarterly)* (autumn–winter, 2001–02): 97–102.

Bracken, Paul. "War Termination." In Ashton B. Carter, John D. Steinbruner, and Charles A. Zraket, eds. *Managing Nuclear Operations*. Washington, DC: Brookings Institute, 1987, 197–214.

Braestrup, Peter. "Limited Wars and the Lessons of Lebanon." *The Reporter*, Vol. 20 (April 30, 1959): 25–27.

Braim, Paul F. *The Will to Win: The Life of General James A. Van Fleet*. Annapolis, MD: Naval Institute Press, 2001.

Brands, Hal. "American Grand Strategy: Lessons from the Cold War." *Foreign Policy Research Institute* (August 2015), www.fpri.org/article/2015/08/ american-grand-strategy-lessons-from-the-cold-war/

"Paradoxes of the Gray Zone." *Foreign Policy Research Institute* (February 2016), www.fpri.org/article/2016/02/paradoxes-gray-zone/

What Good Is Grand Strategy? Power and Purpose in American Statecraft from Harry S. Truman to George W. Bush. Ithaca, NY: Cornell University Press, 2014.

Brannen, Kate. "Obama Warns against Exaggerating the Islamic State Threat." *Foreign Policy* (February 1, 2015), http://foreignpolicy.com/2015/02/01/obama-warns-against-exaggerating-the-islamic-state-threat/

Bratton, Patrick C. "When Is Coercion Successful? And Why Can't We Agree on It?" *Naval War College Review*, Vol. 58, No. 3 (summer 2005): 99–120.

Brazier-Creagh, K. R. "Limited War." *Brassey's Annual* (1957): 35–45.

Breines, Norman. "The Debate on Limited War, 1957–1959: A Study of Attitudes." MA thesis, University of Massachusetts-Amherst, 1961.

Brennan, Brian W. "Limited vs. Total War." *Armor*, Vol. 111, No. 5 (September–October 2002): 8–11.

Brodie, Bernard. *Escalation and the Nuclear Option.* Princeton University Press, 1966.

General André Beaufre on Strategy: A Review of Two Books. Santa Monica, CA: RAND, 1965.

"Learning to Fight a Limited War." In William P. Gerbering and Bernard Brodie. *The Political Dimension in Strategy: Five Papers.* Los Angeles, CA: UCLA Press, 1968, 26–32. Reprinted from *Los Angeles Times* (December 3, 1967).

The Meaning of Limited War. US Air Force Project Rand Research Memorandum, RM-2224. Santa Monica CA: RAND, 1958.

"Politique de dissuasion et guerre limitée." *Politique étrangère*, No. 6 (1990): 543–552.

Review essay, "More about Limited War." *World Politics*, Vol. 10, No. 1 (October 1957): 112–122.

Strategy in the Missile Age. Santa Monica, CA: RAND, 1959.

Strategy in the Nuclear Age. Princeton University Press, 1965.

"Unlimited Weapons and Limited War." *The Reporter*, Vol. 8 (November 18, 1954): 16–21.

War and Politics. New York: Macmillan, 1973.

Brom, Shlomo and Meir Elran, eds. *The Second Lebanon War: Strategic Perspectives.* Tel Aviv: Institute for National Security Studies, 2007.

Brooks, David C. "Lessons from Limited Wars. Cutting Losses: Ending Limited Interventions." *Parameters*, Vol. 43, No. 3 (2013): 99–110.

Brown, Arthur E. "The Strategy of Limited War." In Arthur F. Lykke Jr., ed. *Military Strategy: Theory and Application* (Carlisle Barracks, PA: United

States Army War College, 1993), 213–227. Reprinted from *Military Strategy*, Vol. 3 (August 1973): 25–40.

Brown, Neville. *Limited World War?* Canberra Papers on Strategy and Defence, No. 32. Canberra: Australian National University, 1984.

Broyles, Arthur A., Eugene P. Wigner, and Sidney D. Drell. "Civil Defense in Limited War – A Debate." *Physics Today*, Vol. 29, No. 44 (1976): 44–57.

Bru, Alain and Jean-Baptiste Margeride. "Des Armes pour des guerres limitées: Essai de prospective." *Stratégique*, Vol. 54, No. 2 (1992), www.institut-strategie.fr/strat_054_BRUMARGERI.html

Bruce, Robert B. "Tethered Eagle: Lt. General James A. Van Fleet and the Quest for Military Victory in the Korean War." *Army History* (winter 2012): 6–29.

Bull, Hedley. "Bureaucracy Keeps Doing Its Thing." *The XX Committee* (December 30, 2014), http://20committee.com/2014/12/30/bureaucracy-keeps-doing-its-thing/

"Limited and Nuclear War." *Survival: Global Politics and Strategy*, Vol. 5, No. 2 (1963): 54–57.

Burns, Richard Dean. "Regulating Submarine Warfare, 1921–41: A Case Study in Arms Control and Limited War." *Military Affairs*, Vol. 35, No. 2 (April 1971): 56–63.

Bush, George and Brent Scowcroft. *A World Transformed*. New York: Vintage Books, 1999.

Buzzard, Anthony. "On Limiting Atomic War." *Bulletin of Atomic Scientists*, Vol. 13 (June 1957): 216–232.

Buzzard, Anthony, P. M. S. Blackett, Denis Healey, and Richard Goold-Adams. *On Limiting Atomic War*. London: Royal Institute of International Affairs, 1956.

Byman, Daniel. "'Death Solves All Problems': The Authoritarian Model of Counterinsurgency." *Journal of Strategic Studies*, Vol. 39, No. 1 (2016): 62–93.

Byman, Daniel and Matthew Waxman. *The Dynamics of Coercion: American Foreign Policy and the Limits of Military Might*. Cambridge University Press, 2002.

Cable, James. "De la Guerre limitée." *Stratégique*, Vol. 54, No.2 (1992), www.institut-strategie.fr/strat_054_Cable.html

"Limited War." *International Relations*, Vol. 11, No.6 (1993): 555–569.

Navies in Violent Peace. New York: St. Martin's Press, 1989.

Cagle, Malcolm W. "Sea Power and Limited War." *The United States Naval Institute Proceedings*, Vol. 84, No. 7 (July 1958): 23–27.

Calahan, H. A. *What Makes a War End?* New York: Vanguard Press, 1944.

Callwell, C. E. *Small Wars: Their Principles and Practice*. 3rd edn. Introduction by Douglas Porch. Lincoln, NE: University of Nebraska Press, 1996.

Cannon, Michael W. *The Development of the American Theory of Limited War, 1945–1963.* MA thesis, School of Advanced Military Studies, United States Army Command and General Staff College, 1989.

"The Development of the American Theory of Limited War, 1945–1963." *Armed Forces and Society,* Vol. 19, No. 1 (fall 1992): 71–104.

Carignan, Jennie. "Victory as a Strategic Objective: An Ambiguous and Counter-Productive Concept for the High Command." *Canadian Military Journal,* Vol. 7, No.2 (spring 2017): 5–14.

Carpenter, Ted Galen. "A Really Bad Idea: A 'Limited' War with Iran." *The National Interest* (April 14, 2015), http://nationalinterest.org/feature/really-bad-idea-limited-war-iran–12623

Carr, Eldon. *The Role of the Military in Ending Limited War.* USAWC Research Paper. Carlisle Barracks, PA: US Army War College, 1973.

Carroll, Berenice A. "How Wars End: An Analysis of Some Current Hypotheses." *Journal of Peace Research,* Vol. 6, No. 4 (1969): 295–321.

"War Termination and Conflict Theory: Value Premises, Theories, and Policies." *The Annals of the American Academy of Political and Social Science,* Vol. 392 (November 1970): 14–29.

Casey, Steven. *Selling the Korean War: Propaganda, Politics, and Public Opinion in the United States, 1950–1953.* Oxford University Press, 2008.

Cassidy, Robert. M. "Why Great Powers Fight Small Wars Badly." *Military Review,* Vol. 82, No. 5 (September–October 2000): 41–53.

Catudal, Honoré M. *Soviet Nuclear Strategy from Stalin to Gorbachev: A Revolution in Soviet Military and Political Thinking.* Berlin: Arno Spitz, 1988.

Cesa, Marco, ed. *Machiavelli on International Relations.* Oxford University Press, 2014.

Chance Vought Corporation. *Limited War.* Dallas, TX: Aeronautics and Missile Division, Chance Vought Corp., 1962.

Chandran, D. Suba. "An Inquiry into Limited War – II: Limited War; Unlimited Questions." *Institute of Peace and Conflict Studies,* Nuclear – Articles, No. 884 (October 4, 2002), http://webcache.googleusercontent.com/search?q=cache:d-1AN81BaQQJ:www.ipcs.org/article/nuclear/an-inquiry-into-limited-war-ii-limited-war-unlimited-questions-884.html+&cd=1&hl=en&ct=clnk&gl=us

Limited War: Revisiting Kargil in the Indo–Pak Conflict. Safdarjung Enclave, India: India Research Press, 2005.

"Limited War with Pakistan: Will It Secure India's Interests?" ACDIS Occasional Paper. University of Illinois at Urbana-Champagne: Program in Arms Control, Disarmament, and International Security, August 2004.

Changwen, Chai. "The Korean Truce Negotiations." In Li, Millett, and Yu, trans. and eds. *Mao's Generals Remember Korea,* 184–232.

Chatterjee, Partha. "On the Rational Choice Theory of Limited Strategic War." *The Journal of Political Science*, Vol. 34, No. 2 (April–June 1973): 157–172.

Check, Terence. "'Clean' Bombs and 'Limited' War: Edward Teller's Cold War Arguments." In James F. Klumpp, ed. *Argument in a Time of Change: Definitions, Frameworks, and Critiques.* Annandale, VA: National Communications Association, 1998, 304–309.

Cheema, Zafar Iqbal. "The Strategic Context of the Kargil Conflict: A Pakistani Perspective." In Lavoy, ed. *Asymmetric Warfare in South Asia*, 41–63.

Chickering, Roger. "Total War: The Use and Abuse of a Concept." In Boemke, Chickering, and Förster, eds. *Anticipating Total War*, 13–28.

Chickering, Roger and Stig Förster. "Introduction." In Chickering and Förster, eds., *The Shadows of Total War*, 1–9.

Chickering, Roger and Stig Förster, eds. *Great War, Total War: Combat and Mobilization on the Western Front, 1914–1918* (Cambridge University Press, 2000).

The Shadows of Total War: Europe, East Asia, and the United States, 1919–1939. German Historical Institute. Cambridge University Press, 2003.

Chickering, Roger, Stig Försterand Bernd Greinder, eds. *A World at Total War: Global Conflict and the Politics of Destruction, 1937–1945* (Cambridge University Press, 2010).

Chu, Shulong, "The PRC Girds for Limited, High-Tech War." *Orbis* (spring 1994): 177–191.

Cigar, Norman. "Croatia's War of Independence: The Parameters of War Termination." *The Journal of Slavic Military Studies*, Vol. 10, No. 2 (1997): 34–70.

Cimbala, Stephen J., ed. *Strategic War Termination.* New York: Praeger, 1986.

Clark, Ian. *Limited Nuclear War: Political Theory and Conventions.* Princeton University Press, 1982.

Waging War: A Philosophical Introduction. Oxford: Clarendon Press, 1990.

Clarke, Bruce B. G. "Conflict Termination: A Rational Model." *Studies in Conflict & Terrorism*, Vol. 16, No. 1 (1993): 25–60.

Clarke, Bruce C., Thomas Gates, and James H. Douglas. "Limited War: Where Do They Stand?" *The Army, Navy, Air Force Register and Defense Times* (May 23, 1959): 24–25.

Clarke, Michael. "The Ending of Wars and the Ending of Eras." *The RUSI Journal*, Vol. 160, No. 4 (2015): 4–9.

Clausewitz, Carl von. *Carl von Clausewitz: Two Letters on Strategy.* Peter Paret and Dan Moran, trans. and eds. Fort Leavenworth, KS: Combat Studies Institute, US Army Command and General Staff College, 1984.

On War. Michael Howard and Peter Paret, trans. and eds. Princeton University Press, 1984.

Strategie . Marc Guarin, trans., Donald Stoker and Christopher Bassford, eds. Fort Bragg, NC: Clausewitz.com, 2019.

Clayton, Anthony. *The Wars of French Decolonization.* London: Routledge, 1994.

Clayton, David. "British Foreign Economic Policy towards China, 1949–60," *Electronic Journal of International History*, Article 6, http://sas-space.sas.ac .uk/3393/1/Journal_of_International_History_2000_n6_Clayton.pdf

Clodfelter, Mark. "Air Power and Limited War: An Analysis of the Air Campaigns against North Vietnam as Instruments of National Policy." Ph.D. dissertation, University of North Carolina, Chapel Hill, 1987.

The Limits of Air Power: The American Bombing of North Vietnam. New York: Free Press, 1989.

"Nixon and the Air Weapon." In Dennis E. Showalter and John G. Albert, eds. *An American Dilemma: Vietnam, 1964–1973.* Chicago: Imprint Publications, 1993, 167–186.

Cochrane, Feargal. *Ending Wars.* Cambridge, UK: Polity Press, 2008.

Codevilla, Angelo M. "Make America Victorious Again." *Claremont Review of Books* (October 18, 2016), www.claremont.org/crb/basicpage/make-amer ica-victorious-again/

Codevilla, Angelo M. and Paul Seabury. *War: Ends and Means.* 2nd edn. Dulles, VA: Potomac Books, 2006.

Cohen, Eliot A. "Constraints on America's Conduct of Small Wars." *International Security*, Vol. 9, No. 2 (1984): 151–181.

Colby, Elbridge. "America Must Prepare for Limited War." *The National Interest* (November–December 2015), http://nationalinterest.org/print/feature/ america-must-prepare-limited-war–14104

Collins, Bruce. "Defining Victory in Victorian Warfare, 1860–1882." *The Journal of Modern History*, Vol. 77, No. 3 (July 2013): 895–929.

Collins, J. Lawton. *War in Peacetime: The History and Lessons of Korea.* Boston: Houghton Mifflin, 1969.

Collins, John M. *Grand Strategy: Principle and Practices.* Annapolis, MD: Naval Institute Press, 1973.

Communist Government of North Vietnam. *Initial Failure of the US "Limited War."* Hanoi: Foreign Language Publishing House, 1967.

Corbett, Julian S. *Some Principles of Maritime Strategy.* Eric Grove, introduction and notes. Annapolis, MD: Naval Institute Press, 1988 [1911].

Cordesmann, Anthony H. *Creeping Incrementalism: US Strategy in Iraq and Syria from 2011 to 2015.* Washington, DC: CSIS, 2015.

The "End State" Fallacy: Setting the Wrong Goals for War Fighting. Washington, DC: CSIS, 2016.

"Losing by 'Winning': America's Wars in Afghanistan, Iraq, and Syria." Washington, DC: CSIS, 2018, https://csis-prod.s3.amazonaws.com/s3fs-pub

lic/publication/180813_Losing_By_Winning.pdf?nyp_LojotpQsEquc1mtmn8
OpRwQcnYWW

Cordesmann, Anthony H. and Michael Wang. *Chinese Military Strategy and Military Modernization in 2015: A Comparative Analysis*. Washington, DC: CSIS, 2015.

Corum, James S. "Building the Malayan Army and Police – Britain's Experience during the Malayan Emergency, 1948–1960." In Kendall D. Gott, ed. *Security Assistance: US and International Historical Perspectives*. Leavenworth, KS: Combat Studies Institute Press, 2006.

Coser, Lewis A. "The Termination of Conflict." *The Journal of Conflict Resolution*, Vol. 5, No. 4 (December 1961): 347–353.

Coutau-Bégarie, Hervé. "L'Ancien Regime militaire: Un modèle de guerre limitée?" *Stratégique*, Vol. 54, No. 2 (1992), www.institut-strategie.fr/strat_054_HCBANCIENR.html

Craig, Gordon A. *The Politics of the Prussian Army, 1640–1945*. London: Oxford University Press, 1955.

Review of *Nuclear Weapons and Foreign Policy* by Henry A. Kissinger and *Limited War: The Challenge to American Strategy* by Robert Endicott Osgood. *Commentary* (February 1, 1958), www.commentarymagazine.com/articles/nuclear-weapons-and-foreign-policy-by-henry-a-kissinger-limited- wa r-the-challenge-to-american-strategy-by-robert-endicott-osgood/

Crane, Conrad C. "Exerting Air Pressure and Globalizing Containment: War Termination in Korea." In Moten, ed. *Between War and Peace*, 237–258.

"From Korea to Kosovo: Matching Expectation with Reality for Modern Airpower in Limited Wars." In Jeffrey S. Morton, R. Craig Nation, Paul Forage, and Stefano Bianchi, eds. *Reflections on the Balkan Wars: Ten Years after the Break-up of Yugoslavia*. New York: Palgrave Macmillan, 2004, 211–225.

"To Avert Impending Disaster: American Military Plans to Use Atomic Weapons during the Korean War." *Journal of Strategic Studies*, Vol. 23, No.2 (2000): 72–88.

Cronin, Audrey Kurth. "The 'War on Terrorism': What Does It Mean to Win?" *Journal of Strategic Studies*, Vol. 37, No. 2 (2014): 174–197.

Crozier, Brian. *A Theory of Conflict*. New York: Charles Scribner's Sons, 1974.

Daalder, Ivo H. and Michael E. O'Hanlan. *Winning Ugly: NATO's War to Save Kosovo*. Washington, DC: Brookings Institution Press, 2000.

Dabezies, Pierre. "La Guerre limitée: Notion fourre-tout, obscure clarte." *Stratégique*, Vol. 54, No. 2 (1992), www.institut-strategie.fr/strat_054_Dabezies.html

Daddis, Gregory. "'A Better War?' – The View from the Nixon White House." *Journal of Strategic Studies*, Vol. 36, No. 3 (2013): 357–384.

"Out of Balance: Evaluating American Strategy in Vietnam, 1968–72." *War and Society*, Vol. 32, No. 3 (2013): 252–270.

Westmoreland's War: Reassessing American Strategy in Vietnam. Oxford University Press, 2014.

The Daily Beast (September 11, 2014), www.thedailybeast.com/cheats/2014/09/11/kerry-u-s-is-not-at-war-with-isis.html

Danchev, Alex and Dan Keohane, eds. *International Perspectives on the Gulf Conflict, 1990–91*. Houndsmill, UK: Palgrave Macmillan, 2003.

Darling, Roger. "A New Conceptual Scheme for Analyzing Counterinsurgency." *Military Review*, Vol. 54, No. 6 (June 1974): 54–66.

"A New Conceptual Scheme for Analyzing Insurgency." *Military Review*, Vol. 54, No. 2 (February 1974): 27–38.

Daugherty, William, Barbara Levi, and Frank von Hippel. "The Consequences of 'Limited' Nuclear Attack on the United States." *International Security*, Vol. 10, No. 4 (spring 1986): 3–45.

David, Charles-Philippe and Jean-Jacques Roche. *Théories de la sécurité: Définitions, approches et concepts de la sécurité internationale*. Paris: Montchrestien, 2002.

Davis, Anthony. "When Words Hurt: No Limits on a Limited War." *Asiaweek.com*, Vol. 26, No. 12 (March 31, 2000), http://edition.cnn.com/ASIANOW/asiaweek/magazine/2000/0331/nat.indiapak.war.html

Davis, Julie Hirschfeld and Mark Landler. "Trump Outlines New Afghan War Strategy with Few Details." *The New York Times* (August 21, 2017), www.nytimes.com/2017/08/21/world/asia/afghanistan-troops-trump.html

Davis, Lynn Etheridge. "Limited Nuclear Options: Deterrence and the New American Doctrine: Introduction." *The Adelphi Papers*, Vol. 16, No. 121 (winter 1975–76): 1–22.

Davis, W. V. "The Navy in Limited War." *Ordnance*, Vol. 42 (March–April 1958): 802–805.

Dawson, Joseph G., III. "The US War with Mexico: The Difficulties of Concluding a Victorious War." In Moten, ed. *Between War and Peace*, 85–106.

Deist, Wilhelm. "Foreword." In Wilhelm Deist, ed. *The German Military in the Age of Total War*. Leamington Spa, UK: Berg Publishers, 1985, 5–21.

Deitchman, Seymour J. "Limited War." *Military Review*, Vol. 51 (July 1971): 3–16. *Limited War and American Defense Policy*. Cambridge, MA: MIT Press, 1964.

Dempsey, Martin. "Keynote Speech on Civil–Military Relations at the Center for a New American Security." (December 1, 2014), www.youtube.com/watch?v=8ORRt-lSRwU

Desai, G. "'Wars May Erupt without Warning.'" *The Times of India* (January 7, 2000).

Desportes, Vincent. *Comprendre la guerre*. 2nd edn. Paris: Economica, 2001.

DeWeerd, H. A. "The Triumph of the Limiters: Korea." Santa Monica, CA: RAND, 1968.

Dickey, Jeffrey V., Thomas B. Everett, Zane M. Galvach, Matthew J. Mesko, and Anton V. Soltis. "Russian Political Warfare: Origin, Evolution, and Application." MA thesis, Naval Postgraduate School, 2015.

Diehl, Paul F., ed. *War*. 6 vols. London: Sage Publications, 2005.

Dinerman, Taylor. "The Limits of Limited War." *Gatestone Institute* (October 27, 2011), www.gatestoneinstitute.org/2539/limits-of-limited-war

Dolman, Everett Carl. *Pure Strategy: Power and Principle in the Space and Information Age*. Abingdon, UK: Frank Cass, 2005.

Donner, Michael. *Die neutrale Handelsschiffahrt im begrenzten militärischen Konflikt: Eine völkerrechtliche Untersuchung am Beispiel des Konfliktes zwischen Irak und Iran (1980–1988)*. Kehl am Rhein, Germany: N. P. Engel Verlag, 1993.

Doughart, Jackson. "Neoconservatism in the Political Thought of Albert Camus: A Preliminary Inquiry." *The Journal of Camus Studies* (2012): 41–52.

Dougherty, Kevin. *The United States Military in Limited War: Case Studies in Success and Failure*. Jefferson, NC: McFarland, 2012.

Downs, Chuck. "Limited War: The Initial Failures of Appeasement Policy toward North Korea." *The Heritage Foundation* (August 8, 2000), www.heritage .org/asia/report/limited-war-the-initial-failures-appeasement-policy-toward-north-korea

Drell, Sidney D. and Frank von Hippel. "Limited Nuclear War." *Scientific American*, Vol. 235, No. 5 (November 1976): 27–35.

Dubik, James M. "By Any Other Name, War Is Still War." *Army Magazine*, Vol. 66, No. 6 (June 2016), www.armymagazine.org/2016/05/13/by-any-other-name-war-is-still-war/

Dueck, Colin and Roger Zakheim. "Why We Like Ike." *National Review Online* (January 13, 2015), www.nationalreview.com/article/411482/why-we-ike-colin-dueck-roger-zakheim

Dupuy, T. N. "Can America Fight a Limited Nuclear War?" *Survival: Global Politics and Strategy*, Vol. 3, No. 5 (1961): 220–234.

Durst, Jay B. "Limited Conventional War – Can It Be Successful?" *Military Review*, Vol. 50, No. 1 (January 1970): 56–63.

Duyvesten, Isabelle and James E. Worrall. "Global Strategic Studies: A Manifesto." *Journal of Strategic Studies* (2016): 1–11, www.tandfon-line.com/doi/full/10.1080/01402390.2016.1269228

Dwyer, Philip G. "Total War or Traditional War." *The International History Review*, Vol. 31, No. 1 (March 2009): 72–84.

Earle, Edward Meade, Gordon Craig, and Felix Gilbert, eds. *Makers of Modern Strategy: Military Thought from Machiavelli to Hitler.* Princeton University Press, 1943.

Echevarria, Antulio J., II. *Fourth Generation War and Other Myths.* Carlisle Barracks, PA: US Army War College Press, 2005.

  Operating in the Gray Zone: An Alternative Paradigm for US Military Strategy. Carlisle Barracks, PA: US Army War College Press, 2016.

  Reconsidering the American Way of War: US Military Practice from the Revolution to Afghanistan. Washington, DC: Georgetown University Press, 2014.

Ehrhart, Hans-Georg. "Post-Modern Warfare and the Blurred Boundaries between War and Peace." *Defence & Security Analysis*, Vol. 33, No. 3 (2017): 263–275.

Eichenberg, Richard C. "Victory Has Many Friends: US Public Opinion and the Use of Military Force, 1981–2005." *International Security*, Vol. 30, No.1 (summer 2005): 140–177.

Elkus, Adam. "Abandon All Hope, Ye Who Enter Here: You Cannot Save the Gray Zone Concept." *War on the Rocks* (December 30, 2015), http://waronther ocks.com/2015/12/abandon-all-hope-ye-who-enter-here-you-cannot-save-the-gray-zone-concept/

  "50 Shades of Gray: Why the Gray Wars Concept Lacks Strategic Sense." *War on the Rocks* (December 15, 2015), http://warontherocks.com/2015/12/50-shades-of-gray-why-the-gray-wars-concept-lacks-strategic-sense/

  "The Shadow of Limited War." *Red Team Journal* (July 15, 2010), http://redteamjournal.com/2010/07/the-shadow-of-limited-war/

  "The Strategic and Operational Dynamics of Limited War." *Small Wars Journal* (April 17, 2012), http://smallwarsjournal.com/jrnl/art/the-strategic-and-operational-dynamics-of-limited-war

Ellis, J. W., Jr. and T. E. Greene, "The Contextual Study: A Structured Approach to the Study of Political and Military Aspects of Limited War." *Operations Research*, Vol. 8, No. 5 (September–October 1960): 639–651.

Elowitz, Larry. "Korea and Vietnam: Limited War and the American Political System." Ph.D. dissertation, The University of Florida, 1972.

Evans, Martin. *Algeria: France's Undeclared War.* Oxford University Press, 2012.

Fabre, Cécile. "War Exit." *Ethics*, Vol. 125, No. 3 (April 2015): 631–652.

Fall, Bernard B. "The Theory and Practice of Insurgency and Counter-Insurgency." *Military Review* (September–October 2015): 40–48.

Fairweather, Jack. *The Good War: Why We Couldn't Win the War or the Peace in Afghanistan.* New York: Basic Books, 2014.

Fazal, Tanisha M. and Sarah Kreps. "The United States' Perpetual War in Afghanistan: Why Long Wars No Longer Generate a Backlash at Home."

Foreign Affairs (August 20, 2018), www.foreignaffairs.com/articles/north-america/2018–08–20/united-states-perpetual-war-afghanistan

Fehling, Gregory E. "America's First Limited War." *Naval War College Review*, Vol. 53, No. 3 (summer 2000): 101–143.

Fenenko, Alexey. "Donbas: A Limited War for a Total Revision of the Cold War Order." *Russia Direct* (April 21, 2015), www.russia-direct.org/opinion/donbas-limited-war-total-revision-cold-war-order

Finletter, Thomas K. *Power and Policy: US Foreign and Military Policy in the Hydrogen Age*. San Diego: Harcourt, Brace and Co., 1954.

Fisher, Thomas L. "Limited War – What Is It?" *Air University Quarterly Review*, Vol. 9 (winter 1957–58): 127–142.

Flavin, William. "Planning for Conflict Termination and Post-Conflict Success." *Parameters* (autumn 2003): 95–112.

Fleck, Janice. *Limited War Theory in Vietnam: A Critique according to Clausewitz*. Washington, DC: National Defense University, National War College, 1994.

Flynn, Michael T. "How about Winning Our Nation's Wars instead of Just Participating in Them?" *Military Review* (March–April 2016): 8–15.

Foot, Rosemary. *A Substitute for Victory: The Politics of Peacemaking at the Korean Armistice Talks*. Ithaca, NY: Cornell University Press, 1990.

Forsén, Björn and Annette Forsén. "German Secret Submarine Exports, 1919–35." In Donald J. Stoker Jr. and Jonathan A. Grant, eds. *Girding for Battle: The Arms Trade in a Global Perspective*. Westport, CT: Praeger, 2003, 113–134.

Förster, Stig and Jörg Nagler. "Introduction." In Förster and Nagler, eds., *On the Road to Total War*, 1–25.

On the Road to Total War: The American Civil War and the German Wars of Unification, 1861–1871. German Historical Institute. Cambridge University Press, 1997.

Fortna, Virginia Page. "Scraps of Paper? Agreements and the Durability of Peace." *International Organization*, No. 57 (spring 2003): 337–372.

Foster, James L. and Garry D. Brewer. "And the Clocks Were Striking Thirteen: The Termination of War." *Policy Sciences*, Vol. 7, No. 2 (June 1976): 225–243.

Fox, Amos C. and Andrew J. Rossow. "Assesing Russian Hybrid Warfare: A Successful Tool for Limited War." *Small Wars Journal* (August 8, 2016), https://smallwarsjournal.com/jrnl/art/assessing-russian-hybrid-warfare-a-successful-tool-for-limited-war

Fox, William T.R. "The Causes of Peace and Conditions of War." *The Annals of the American Academy of Political and Social Science*, Vol. 392 (November 1970): 1–13.

"Foreword." *The Annals of the American Academy of Political and Social Science*, Vol. 392 (November 1970): viii.

Frank, Richard. "Ending the Pacific War: 'No Alternative to Annihilation.'" In Daniel Marston, ed. *The Pacific War Companion*. Oxford, UK: Osprey Publishing, 2005, 227–245.

Franklin, William D. "Clausewitz on Limited War." *Military Review*, Vol. 47, No. 6 (1967): 23–29.

Fravel, M. Taylor. "China's Changing Approach to Military Strategy: The Science of Military Strategy from 2001 to 2013." In Joe McReynolds, ed. *China's Evolving Military Strategy*. Washington, DC: Brookings, 2016, 40–73.

Freedberg, Sydney J. Jr., "No Longer Unthinkable: Should the US Ready for 'Limited' Nuclear War?" *Breaking Defense* (May 30, 2013), http://breaking defense.com/2013/05/no-longer-unthinkable-should-us-ready-for-limited-nuclear-war/

Freedman, Lawrence. *The Evolution of Nuclear Strategy*. New York: St. Martin's Press, 1983.

"On War and Choice." *The National Interest* (May–June 2010): 9–16.

Strategy . Oxford University Press, 2013.

"The Theory of Limited War." In Danchev and Keohane, eds. *International Perspectives on the Gulf Conflict, 1990–91*, 201–223.

"Ukraine and the Art of Limited War." *War on the Rocks* (October 2014), http://warontherocks.com/2014/10/ukraine-and-the-art-of-limited-war/#_

Freedman, Lawrence and Efraim Karsh. *The Gulf Conflict, 1990–1991: Diplomacy and War in the New World Order*. Princeton University Press, 1995.

Freier, Nathan P., et al. *Outplayed: Regaining Strategic Initiative in the Gray Zone*. Carlisle, PA: Strategic Studies Institute, United States Army War College Press, 2016.

French, David. "Vietnam and the Legacy of Limited War." *The National Review* (April 30, 2015), www.nationalreview.com/article/417743/vietnam-and-legacy-limited-war-david-french

Freudenberg, Dirk. *Theorie des Irregulären: Partisanen, Guerillas, und Terroristen im modernen Kleinkrieg*. Wiesbaden: Verlag für Sozialwissenschaften, 2008.

Frkovich, James. "Limited War and the Ugandan Experience: Implications for African Security." *African Security*, Vol. 3, No. 3 (2010): 148–167.

Fuller, William C., Jr. *Strategy and Power in Russia, 1600–1914*. New York: The Free Press, 1992.

Gabrielson, Iver. "Military Strategy and the Conduct of the 2006 Israel–Hezbollah War." *Comparative Strategy*, Vol. 32, No. 5 (2013): 435–442.

Gacek, Christopher M. *The Logic of Force: The Dilemma of Limited War in American Foreign Policy*. New York: Columbia University Press, 1994.

Gaddis, John Lewis. *Strategies of Containment*. 2nd edn. Oxford University Press, 2005.

Gallois, Pierre. *The Balance of Terror: Strategy for the Nuclear Age.* Richard Howard, trans. Boston: Houghton Mifflin, 1961.

Galula, David. *Counterinsurgency Warfare: Theory and Practice.* Westport, CT: Praeger Security International, 1964, 2006.

Pacification in Algeria, 1956–1958. Santa Monica, CA: Rand, 1963, 2006.

Gannon, Michael V. "Limited vs. Total War." *Commonweal,* Vol. 48 (August 22, 1958): 510–513.

Ganor, Boaz. "Defining Terrorism – Is One Man's Terrorist Another Man's Freedom Fighter?" *International Institute for Counterterrorism* (January 1, 2010), www.ict.org.il/Article/1123/Defining-Terrorism-Is-One-Mans-Terrorist-Another-Mans-Freedom-Fighter#gsc.tab=0

Garg, Rahul. "Positive Prospects for Limited War in South Asia." *Journal of Defence Studies,* Vol. 5, No. 2 (April 2011): 90–108.

Garnett, John C. "Limited 'Conventional' War in the Nuclear Age." In Michael Howard, ed. *Restraints on War: Studies in the Limitation of Armed Conflict.* Oxford University Press, 1979, 79–102.

"Limited War." In John Baylis, Ken Booth, John Garnett, and Phil Williams. *Contemporary Strategy: Theories and Policies.* New York: Holmes & Meier, 1982, 114–131.

Garnter, Scott Sigmund. *Strategic Assessment in War.* New Haven: Yale University Press, 1997.

Gat, Azar. *A History of Military Thought: From the Enlightenment to the Cold War.* Oxford University Press, 2001.

Gates, Robert M. *Duty: Memoirs of a Secretary at War.* New York: Knopf, 2014.

Gavin, James M. "Why Limited War?" *Ordnance,* Vol. 42 (April 1958): 809–813.

Gelpi, Christopher, Peter D. Feaver, and Jason Reifler. "Success Matters: Casualty Sensitivity and the War in Iraq." *International Security,* Vol. 30, No. 3 (winter 2005–06): 7–46.

Géré, François. "Limiter la guerre, Clausewitz, encore." *Stratégique,* Vol. 54, No. 2 (1992), www.institut-strategie.fr/strat_054_GR_tdm.html

Giap, Vo Nguyen and Van Tien Dung. *How We Won the War.* Philadelphia: Recon Publishers, 1976.

Gietschier, Steven Philip. "Limited War and the Home Front: Ohio during the Korean War." Ph.D. dissertation, The Ohio State University, 1977.

Gill, Bates. "Limited Engagement." *Foreign Affairs,* Vol. 78, No. 4 (July–August 1999): 65–76.

Gillcrist, Paul Thomas. "Limited War and American Foreign Policy." MA thesis, Washington, DC: The American University, 1965.

Glavin, Terry. "The American Epoch Is Over. It Ended on Obama's Watch." *National Post* (January 18, 2017), https://nationalpost.com/opinion/the-american-epoch-is-over-it-ended-on-obamas-watch

Godwin, Paul H. B. "Chinese Military Strategy Revised: Local and Limited War." *The Annals of the American Academy of Political and Social Science*, Vol. 519 (January 1992): 191–201.

Goemans, H. E. *War and Punishment: The Causes of War Termination and the First World War*. Princeton University Press, 2000.

Gordon, Andrew. "Social Protest in Imperial Japan: The Hibiya Riot of 1905," *The Asia-Pacific Journal*, Vol. 12, No. 3 (July 20, 2014): 1–22.

Gordon, Michael R. "Powell Delivers a Resounding No on Using Limited Force in Bosnia." *The New York Times* (September 28, 1992), www.nytimes.com/1992/09/28/world/powell-delivers-a-resounding-no-on-using-limited-force-in-bosnia.html?pagewanted=all

  "US Outlines Plans on Nuclear-Weapons Use." *The Wall Street Journal* (February 2, 2018), www.wsj.com/articles/u-s-outlines-plan-on-nuclear-weapons-use-1517621791

Gordon, Michael R. and Bernard E. Trainor. *Cobra II: The Inside Story of the Invasion and Occupation of Iraq*. New York: Vintage, 2007.

  Endgame: The Inside Story of the Struggle for Iraq, from George W. Bush to Barack Obama. New York: Pantheon, 2012.

  The Generals' War: The Inside Story of the Conflict in the Gulf. New York: Back Bay Books, 1995.

Gorman, Paul F. "Limited War: Korea, 1950." Paper for Government 285, Harvard University, fall 1953, http://usacac.army.mil/cac2/csi/docs/Gorman/02_Army_1950_72/b_Harvard/02_53_LimitedWar_Nov.pdf

Gormley, Robert H. "Limited War and the Striking Fleets." *US Naval Institute Proceedings*, Vol. 89, No. 2 (February 1963): 53–59.

Gortzak, Yoav. "Using Indigenous Forces in Counterinsurgency Operations: The French in Algeria, 1954–1962." *Journal of Strategic Studies*, Vol. 32, No. 2 (2009): 307–333.

Gouré, Leon. *Soviet Limited War Doctrine*. Santa Monica, CA: RAND, 1963.

Gourevitch, Philip. "What Obama Didn't Say." *The New Yorker* (September 11, 2014), www.newyorker.com/news/daily-comment/obama-didnt-say

Gray, Colin S. *Categorical Confusion? The Strategic Implications of Recognizing Challenges Either as Irregular or Traditional*. Carlisle, PA: Strategic Studies Institute, US Army War College, 2012.

  Defining and Achieving Decisive Victory. Carlisle, PA: Strategic Studies Institute, US Army War College, 2002.

Gray, Colin S. and Keith Payne. "Victory is Possible." *Foreign Policy*, No. 39 (summer 1980): 14–27.

Greathouse, Ronald. H. "Profile of a Dilemma: Limited Nuclear War." *The Marine Corps Gazette*, Vol. 43 (January 1959): 24–26.

Greentree, Todd R. "A War Examined: Afghanistan." *Parameters*, Vol. 43, No. 3 (2013): 87–97.

Greenwalt, Charles. "Limited War Authority Would Tie Hands of Obama's Successors." *Lancaster Online* (March 1, 2015), https://lancasteronline .com/opinion/columnists/limited-war-authority-would-tie-hands-of-obama -s-successors/article_035c6646-bdfa-11e4-ba5e-831fbfbe29e9.html

Griffin, Christopher. "From Limited War to Limited Victory: Clausewitz and Allied Strategy in Afghanistan." *Contemporary Security Policy*, Vol. 35, No. 3 (2014): 446–467.

Griffith, Michael C. *War Termination: Theory, Doctrine, and Practice*. Fort Leavenworth, KS: School of Advance Military Studies, 1992.

Griswald, Alex. "NY Times Stealth-Edits Article to Remove Embarrassing Obama Admission." *Mediaite.com* (December 29, 2015), www.mediaite .com/online/ny-times-stealth-edits-article-to-remove-embarrassing-obama- admission/

Grygiel, Jacob and A. Wess Mitchell. "Limited War Is Back." *The National Interest* (August 28, 2014): 37–44, http://nationalinterest.org/feature/ limited-war-back–11128

Gsponer, André. "The Neutron Bomb and Other Limited Nuclear War Weapons." *Bulletin of Peace Proposals*, Vol. 13, No. 3 (1982): 221–225.

Guevara, Che. *Guerrilla Warfare*. Lincoln, NE: University of Nebraska Press, 1998.

Gurtov, Mel. "Endless War, Undeclared and Undebated." *LobeLog* (December 29, 2015), https://lobelog.com/endless-war-undeclared-and-undebated/

Guttmann, Allen, ed. *Korea and the Theory of Limited War*. Boston: D. C. Heath, 1967.

Gwynn, Charles W. *Imperial Policing*. London: Macmillan, 1939.

Haass, Richard N. *War of Necessity, War of Choice: A Memoir of Two Iraq Wars*. New York: Simon & Schuster, 2009.

Haider, Muhammed Zarrar. "Misconception of Limited War." Unpublished paper on *Academia.edu*, undated (downloaded February 2017), www.aca- demia.edu/6948557/Misconception_of_Limited_War

Hall, John. "An Irregular Reconsideration of George Washington and the American Military Tradition." *The Journal of Military History*, Vol. 78, No. 3 (2014): 961–993.

Halperin, Morton H. "Limited War: An Essay on the Development of the Theory and an Annotated Bibliography." *Occasional Papers in International Affairs*, No. 3 (May 1962): 1–67.

Limited War in the Nuclear Age. Cambridge, MA: Harvard University Press, 1963.

"Nuclear Weapons and Limited War." *The Journal of Conflict Resolution*, Vol. 5, No. 2 (June 1961): 146–166.

"War Termination as a Problem in Civil–Military Relations." *Annals of the American Academy of Political and Social Science*, Vol. 392, No.1 (1970): 86–95.

Hampton, Ephraim M. "Unlimited Confusion over Limited War." *Air University Quarterly Review*, Vol. 9 (spring 1957): 28–47.

Handel, Michael I. *Masters of War: Classical Strategic Thought*. 3rd edn. London: Frank Cass, 2001.

"The Study of War Termination." *Journal of Strategic Studies*, Vol. 1, No. 1 (1978): 51–75.

Harari, Yuval Noah. "Why It's No Longer Possible for Any Country to Win a War." *Time* (June 23, 2017), http://time.com/4826856/russia-trump-north-korea-china-war/

Hashim, Ahmed S. *Insurgency and Counterinsurgency in Iraq*. Ithaca, NY: Cornell University Press, 2006.

Haslam, Jonathan. *Russia's Cold War: From the October Revolution to the Fall of the Wall*. New Haven, CT: Yale University Press, 2011.

Hassan, Hassan. "ISIS Is Ready for a Resurgence," *The Atlantic* (August 26, 2018), www.theatlantic.com/international/archive/2018/08/baghdadi-recording-iraq-syria-terrorism/568471/

Haun, Phil and Colin Jackson. "Breaker of Armies: Air Power in the Easter Offensive and the Myth of Linebacker I and II in the Vietnam War." *International Security*, Vol. 40, No. 3 (winter 2015–16): 139–178.

Hawkins, William R. "Imposing Peace: Total vs. Limited Wars, and the Need to Put Boots on the Ground." *Parameters* (summer 2000): 72–82.

"The Man Who Invented Limited War." *MHQ: The Quarterly Journal of Military History*, Vol. 4, No. 1 (autumn 1991): 105–109.

Hayden, Bill. "Opening Address." In Young, ed. *Defence and the Media in the Time of Limited War*, 5–14.

Hayes, John D. "Peripheral Strategy … Littoral Tactics … Limited War." *The Army Combat Forces Journal*, Vol. 5 (September 1954): 36–39.

Healy, Gene. "Goodbye, Obama: The Outgoing President Leaves a Loaded Gun in the Oval Office." *Reason.com* (February 2017), http://reason.com/archives/2017/01/10/goodbye-obama

Hedstrom, Jr., Marvin A. "Limited War in the Precision Engagement Era: The Balance between Dominant Maneuver and Precision Engagement." MA thesis, School of Advanced Military Studies, 2001.

Heilbrunn, Otto. "When the Counter-Insurgents Cannot Win." *Royal United Services Institution Journal*, Vol. 114, No. 653 (March 1969): 55–58.

Hellborn, Rudolph. "Die bonner Theses des begrenzten Krieges." *Deutsche Aussenpolitik* (June 1960): 602–617.

Hémez, Rémy. "Operation Sangrais: A Case Study in Limited Military Intervention." *Military Review* (November–December 2016): 72–80.

nderson, Errol A and J. David Singer, "'New Wars' and Rumors of 'New Wars.'" In Diehl, ed., *War*, Vol. I, 398–425.

ring, George C. *America's Longest War: The United States and Vietnam, 1950–1975.* 3rd edn. New York: McGraw-Hill, 1996.

'In Cold Blood': LBJ's Conduct of Limited War in Vietnam." *The Harmon Memorial Lectures*, No. 93. Colorado Springs, CO: US Air Force Academy, 1990.

om Colony to Superpower: US Foreign Relations since 1776 (New York: Oxford University Press, 2008).

Hershberger, W. D. "EMP and a Limited Nuclear War." *Science*, Vol. 213, No. 4510 (August 21, 1981): 816.

Herwig, Holger. "Total Rhetoric, Limited War: Germany's U-Boat Campaign, 1917–1918." *Journal of Military and Strategic Studies*, Vol. 1, No. 1 (1998), http://jmss.journalhosting.ucalgary.ca/jmss/index.php/jmss/article/view/19/18

Hess, Gary R. *Presidential Decisions for War: Korea, Vietnam, and the Persian Gulf.* Baltimore, MD: Johns Hopkins University Press, 2001.

Heuser, Beatrice. *The Evolution of Strategy: Thinking about War from Antiquity to the Present.* Cambridge University Press, 2010.

"*Regina Maris* and the Command of the Sea: The Sixteenth-Century Origins of Modern Maritime Strategy." *Journal of Strategic Studies* (2015): 1–38.

Higgins, Trumbull. *Korea and the Fall of MacArthur: A Précis in Limited War.* New York: Oxford University Press, 1960.

Highland, H. M. Curteis. "The Doctrine of Limited Liability." *Royal United Services Institution*, Vol. 83, No. 532 (1938): 695–701.

Hildreth, Charles H. *USAF Logistics Preparations for Limited War, 1958–1961.* Washington, DC: USAF Historical Division Liaison Office, October 1962.

Hilsman, Roger. *From Nuclear Military Strategy to a World Without War: A History and a Proposal.* Westport, CT: Praeger, 1999.

Hirano, Ryuji. "The First Sino–Japanese and the Russo–Japanese War from the Viewpoint of a 'Maritime Limited War': From the Perspective of Julian Corbett's Strategic Theory." Briefing Memorandum. *National Institute for Defense Studies (NIDS) News.* Japan Ministry of Defense (June 12, 2015).

Hoag, Malcolm W. *On Local War Doctrine.* Santa Monica, CA: RAND, 1961.

Hoffman, Frank G. *Conflict in the 21st Century: The Rise of Hybrid Wars.* Arlington, VA: Potomac Institute for Policy Studies, 2007.

"The Contemporary Spectrum of Conflict: Protracted, Gray Zone, Ambiguous, and Hybrid Modes of Warfare." *The Heritage Foundation: 2016 Index of US Military Strength*, 25–36, http://index.heritage.org/military/2016/essays/contemporary-spectrum-of-conflict/

Decisive Force – The New American Way of War? National Security Decision-Making paper. Newport, RI: US Naval War College, March 1994.

"Further Thoughts on Hybrid Threats." *Small Wars Journal* (March 2, 2009), http://smallwarsjournal.com/jrnl/art/further-thoughts-on-hybrid-threats

"Hybrid vs. Compound War." *Armed Forces Journal* (October 1, 2009), http://armedforcesjournal.com/hybrid-vs-compound-war/

"On Not-So-New Warfare: Political Warfare vs. Hybrid Threats." *War on the Rocks* (July 28, 2014), https://warontherocks.com/2014/07/on-not-so-new-warfare-political-warfare-vs-hybrid-threats/

Holden Reid, Brian. "The Cold War US Army: Building Deterrence for Limited War." *Cold War History*, Vol. 10, No. 3 (August 2010): 464–465.

"Michael Howard and Evolving Ideas about Strategy." *Annual Liddell Hart Lecture*. London, King's College (November 27, 2012).

Holdorf, Polly M. "Limited Nuclear War in the 21st Century." In Mark Jansson, ed. *A Collection of Papers from the 2010 Nuclear Scholars Initiative*. Washington, DC: CSIS, 2010), 137–149, http://csis.org/files/publication/110916_Holdorf.pdf

Holmes, Terence M. "The Clausewitzian Fallacy of Absolute War." *Journal of Strategic Studies* (April 2017), www.tandfonline.com/doi/abs/10.1080/01402390.2017.1307742

Holmqvist, Caroline. *Policing Wars: On Military Intervention in the Twenty-First Century*. Houndsmill, UK: Palgrave Macmillan, 2014.

Holsti, Kalevi J. *The State, War, and the State of War*. Cambridge University Press, 1996.

Homan, C. "Nucleaire Strategie." In Teitler, Bosch, and Klinkert, eds. *Militaire Strategie*, 231–260.

Honig, Jan Willem. "Problems of Text and Translation." In Hew Strachan and Andreas Herberg-Rothe, eds. *Clausewitz in the Twenty-First Century*. Oxford University Press, 2007, 57–73.

Horne, Alistair. *A Savage War of Peace: Algeria, 1954–1962*. New York: New York Review of Books, 2006.

Horne, John. "Introduction: Mobilizing for 'Total War,' 1914–1918." In John Horne, ed. *State, Society, and Mobilization in Europe during the First World War*. Cambridge University Press, 1997, 1–17.

Howard, Michael. "The Classical Strategists." *The Adelphi Papers*, Vol. 9, No. 54 (1969): 18–32.

"Constraints on War." In Michael Howard, George J. Andreopolous, and Mark R. Shulman, eds. *The Laws of War: Constraints on Warfare in the Western World*. New Haven, CT: Yale University Press, 1994, 1–11.

"The Forgotten Dimension of Strategy." *Foreign Affairs*, Vol. 57, No. 5 (1979): 975–986.

ed. *Restraints on War: Studies in the Limitation of Armed Conflict*. Oxford University Press, 1979.

"*Temperamenta Belli*: Can War be Controlled?" In Howard, ed. *Restraints on War*, 1–16.

"The Transformation of Strategy." *The RUSI Journal*, Vol. 156, No. 4 (2011):12–16.

Hsieh, Wayne Wei-Siang. "Total War and the American Civil War Reconsidered: The End of an Outdated 'Master Narrative.'" *The Journal of the Civil War Era*, Vol. 1, No. 3 (September 2011): 394–408.

Hua, Hongxun. "China's Strategic Missile Programs: Limited Aims, Not 'Limited Deterrence.'" *The Nonproliferation Review*, Vol. 5, No. 2 (1998): 60–68.

Hume, Robert S. and Nathan P. Freier. "Confronting Conflict in the 'Gray Zone.'" *Breaking Defense* (June 23, 2016), http://breakingdefense.com /2016/06/confronting-conflict-in-the-gray-zone/

Hunt, Michael C. "Beijing and the Korean Crisis, June 1950–June 1951," *Political Science Quarterly*, Vol. 107, No. 3 (autumn, 1992): 453–478.

Ignatius, David. "The Problem with America's Limited Wars." *Washington Post* (October 9, 2014), www.washingtonpost.com/opinions/david-ignatius-real-ity-check-on-limited-war/2014/10/09/19c8c95e-4ff2-11e4-babe-e91da079c-b8a_story.html

Iklé, Fred Charles. *Every War Must End*. New York: Columbia University Press, 1971. *How Nations Negotiate*. New York: Harper & Row, 1964, 1987.

Imlay, Talbot. Review essay, "Total War." *Journal of Strategic Studies*, Vol. 30, No. 3 (2007): 547–570.

Ingram, Haroro J. "Three Lessons from the Modern Era of Small Wars." *The International Relations and Security Network* (May 26, 2014), www.isn .ethz.ch/Digital-Library/Articles/Detail/?id=180191

Ingram, Haroro J. and Craig Whiteside. "Outshouting the Flea: Islamic State and Modern Asymmetric Strategic Communications." In Andrea Dew, Marc Genest, and S. C. M. Payne, eds. *From Quills to Tweets: How America Communicates War and Revolution*. Washington, DC: Georgetown University Press, 2019.

Interavia Study Group. "'Little Wars' Need Big Battalions." *Interavia*, Vol. 11, No. 10 (October 1956): 773–776.

Ivey, Ramon A. "Limited War, National Will, and the All Volunteer Army." Study Project. Carlisle Barracks, PA: US Army War College, 1988.

Jack, Tan Kwoh. "The Korean War June–October 1950: Inchon and Stalin in the 'Trigger vs. Justification' Debate." Working Paper No. 105. Singapore Institute of Defence and Strategic Studies (January 2006).

Jackson, Ashley. "The Taliban's Fight for Hearts and Minds." *Foreign Policy* (September 12, 2018), https://foreignpolicy.com/2018/09/12/the-talibans-fight-for-hearts-and-minds-aghanistan/

Jackson, Colin F. "Lost Chance or Lost Horizon? Strategic Opportunity and Escalation Risk in the Korean War, April–July 1951." *Journal of Strategic Studies*, Vol. 33, No. 2 (2010): 255–289.

James, D. Clayton, with Anne Sharp Wells. *Refighting the Last War: Command and Crisis in Korea*. New York: Free Press, 1993.

Janda, Lance. "Shutting the Gates of Mercy: The American Origins of Total War, 1860–1880." *Journal of Military History*, Vol. 59, No. 1 (January 1995): 7–26.

Janecek, Frank P. "In Limited War – Victory before the Culminating Point." Joint Maritime Operations paper. Newport, RI: US Naval War College, May 1995.

Jarausch, Konrad H. "The Illusion of Limited War: Chancellor Bethmann Hollweg's Calculated Risk, July 1914." *Central European History*, Vol. 2, No. 1 (March 1969): 48–76.

Jian, Chen. *China's Road to the Korean War: The Making of the Sino-American Confrontation*. New York: Columbia University Press, 1994.

Jocelyn, Thomas. "Losing a War." *The Weekly Standard* (August 27, 2018), www.weeklystandard.com/thomas-joscelyn/losing-a-war

Johnson, Dominic D. P. *Failing to Win: Perceptions of Victory and Defeat in International Politics*. Cambridge, MA: Harvard University Press, 2006.

Johnson, James T. *Ideology, Reason, and the Limitation of War: Religious and Secular Concepts, 1200–1740*. Princeton University Press, 1975.

Just War Tradition and the Restraint of War: A Moral and Historical Inquiry. Princeton University Press, 1981.

"The Meaning of Non-Combatant Immunity in the Just War/Limited War Tradition." *Journal of the American Academy of Religion*, Vol. 39, No.2 (June 1971): 151–170.

Johnson, Robert. "Hybrid War and Its Countermeasures: A Critique of the Literature." *Small Wars & Insurgencies*, Vol. 29, No. 1 (2018): 141–163.

Johnson, Robert B. "Tactical Warfare and the Limited War Dilemma." *TEMPO Review Paper*. Santa Barbara, CA: General Electric Company, 1961.

Johnston, Herbert. "Limited War." *Review of Politics*, Vol. 27, No. 2 (April 1965): 246–247.

Johnston, Patrick B. "Does Decapitation Work? Assessing the Effectiveness of Leadership Targeting in Counterinsurgency Campaigns." *International Security*. Vol. 36, No. 4 (spring 2012): 47–79.

Johnston, Patrick B. and Brian R. Urlacher. "Explaining the Duration of Counterinsurgency Campaigns," (February 25, 2012), http://patrickjohnston.info/materials/duration.pdf

Jomini, Antoine-Henri. *The Art of War*. G. H. Mendell and W. P. Craighill, trans. Westport, CT: Greenwood, 1971 [1862].

Jones, Christopher. "Just and Limited Wars: Restraints on the Use of the Soviet Armed Forces." *World Politics*, Vol.28, No. 1 (October 1975): 44–68.

Jones, Terry. "Why Grammar Is the First Casualty of War." *The Daily Telegraph* (December 1, 2001), www.telegraph.co.uk/news/uknews/1364012/Why-grammar-is-the-first-casualty-of-war.html

Jordan, Jenna. "Attacking the Leader, Missing the Mark: Why Terrorist Groups Survive Decapitation Strikes." *International Security*, Vol. 38, No. 4 (spring 2014): 7–38.

Josephson, Matthew. "The Fantasy of Limited War." *The Nation* (August 31, 1957): 89–91.

Joshi, Shashank, "India's Military Instrument: A Doctrine Stillborn." *Journal of Strategic Studies*, Vol. 36, No. 4 (2013): 512–540.

Joy, C. Turner. *How Communists Negotiate*. New York: Macmillan, 2013 [1955].

Kagan, Donald, Eliot Cohen, Charles F. Doran, and Michael Mandelbaum. "Is Major War Obsolete? An Exchange." *Survival: Global Politics and Strategy*, Vol. 41, No. 2 (1999): 139–152.

Kahn, Herman. "Issues of Thermonuclear War Termination." *The Annals of the American Academy of Political and Social Science*, Vol. 392 (November 1970): 133–172.

On Escalation. New York: Praeger, 1967.

Kalamanowitz, Pablo. "Regular War, *Jus in Bello*, and the Ideal of Limited War." Paper prepared for the ECPR General Conference (2015).

Kaldor, Mary. "In Defence of New Wars." *Stability*, Vol. 2, No. 1 (2013): 1–16.

New and Old Wars: Organised Violence in a Global Era. 3rd edn. Cambridge: Polity Press, 2012.

Kaplan, Morton A. *The Strategy of Limited Retaliation*. Policy Memorandum No. 19. Princeton, NJ: Center of International Studies, 1959.

"Kargil, a 'test for limited n-war.'" *The Hindu* (August 20, 2003), http://www.thehindu.com/2003/08/20/stories/2003082006001200.htm

Karon, Tony. "Obama Promises a Long and Limited War on Islamic State." *Al Jazeera America* (September 11, 2014), http://america.aljazeera.com/articles/2014/9/10/islamic-state-obama.html

Kartchner, Kerry M. "Escalation to Limited Nuclear War in the 21st Century." In Larsen and Kartchner, eds. *On Limited Nuclear War in the 21st Century*, 144–171.

Kaufmann, William W. *Policy Objectives and Military Action in the Korean War*. Santa Monica, CA; RAND, 1956.

Kawamura, Kouki. "Briefing Memo: Limited War and Escalation." *The National Institute for Defense Studies News* (April 2016), www.nids.mod.go.jp/english/publication/briefing/pdf/2016/briefing_e201604

Kecskemeti, Paul. "Political Rationality in Ending War." *The Annals of the American Academy of Political and Social Science*, Vol. 392 (November 1970): 105–115.

  Strategic Surrender: The Politics of Victory and Defeat. Stanford University Press, 1958.

Kempf, Olivier. "L'Indirection de la guerre ou le retour de la guerre limitée." *Institut français des relations internationals (IFRI)*, No. 4 (winter 2015): 157–169.

Kerin, James R., Jr. *Remembering Limited War: Reflections on the Korean War in Selected American Novels.* Carlisle Barracks, PA: US Army War College, 2000.

Khan, Feroz Hassan, Peter R. Lavoy, and Christopher Clary. "Pakistan's Motivations and Calculations for the Kargil Conflict." In Lavoy, ed. *Asymmetric Warfare in South Asia*, 64–91.

Khan, Khurshid. "Limited War under the Nuclear Umbrella and Its Implications for South Asia," (2005), http://sacw.pagesperso-orange.fr/saan/2005/khurshidkhan.pdf

Kiesling, Eugenia C. "'Total War, Total Nonsense' or 'The Military Historian's Fetish.'" In Michael S. Neiberg, ed. *Arms and the Man: Military History Essays in Honor of Dennis Showalter.* Leiden: Brill, 2011, 223–227.

Kilgour, D. Marc and Frank C. Zagare. "Explaining Limited Conflicts." *Conflict Management and Peace Science*, Vol. 24, No. 1 (2007): 65–82.

Kim, Arm-San. "A Note on Sunzi's Art of War and Limited War: A Modern Interpretation." *Korean Journal of Defense Analysis*, Vol.6, No. 1 (1994): 245–257.

Kim, Taewoo. "Limited War, Unlimited Targets: US Air Force Bombing of North Korea during the Korean War, 1950–1953." *Critical Asian Studies*, Vol. 44, No. 3 (2012): 467–492.

King, Jr., James E. "Deterrence and Limited War." *Army*, Vol. 8 (August 1957): 21–26.

  "Nuclear Plenty and Limited War." *Foreign Affairs*, Vol. 35, No. 2 (January 1957): 238–256.

Kissinger, Henry A. "Controls, Inspection, and Limited War." *The Reporter*, Vol. 16, No. 12 (June 13, 1957): 14–19.

  Diplomacy . New York: Simon and Schuster, 1994.

  "Limited War: Conventional or Nuclear?" *Survival: Global Politics and Strategy*, Vol. 3, No. 1 (1961): 2–11.

  "Military Policy and the Defense of the 'Grey Areas.'" *Foreign Affairs*, Vol. 33, No. 3 (April 1958): 416–428.

  The Necessity for Choice: Prospects of American Foreign Policy. New York: Harper, 1960.

  "Nuclear Testing and the Problem of Peace." *Foreign Affairs*, Vol. 37, No. 1 (October 1958): 1–18.

Nuclear Weapons and Foreign Policy. New York: Harper & Brothers, 1957.

Kitson, Frank. *Low-Intensity Operations: Subversion, Insurgency, Peace-Keeping*. Harrisburg, PA: Stackpole Books, 1971.

Knorr, Klaus. "Limited Strategic War." In Knorr and Read, eds. *Limited Strategic War*, 3–31.

Knorr, Klaus and Thornton Read, eds. *Limited Strategic War*. New York: Praeger, 1962.

Kolb, Avery E. *Emergency Resource Management: Limited War*. Washington, DC: Industrial College of the Armed Forces of the United States, 1969.

Kolodziej, Edward A. Review of *Limited War Revisited* by Robert E. Osgood. *The Journal of Politics*, Vol. 43, No. 1 (February 1981): 247–48.

Kolton, Randy J. *Isolating the Theater of War: Operational Implications of Border Sanctuaries in Limited War*. Fort Leavenworth, KS: US Army Command and Staff College, 1990.

Kondratov, T. "What Is 'Limited War'?" *Soviet Military Review*, No. 1 (August 1973): 48–49.

Krebs, Gerhard. "Super Sunrise? Japanese–United States Peace Feelers in Switzerland, 1945." *The Journal of Military History*, Vol. 69, No. 4 (October 2005): 1081–1120.

Krepon, Michael. "Limited War, Escalation Control, and the Nuclear Option in South Asia." In Michael Krepon, Rodney W. Jones, and Ziad Haider, eds., *Escalation Control and the Nuclear Option in South Asia*. Washington, DC: Stimson Center, 149–166, www.stimson.org/sites/default/files/file ... /Escalation%20Control%20FINAL_0.pdf

Kriner, Douglas and Francis Shen. "Limited War and American Political Engagement." *Journal of Politics*, Vol. 71, No. 4 (October 2009): 1514–1529.

Krizanovic, Gary. *Operational Art in Limited War Termination: The Bridge between the Strategic and the Operational Levels of War*. Joint Maritime Operations paper. Newport, RI: US Naval War College, 1994.

Kroenig, Matthew. "The Case for US Tactical Nukes." *The Wall Street Journal* (January 24, 2018), www.wsj.com/articles/the-case-for-tactical-u-s-nukes–1516836395

Kuklick, Bruce. *Blind Oracles: Intellectuals and War from Kennan to Kissinger*. Princeton University Press, 2006.

Ladwig, Walter C., III. "A Cold Start for Hot Wars? The Indian Army's New Limited War Doctrine." *International Security*, Vol. 32, No. 3 (winter 2007–08): 158–190.

Lai, Nathan Yu-jen. "United States Policy and the Diplomacy of Limited War in Korea, 1950–1951." Ph.D. dissertation, University of Massachusetts, 1974.

Lambert, Nicholas. Review essay, "False Prophet?: The Maritime Theory of Julian Corbett and Professional Military Education." *The Journal of Military History*, Vol. 77, No. 3 (July 2013): 1055–1078.

Landler, Mark. "Obama, in Speech on ISIS, Promises Sustained Effort to Rout Militants." *The New York Times* (September 10, 2014), www.nytimes .com/2014/09/11/world/middleeast/obama-speech-isis.html

Langbaum, Robert. "Democratic Strategy to Halt the Soviet Threat: 'Limited War' as the Path to Peace." *Commentary* (July 1, 1951), www.commentarymaga- zine.com/articles/democratic-strategy-to-halt-the-soviet-threat-lim ited-war- as-the-path-to-peace/

Lange, Sven. *Hans Delbrück und der "Strategiestreit": Kriegführung und Kriegsgeschichte in der Kontroverse, 1879–1914*. Freiburg im Breisgau: Rombach, 1995.

Larison, Daniel. "Obama's 'Limited' Perpetual War." *The American Conservative* (February 12, 2015), www.theamericanconservative.com/lar ison/obamas-limited-perpetual-war/

"Why 'Limited' Wars Fail." *The American Conservative* (October 10, 2014), www.theamericanconservative.com/larison/why-limited-wars-fail/

Larsen, Jeffrey A. "Limited War and the Advent of Nuclear Weapons." In Larsen and Kartchner, eds. *On Limited Nuclear War in the 21st Century*, 3–20.

Larsen, Jeffrey A. and Kerry M. Kartchner, eds. *On Limited Nuclear War in the 21st Century*. Stanford University Press, 2014.

Larson, Robert. "B. H. Liddell Hart: Apostle of Limited War." *Military Affairs*, Vol. 44, No. 2 (April 1980).

Lavoy, Peter R., ed. *Asymmetric Warfare in South Asia: The Causes and Consequences of the Kargil Conflict*. Cambridge University Press, 2009.

Lawrence, T. E. "The 27 Articles of T. E. Lawrence." *The Arab Bulletin* (August 20, 1917), https://wwi.lib.byu.edu/index.php/The_27_Articles_of_T.E._Lawrence

Layton, Peter. "The Idea of Grand Strategy." *The RUSI Journal*, Vol. 157, No. 4 (2012): 56–61.

LeBow, Richard Ned. "Thomas Schelling and Strategic Bargaining." *International Journal*, Vol. 51, No. 3 (summer 1996): 555–576.

"Reason Divorced from Reality: Thomas Schelling and Strategic Bargaining." *International Politics*, Vol. 43 (2006): 429–452.

Le Cheminant, P. de L. "Tactical Deterrence or Limited War?" *Brassey's Annual* (1961): 112–121.

Lee, Bradford A. "Strategic Interaction: Theory and History for Practitioners." In Thomas Mahnken, ed. *Competitive Strategies for the 21st Century*. Palo Alto, CA: Stanford University Press, 2012, 28–46.

"Winning the War but Losing the Peace? The United States and the Strategic Issues of War Termination." In Bradford A. Lee and Karl F. Walling eds. *Strategic Logic and Political Rationality: Essays in Honor of Michael I. Handel*. London: Frank Cass, 2003, 248–273.

Lee, Steven. "Morality, the SDI, and Limited Nuclear War." *Philosophy and Public Affairs*, Vol. 17, No. 1 (winter 1988): 15–43.

Lee, Wayne E. "Plattsburgh 1814: Warring for Bargaining Chips." In Moten, ed. *Between War and Peace*, 43–63.

LeGro, William E. "The Why and How of Limited War." *Military Review*, Vol. 50, No. 7 (July 1970): 32–39.

Lemmer, George F. "USAF Manpower in Limited War, 1964–1967." USAF Historical Division Liaison Office, 1968.

Lepgold, Joseph and Brent L. Sterling. "When Do States Fight Limited Wars? Political Risk, Policy Risk, and Policy Choice." *Security Studies*, Vol. 9, No. 4 (2000): 127–166.

Lesh, Bruce A. "Limited War or Rollback of Communism?: Truman, MacArthur, and the Korean Conflict." *OAH Magazine of History*, Vol. 22, No. 4 (October 2008): 47–53.

Levinson, Irving W. "A New Paradigm for an Old Conflict: The Mexico–United States War." *The Journal of Military History*, Vol. 73, No. 2 (April 2009): 393–416.

Lévy, Bernard-Henri. "Thinking the Unthinkable: This Is War." Steven B. Kennedy, trans. *Globe and Mail* (November 16, 2015), www.theglobeandmail.com/globe-debate/thinking-the-unthinkable-this-is-war/article27284617/

Levy, Jack S. "Big Wars, Little Wars, and Theory Construction." *International Relations*, Vol. 16, No. 3 (1990): 215–224.

Lewis, Adrian. *The American Culture of War: The History of US Military Force from World War II to Operation Iraqi Freedom*. New York: Routledge, 2007.

Lewy, Guenter. *America in Vietnam*. Oxford University Press, 1980.

Li, Xiaobing. *China's Battle for Korea: The 1951 Spring Offensive*. Bloomington, IN: Indiana University Press, 2014.

Li, Xiaobing, Allan R. Millett, and Bin Yu, trans. and eds. *Mao's Generals Remember Korea*. Lawrence, KS: University Press of Kansas, 2001.

Liddell Hart, B. H. *Defence of the West*. New York: Morrow & Co., 1950.
   The Revolution in Warfare. New Haven, CT: Yale University Press, 1947.
   Strategy. 2nd edn. New York: Meridian, 1991 [1967].
   "War, Limited." *Harper's*, Vol. 192, No. 1150 (March 1946): 193–203.

"Limited War: Prospects and Possibilities." *Army Information Digest*, Vol. 13 (June 1958): 6–20.

Loan, Eugene Van. "Limited to Defeat." *Claremont Review of Books Digital* (March 1, 2016), www.claremont.org/crb/basicpage/limited- to-defeat/

Lockwood, Jonathan Samuel. *The Soviet View of US Strategic Doctrine: Implications for Decision Making*. Foreword by Leon Gouré. New Brunswick: Transaction Books, 1983.

Lockyer, Adam. "How Democracies Exit Small Wars: The Role of Opposition Parties in War Termination." *The Australian Journal of International Affairs*, Vol. 66, No. 3 (2012): 381–396.

Lofgren, Charles A. "How New Is Limited War?" *Military Review* (July 1967): 16–23.

Lohaus, Phillip. "A Missing Shade of Gray: Political Will and Waging Something Short of War." *War on the Rocks* (January 11, 2017), https://warontherocks .com/2017/01/a-missing-shade-of-gray-political-will-and-waging-something -short-of-war/

Long, Austin. *On "Other War": Lessons from Five Decades of RAND Counterinsurgency Research.* Santa Monica, CA: RAND, 2006.

Lucas, George R. "Postmodern War." *Journal of Military Ethics*, Vol. 9, No. 4 (2010): 289–298.

Luck, Edward C. and Stuart Albert. "Introduction." In Stuart Albert and Edward C. Luck, eds. *On the Endings of Wars.* Port Washington, NY: Kennikat Press, 1980, 3–6.

Luttwak, Edward N. *On the Meaning of Victory: Essays on Strategy.* New York: Simon and Schuster, 1986.

  Strategy: The Logic of War and Peace. Cambridge, MA: Belknap Press of Harvard, 1987.

Lyall, Jason. "Do Democracies Make Inferior Counterinsurgents? Reassessing Democracy's Impact on War Outcomes and Duration." *International Organization*, Vol. 64, No. 1 (2010): 167–192.

Lybrand, William A., ed. *Proceedings of the Symposium: The US Army's Limited-War Mission and Social Science Research, March 26, 27, 28, 1962.* Washington, DC: Special Operations Research Office, American University, 1962.

Lynn, John A. "Patterns of Insurgency and Counterinsurgency." *Military Review* (July–August 2005): 22–27.

MacArthur, Douglas. "Farewell Address to Congress, April 19, 1951," www.amer- icanrhetoric.com/speeches/douglasmacarthurfarewelladdress.htm

  Reminiscences . New York: McGraw-Hill, 1964.

Machiavelli, Niccolò. *Discourses on Livy.* Ninnian Hill Thomson, trans. Mineola, NY: Dover Publications, 2007.

Mack, Andrew. "Why Big Nations Lose Small Wars: The Politics of Asymmetric Conflict." *World Politics*, Vol. 27, No. 2 (1975): 175–200.

Mahan, Alfred Thayer. *Naval Strategy Compared and Contrasted with the Principles and Practice of Military Operations on Land.* Boston: Little, Brown, 1911.

Mahnken, Thomas C. "Future Scenarios of Limited Nuclear Conflict." In Larsen and Kartchner, eds. *On Limited Nuclear War in the 21st Century*, 129–143.

Malkasian, Carter. "Toward a Better Understanding of Attrition: The Korean and Vietnam Wars." *The Journal of Military History*, Vol. 68, No. 3 (July 2004): 911–942.

Mallison, Jr., W. Thomas. *Studies in the Law of Naval Warfare: Submarines in General and Limited Wars*. International Law Studies, 1966, Vol. LVIII. Washington, DC: USGPO, 1968.

Mandelbaum, Michael. "Is Major War Obsolete?" *Survival: Global Politics and Strategy*, Vol. 40, No. 4 (1998): 20–38.

Manea, Octavian. "NATO in the Age of Limited Wars." *Defence Matters* (April 4, 2016), http://defencematters.org/news/nato-in-the-age-of-limited-wars/343/

Mao Tse-Tung. *On Guerrilla Warfare*. Samuel B. Griffith II, trans. Urbana, IL: University of Illinois Press, 2000.

   "The Three Stages of Protracted War." In *Selected Military Writings*. Peking: Foreign Language Press, 1967, 210–219.

Marighella, Carlos. "The Minimanual of the Urban Guerrilla." In Sam. C. Sarkesian, ed. *Revolutionary Guerrilla Warfare*. Chicago: Precedent Publishing, 1975, 507–530.

Marolda, Edward J. "The Influence of Burke's Boys on Limited War." *US Naval Institute Proceedings*, Vol. 107, No. 942 (August 1981): 36–41.

Marquis, Jefferson P. "The 'Other War': An Intellectual History of American Nation-Building in South Vietnam, 1954–1975." Ph.D. dissertation, Ohio State University, 1997.

Martel, William C. *Victory in War: Foundations of Modern Military Policy*. Cambridge University Press, 2007.

Martin, Lawrence. "Limited Nuclear War." In Howard, ed. *Restraints on War*, 103–122.

Martin, Wayne Richard. "An Analysis of United States International Relations before and during Limited War." Ph.D. dissertation, University of Southern California, 1970.

Matray, James I. "Truman's Plan for Victory: National Self-Determination and the Thirty-Eighth Parallel Decision in Korea." *The Journal of American History*, Vol. 66, No. 2 (September 1979): 314–333.

Maxwell, Neville. *China's "Aggression" of 1962 and the Unresolved Border Dispute*. Oxford: Court Place Books, 1999.

Mazarr, Michael J. "The Folly of 'Asymmetric' War." *The Washington Quarterly*, Vol. 31, No. 3 (July 2008): 33–53.

   Mastering the Gray Zone: Understanding a Changing Era of Conflict. Carlisle, PA: US Army War College Press, 2015.

   "The Strange Debates of Strategy." *War on the Rocks* (January 14, 2016), http://warontherocks.com/2016/01/the-strange-debates-of-strategy/

   "Struggle in the Gray Zone and World Order." *War on the Rocks* (December 22, 2015), http://warontherocks.com/2015/12/struggle-in-the-gray-zone-and-world-order/

McCallion, Joseph, Jr. "Achieving Total War Goals with a Limited War Force: Convincing the Enemy to Accept Defeat." MA thesis, School of Advanced Military Studies, United States Army Command and General Staff College, 2005.

McClintock, Robert. *The Meaning of Limited War*. Boston: Houghton Mifflin, 1967.

McCuen, John J. *The Art of Counter-Revolutionary Warfare: A Psycho-Politico - Military Strategy of Counter-insurgency*. Harrisburg, PA: Stackpole, 1966.

McIntyre, Jamie. "Top US Commander: Trump's Afghanistan Plan a 'Game Changer.'" *Washington Examiner* (November 28, 2017), www.washingtonexaminer.com/top-us-commander-trumps-afghanistan-plan-a-game-changer

McIntyre, William R. "Limited War." *Editorial Research Reports*, Vol. 2 (July 23, 1958): 549–568.

Meiser, Jeffrey W. "Ends + Ways + Means = (Bad) Strategy." *Parameters*, Vol. 46, No. 4 (winter 2016–17): 81–91.

Mercer, Jonathan. "Emotion and Strategy in the Korean War." *International Organization*, Vol. 67, No. 2 (spring 2013): 221–252.

Mesquita, Bruce Bueno de. "Big Wars, Little Wars: Avoiding Selection Bias." *International Relations*, Vol. 16, No. 3 (1990): 159–169.

Metz, Steven. "A Tale of Two Strategies: Limited War in US and Russian Strategic Culture." *World Politics Review* (April 5, 2015), www.worldpoliticsreview.com/articles/18393/ataleoftwostrategieslimitedwarinusandrussianstrategicculture

Milevski, Lukas. *The Evolution of Modern Grand Strategic Thought*. Oxford University Press, 2016.

  "The Modern Evolution of Grand Strategic Thought." Ph.D. thesis, University of Reading, 2014.

  "The Nature of Strategy versus the Character of War." *Comparative Strategy*, Vol. 35, No. 5 (2016): 438–446.

  "Prospective Strategy for Baltic Defense: The Russian Public and War Termination in the Baltic States." *Military Review* (January–February 2018): 58–70.

  "Revisiting Wiley's Dichotomy of Strategy: The Effects of Sequential and Cumulative Patterns of Operations." *Journal of Strategic Studies*, Vol. 35, No. 2 (2012): 223–242.

  The West's East: Contemporary Baltic Defense in Strategic Perspective. Oxford University Press, 2018.

Millham, Matt, "Obama Refocuses the Mission with Drawdown." *Stars & Stripes* (June 23, 2011), www.stripes.com/news/obama-refocuses-the-mission-with-drawdown-1.147315

Miller, Paul D. *Armed State Building: Confronting State Failure, 1898–2012.* Ithaca: Cornell University Press, 2013.

Millett, Alan R. *The Korean War: The Essential Bibliography Series.* Washington, DC: Potomac Books, 2007.

   The War for Korea, 1945–1950: A House Burning. Lawrence, KS: University Press of Kansas, 2005.

   The War for Korea, 1950–1951: They Came from the North. Lawrence, KS: University Press of Kansas, 2010.

Millett, Allan R. and Peter Maslowski. *For the Common Defense: A Military History of the United States of America.* 2nd edn. New York: Free Press, 1994.

Millstein (Mil'shtein), M. and A. Slobodenko. "'Limited War' – Weapon of Unlimited Aggression." *New Times* (October 1958): 13–15.

Milne, David. "'Our Equivalent of Guerrilla Warfare': Walt Rostow and the Bombing of Vietnam, 1961–1968." *The Journal of Military History*, Vol. 71, No. 1 (January 2007): 169–203.

Mlyn, Eric. *The State, Society, and Limited Nuclear War.* Albany, NY: State University of New York Press, 1995.

Mochalov, V. "Concerning the 'Theory of Limited Wars.'" *Soviet Military Review*, No. 2 (February 1965): 40–42.

   "What Lies behind the Theory of 'Limited Wars'?" *Soviet Military Review*, No. 8 (August 1969): 54–56.

Mochalov, V. and V. Dashichev, "The Smoke Screen of the American Imperialists." *Red Star* (December 17, 1957). Leon Gouré, trans. Published as *Soviet Commentary on the Doctrine of Limited Nuclear War.* Santa Monica, CA: RAND, 1958.

Mohan, C. Raja. "Fernandes Unveils 'Limited War' Doctrine." *The Hindu* (January 25, 2000), www.thehindu.com/2000/01/25/stories/01250001.htm

Möise, Ed. "Vietnam War Bibliography: Theories of Limited War and Counterinsurgency," http://edmoise.sites.clemson.edu/limited.html

Monaghan, Andrew. "Putin's Way of War: The 'War' in Russia's 'Hybrid Warfare.'" *Parameters*, Vol. 45, No. 4 (winter 2015–16): 65–74.

Monroe, Robert Rawson. "Limited War Strategy of the United States." MA thesis, Stanford University, 1962.

Morton, Louis. "The Twin Essentials of Limited War." *Survival: Global Politics and Strategy*, Vol. 3, No. 3 (1961): 135–138.

Moten, Matthew, ed. *Between War and Peace: How America Ends Its Wars.* New York: Free Press, 2011.

   War Termination: The Proceedings of the War Termination Conference, United States Military Academy, West Point. Fort Leavenworth, KS: Combat Studies Institute Press, 2010.

Mueller, John. *Retreat from Doomsday: The Obsolescence of Major War.* New York: Basic Books, 1989.

Mulrine, Anna. "Why America Isn't Winning Its Wars." *Christian Science Monitor* (December 12, 2015), www.csmonitor.com/USA/Military/2015/1211/Why-America-isn-t-winning-its-wars

Murdock, Deroy. "Bush Didn't Lie: Then Why Did His Administration Sit on the Evidence of Saddam Hussein's WMDs?" *National Review* (October 16, 2014), www.nationalreview.com/2014/10/bush-didnt-lie-deroy-murdock/

Nalapat, Madhav. "PLA Hawks Fuel Pakistan's Push for Limited War." *Sunday Guardian* (August 14, 2016), www.sundayguardianlive.com/news/6095-pla-hawks-fuel-pakistan-s-push-limited-war

Nalls, John C. "Resurrecting Limited War Theory." MA thesis, School of Advanced Military Studies. United States Army Command and General Staff College, 2008.

National Security Council Report, NSC 81/1, "United States Courses of Action with Respect to Korea," September 9, 1950, History and Public Policy Program Digital Archive, Truman Presidential Museum and Library, http://digitalarchive.wilsoncenter.org/document/116194.pdf?v=b5f4cbf0ae773fe6970014edb854029e

Navias, Martin and Tim Moreman. "Limited War and Developing Countries." In Lawrence Freedman, ed. *War*. Oxford University Press, 1994, 309–314.

Neely, Mark E. "Was the Civil War a Total War?" *Civil War History*, Vol. 50, No. 4 (December 2004): 434–458.

Neiberg, Michael S. "To End All Wars? A Case Study of Conflict Termination in World War I." In Bartholomees Jr., ed. *US Army War College Guide to National Security Issues*, Vol. II, 337–347.

Neresov, Timur. "What Size Is My War? Examining the Concepts of Total and Limited War." *The Strategy Bridge* (November 3, 2016), http://thestrategybridge.org/the-bridge/2016/11/3/what-size-is-my-war-examining-the-concepts-of-total-and-limited-war

Nerheim, Steven William. "NSC-81/1 and the Evolution of US War Aims in Korea, June–October 1950." *Strategy Research Project*. Carlisle, PA: US Army War College, 2000.

Neumann, Peter R. and M. L. R. Smith. "Strategic Terrorism: The Framework and Its Fallacies." *Journal of Strategic Studies*, Vol. 28, No. 4 (2005): 571–595.

Neustadt, Richard E. "The Exercise of Presidential Power." In Guttmann, ed. *Korea and the Theory of Limited War*, 351–365.

New York Times (December 19, 2014), www.nytimes.com/2014/12/20/world/fbi-accuses-north-korean-government-in-cyberattack-on-sony-pictures.html

Nguyen, Lien-Hang T. *Hanoi's War: An International History of the War for Peace in Vietnam*. Chapel Hill, NC: University of North Carolina Press, 2012.

Nichols, Thomas M. *Eve of Destruction: The Coming Age of Preventive War.* Philadelphia: University of Pennsylvania Press, 2008.

Nickerson, Hoffman. *Can We Limit War?* Port Washington, NY: Kennikat Press, 1977 [1933].

"Limited War, 1957." *Ordnance* (November–December 1957): 428–429.

Niedringhaus, David A. "US Army Armor in Limited War: Armor Employment Techniques in Korea and Vietnam." MA thesis, Ohio State University, 1987.

Nish, Ian. *The Origins of the Russo-Japanese War.* Abingdon, UK: Routledge, 1985.

Nishank, Motwani. "Be Prepared for an India–Pakistan Limited War." *The Diplomat* (October 5, 2018), https://thediplomat.com/2018/10/be-prepared-for-an-india-pakistan-limited-war/

Nitze, Paul. H., with Ann M. Smith and Steven L. Rearden. *From Hiroshima to Glasnost: At the Center of Decision – A Memoir.* New York: Grove Weidenfeld, 1989.

"Limited Wars or Massive Retaliation?" Review of Henry A. Kissinger, *Nuclear Weapons and Foreign Policy. The Reporter* (September 5, 1957): 40–41.

Nowlin, David V. and Ronald J. Stupak. *War as an Instrument of Policy: Past, Present, and Future.* Lanham, MD: University Press of America, 1998.

"NSC 68: A Report to the National Security Council, 14 April 1950." *Naval War College Review*, Vol. 27, No. 6 (May–June 1975): 51–108.

Obama, Barack. "Address to the Nation on the Islamic State of Iraq and the Levant" (September 10, 2014), www.americanrhetoric.com/speeches/barackobama/barackobamaisilspeechtonation.htm

"President Obama's Speech on Combating ISIS and Terrorism" (September 10, 2014), www.cnn.com/2014/09/10/politics/transcript-obama-syria-isis-speech/

"Press Conference by President Obama – Antalya, Turkey" (November 16, 2015), www.whitehouse.gov/the-press-office/2015/11/16/press-conference-president-obama-antalya-turkey

"Remarks by the President in Address to the Nation on the Way forward in Afghanistan and Pakistan" (December 1, 2009), www.whitehouse.gov/the-press-office/remarks-president-address-nation-way-forward-afghanistan-and-pakistan

"Transcript of Obama Speech on Afghanistan" (December 2, 2009), http://edition.cnn.com/2009/POLITICS/12/01/obama.afghanistan.speech.transcript/index.html

Oberst, David J. *Why Wars End: An Expected Utility War Termination Model.* Carlisle Barracks, PA: US Army War College, 1991

O'Brien, William. *The Conduct of Just and Limited War.* New York: Praeger, 1981.

"Guidelines for Limited War." *Military Review*, Vol. 59, No.2 (February 1979): 64–72.

"Just War, Limited War, and Vietnam." *Journal of Social Philosophy*, Vol. 1, No. 4 (January 1973): 16–18.

O'Connell, D.P. "Limited War at Sea since 1945." In Howard, ed. *Restraints on War*, 123–134.

O'Connor, Raymond G. "Victory in Modern War." *Journal of Peace Research*, Vol. 6, No. 4 (1969): 367–384.

Olson, William. "The Concept of Small Wars." *Small Wars & Insurgencies*, Vol.1, No. 1 (1990): 39–46.

Osgood, Robert E. "Limited War and Korea." In Lawrence Freedman, ed. *War*. Oxford University Press, 1994, 336–341.

Limited War Revisited. Boulder, CO: Westview Press, 1979.

"Limited War Strategy." *Army*, Vol. 9 (December 1958): 53–54.

Limited War: The Challenge to American Strategy. Chicago University Press, 1957.

"Nuclear Arms: Uses and Limits." *The New Republic* (September 10, 1962): 15–18.

"The Post-War Strategy of Limited War: Before, during and after Vietnam." In Laurence Martin, ed. *Strategic Thought in the Nuclear Age.* Baltimore, MD: Johns Hopkins University Press, 1979, 93–130.

"The Reappraisal of Limited War." *The Adelphi Papers*, Vol. 9, No. 54 (1969): 41–54.

"The Reappraisal of Limited War." In *Problems of Modern Strategy.* New York: Praeger Publishers, 1970, 92–120.

"The Reappraisal of Limited War." In Lawrence Freedman, ed. *War.* Oxford University Press, 1994, 348–351.

Palit, D. K. *War in the Deterrent Age.* London: Macdonald, 1966.

Pape, Robert. *Bombing to Win: Air Power and Coercion in War.* Ithaca, NY: Cornell University Press, 1996.

Paret, Peter. "A Total Weapon of Limited War." *Royal United Services Institute*, Vol. 105, No. 617 (1960): 62–69.

"Eine totale Waffe in begrenzten Krieg." *Wehrwissenschaftliche Rundschau: Zeitschrift für die europäische Sicherheit*, Vol. 9, No. 10 (1959): 555–564. *French Revolutionary Warfare from Indochina to Algeria.* London: Pall Mall Press, 1964.

ed. *Makers of Modern Strategy: From Machiavelli to the Nuclear Age.* Princeton University Press, 1984.

Understanding War: Essays on Clausewitz and the History of Military Power. Princeton University Press, 1992.

Park, Tae-Gyun, "US Policy Change toward South Korea in the 1940s and the 1950s." *Journal of International and Area Studies*, Vol. 7, No. 2 (2000): 89–104.

Paschall, Rod. "Low-Intensity Conflict Doctrine: Who Needs It?" *Parameters*, Vol. 15, No. 3 (fall 1985): 33–45.

Pate, Randolph McC. "How Can We Cope with Limited War?" *The Army, Navy, Air Force Register and Defense Times*, Vol. 80 (November 28, 1959): 16–17.

"Peace or Piecemeal? The Army's Role in Limited War." *Army Information Digest*, Vol. 13 (June 1958): 2–3.

Pedroncini, Guy. "La Guerre de 1870–1871: Une guerre limitée." *Stratégique*, Vol. 54, No. 2 (1992), www.institut-strategie.fr/strat_054_PEDRONCINI.html

Peierls, Rudolf. "Limited Nuclear War?" *The Bulletin of Atomic Scientists*, Vol. 38, No. 5 (1982): 2.

Perry, William J. "There Is No Such Thing as 'Limited' Nuclear War." *William J. Perry Project* (March 7, 2017), www.wjperryproject.org/notes-from-the-brink/no-such-thing-as-limited-nuclear-war

Pike, Douglas. *Viet Cong: The Organization and Techniques of the National Liberation Front of South Vietnam*. Cambridge, MA: MIT Press, 1966.

Pillar, Paul R. *Negotiating Peace: War Termination as a Bargaining Process*. Princeton University Press, 1983.

Pimentel, David and Michael Burgess. "Nuclear War Investigation Related to a Limited Nuclear Battle with Emphasis on Agricultural Impacts in the United States." *Ambio*, Vol. 41, No.8 (December 2012): 894–899.

Pohl, James W. Exhibition review of *Korea: America's First Limited War*. Exhibition at the Lyndon Baines Johnson Library and Museum, Austin, Texas, May 12, 1988 – January 8, 1989. *The Southwest Historical Quarterly*, Vol. 92, No. 2 (October 1988): 389–392.

Poirier, Lucien. "Stratégie intégrale et guerre limitée." *Stratégique*, Vol. 54, No. 2 (1992), www.institut-strategie.fr/strat_054_Poirier_tdm.html

Pollack, Kenneth M. The Threatening Storm. New York: Random House, 2002.

Porch, Douglas. *Counterinsurgency: Exposing the Myths of the New Way of War*. Cambridge University Press, 2013.

  The French Secret Services: A History of French Intelligence from the Dreyfus Affair to the Gulf War. New York: Farrar, Straus, and Giroux, 2003.

Poussou, Jean Pierre. "Une Guerre civile limitée: La guerre civile anglaise (1642–1651)." *Stratégique*, Vol. 54, No. 2 (1992), www.institut-strategie.fr/strat_054_Poussou.html

Powell, Colin L. *My American Journey*. New York: Random House Ballantine, 1996.

Powell, Robert. "Nuclear Brinksmanship, Limited War, and Military Power." *International Organization*, Vol. 69, No. 3 (June 2015): 589–626.

"Nuclear Deterrence and the Strategy of Limited Retaliation." *The American Political Science Review*, Vol. 83, No. 2 (June 1989): 503–519.

Powers, Thomas and Rothven Tremain. *Total War: What It Is, How It Got That Way*. New York: W. Morrow, 1988.

Pruitt, John M., Jr. "Limited War: A Model for Entry, Conduct, and Termination." MA thesis, Naval Postgraduate School, 1984.

Puzzanghera, Jim. "Feinstein Criticizes Obama's Islamic State Strategy, Urges More US Special Forces in Syria," *Los Angeles Times* (November 22, 2015), www.latimes.com/world/la-fg-obama-isis-criticism-20151122-story.html

Quester, George H. "Wars Prolonged by Misunderstood Signals." *The Annals of the American Academy of Political and Social Science*, Vol. 392 (November 1970): 30–39.

Raghavan, V. R. "Limited War and Nuclear Escalation in South Asia." *The Nonproliferation Review*, Vol. 8, No. 3 (2001): 82–98.

Ramsey, Kristopher W. "Settling It on the Field: Battlefield Events and War Termination." *Journal of Conflict Resolution*, Vol. 52, No. 6 (December 2008): 850–879.

Randle, Robert. "Peace in Vietnam and Laos: 1954, 1962, 1973." In David Smith and Robert Randle, eds. *From War to Peace: Essays in Peacemaking and War Termination*. New York: Trustees of Columbia University, 1974, 42–67.

Ranft, Brian. "Restraints on War at Sea before 1945." In Howard, ed. *Restraints on War*, 39–56.

Rauchensteiner, Manfried and Erwin A. Schmidl, eds. *Formen des Krieges: Vom Mittelalter zum "Low Intensity Conflict."* Graz: Verlag Styria, 1991.

Read, Thornton. "Limited Strategic War and Tactical Nuclear War." In Knorr and Read, eds. *Limited Strategic War*, 67–116.

Record, Jeffrey. *Beating Goliath: Why Insurgencies Win*. Washington, DC: Potomac Books, 2007.
  Bounding the Global War on Terrorism. Carlisle Barracks, PA: Strategic Studies Institute, 2003.

Reed, James W. "Should Deterrence Fail: War Termination in Campaign Planning." *Parameters* (summer 1993): 41–52.

Rees, David. *Korea: The Limited War*. New York: St. Martin's Press, 1964.

Reinhardt, G. C. *Nuclear Weapons and Limited War: A Sketchbook History*. Santa Monica, CA: RAND, November 1964.

Reiter, Dan. *How Wars End*. Princeton University Press, 2009.

"Response to Suzanne Werner and Amy Yuen, 'Making and Keeping Peace.'" *Organization*, Vol. 59, No. 2 (spring 2005): 261–292, 8 pages, www.columbia.edu/~vpf4/Response%20to%20Werner%20and%20Yuen.pdf

Rhodes, Quinn J. "Limited War under the Nuclear Umbrella: An Analysis of India's Cold Start Doctrine and Its Implications for Stability on the Subcontinent." MA thesis, Naval Postgraduate School, 2010.

Richardson, James L. Review of Klaus Knorr and Thornton Read, eds., *Limited Strategic War*. *The Journal of Conflict Resolution*, Vol. 7, No. 4 (December 1963): 781–785.

Richardson, Robert C., III. "Do We Need Unlimited Forces for Limited War?" *Air Force*, Vol. 42 (March 1959): 53–56.

Richelson, Jeffrey T. "Soviet Strategic Doctrine and Limited Nuclear Operations: A Metagame Analysis." *The Journal of Conflict Resolution*, Vol. 23, No. 2 (June 1979): 326–336.

Rid, Thomas. "Cyber War Will Not Take Place." *Journal of Strategic Studies*, Vol. 35, No. 1 (2012): 5–32.

Ridgway, Matthew B. *The Korean War*. New York: Da Capo, 1967.

   The War in Korea: How We Met the Challenge, How All-Out Asian War Was Averted, Why MacArthur Was Dismissed, Why Today's War Objectives Must Be Limited. London: Barrie and Rockliff, 1967.

Ritter, Gerhard. *Frederick the Great: A Historical Profile*. Peter Paret, ed. and trans. Berkeley: University of California Press, 1968.

Robinson, Julian. "'ISIS to Outlast Obama's Presidency': Military Campaign to Destroy Terror Group Could Take THREE Years, Senior US Officials Warn." *The Daily Mail* (September 8, 2014), www.dailymail.co.uk/news/ article-2747640/ISIS-outlast-Obama-s-presidency-Military-campaign-destroy -terror-group-years-senior-U-S-officials-warn.html

Romer, Jean-Christophe. "L'URSS et la guerre limitée." *Stratégique*, Vol. 54, No. 2 (1992), www.institut-strategie.fr/strat_054_ROMER.html

Rongzhen, Nie. "Beijing's Decision to Intervene." In Li, Millett, and Yu, trans. and eds. *Mao's Generals Remember Korea*, 38–60.

Roosevelt, Franklin D. "State of the Union Address" (January 6, 1942). In Gerhard Peters and John T. Woolley, eds. *The American Presidency Project*, www.presidency.ucsb.edu/documents/state-the-union-address-1

Rose, Gideon. "The Exit Strategy Delusion." *Foreign Affairs*, Vol. 77, No. 1 (January–February 1998): 56–67.

   How Wars End: Why We Always Fight the Last Battle. New York: Simon and Schuster, 2010.

Rosen, Stephen Peter. *Vietnam and the American Theory of Limited War*. Harvard Center for International Affairs. Washington, DC: Office of the Secretary of Defense, December 1981.

   "Vietnam and the American Theory of Limited War." *International Security*, Vol. 7, No. 2 (fall 1982): 83–113.

Rosenau, William. "The Kennedy Administration, US Foreign Internal Security Assistance, and the Challenge of 'Subterranean War,' 1961–63." *Small Wars & Insurgencies*, Vol. 14, No. 3 (2003): 65–99.

Rosencrance, R. N. "Can We Limit Nuclear War?" *Military Review*, Vol. 38 (March 1959): 51–59.

Ross, Andrew L. "The Origins of Limited Nuclear War Theory." In Larsen and Kartchner, eds. *On Limited Nuclear War in the 21st Century*, 21–48.

Rostow, W. W. *The Stages of Economic Growth: A Non-Communist Manifesto*. Cambridge University Press, 1960.

Rovner, Joshua. "Delusion of Defeat: The United States and Iraq, 1990–1998." *Journal of Strategic Studies*, Vol. 37, No. 4 (2014): 482–507.

Rubin, Jennifer. "Obama's Limited War against the Islamic State Is Faltering." *Washington Post* (October 8, 2014), www.washingtonpost.com/blogs/right-turn/wp/2014/10/08/obamas-limited-war-against-the-islamic-state-is-faltering/

"Rules for Limited War: The Falklands Islands Conflict Marks a Step towards the Automation of Conventional War." *Nature*, Vol. 297 (May 1982): 253–254.

Russell, James A. Review of *On Limited Nuclear War in the 21st Century* by Jeffrey A. Larsen and Kerry M. Kartchner, eds. *H-Diplo, H-Net Reviews* (November 2014), www.h-net.org/reviews/showrev.php?id=42207

Sachdev, A. K. "Chinese Missiles: Winning the Limited War." *Strategic Analysis*, Vol. 24, No. 3 (2000): 525–538.

Salkin, Yves. "Une Petite Guerre en Amerique Centrale (1969)." *Stratégique*, Vol. 54, No. 2 (1992), www.institut-strategie.fr/strat_054_Salkin.html

Sarkesian, Sam. C., ed. *Revolutionary Guerrilla Warfare*. Chicago: Precedent Publishing, 1975.

Saundby, Robert. "Air Power in Limited Wars." *Royal United Services Institute*, Vol. 103, No. 611 (1958): 378–383.

"The Doctrine of Proportional Force." *Military Review*, Vol. 37 (October 1957): 84–89.

"War – Limited or Unlimited?" *Air Power*, Vol. 2 (1955): 100–102.

Saunders, Paul J. "Choosing Not to Choose: Obama's Dithering on Syria." *The National Interest* (December 16, 2015), http://nationalinterest.org/feature/choosing-not-choose-obamas-dithering-syria-14633?page=show

Savage, Charlie. "Barack Obama's Q&A." *Boston Globe* (December 20, 2007), http://archive.boston.com/news/politics/2008/specials/CandidateQA/ObamaQA/

Scales, Robert H., Jr. *Firepower in Limited War*. Revised edn. Novato, CA: Presidio, 1995.

Schadlow, Nadia. "The Problem with Hybrid Warfare." *War on the Rocks* (April 2, 2015), https://warontherocks.com/2015/04/the-problem-with-hybrid-warfare/

War and the Art of Governance: Consolidating Combat Success into Political Victory. Washington, DC: Georgetown University Press, 2017.

Schake, Kori. "The Perils of Limiting Our Wars." *War on the Rocks* (October 16, 2014), http://warontherocks.com/2014/10/the-perils-of-limiting-our-wars/

Sharp, U. S. Grant. *Strategy for Defeat: Vietnam in Retrospect* (Novato, CA: Presidio, 1998).

Scharre, Paul. "Spectrum of What?" *Military Review* (November–December 2012): 73–79.

Scheipers, Sibylle. "Counterinsurgency or Irregular Warfare? Historiography and the Study of 'Small Wars.'" *Small Wars & Insurgencies*, Vol. 25, Nos. 5–6 (2014): 879–899.

  "'The Most Beautiful of Wars': Carl von Clausewitz and Small Wars." *European Journal of International Security*, Vol. 2, No. 1 (February 2017): 47–63.

Schelling, Thomas C. *Arms and Influence*. New Haven, CT: Yale University Press, 1966.

  "Bargaining, Communication, and Limited War." *Conflict Resolution*, Vol. 1, No. 1 (March 1957): 19–36.

  Nuclear Weapons and Limited War. Santa Monica, CA: RAND, 1959.

  The Strategy of Conflict. Cambridge, MA: Harvard University Press, 1963 [1960].

  "The Strategy of Conflict: Prospectus for a Reorientation of Game Theory." *Conflict Resolution*, Vol. 2, No. 3 (1958): 203–246.

Schleifer, Ron. "Democracies, Limited War, and Psychological Operations." In Efraim Inbar, ed., *Democracies and Small Wars*. London: Frank Cass, 2003, 40–52.

Schnabel, James F. *Policy and Direction: The First Year*. Washington, DC: Center of Military History, 1992.

Schroden, Jonathan. "A Best Practice for Assessment in Counterinsurgency." *Small Wars Insurgencies*, Vol. 25, No. 2 (2014): 479–486.

Schwarz, Urs. *American Strategy: A New Perspective. The Growth of Politico-Military Thinking in the United States*. Garden City, NY: Anchor/Doubleday, 1967.

Schwarzkopf, Norman H. and Peter Petre. *It Doesn't Take a Hero*. New York: Bantam, 1992.

Seabury, Paul. "Provisionality and Finality." *The Annals of the American Academy of Political and Social Science*, Vol. 392 (November 1970): 96–104.

Seim, Harvey B. "Are We Ready to Wage Limited War?" *US Naval Institute Proceedings*, Vol. 87, No. 3 (March 1961): 27–32.

  "The Navy and the Fringe War." *US Naval Institute Proceedings*, Vol. 77 (August 1951): 835–841.

Sent, Esther-Mirjam. "Some Like it Cold: Thomas Schelling as a Cold Warrior." *Journal of Economic Methodology*, Vol. 14, No. 4 (December 2007): 455–471.

Sethi, Manpreet. "Conventional War in the Presence of Nuclear Weapons." *Strategic Analysis*, Vol. 33, No. 3 (2009): 415–425.

Seymour-Ure, Colin. "British 'War Cabinets' in Limited Wars: Korea, Suez, and the Falklands." *Public Administration*, Vol. 62 (summer 1984): 181–200.

Shane, Leo, III. "DoD to Deploy 'Targeting Force' to Hunt Down ISIS Leaders." *Military Times* (December 1, 2015), www.militarytimes.com/story/military/capitol-hill/2015/12/01/carter-isil-hasc-war/76609562/

Shoemaker, Raymond L., Peter L. Urban, John Clapper Jr., et al., "Readiness for the Little War: Optimum Integrated Strategy." *Military Review*, Vol. 37, No. 1 (April 1957): 14–26.

Shy, John. *A People Numerous and Armed: Reflections on the Military Struggle for American Independence*. Ann Arbor: University of Michigan Press, 1990.

Sigler, John H. "The Iran–Iraq Conflict: The Tragedy of Limited Conventional War." *International Journal*, Vol. 41, No. 2 (spring 1986): 424–456.

Simpson, Emile. *War from the Ground up: Twenty-First Century Combat as Politics*. Oxford University Press, 2013.

Singh, Jasjit. "Dynamics of Limited War." *Strategic Analysis*, Vol. 24, No. 7 (2000): 1205–1220.

Singh, Sushant. "Limited War, Limited Sense." *The Indian Express* (September 24, 2015), http://indianexpress.com/article/opinion/columns/limited-war-limited-sense/

Singh, Swaran. "Indian Debate on Limited War Doctrine." *Strategic Analysis*, Vol. 23, No. 12 (2000): 2179–1285.

   Limited War: The Challenge of US Military Strategy. New Delhi: Lancers Books, 1995.

Sisk, Richard. "Mattis: There Is No Such Thing as a 'Tactical' Nuke.'" *Military.com* (February 6, 2018), www.military.com/defensetech/2018/02/06/mattis-there-no-such-thing-tactical-nuke.html

Smith, Dale O. "Air Power in Limited War." *Air Force*, Vol. 38 (May 1955): 43–44, 47.

Smith, David and Robert Randle, eds. *From War to Peace: Essays in Peacemaking and War Termination*. New York: Trustees of Columbia University, 1974.

Smith, Frederic H. "Nuclear Weapons and Limited War." *Air University Review Quarterly*, Vol. 12, No. 1 (spring 1960): 3–27.

Smith, James M. "Limited Nuclear Conflict and the American Way of War." In Larsen and Kartchner, eds. *On Limited Nuclear War in the 21st Century*, 244–262.

Smith, R. J. "A Defect in the Limited War Theory." *Science*, Vol. 223, No. 4642 (March 1984): 1271.

Smith, Rupert. *The Utility of Force: The Art of War in the Modern World*. New York: Knopf, 2007.

odgrass, Thomas. "Limited War Doctrine: A Fatal Flaw." *The Embattled Catholic American Thinker* (December 29, 2006), www.catholicameri-canthinker.com/limited-war-doctrine.html

ayder, Jack L. *The Soviet Strategic Culture: Implications for Limited Nuclear Operations*. Santa Monica, CA: RAND, 1977.

ohdi, H. P. S. "China's White Paper on Military Strategy." *Centre for Air Power Studies (CAPS)* (June 5, 2015).

Sokolovskii, V. D. *Soviet Military Strategy*. H. Dinerstein, L. Gouré, and T. Wolfe, eds. Santa Monica, CA: RAND, 1963.

Spaight, J. M. "Limited and Unlimited War." *Royal Air Force Quarterly and Commonwealth Air Forces Journal*, Vol. 4 (1952): 6–8.

Speier, Hans. *Social Order and Risks of War: Papers in Political Sociology*. New York: George W. Stewart, 1952.

Stein, Harold. Review of *Limited War: The Challenge to American Strategy* by Robert E. Osgood. *The American Political Science Review*, Vol. 52, No. 2 (June 1958): 533–535.

Steinmeyer, Walter. "The Intelligence Role in Counterinsurgency." *Studies in Intelligence*, Vol. 59, No. 4 (December 2015): 21–27.

Stephens, Brett. "Normalizing Iran." *Wall Street Journal* (January 18, 2016), www.wsj.com/articles/normalizing-iran–1453162144

Stephens, Hampton. "Adapting the Powell Doctrine to Limited Wars." *World Politics Review* (Dec. 2018), www.worldpoliticsreview.com/insights/25084/adapting-the-powell-doctrine-to-limited-wars

Stockton, Paul. "Strategic Stability between the Super-Powers." *The Adelphi Papers*, Vol. 26, No. 213 (winter 1986).

Stoker, Donald. *Clausewitz: His Life and Work*. Oxford University Press, 2014.

"Everything You Think You Know about Limited War is Wrong." *War on the Rocks* (December 22, 2006), https://warontherocks.com/2016/12/every thing-you-think-you-know-about-limited-war-is-wrong/

The Grand Design: Strategy and the US Civil War. Oxford University Press, 2010.

"Insurgencies Rarely Win and Iraq Won't Be Any Different (Maybe)," *Foreign Policy* (January 15, 2007), http://foreignpolicy.com/2007/01/15/insurgen cies-rarely-win-and-iraq-wont-be-any-different-maybe/

"The Myth of Total War." *The Strategy Bridge* (December 17, 2006), https://thestrategybridge.org/the-bridge/2016/12/17/the-myth-of-total-war

"Six Reasons Insurgencies Lose: A Contrarian View." *Small Wars Journal* (July 4, 2009): 1–11, http://smallwarsjournal.com/jrnl/art/six-reasons-insurgencies-lose

"What's in a Name? Clausewitz's Search to Define 'Strategy.'" *Infinity Journal*, Vol. 5, No. 2 (spring 2016): 11–15.

"What's in a Name II: 'Total War' and Other Terms that Mean Nothing." *Infinity Journal*, Vol. 5, No. 3 (fall 2016): 21–23.

Stoker, Donald and Edward B. Westermann, eds. *Expeditionary Police Advising and Militarization: Building Security in a Fractured World*. Solihull, UK: Helion & Co., 2018.

Stoker, Donald and Michael W. Jones. "Colonial Military Strategy." In Donald Stoker, Kenneth J. Hagan, and Michael T. McMaster, eds. *Strategy in the War of American Independence: A Global Approach*. London: Routledge, 2010, 5–34.

Stokes, Doug and Kit Waterman, "Beyond Balancing? Intrastate Conflict and US Grand Strategy." *Journal of Strategic Studies* (June 12, 2017), www.tand-fonline.com/doi/full/10.1080/01402390.2017.1330682

Strachan, Hew. *Clausewitz's On War: A Biography* (New York: Atlantic Monthly Press, 2007).

The Direction of War: Contemporary Strategy in Historical Perspective. Cambridge University Press, 2013.

"Strategy and the Limitation of War." *Survival: Global Politics and Strategy*, Vol. 50, No. 1 (2008): 31–54.

Strassler, Robert B., ed., *The Landmark Thucydides: A Comprehensive Guide to the Peloponnesian War*. New York: Touchstone, 1996.

Strausz-Hupé, Robert. "Limits of Limited War." *The Reporter*, Vol. 17 (November 1957): 30–34.

"Nuclear Blackmail and Limited War." *Yale Review*, Vol. 48 (winter 1959): 174–181.

Stueck, William. *Rethinking the Korean War: A New Diplomatic and Strategic History*. Princeton University Press, 2002.

Sullivan, Patricia L. "War Aims and War Outcomes: Why Powerful States Lose Limited Wars." *Journal of Conflict Resolution*, Vol. 51, No.3 (2007): 496–524.

Summers, Harry G. Jr. "Full Circle – World War II to the Persian Gulf." *Military Review* (February 1992): 38–48.

On Strategy: A Critical Analysis of the Vietnam War. Novato, CA: Presidio Press, 1984.

"Vietnam: Lessons Learned, Unlearned and Relearned." *Art of War Colloquium*. Carlisle Barracks, PA: US Army War College, June 1983, 28–43.

"War: Deter, Fight, Terminate, the Purpose of War Is a Better Peace." *Naval War College Review*, Vol. 39, No. 1 (1986): 18–29.

Sun Tzu. *The Art of War*. Samuel B. Griffith, trans. London: Oxford University Press, 1961.

Surmeier, John J. *Alternative Approaches to Using Peacetime and Wartime Costs in Limited War Cost-Effectiveness Studies*. Santa Monica, CA: RAND, 1969.

Taber, Robert. *The War of the Flea: A Study of Guerrilla Warfare Theory and Practice*. St. Albans, UK: Paladin, 1970.

Talbot, Strobe. "Unilateralism: Anatomy of a Foreign Policy Disaster." *Brookings Institute* (February 21, 2007), www.brookings.edu/opinions/unilateralism-anatomy-of-a-foreign-policy-disaster/

Talensky, N. "On the Character of Modern Warfare." *International Affairs* (October 1969): 23–27.

Tapper, Jake. "Senate Regrets the Vote to Enter Iraq." *ABC News* (January 5, 2007), https://abcnews.go.com/GMA/Politics/story?id=2771519&page=1

Tarapore, Arzan. *Holocaust or Hollow Victory: Limited War in Nuclear South Asia.* New Delhi: Institute of Peace and Conflict Studies, 2005.

Taylor, Maxwell D. "Improving Our Capabilities for Limited War." *Army Information Digest*, Vol. 14 (February 1959): 2–9.

"On Limited War." *Army Information Digest*, Vol. 13 (June 1958): 4–5.

The Uncertain Trumpet. New York: Harper, 1960.

Teitler, G. "Oorlogvoering: Eenvormigheid en Verscheidenheid." In Teitler, Bosch, and Klinkert, eds. *Militaire Stratégie*, 77–106.

Teitler, G., J. M. J. Bosch, and W. Klinkert, eds. *Militaire Stratégie.* Amsterdam: Mets & Schilt, 2002.

Teller, Edward. "The Way the US Army Would Fight in Little Wars." *US News & World Report* (November 9, 1956): 56–59.

Tellis, Ashley J., C. Christine Fair, Jamison Jo Medby. *Limited Conflicts under the Nuclear Umbrella: Indian and Pakistani Lessons from the Kargil Crisis.* Santa Monica, CA: RAND, 2002.

Terhune, Kenneth W. and Joseph M. Firestone. "Global War, Limited War, and Peace: Hypotheses from Three Experimental Worlds." *International Studies Quarterly*, Vol. 14, No. 2 (June 1970): 195–218.

Terrill, W. Andrew. *Escalation and Intrawar Deterrence during Limited Wars in the Middle East.* Carlisle, PA: Strategic Studies Institute, US Army War College, 2009.

Tertrais, Bruno. "Leçons de l'exemple indo-pakistanais pour la dissuasion nucleaire." *Fondation pour la recherché stratégique (FRS)*, No. 75 (October 2003), www.iaea.org/inis/collection/nclcollectionstore/_public/37/066/37066502.pdf?r=1

Thies, Wallace J. "Searching for Peace: Vietnam and the Question of How Wars End." *Polity*, Vol. 7, No. 3 (spring 1975): 304–333.

Thomas, John R. "Limited Nuclear War in Soviet Strategic Thinking." *Orbis* (spring 1966): 184–202.

Thompson, John A. *A Sense of Power: The Roots of America's Global Role.* Ithaca, NY: Cornell University Press, 2015.

Tierney, Dominic. *How We Fight: Crusades, Quagmires, and the American Way of War.* New York: Little Brown, 2010.

The Right Way to Lose a War: America in an Age of Unwinnable Conflicts. New York: Little, Brown, 2015.

"Why Has America Stopped Winning Wars?" *The Atlantic* (June 2, 2015), www
.theatlantic.com/international/archive/2015/06/america-win-loss-iraq-afghani
stan/394559/

Tinch, Clark W. "Quasi-War between Japan and the USSR, 1937–1939." *World
Politics*, Vol. 2, No. 2 (January 1951): 174–199.

Trachtenberg, Marc, ed. *The Development of American Strategic Thought*. Vol. I.
*Basic Documents from the Eisenhower and Kennedy Periods, including the
Basic National Security Policy Papers from 1953 to 1959*. New York:
Garland, 1987.

The Development of American Strategic Thought. Vol. II. *Writings on
Strategy, 1945–1951*. New York: Garland, 1987.

The Development of American Strategic Thought. Vol. III (in three volumes).
Writings on Strategy, 1952–1960. New York: Garland, 1987.

The Development of American Strategic Thought. Vol. IV. *Writings on
Strategy, 1961–1969, and Retrospectives*. New York: Garland, 1987.

History and Strategy. Princeton University Press, 1991.

"Strategic Thought in America, 1952–1966." *Political Science Quarterly*, Vol.
104, No. 2 (summer 1989): 301–344.

Tracinski, Robert. "Barack Obama: Worst. President. Ever." *The Federalist*
(November 19, 2015), http://thefederalist.com/2015/11/19/barack-obama-
worst-president-ever/

Trauschweizer, Ingo Wolfgang. "Creating Deterrence for Limited War: The US
Army and the Defense of West Germany, 1953–1982." Ph.D. dissertation,
University of Maryland, College Park, 2006.

Traverso, Edmund., ed. *Korea and the Limits of Limited War*. Menlo Park, CA:
Addison-Wesley Publishing, 1970.

Trinquier, Roger. *A French View of Counterinsurgency*. Daniel Lee, trans.
London: Pall Mall Press, 1964. Reprint: Fort Leavenworth: Combat
Studies Institute, 1985.

Truman, Harry S. *Memoirs by Harry S. Truman*. 2 vols. New York: Doubleday,
1955.

Trump, Donald. "Remarks by President Trump on the Strategy in Afghanistan
and South Asia" (August 21, 2017), www.whitehouse.gov/briefings-
statements/remarks-president-trump-strategy-afghanistan-south-asia/

Tsou, Tang. "Mao's Limited War in the Taiwan Strait." *Orbis*, Vol. 3 (fall 1959):
332–350.

Tuck, Christopher. "Afghanistan: Strategy and War Termination." *Parameters*
(autumn 2012): 44–61.

Turley, William S. *The Second Indochina War: A Concise Political and Military
History*. 2nd edn. Lanham, MD: Rowan and Littlefield, 2009.

Ucko, David H. "'The People Are Revolting': An Anatomy of Authoritarian
Counterinsurgency." *Journal of Strategic Studies*, Vol. 39, No. 1 (2016):

29–61. United States, Central Intelligence Agency. "The Evolution of Soviet Doctrine on Limited War," (October 9, 1967), www.cia.gov/library/readingroom/docs/DOC_0000309808.pdf

Department of the Army. *ADP 3–0: Unified Land Operations*. Washington, DC: Dept. of the Army, October 2011, www.army.mil/e2/rv5_downloads/info/references/ADP_3–0_ULO_Oct_2011_APD.pdf

Bibliography on Limited War. Dept. of the Army Pamphlet 20–60. Washington, DC: Government Printing Office, February 1958.

Department of Defense. Defense Science Board. *Report on Limited War*. Vol. I. Washington, DC: Office of the Under Secretary of Defense for Acquisition, 1958.

Department of the Navy. USMC. *Small Wars Manual*. Washington, DC: USGPO, 1940, 1987.

Department of State, "Authority of the President to Repel the Attack in Korea." Department of State Memorandum of July 3, 1950. *Department of State Bulletin*, Vol. 23 (July 31, 1950): 173–178.

Foreign Relations of the United States [FRUS], 1951, Asia and the Pacific. Washington, DC: USGPO, 1977.

Foreign Relations of the United States [FRUS], 1951, Korea and China. Washington, DC: USGPO, 1983.

Foreign Relations of the United States [FRUS], Vietnam, 1964. Washington, DC: USGPO, 1992.

Joint Chiefs of Staff (JCS). *The National Military Strategy of the United States of America 2015* (June 2015).

Senate. *Effects of Limited Nuclear War. Hearing Before the Subcommittee on Arms Control, International Organizations, and Security Agreements of the Committee on Foreign Relations (September 18, 1975)*. Washington, DC: USGPO, 1976.

White House. "Authorization for Use of Military Force against the Islamic State of Iraq and the Levant," (February 11, 2015), www.whitehouse.gov/sites/default/files/docs/aumf_02112015.pdf

Van Fleet, James A. "The Truth about Korea: From a Man Now Free to Speak." Part 1. *Life*, Vol. 34, No. 19 (May 11, 1953): 126–128, 131–132, 134, 137–138, 140, 142.

"The Truth about Korea: How We Can Win with What We Have." Part II. *Life* (May 8, 1953): 156–172.

Van Loan, Eugene, "Limited to Defeat." *Claremont Review of Books Digital* (March 1, 2016), www.claremont.org/crb/basicpage/limited-to-defeat/

Vennesson, Pascal. "Is Strategic Studies Narrow? Critical Security and the Misunderstood Scope of Strategy." *Journal of Strategic Studies* (2017): 1–34, www.tandfonline.com/doi/full/10.1080/01402390.2017.1288108

Walton, Dale. *The Myth of Inevitable US Defeat in Vietnam*. Abingdon, UK: Routledge, 2002.

Warden, John K. *Limited Nuclear War: The 21st-Century Challenge for the United States*. Livermore Papers on National Security, No. 4. Livermore, CA: Livermore National Laboratory, 2018.

Warner, Denis and Peggy Warner. *The Tide at Sunrise: A History of the Russo-Japanese War, 1904–1905*. Abingdon, UK: Routledge, 2004.

Warrington, Bob. "The American Approach to Limited War." MA thesis, National Defense University, National War College, 1994.

Watson, Mark. S. "Can We Limit an 'A-War'?" *The Nation*, Vol. 161 (December 24, 1955): 550–551.

Watt, Donald Cameron. "Restraints on War in the Air before 1945." In Howard, ed. *Restraints on War*, 57–78.

Watts, Stephen, Caroline Baxter, Molly Dunigan, and Christopher Rizzi. *The Use and Limits of Small-Scale Military Interventions*. Santa Monica: RAND, 2002.

Waxman, Matthew C. "The Power to Wage War Successfully." *Columbia Law Review*, Vol. 117, No. 3 (April 2017): 613–686.

Wein, Matthew. "Go Big or Go Home: Applying the Full Force of the US National Security Apparatus." *War on the Rocks* (May 20, 2016), http://waronther ocks.com/2016/05/go-big-or-go-home-applying-the-full-force-of-the -u-s-national-security-apparatus/

Weinberger, Caspar. "The Uses of Military Power." *Defense* (January 1985): 2–11.

Weisiger, Alex. *Logics of War: Explanations for Limited and Unlimited Conflicts*. Cornell University Press, 2013.

Welna, David. "As Fighting Season Begins in Afghanistan, Trump Administration Aims for Peace Talks." *NPR* (March 23, 2018), www.npr.org/2018/03/23/ 596529860/as-fighting-season-begins-in-afghanistan-trump-administration-aims-for-peace-tal

Werner, Suzanne. "Absolute and Limited War: The Possibility of Foreign-Imposed Regime Change." *International Interactions*, Vol. 22, No. 1 (1996): 67–88.

  "Negotiating the Terms of Settlement: War Aims and Bargaining Leverage." *The Journal of Conflict Resolution*, Vol. 42, No. 3 (June 1998): 321–343.
  "The Precarious Nature of Peace: Resolving the Issues, Enforcing the Settlement, and Renegotiating the Terms." *American Journal of Political Science*, Vol. 43, No. 3 (July 1999): 912–934.

Werner, Suzanne and Amy Yuen. "Making and Keeping Peace." *International Organization*, Vol. 59, No. 2 (spring 2005): 261–292.

West, Diana. "Limited War vs. Total War." *RealClearPolitics* (August 31, 2007), www.realclearpolitics.com/articles/2007/08/limited_war_vs_total_war.html

Westad, Odd Arne. *The Global Cold War*. Cambridge University Press, 2007.

Weyland, Otto P. "Air Power in Limited War." *Ordnance*, Vol. 44 (July–August 1959): 40–43.

"How TAC Stops Limited War before It Starts." *Armed Force Management*, Vol. 5 (April 1959): 24–25.

White, Jonathan Mark. "The Case for Limited War: Lyndon B. Johnson's Vietnam War Rhetoric." BA honors thesis, Vanderbilt University, 2007.

Whiteley, E.A. "Limited War – Brute Force or Subtle Pressure?" *Royal United Services Institution Journal*, Vol. 104, No. 615 (1959): 315–319.

Whiteside, Craig. "The Islamic State and the Return of Revolutionary Warfare." *Small Wars & Insurgencies*, Vol. 27, No.5 (2016): 743–776.

Widen, J. J. "Sir Julian Corbett and the Theoretical Study of War." *Journal of Strategic Studies*, Vol. 30, No. 1 (2007): 109–127.

de Wijk, Rob. *The Art of Military Coercion: Why the West's Military Superiority Scarcely Matters*. Amsterdam: Mets & Schilt, 2005.

Will, George, "Obama Is Defying the Constitution on War." *The Washington Post* (September 17, 2014), www.washingtonpost.com/opinions/george-will-obama-needs-congress-to-approve-this-war/2014/09/17/26de9d3e-3d c9-11e4-boea-8141703bbf6f_story.html?noredirect=on&utm_term=.4ce4 073c2 ba

Williamson, Corbin. "Fighting with Friends: Coalition Warfare in Korean Waters, 1950–1953." *Joint Force Quarterly*, No. 83 (2016): 99–104.

Wilson, Geoff and Will Saetren. "Could America Really Win a 'Limited' Nuclear War?" *The National Interest* (February 18, 2017), http://nationalinterest.org /blog/the-buzz/could-america-really-win-limited-nuclear-war-19503? page=show

Wilson, George G. "Limited Use of Force." *The American Journal of International Law*, Vol. 11, No. 2 (April 1917): 384–387.

Wilson, Isaiah, III, and Scott Smitson. "Solving America's Gray-Zone Puzzle." *Parameters*, Vol. 46, No. 4 (2017): 55–67.

Wilson, Scott and Al Kamen, "'Global War on Terror' Is Given New Name," *Washington Post* (March 25, 2009), www.washingtonpost.com/wp-dyn /content/article/2009/03/24/AR2009032402818.html

Wimmer, Andrea and Brian Min. "The Location and Purpose of Wars around the World: A New Global Dataset, 1816–2001." *International Interactions*, Vol. 35, No. 4 (2009): 390–417.

Wirtz, James J. "Limited Nuclear War Reconsidered." In Larsen and Kartchner, eds. *On Limited Nuclear War in the 21st Century*, 263–271.

Wittman, Donald. "How a War Ends: A Rational Model Approach." *The Journal of Conflict Resolution*, Vol. 23, No. 4 (December 1979): 743–763.

Wohlstetter, Albert. "The Delicate Balance of Terror." *Foreign Affairs* (January 1959): 211–234.

Wolfers, Arnold. "Could a War in Europe Be Limited?" *Yale Review*, Vol. 45 (winter 1956): 214–288.

Wood, Bryce. "How Wars End in Latin America." *The Annals of the American Academy of Political and Social Science*, Vol. 392 (November 1970): 40–50.

Wood, Hugh G. "American Reaction to Limited War in Asia: Korea and Vietnam, 1950–1968." Ph.D. dissertation, University of Colorado, 1974.

Woodman, Stewart. "Defining Limited Conflict: A Case of Mistaken Identity." In Young, ed. *Defence and the Media in the Time of Limited War*, 24–43.

Woods, Kevin M. *The Mother of All Battles: Saddam Hussein's Strategic Plan for the Persian Gulf War*. Annapolis, MD: Naval Institute Press, 2008.

Woods, Kevin M., Michael R. Pease, Mark E. Stout, Williamson Murray, and James G. Lacey. *The Iraqi Perspectives Project: A View of Operation Iraqi Freedom from Saddam's Senior Leadership*. Washington, DC: Joint Center for Operational Analysis, 2013.

Wright, Quincy. *A Study of War*. 2nd edn. University of Chicago Press, 1965.

"How Hostilities Have Ended: Peace Treaties and Alternatives." *The Annals of the American Academy of Political and Social Science*, Vol. 392 (November 1970): 51–61.

Wylie, J. C. *Military Strategy: A General Theory of Power Control*. New Brunswick, NJ: Rutgers University Press, 1967.

Wynne, G. C. "Pattern for Limited (Nuclear) War: The Riddle of the Schlieffen Plan-I." *Royal United Services Institution*, Vol. 102, No. 608 (1957): 488–499.

"Pattern for Limited (Nuclear) War: The Riddle of the Schlieffen Plan-II." *Royal United Services Institution*, Vol. 103, No. 609 (1958): 40–50.

"Pattern for Limited (Nuclear) War: The Riddle of the Schlieffen Plan-III." *Royal United Services Institution*, Vol. 103, No. 610 (1958): 215–222.

Yarrington, Gary A, Curator. *Korea: America's First Limited War. An Exhibition at the Lyndon Baines Johnson Library and Museum, May 12, 1988 – January 8, 1989*. Austin, TX: Lyndon Baines Johnson Library and Museum, 1988.

Yglesias, Matthew. "Obama's Biggest Terrorism Struggle: How to Sell 'Don't do stupid shit' as a Strategy" (November 18, 2015), www.vox.com/2015/11/18/9751340/paris-attack-dont-do-stupid-shit

Young, Marilyn B. "Historian Marilyn B. Young Discusses 'Limited War, Unlimited.'" Webcast. *Library of Congress*, Washington, DC (July 8, 2009), www.loc.gov/today/cyberlc/feature_wdesc.php?rec=4683

Young, Peter R., ed. *Defence and the Media in the Time of Limited War*. London: Frank Cass, 1992.

Zeisberg, Mariah. *War Powers: The Politics of Constitutional Authority*. Princeton University Press, 2013.

Zenko, Micah. *Between Threats and War: US Discrete Military Operations in the Post-Cold War World*. Stanford University Press, 2010.

Zhai, Qiang. *China and the Vietnam Wars, 1950–1975*. Chapel Hill, NC: University of North Carolina Press, 2000.

Zhang, Xiaoming. "China's 1979 War with Vietnam: A Reassessment." *The China Quarterly*, Vol. 184 (December 2005): 851–874.

INDEX

Printed in the United States
by Baker & Taylor Publisher Services